LEARN BY MAKING THE COMPLICATED SIMPLE

Other publications by the authors:

Test Development and Item Writing for *NCLEX*® Success—2013
***NCLEX-RN*® Review: Keeping It Real!® *Simplified—eBook* 2013**
Dr. Peck's Pediatric Review *Simplified—eBook* 2013
www.sylviarayfield.com

Nursing Made Insanely Easy—2011
Pharmacology Made Insanely Easy—2013
***NCLEX-RN*® 101: How to Pass—2013**
***NCLEX-PN*® 101: How to Pass—2011**
Pathways of Teaching Nursing: *Keeping It Real!*
www.icanpublishing.com

NCLEX-RN® Review: Keeping It Real!® *Simplified*

Sylvia Rayfield & Associates, Inc.

Tina Rayfield, RN, PA-C
President
Sylvia Rayfield & Associates, Inc.

Sylvia Rayfield, MN, RN, CNS
Founder
Sylvia Rayfield & Associates, Inc.
Co-Founder
I CAN Publishing, Inc.

12480 Seratine Drive
Pensacola, Florida 32506
www.sylviarayfield.com

Cover Design: Elliot Bern, Gainesville, GA
Images Courtesy of: I CAN Publishing, Inc.
Photography: Sylvia Rayfield

ISBN: 978-0-9891688-1-6
Library of Congress Control Number: applied for
Printed in the United States of America

Nursing education, practice, and pharmacology is an every changing science. For purposes
of this publication, the authors and publisher have reviewed current and reliable sources and
care has been taken to confirm the accuracy of the information presented; however, the authors,
editor, and publisher disclaim all responsibility for errors, omissions, or consequences from
application of the information in this publication. This publication is
written to assist nursing students in their understanding of nursing concepts, to assist nursing faculty
in teaching in a simplified manner, and to help new graduates pass the
NCLEX® exam.

The accelerated learning of vital minimum standards in nursing is the backbone and strength of
this book. The videos and other online information are supplements that enhance the presentation
but are not essential to the content. There is uncertainty in utilizing the videos as they may become
technically ineffective. This publisher is not responsible for websites (or their content) that are not
owned by the publisher.

Cover Design: Elliot Bern, Gainesville, GA
Conversion Services: eBook Architects, Austin, TX
Images Courtesy of: I CAN Publishing, Inc., Duluth, GA
Photography: Sylvia Rayfield

This book may be purchased at Sylvia Rayfield & Associates, Inc., www.sylviarayfield.com.

The eBook may be purchased through the following retail distributors and Sylvia Rayfield &
Associates, Inc. www.sylviarayfield.com
    Amazon (Kindle)
    Apple iBookstore (iPad)
    Baker & Taylor (leading distributor)
    Barnes & Noble (Nook)
    Gardner's (Britain's largest bookstore)
    eSental (Southeast Asia's biggest bookstore)
    Scribd (the world's largest on-line library)
    Sony Reader Store (Reader)

DEDICATION

This book is dedicated to the Associates of Sylvia Rayfield & Associates. Their expertise in accelerated learning and their joy for teaching are models of inspiration. Their expert contributions make this eBook innovative, accurate, and the complicated simple. They take our work to thousands of people a year in the United States, Bangladesh, Canada, England, Ireland, the Philippines, and South Africa. It is a pleasure to work with Judy Duvall, Darlene Franklin, Melissa Geist, Loretta Manning, Stephanie Mitchell Jessica Roberts, Marcia Russell, and Mayola Villarruel.

Retired Associates Marie Bremner, Phoebe Helm, Vanice Roberts, and Martha Sherman

In Memory

Alita Rayfield Caskey Maddox—daughter, sister, mother, Associate, and Pediatric Nurse Practitioner extraordinaire.

> To give beyond reason, to care beyond hope, to love without limit: to reach, stretch, and dream, in spite of your fears. These are the hallmarks of divinity—traits of the immortal—your badges of honor. May you wear them with a pride as great as the immeasurable pride we feel for you.
>
> Michael Dooley

Introduction

What makes this book different from all other review books?
Utilizing Accelerated Learning Methods, we have blended a smorgasbord of learning into one book.

- ⸙ There is opportunity to visit a large number of audio and video URLs for virtual learning.

- ⸙ Current NCLEX® STANDARDS from research provide the complete structure for this book and make it significant.

- ⸙ The unique arrangement of factual nursing concepts ties the simple to the complex to make learning easier.

- ⸙ The style is "bottom line," often in columns or tables.

- ⸙ Practice questions are clinical reasoning, high difficulty level NCLEX® style items structured with the same percentages that are in the current test plan. Quality over quantity lessens the number of items needed for practice.

- ⸙ Authors are NCLEX® specialists with years of experience and current information.

- ⸙ Author experiences provide a look at the "unseen and unspoken" that make nursing an art as well as a science.

This Book Was Written to Assist in the Preparation for:

- 𝄞 *NCLEX®* Success
- 𝄞 **Study Guide for Nursing School Exams**
- 𝄞 **Refresher Course**
- 𝄞 **Nursing Faculty Guide for "What Must Be Taught"!**
- 𝄞 **New Graduates Preparing for a New Job**
- 𝄞 **Preparation for *CGFNS QUALIFYING EXAM®***

Key Concepts

- 𝄞 **Readiness for Success**
- 𝄞 **Follow These Steps**
- 𝄞 **Test Taking Strategies**
- 𝄞 **What's on *NCLEX®*?**

Table of Contents

Introduction to a new way of learning using *NCLEX*® Standards, music, acronyms, YouTube video opportunities, and images.

Adults and Children:

Abbreviations Glossary

Use approved abbreviations and standard terminology when documenting care.

AAA	Abdominal Aortic Aneurysm
ABD	Abdomen
ABG	Arterial Blood Gas
ACE	Angiotensin Converting Enzyme
ACLS	Advanced Cardiac Life Support
ACTH	AdrenoCorticoTropic Hormone
ADH	Anti-Diuretic Hormone
ADL	Activities of Daily Living
AF	Atrial Fibrillation
AICD	Automatic Implantable Cardioverter Defibrillator
AKI	Acute Kidney Injury
ALL	Acute Lymphocytic Leukemia
ALS	Amytropic Lateral Sclerosis
AML	Acute Myelogenous Leukemia
AODM	Adult Onset Diabetes Mellitus
APSGN	Acute Post-streptococcal Glomerulonephritis
ARDS	Acute Respiratory Distress Syndrome
ARF	Acute Renal Failure
ASAP	As Soon As Possible
ASD	Atrial Septal Defect
ASHD	Atherosclerotic Heart Disease
ALT	Alanine Transferase
AST	Aspartate Transferase
ATN	Acute Tubular Necrosis
AVF	AtrioVentricular Fistula
A-VO$_2$	ArterioVenous Oxygen

BBB	Bundle Branch Block
BKA	Below the Knee Amputation
BP	Blood Pressure
BPH	Benign Prostatic Hypertrophy
BPM	Beats Per Minute
BS	Bowel or Breath Sounds
BUN	Blood Urea Nitrogen

C&S	Culture and Sensitivity
Ca	Calcium
CABG	Coronary Artery Bypass Graft

CAD	Coronary Artery Disease
CAT	Computerized Axial Tomography
CAUTI	Catheter Associated Urinary Tract Infection
CBC	Complete Blood Count
C. DIFF	Clostridium Difficile
CF	Cystic Fibrosis
CHB	Complete Heart Block
CHF	Congestive Heart Failure
CKD	Chronic Kidney Disease
CML	Chronic Myelogenous Leukemia
CMV	CytoMegaloVirus
CNA	Certified Nurse Assistant
CNS	Central Nervous System
CO	Cardiac Output
CO_2	Carbon Dioxide
C/O	Complaining Of
COP	Colloid Osmotic Pressure
COPD	Chronic Obstructive Pulmonary Disease
CPAP	Continuous Positive Airway Pressure
CPK	Creatine PhosphoKinase
CPR	CardioPulmonary Resuscitation
CRCL	CReatinine CLearance
CRF	Chronic Renal Failure
CRI	Chronic Renal Insufficiency
CRP	C-Reactive Protein
CSF	CerebroSpinal Fluid
CT	Computerized Tomography
CVA	CerebroVascular Accident/Cerebral Vascular Accident
CVP	Central Venous Pressure

D5W	5% Dextrose in Water
DI	Diabetes Insipidus
DIC	Disseminated Intravascular Coagulopathy
DJD	Degenerative Joint Disease
DKA	Diabetic KetoAcidosis
DM	Diabetes Mellitus
DNR	Do Not Resuscitate
DOE	Dyspnea On Exertion
DPT	Diphtheria, Pertussis, Tetanus
DTs	Delirium Tremens
DTR	Deep Tendon Reflexes
DVT	Deep Venous Thrombosis
DX	Diagnosis

ECG/EKG	ElectroCardioGram
ECT	ElectroConvulsive Therapy
EEG	ElectroEncephaloGram
EKG	ElectroCardioGram
EMG	ElectroMyoGram
ENT	Ears, Nose, and Throat
ER/ED	Emergency Room/Department
ESR	Erythrocyte Sedimentation Rate
ESRD	End Stage Renal Disease
ET	EndoTracheal
ETT	EndoTracheal Tube
EtOH	Ethanol

FBS	Fasting Blood Sugar
F&E	Fluid and Electrolytes
FFP	Fresh Frozen Plasma
FTT	Failure to Thrive
FSBS	FingerStick Blood Sugar
FUO	Fever of Unknown Origin
FVD	Fluid Volume Deficit
FVO	Fluid Volume Overload
Fx	Fracture

GAD	Generalized Anxiety Disorder
GFR	Glomerular Filtration Rate
GJ tube	Gastrojejunal Feeding Tube
GI	GastroIntestinal
gm/dl	grams per deciliter
gr	grain; 1 grain= 6mg, therefore, Vgr=325mg
GSW	Gun Shot Wound
gtt	drops
GTT	Glucose Tolerance Test
GU	GenitoUrinary

HA	Headache
HCT	HematoCriT
Hgb	HemoGloBin
HIPAA	Health Insurance Portability and Accountability Act
HIV	Human Immunodeficiency Virus
HOB	Head Of Bed
HR	Heart Rate
HS	Hour of Sleep
HTN	Hypertension
Hx	History
H_2O	Water

I&D	Incision and Drainage
I&O	Intake and Output
ICP	IntraCranial Pressure
ICS	Intercostal Space
ICU	Intensive Care Unit
IDDM	Insulin Dependent Diabetes Mellitus
IED	Intermittent Explosive Disorder
IHI	Institute for Healthcare Improvement
IICP	Increased InterCranial Pressure
INR	International Normalized Ratio
IOP	Increased Ocular Pressure/Intraocular Pressure
IPPB	Intermittent Positive Pressure Breathing
IRDM	Insulin Resistant Diabetes Mellitus
IT	InterThecal
ITP	Idiopathic Thrombocytopenic Purpura
IV	Intravenous
IVF	Intravascular Fluids
IVP	Intravenous Pyelogram

JODM	Juvenile Onset Diabetes Mellitus
JVD	Jugular Venous Distention

Kg/hr	kilograms per hour
KUB	Kidneys, Ureters, Bladder
KVO	Keep Vein Open

LAD	Lymphadenopathy
LE	Lupus Erythematosus
LLL	Left Lower Lobe
LMP	Last Menstrual Period
LMWH	Low Molecular Weight Heparins
LOC	Level Of Consciousness
LP	Lumbar Puncture
LPN/LVN	Licensed Practical/Vocational Nurse
LVH	Left Ventricular Hypertrophy

MAOI	MonoAmine Oxidase Inhibitor
MAP	Mean Arterial Pressure
Meq/L	Milliequivalents per Liter
MI	Myocardial Infarction
mL	Milliliter
MODS	Multi-Organ Dysfunction Syndrome
MMR	Measles, Mumps, Rubella
MRI	Magnetic Resonance Imagine
MRSA	Methicillin Resistant Staph Aureus
MS	Multiple Sclerosis

MVA	Motor Vehicle Accident

NCLEX®	National Council Licensure Examination
NG	NasoGastric
NIDDM	Non-Insulin Dependent Diabetes Mellitus
NKA	No Known Allergies
NKDA	No Known Drug Allergies
NMR	Nuclear Magnetic Resonance
NPO	Nothing by mouth
NSAID	Non-Steroidal Anti-Inflammatory Drugs
NSR	Normal Sinus Rhythm
NT	NasoTracheal

OCD	Obsessive Compulsive Disorder
OD	right eye
OG	Oral Gastric
OOB	Out Of Bed
OR	Operating Room
OS	left eye
OSHA	Occupational Safety and Health Administration
OTC	Over The Counter
OU	both eyes
O_2	Oxygen

PAC	Pulmonary Artery Catheter
PAC	Pulmonary Artery Catheterization
PAC	Premature Atrial Contraction
PAO_2	Alveolar Oxygen
PaO_2	Peripheral Arterial Oxygen content
PAP	Pulmonary Artery Pressure
PCA	Patient Controlled Analgesia
PCWP	Pulmonary Capillary Wedge Pressure
PDA	Patent Ductus Arteriosus
PE	Pulmonary Embolus
PEEP	Positive End Expiratory Pressure
PFT	Pulmonary Functions Tests
PICC	Peripherally Inserted Central Catheter
PKU	Phenylketonuria
PRN	as needed
PT	Prothrombin Time
PTH	ParaThyroid Hormone
PTSD	Post-Traumatic Stress Disorder
PTT	Partial Thromboplastin Time
PUD	Peptic Ulcer Disease
PVC	Premature Ventricular Contraction

PVD	Peripheral Vascular Disease

q	every (q6h = Every 6 hours
qd	every day
qh	every hour
qid	four times a day

RA	Rheumatoid Arthritis
RBC	Red Blood Cell
RLQ	Right Lower Quadrant
R/O	Rule Out
ROM	Range of Motion
RR	Respiratory Rate
RVH	Right Ventricular Hyperthrophy
Rx	treatment

SBE	Subacute Bacterial Endocarditis
SCI	Spinal Cord Injury
SG	Swan-Ganz
SGA	Small for Gestational Age
SGOT	Serum Glutamic-Oxaloacetic Transaminase
SGPT	Serum Glutamic-Pyruvic Transaminase
SIADH	Syndrome of Inappropriate AntiDiuretic Hormone
SJS	Steven Johnson's Syndrome
SLE	Systemic Lupus Erythematous
SOB	Shortness Of Breath
SOBOE	Shortness Of Breath On Exertion
SPO_2	Saturation of Peripheral Oxygen
STAT	immediately
SUBQ	SubCUtaneous
Sx	Symptoms

T	Temperature
T&C	Type and Crossmatch
TB	TuBerculosis
TBI	Traumatic Brain Injury
TIA	Transient Ischemic Attack
tid	three times a day
TJC	The Joint Commission
TPN	Total Parenteral Nutrition
TSH	Thyroid Stimulating Hormone
TTE	TransThoracic Echocardiogram
TURP	TransUrethral Resection of Prostate

UC	Ulcerative Colitis
UGI	Upper GastroIntestinal
u/l	Units per Liter
UOP	Urinary OutPut
URI	Upper Respiratory Infection
URQ	Upper Right Quadrant
US	UltraSound
UTI	Urinary Tract Infection

VDRL	Venereal Disease Research Laboratory (test for Syphilis)
VF	Ventricular Fibrillation
VS	Vital Signs
VT	Ventricular Tachycardia

WBC	White Blood Cell
WN	Well Nourished
WNL	Within Normal Limits
WT	Weight

XI	eleven
XII	twelve

yo	Years Old

This book is written to help nursing students learn concepts that are vital to safe clinical practice and to help prepare for nursing school exams and the *NCLEX*®. This is a different review book than any you have ever seen. Why? Because we teach so that you can remember and we make complicated concepts simple! We also connect with our learners and will do that in various ways. One way is to provide some of our own and other nurse friends' experiences so that you can get the "feel." Learning research shows that what goes through the feeling part of our brain stays. We are strong believers in Accelerated Learning Techniques and will use YouTube video opportunities, images, acronyms, poems, and anything else creative to help you remember.

We know this works! Our experience with these techniques has provided us with evidence based research of more than 30 years at over a 98% pass rate!

We also know that practice questions are important, *but you don't have to do 5000 of them,* you just have to practice advanced *NCLEX*® type items that bring your thinking to clinical reasoning. Every state does not contract with the National Council of State Boards of Nursing (the *NCLEX*® writers) without reason. They are responsible for the **SAFETY** of the citizens of their state and want an exam that reflects exactly that. This is not an exam about facts (but you had better know the facts). It is an exam of what you assess, analyze, plan, implement, and evaluate with a client once you are given their clinical picture. You just cannot stand at the end of the bed and say, "Oh, I know what arrhythmia the patient is in." Name the arrhythmia and watch them die.

> YOU CAN'T JUST NAME IT, YOU HAVE TO DO SOMETHING
> SO THE CLIENT WILL NOT DIE!

Our questions are different too because they are ALL clinical reasoning *NCLEX*® type questions for your practice. Find them at the end of each chapter.

NCLEX® Organization and You

The National Council of State Boards of Nursing (NCSBN®) is the professional nursing organization responsible for writing the *NCLEX*® exam for both registered and practical nurses. The profession of nursing is proud of the research that is completed by the National Council of State Boards of Nursing. This ongoing research, published every three years, is titled *Report of Findings from the 2011 RN Practice Analysis: Linking the NCLEX-RN® Examination to Practice* (NCSBN®, 2012). This research is the backbone of the *NCLEX*® Examination and this review book. **It will be implemented for the 2013-2016 *NCLEX*® exam.** We are grateful to the NCSBN® for this excellent research and for their contributions to the profession. The NCSBN® (www.ncsbn.org) research indicated that the majority of registered nurse graduates begin their careers in hospital type agencies. For this reason, the majority of the *NCLEX®* questions are written to evaluate the ability of the new graduate to keep the public safe in clinical related situations.

NCLEX-RN® REVIEW: Keeping It Real! *Simplified* **is written about real clinical situations with real clinical reasoning questions for your practice.**

Research on learning has determined that the more we associate new learning with information that we already know, the easier it is to recall. In this edition, we "connect the dots" for you so that you can remember the concepts easily and apply them to many different clinical reasoning situations.

Follow These Steps and You Will Be Well on the Way to Passing the *NCLEX®*

1. **Complete all course work** from your school of nursing and apply for graduation. Your school is not obligated to send your transcripts to the exam people until you have met all course requirements, paid all fees, returned all library books, and graduated. They should be committed to send your transcripts to your state board of nursing within 30 days. (Sometimes this takes longer.) It is a good thing to check with the school's registrar to determine when your transcripts may be sent.

2. **Complete an application** to take the *NCLEX®* exam. This can be accomplished at The National Council of State Boards of Nursing website, www.ncsbn.org. There is an **NCLEX® Examination Candidate Bulletin at a Glance** on this site that gives you a step-by-step process for completing the registration. This bulletin also explains the association of the National Council of State Boards of Nursing with Pearson Vue. Pearson Vue is the company that provides the venues and computers where you will take the exam. Their website is www.pearsonvue.com/nclex. Be sure to add *NCLEX®* onto this address as Pearson Vue provides the venue for many other types of exams. Once Pearson Vue and you receive the *Authority to Test* (ATT) from your board of nursing, you should have the right to schedule a testing date. It is important to take the exam within 30 days of your ATT. It is always smart to check with the closest Pearson Vue testing center to determine that they have received your application and all materials are in order. All telephone numbers and addresses are on their website. **It is up to you to schedule the time and date that you wish to take the exam.** Pearson Vue has over 200 testing centers in the United States and approximately 19 international testing centers.

3. **Critical tips on the application process**
   Read carefully and follow every step of the candidate bulletin—they mean every word. Always use the same name and ID number when you talk with the testing group. For example, if you complete the application using Nancy Sue Brown and the next time you

send additional papers or a check and you use Nancy S. Brown, it **will** get lost and your application will become screwed up.

4. **Even if your name changes legally** by marriage, you will need to send the testing group a name change application to make certain that all of your paperwork is appropriate for exam time. Be consistent!

   Every school of nursing has a program code and your name is associated with your school. Get it right the first time and always use the same code for each piece of paper you are sending in.

   Send guaranteed payment for your application. There is nothing like the delay that you will have to live with if you send in an insufficient funds check.

   If an agency is paying your exam fee, be sure that they have your correct name, correct email, correct school code, your valid picture identification, and that they fill out a separate form just for you. When your name appears on a check with other names that the agency is paying for, things can get messed up. Ask the agency to write a separate check for each individual.

5. **The most important tip of all—time is of the essence! Research indicates that the closer you take the *NCLEX®* to your graduation date, the better your opportunity for passing. Do not delay! As Nike® says, "Just Do It!"**

6. **Once you receive the Authority to Test** document from Pearson Vue and, if space allows, you can take the exam within 48 hours. We recommend taking a review course and, of course, we believe that we have the #1 in Quality available in the world. www.sylviarayfied.com

7. Once you have received the Authority to Test, you have 3 months to schedule your exam. *If you do not schedule during this time period, you will have to start this whole process all over again.*

Test Taking Strategies

There are many books available on test taking that discuss strategies to help you think about how to answer the questions. The first chapter in the *NCLEX-RN® 101: How To Pass* (I CAN Publishing, Inc.) is the best! It includes successful strategies that we have been using for over 20 years and they work. **Bottom line: You can only trust the question. Answer the question in your head before looking at the distractors.**

Test taking strategies alone will not help you to pass *NCLEX®*. In this publication, we are utilizing another important strategy that includes what the *NCLEX®* items are written about.

What's on *NCLEX®*?

The National Council of State Boards of Nursing (NCSBN®) has completed research that indicates the following categories and percentages for the existing standards for the *NCLEX-RN®* examination. (Copyright National Council of State Boards of Nursing Detailed Test Plan, www.ncsbn.org)

Management	17–23%
Pharmacology	12–18%
Physiological Adaptation	11–17%
Risk Reduction	9–15%
Infection Control	9–15%
Basic Care & Comfort	6–12%
Health Promotion	6–12%
Psycho-social	6–12%

By analyzing the chart, it is easy to determine where to place your study and preparation emphasis. When you can see that management and pharmacology makes up as much as 41% of the entire exam and basic care and comfort, health promotion, and psycho-social altogether make up only 36% of the exam, **where do you want to put your time?**

Currently, there are 141 "activities" that fall within the chart above. These are from the *2011 RN Practice Analysis: Linking the NCLEX-RN® Examination to Practice* NCSBN® Research Brief published January 2012 and found at www.ncsbn.org.

Some research studies show that iatrogenic damage (a form of medical error) is a leading cause of hospital deaths.

As much as 38% of the *NCLEX®* exam includes both management and infection control and may be defined within the standards in this first FREE INTRODUCTORY UNIT.

The NCSBN® (www.ncsbn.org) research indicates that the majority of new graduates from RN programs begin their careers in hospitals or similar agencies. For this reason, to keep the public safe, the **backbone** of nursing standards is related to national health care standards that are set by agencies such as:

State Boards of Nursing—Sets the standards for the regulation of the practice of nursing and issues licenses for practice. This includes legal standards, priorities for nursing care, implementation and evaluation of nursing care, ethics, and many other standards.

Joint Commission—The Joint Commission (TJC), www.jointcommission.org, formerly the Joint Commission on Accreditation of Healthcare Organizations. TJC operates accreditation programs for hospitals and other health care organizations that wish accreditation status. Most states recognize Joint Commission accreditation as a condition of licensure and the receipt of Medicaid reimbursement. What does this mean? **Money**—if there is no Joint Commission accreditation for the hospital agency, there is no money from Medicaid. Most hospitals that are currently not accredited are seeking accreditation.

HIPAA—Health Insurance Portability and Accountability Act, www.hipaa.com, prescribes standards that are used in hospital agencies including privacy, confidentiality, and safeguards to patient data on charts and computers.

OSHA—Occupational Safety and Health Administration (United States Department of Labor), www.osha.com, sets standards including blood borne pathogens, biological hazards, potential chemical and drug exposures, respiratory hazards, ergonomic hazards from lifting, hazards associated with laboratories, medical equipment maintenance, and administrative staff, to name a few.

The National Council of State Boards of Nursing research standards are the basis for this book and for the NCLEX® exam. These standards were used to formulate each chapter and every review question.

PASS NCLEX®!

Ensure proper identification of the client.

Provide care within the legal scope of practice.

Protect the client from injury/falls, electrical hazards, malfunctioning equipment or malfunctioning staff.

Practice in a manner consistent with a code of ethics for RNs.

Verify appropriateness/accuracy of order.

Maintain client confidentiality and privacy.

Evaluate/document response to treatment.

Collaborate with health care members in other disciplines when providing care.

Prioritize workload to manage time effectively.

Acknowledge/document practice error.

Supervise care provided by others (other RNs, LPNs, CNAs).

These commonalities listed flow through the client safety of every body system and are heavily weighted on the *NCLEX®* exam. We have condensed them into the following box on MANAGE. You will note the **manage box** in each chapter.

PASS *NCLEX®*!

M	**Make sure of identity, accuracy of orders**
A	**Arrange privacy/confidentiality/consent/collaboration with other team**
N	**No injuries, falls, malfunctioning equipment or staff or hazards**
A	**Address errors, abuse, legalities, scope of practice—document**
G	**Give (delegate) orders to appropriate people**
E	**Evaluate priorities/response to treatment**

THIS SAFETY **ACRONYM IS A GREAT WAY TO ORGANIZE:**
- **Safe client care**
- **Study of heaviest weighted NCLEX® standards**
- **All body systems**

You will recognize this acronym in all of the chapters.

PASS *NCLEX®*!

S   **System specific assessment**

A   **Assess for risk and respond**

F   **Find change/trends and intervene**

E   **Evaluate pharmacology**

T   **Teach infection control, health promotion using psycho-social**

Y   **Your management—legal/ethical/scope of practice, identity, errors, delegation, faulty equipment/staff, privacy/confidentiality, falls/hazards**

A Story

The following is an account of one graduate's experience of taking the *NCLEX®* exam. We hope it will be useful to you.

What a magical day, the day I found out my last clinical grade and knew beyond a doubt that my educational responsibilities were completed for nursing and that school was over for me. That day came the second week of August. Soon there was graduation in October and in November came the paper diploma I was looking for that celebrated all that hard work.

*The next task was the **NCLEX-RN®** exam. First, I had to register with my state and apply to test. This was, for me, accomplished mostly online. The state required an official copy of my diploma so the only paperwork for my state included an official fingerprint card with a notarized copy of my driver's license. Four weeks later, I received my "authority to test" by email. A hard copy followed by mail a week later. In November I was anxious to challenge the exam. I followed the directions at www.ncsbn.org, which linked me to Pierson Vue and allowed me to register and pay the exam fee. While waiting to take the exam, I tried to keep everything fresh from school. I scheduled and attended a live review and spent about 2 hours a day, 5 days a week answering **NCLEX®** questions. The first hour I answered questions and the second hour was spent studying what I missed.*

Everybody prepares for big exams in their own way. I registered but didn't share the date with my friends so they wouldn't ask me when I would receive the results. I don't have a Pierson Vue testing center in my community. The closest one is about one and a half hours away with no traffic. I know that because I drove to the exam center two days before the exam. Parking for me was free and easy to find. I even went up the elevator to the right floor and found not only the testing center but the restroom as well.

I made arrangements to be off from work the day before and the day of the exam. I helped my children be prepared and had them stay overnight with a close family friend the night before I took the test. They were in school while I tested. I spent the day before the exam taking care of me. I made my favorite meal, I had a pedicure, I watched a movie (a comedy), and I went to bed early.

EXAM DAY—I had an early start. I know because I set 3 different alarm clocks so I could tell myself to fall asleep and not worry that I would miss the test. The drive went by like the blink of an eye and there I was opening the door to the exam center. I had my Authority to Test (ATT), my wallet with my ID and a protein bar. The staff gave me a laminated copy of the rules of Pierson Vue for me to read and they took my paperwork and ID. Next, they scanned the palm vein of my right hand with a very cool device set up on the table up front. Next, it was time for my close-up picture that was attached to my ATT and palm vein online.

I waited about 10 minutes for the next staff member to be ready to take me into the test room. I emptied all my pockets into a personal locker and took the key with me. I found the rooms to be cold so don't forget to bring a sweater to stay warm. A new staff member asked me again if I understood the rules, and then she handed me a white board, something to write with, and a headphone set. Since there were people at most of the stations in the test room, she showed me where to sit. Then she scanned my palm again to open the computer Terminal. Once the computer was opened, I began the pretest that was at the front of the exam. I recognized this pretest as the same one as the candidate tutorial on the web site at registration. I was focused. I was in it. That was at least until the person in the next cubby kept tapping his pencil on the table as some kind of nervous twitch. I put my headphones on and, believe it or not, the noise was gone.

It is startling when the computer shuts down. There is a small noise and the screen goes blank before a prompt tells you that your exam is complete. This is when I got nervous. The exam was demanding and all my energy was spent. Fortunately, I had registered to get the results online in 48–72 hours (remember that exam day does not count in the 48 hours).

I PASSED!!!

Nursing Management in Cardiovascular and Hematology Disorders

Sylvia Rayfield, MN, RN, CNS
Edited by Sylvia Rayfield & Associates, Inc.

Ischemic heart diseases and congestive heart failure often alternate as the #1 leading cause of admissions and death in hospitals.

That's the scary thing about heart disease. You can be fine one minute and dead the next. You can put up with a little chest pain every once in a while if you know you're not about to die from it.

Mark Hlatky

MOST COMMON TYPES OF CARDIOVASCULAR DISORDERS

Key Concepts:
- Hypertension Leading to Hypertensive Heart Disease
- Coronary Artery Disease/Ischemic Heart Disease
- Arrhythmias
- Congestive Heart Failure
- Cardiogenic Shock
- Blood Disorders
- Practice Questions, Answers and Rationale

is a simplified version of the nursing process, which is a simplified version of a problem solving process. This analogy allows us to make the complicated simple and we will use it in many chapters of this book.

Hypertension

High blood pressure is defined in some sources as a consistent reading of 140/90 or 130/80 for clients with diabetes or renal disease. Hypertension or higher than normal pressure in the arteries leads to hypertensive heart disease, coronary artery disease, heart attacks, and stokes.

SEARCH (Assess, Analysis)	RESCUE (Implementation)	FALLOUT (Outcome—good/bad)
Vital signs Utilize the correct size cuff for BP analysis. Do not use a neonatal cuff on a 350 pound man! Search for symptoms of hypertension, including: • headaches • dizziness • blurred vision • nosebleeds • heart palpitations • fatigue & SOB Risk factors include: • heredity • age • obesity/eating habits that increase total cholesterol above 200mg/dl • LDL (bad) cholesterol should be less than 130mg/dl • HDL (Good) cholesterol should be 60mg/dl or higher • Triglycerides should be less than 150mg/dl	Teach accurate BP testing. High blood pressure does is painless. Encourage the client to keep record of BP at different times of the day. Symptoms must not be ignored. Monitor vital signs. Heredity and age cannot be corrected, but obesity and eating habits can. Think **COLOR** on the plate to get fruits and vegetables, which help reduce cholesterol levels. Think reduction of: • meat over the size of a deck of cards • bacon • cream, dairy products • fried foods	BP control reduces hypertensive disease which can lead to cardiovascular disease. Hypertension leads to other types of heart disease Obesity contributes to hypertension, high cholesterol, coronary artery disease, heart attacks, and strokes. Think **HEALTH PROMOTION!**

MEDICATIONS FOR HYPERTENSIVE DISORDERS

When administering medication nurses are legally responsible and must be CAREFUL!

PASS *NCLEX*®!

C   **Calculate correctly**

A   **Assess for allergies**

R   **Rights of administration**

E   **Evaluate response**

F   **Feel free to call provider if intuition alerts**

U   **Utilize assessments in determining ordered parameters**

L   **Lab data pertinence**

Medication	Prior to Administration	Nursing Actions/ Education	Alerts
ACE INHIBITORS Angiotensin Converting Enzyme the **"pril"** drugs Benaze**pril** (Lotensin) Capto**pril** (Capoten) Enla**pril** (Vasotec) Lisino**pril** (Zestril) Moexi**pril** (Univasc) Rami**pril** (Altace)	Determine baseline BP. Caution with renal or liver impairment Determine other medications that may interact. Determine allergies	Evaluate for first dose BP drop. Report headache, weakness, rash, cough	Verify orders due to some contraindications. Hypotension A tendency to cough. Renal failure Liver failure Angioedema Decrease in WBC's Erectile dysfunction

Medication	Prior to Administration	Nursing Actions/ Education	Alerts
"ARBS" Angiotensin II Receptor Blockers, also called "sartans" Lo**sartin** (Cozaar) Telmi**sartan** (Micardis) Cande**sartan** (Atacand) Epro**sartan** (Teveten) Val**sartan** (Diovan) Olme**sartan** (Benecar)	Determine other medications that may interact, such as Lasix or Lithium. Determine allergies. Caution with renal or liver impairment.	Report headache, weakness, diarrhea, dizziness, and rash. May cause birth defects in pregnant women Decongestants increase BP. Micardis may interact with Lanoxin.	Hypotension Erectile dysfunction
BETA BLOCKERS	Determine allergies **WARNING: May cause airway to constrict in clients with asthma or COPD. Beta blockers increase blood sugar in many clients, causing elevated blood sugar or high risk of becoming diabetic. Beta blockers may mask symptoms of hypoglycemia.** Caution with renal or liver impairment. Determine other medications that may interact, such as Lasix or Lithium.	Evaluate for first dose BP drop. If client is taking antacids, the antacids should be taken 2 hours prior to or after these medications. Educate to keep personal BP record.	GI symptoms Nausea/vomiting Swelling of the face, throat, tongue, lips, eyes, hands, feet, ankles, or lower legs. Hoarseness Difficulty breathing or swallowing. Fainting

Medication	Prior to Administration	Nursing Actions/ Education	Alerts
Beta Blockers slow the heart rate and decrease the BP (end in **LOL**) There are 2 major types of Beta blockers. Think—we have 1 heart (Beta 1 affects primarily the heart) and 2 lungs (Beta 2 affect both the heart and lungs). The following are examples of Beta 1 drugs used to lower BP. • Acebuto**lol** (Sectral) • Ateno**lol** (Tenormin) • Metopro**lol** (Toprol, Lopressor) The following are examples of Beta 2 drugs also used to decrease BP in clients that do not have lung disease. • Nado**lol** (Corgard) • Proprano**lol** (Inderal)	Determine baseline vital signs. Determine allergies. **Extreme caution with the client with asthma or COPD!**	Evaluate the first dose BP drop. If client is taking antacids, the antacids should be taken 2 hours prior to or after these medications. Usually contraindicated in lung disease.	Hypotension Dizziness Weakness Fainting Cold hands and feet Depression
Calcium Channel Blockers relax and enlarge blood vessels causing a decrease in BP. Many of these drugs end in "**pine**." Amlodi**pine** (Norvasc) Amlodi**pine** with Atorvastatin (Caduet) Amlodi**pine** with Benazepril (Lotrel) Amlodi**pine** with Valsartan (Exforge) Felodi**pine** (Plendil) Nicardi**pine** (Cardene) Nisoldi**pine** (Sular) Verapamil (Calan)	Determine baseline vital signs. Note that the combination drugs must be treated as giving both drugs. Since Caduet is given with a statin, the liver enzymes should be determined. If given with a "**pril**," allergies to this med or tendency to cough should be determined. Determine if client is a diabetic; current research indicates that Verapamil may slow diabetes.	Educate client to keep personal BP/pulse record. Educate for dizziness or lightheadedness, flushing, or feeling warm. Monitor heart rate. This drug slows the heart rate. Peripheral edema is a very common side effect.	Hypotension Dizziness Weakness Fainting

Medication	Prior to Administration	Nursing Actions/ Education	Alerts
Drugs that lower BP often are given in combination with each other or with **Diuretics.** Diuretics work by excreting salt and water through the kidney causing a volume loss.	Determine allergies to sulfa drugs. Check renal function Determine baseline vital signs.	Administer during day as urinary frequency will occur. Measure I&O Weigh daily Educate to eat foods that are high in potassium. Avoid foods high in sodium.	**Side effects and adverse reactions to these meds:** Too much fluid may be excreted causing dizziness and light-headedness, hypotension. Causes loss of potassium which can affect the electrical conduction in the heart, hypokalemia Dehydration
Diuretics These are just a few of the common diuretics: • Furosemide (Lasix) • Bumetanide(Bumex) • Torsemide ((Demadex) • Hydrochlorothiazide (Hydrodiuril)	Assess for client allergies especially to sulfa	Educate for daily weights, foods, or drugs that will not interfere with this medication. Educate to eat foods high in potassium Watch for muscle cramps and thirst. Monitor for low potassium <3.5	Hypokalemia Hyponatremia Tinnitus, hearing loss, ototoxicity except with hydrochlorothiazide Hypocalcemia except with hydrochlorothiazide
Common K+ sparing diuretics: • Spironolactone (Aldactone) • Amioloride (Midamor)	Check K+ levels	Educate for frequent K+ checks Educate for GI upsets	Hyperkalemia GI upsets and peptic ulcer

Medication	Prior to Administration	Nursing Actions/ Education	Alerts
		Diuretic side effects can be summed up with these 6 issues: • Dehydration • Hypotension • Diuresis • Electrolyte imbalance • Allergy to sulfa • Tinnitus (except with Thiazides)	Dry mouth Decreased BP, especially on the first dose I&O, daily weights Evaluate muscle cramps and weakness. Evaluate for hives, swelling of lips, tongue, and difficulty breathing

Coronary Artery Disease(CAD)/Ischemic Heart Disease

Coronary Artery Disease (**CAD**) is considered the most common type of heart disease and is caused from atherosclerosis (hardening of the arteries) or the build up over time of fat, cholesterol, and other substances in the arteries. This substance is called plaque, comes from our dietary intake, and narrows the artery, diminishing the needed amount of blood that goes through it. Plaque also increases the likelihood that blood clots will form in the artery, break loose, and plug a smaller artery causing the death of the coronary muscle that this artery serves. **CAD** is currently the most common cause of death.

THE HEART,

WITHOUT IT, WE ARE NOT HERE!

The acronym **HEART** will help us remember some important issues in this system.

H   Heart sounds and pulse rates are vital ways to assess the heart

E   Exercise builds a strong heart and rehabilitates a damaged one

A   Avoiding smoking, high cholesterol foods, and alcohol helps avoid heart disease

R   Response to stress is high on the list of living without heart disease

T   Tests (blood work, EKG, cardiac cath, CT Scan, and MRI) and pain confirm diagnosis

The heart has many arteries that carry oxygen to the muscles so that it will pump blood flow to the body without pain.

- Diminished blood flow in these arteries causes chest pain (**Angina Pectoris**). Watch this 1 minute YouTube for a quick update on angina and nitroglycerin. http://www.youtube.com/watch?v=GIWb4-a7A6A
- Pain is known to extend an infarct (make it worse).
- Pain control must be QUICK!
    - Aspirin is often the first line medication, which interferes with the blood's clotting action.
    - Nitroglycerin under the tongue. Three tablets over 10-15 minutes. Nitroglycerin makes the BP decrease; watch for hypotension. If pain isn't diminished, it's time to head for the emergency department.
    - Oxygen to improve oxygenation of the tissues and reduce pain.

THE SAFETY **ACRONYM IS A GREAT WAY TO ORGANIZE:**
- **Safe client care**
- **Study of heaviest weighted NCLEX® standards**
- **All body systems**

PASS *NCLEX®*!

S   **System specific assessment**

A   **Assess for risk and respond**

F   **Find change/trends and intervene**

E   **Evaluate pharmacology**

T   **Teach/practice infection control, health promotion**

Y   **Your management—legal/ethical/scope of practice, identity, errors, delegation, faulty equipment/staff, privacy, confidentiality, falls/**

SYSTEM SPECIFIC ASSESSMENT

We can't know what's going on with the heart unless we perform a focused assessment and for that we need tools. Start with a watch to take vital signs. This will get a feel for the strength and regularity of the pulse as well as the rate. Second, use a stethoscope; it's like American Express, "Don't leave home without it!" **If there are no heart sounds, there is nothing!**

Use the stethoscope to determine the blood pressure and listen to the heart sounds.

S1 (lub) is the closure of the AV valves or the valves between the atria and the ventricle. We want to hear a good crisp sound without murmurs.

S2 (dub) is the closure of the aortic and pulmonic valves. These are sometimes called the semilunar valves. S1 and S2 are both heard best with the diaphragm of the stethoscope.

S3 is a sound we would prefer not to hear since this may indicate that the client has too much fluid on board and is going into congestive heart failure. If we do hear the S3, it is time to go into clinical reasoning and prioritize nursing care. Discussion on CHF comes later.

S4 is another sound, sometimes called a gallop rhythm, that may indicate hypertrophy or fibrosis of the ventricle, hypertension of long standing, Coronary Artery Disease (CAD) or Congestive Heart Failure (CHF).

ASSESS AND RESPOND TO CHANGES IN CLIENT VITAL SIGNS

For review, we recommend that you go to www.easyauscultation.com. The *NCLEX*® has sounds on the exam that you will need to identify and make a clinical decision regarding what you hear. (Bottom Line: If there are more than 2 heart sounds, it is time to further investigate, and report to the provider.)

After heart sounds, let's take a look at the neck veins that will indicate JVD (Jugular Venous Distention). Raise the head of the bed 30-45 degrees, stand on the client's right, have him lie on his back, and turn his head to the left. With a soft light the jugular vein can be seen. If it is distended as high as the jaw angle, the client may have potential Congestive Heart Failure (CHF).

DIAGNOSTIC TOOLS

Diagnostic Tests are often essential to **assess for risk.**

There are 3 important questions that the nurse should be able to answer regarding any diagnostic test.

1. What should the client be taught prior to the exam and what is the nursing priority?

2. What should the client be taught regarding the procedure itself and what is the nursing priority during the procedure?

3. What should the client be taught after the procedure is completed and what is the nursing priority?

These are vital concepts to know and are often tested on *NCLEX*®.

PULSE OX –Looks like a clothes- pin on the end of the finger or ear lobe that measures oxygen saturation in a client's blood. Pulse ox monitors may vary, but the normal of a healthy client is approximately 90-95%. Older clients or clients with COPD (Chronic Obstructive Pulmonary Disease) may range from 88-94% on pulse oximeter. A quick easy non-invasive way to assess the client with suspected heart disease.

Cardiac Troponin T (cTnT) to determine the protein that identifies cardiovascular problems. The higher the troponins blood level, the higher the risk for cardiac death.

CVP (Central Venous Pressure) reading is another tool that is important to assess right ventricular function and systemic fluid status. The central venous pressure is considered a direct measurement of the blood pressure in the right atrium and vena cava. It is acquired by threading a central venous catheter (subclavian double lumen central line) into any of several large veins. A normal CVP reading is 2-6mm Hg. If the CVP increases or is elevated, this is an indication of fluid overload. If the CVP decreases or is low, this may indicate dehydration or shock. Nursing priority is to have a baseline reading and monitor the status. If the client is receiving IVs and the CVP reading goes from 5mm Hg to 10mm Hg within an hour, it is likely that the IVs are infusing too fast and should be slowed. This client should be monitored closely. This is the time to be listening to the lung sounds for signs of fluid overload. Go to http://www.cvmbs.colostate. edu/clinsci/callan/breath_sounds.html and listen to normal lung sounds first; then listen to other types of lung sounds that indicate fluid overload (crackles). The **CVP** catheter has several additional uses. Fluids and medications can be infused rapidly through the catheter directly into the right atrium which can be life saving.

EKG and **Telemetry** are excellent tools for assessing the heart by determining rate and rhythm. Nurses are responsible for initiating, monitoring, and interpreting arrhythmias seen on telemetry and selecting appropriate drugs from standing protocol for intervention of arrhythmias. These procedures are fairly non-invasive, but as always must be explained to the client.

Cardiac Catheterization is an invasive procedure (requiring informed consent). This exam measures blood pressure within the heart, oxygen in the blood, cardiac output, and, if dye is used, can look at the coronary arteries. View this quick YouTube is a graphic of this procedure. http://www.youtube.com/watch?v=sXrO52vqUQI

Nursing issues:

BEFORE: Consent signed, IV line open, and evaluation of blood work prior to procedure. Is the hematocrit high enough to have surgery? Is the client allergic to the dye? Hold the client NPO. Provide explanations to the client to alleviate fears including the fact that they may have to lie flat for a few hours after the exam.

DURING: Monitor vital signs; keep client warm, these ORs are cold. Reassure that "hot flash" is normal and will pass.

AFTER: Since the coronary cath has been inserted through a limb, usually the leg, there is a good possibility of bleeding at the insertion site as most of these clients have been administered Coumadin prior to the procedure.

Echocardiogram (Transthoracic echocardiogram, TTE) is the most common. A non-invasive test that uses sound waves to look at heart size, valves, identification of blood clots, muscle thickness, movement of the heart wall, and ejection fraction. If the ejection fraction is low, heart failure may be indicated. Since this is non-invasive, an explanation to alleviate fears will be useful, but NPO and IVs are usually not indicated unless a more extensive echo is done.

Magnetic Resonance Imaging (MRI) in a non-invasive test utilizing a powerful magnetic field to produce detailed pictures of the heart or virtually any internal body structure. Non-invasive because it does not hurt, but scary enough to people that are claustrophobic that they may need a sedative. Watch this short YouTube to see an actual MRI being performed if you have not seen one. The first 2 minutes are all that is needed to help you remember. http://www.youtube.com/watch?v=FallWN1uYco

BEFORE: Make sure the client is not pregnant. Remove jewelry, watches, credit cards, hearing aids, zippers, hairpins, body piercings, eyeglasses, **anything metal** that will interfere with the magnetic field. Clients with artificial heart valves, implanted drug infusion ports, implanted devices such as a cardiac pacemaker or defibrillator, metallic joint prosthesis, artificial hips, metal pins, plates, surgical staples, or any type of stent may pose a risk and the nurse should document these findings as well as notify the physician and MRI technologist of these findings. Inform client this test is noisy and this is normal. Client must be able to hold very still.

If contrast is to be used, an IV line is necessary.

After any diagnostic test the bottom line for nursing is to:
FIND TRENDS AND CHANGES IN CLIENT CONDITION AND INTERVENE APPROPRIATELY

Common changes will include:

- Reaction to dye

- Reaction to medications for pre-procedure or pain

- Change in vital signs

These assessments and diagnostic tests will provide the nurse and the physician with a diagnosis and a direction for nursing care and treatment. The entry level nurse graduating with a diploma, ADN or BSN is not responsible for making a medical diagnosis, but is responsible for reacting to the client's symptoms and providing medication from protocol if it is available. One of the most important decisions that a nurse makes is a legal and ethical one. We have to know when we have reached our level of competence. We have completed our assessment, looked at the diagnostic tests, provided the client with health promotion and reassurance, but there definitely comes a time when our responsibility is to notify the health care provider who knows more than we do; otherwise, we will work outside our scope of practice.

A typical scenario of a cardiac client might include the guy who is at his home, mowing his grass and has SOBOE (shortness of breath on exertion). Then he realizes that his chest is feeling like someone is standing on it. He may have had this feeling before (angina—a narrowing of the cardiac arteries that causes a lack of oxygen and pain in the heart muscle) and he may have nitroglycerin tablets that he carries with him that will dilate the coronary arteries and ease the workload of the heart. He will put one under his tongue. In 5 minutes he still has the pain and he puts another under his tongue. In another 5 minutes he tries one more. Nitroglycerin also comes in a spray that releases in the mouth and works well to dilate the coronary arteries. If none of these stop the pain, it is now time to head to the emergency department as the angina may have progressed to a myocardial infarction. Vital sign assessment after a client has take nitroglycerin is likely to show a decreased blood pressure due to arterial dilatation.

A Myocardial infarct (MI) causes muscle death in the myocardium and treatment should be swift and aimed toward preventing further extension of the infarct. The EKG is a great tool to use here as the ST segment is elevated in an MI and provides some confirmation.

An EKG strip of an elevated ST segment is inserted next.

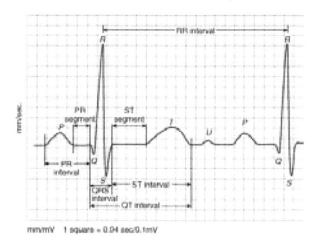

mm/mV   1 square = 0.04 sec/0.1mV

Remember, lack of oxygen causes pain. Pain extends an infarct and the nurse is responsible for providing pain relief through oxygen, morphine and other medications listed on protocol. The narcotic, morphine, is often administered for pain relief.

EVALUATE PHARMACOLOGY

Other medications commonly administered after an MI include:

- ➢ **Oxygen** to re-oxygenate the coronary muscles

- ➢ **Nitroglycerin** to dilate the coronary arteries for better oxygen delivery

- ➢ **Aspirin,** an antiplatelet agent to prolong bleeding and reduce clotting

- ➢ **Morphine,** a narcotic for pain relief

- ➢ **Thrombolytics (Activase, Streptokinase)** to hopefully restore a coronary vessel that has been occluded.

- ➢ **Clopidogrel (Plavix)** to prevent clotting by inhibiting platelet aggregation

- ➢ **Anticoagulants (Heparin, Coumadin, Lovenox)**

- ➢ **ACE Inhibitors,** drugs that end in "**pril**" (reduces the heart rate if needed)

- ➢ **Beta Blockers,** drugs that end in "**lol**" (reduces the heart rate)

Ace Inhibitors and Beta Blockers are discussed more thoroughly in the Hypertension section of this book.

Medication Administration Alert

REMEMBER: When administering medication we must be CAREFUL!

All of these medications and interventions may be utilized while the OR is being scheduled for a possible **coronary artery bypass grafting,** often called **CABG.** Since the arteries have become clogged, the bypass surgery utilizes an artery from another part of the body to bypass a clogged artery and create a new blood flow to the cardiac muscle. This surgery is serious because the sternum is divided, the heart is stopped, and a heart-lung machine is used in most of these procedures to keep the client perfused while the surgeon is affixing new veins.

Monitoring for risk and intervention after a CABG includes:

C	Careful monitoring for arrhythmias; the main cause of death during and after this procedure is ventricular tachycardia and ventricular defibrillation
A	Alert for signs of stroke
B	Bleeding external and internal can lead to "going back in" for additional surgery. Monitor VS and symptoms of shock.
G	GFR (glomerular filtration rate) in the kidney decreases—watch for kidney failure. Urinalysis and blood tests will help determine renal function. Renal failure is a high alert situation when the client is taking medications that are excreted through the kidney.

Myocardial Infarcts, MI, heart attacks lead to arrhythmias. Arrhythmias are changes in the electrical conduction of the heart and can be confirmed on EKG. If you need a refresher, this YouTube will help you remember where the leads should be placed to get an EKG or a rhythm strip and shows exactly how to do an EKG. http://www.youtube.com/watch?v=eA5HmQSMGHE

* This is what a normal heart rhythm should look like. This strip would be a normal sinus rhythm (NSR), Note that the **P waves** indicate atrial activity and the **qrs** complex indicates ventricular activity

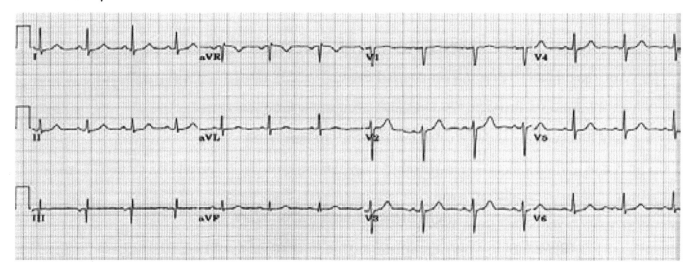

- Visit this YouTube site to see NSR as it appears on a cardiac monitor. http://www.youtube.com/watch?v=Q0JMfIVaDUE

- We will not present a full ACLS course in arrhythmias in this review book because, at this time, it is not currently content specific to the **NCLEX®**. We will, however, present the major fatal dysrhythmias that are most common. We will also suggest those drugs that are most often seen in standing protocol documents currently used to intervene in these aberrations.

ATRIAL FIBRILLATION

- The most common arrhythmia is **Atrial Fibrillation.** When you can't identify a **P wave,** you can deduce that there is a problem in the atria. The good news is that we can live for a while without an identifiable **P wave** as in the case of atrial fibrillation (AF) or atrial flutter. If you have not seen AF on a cardiac monitor watch this: http://www.youtube.com/watch?v=R-Z_S5sVBJA
  If your client has atrial fib what would be your nursing priority?
  - Notify the provider

  - Request an order for an anticoagulant

  - Prepare for possible cardioversion with external direct current at low voltage

  - Prepare for possible cardioversion with medication ordered by the provider.

Pwave - Represent Atrial Activity

QRS Complex - Represents Ventricule Activity

Twave - Represents Repolarization (Recovery) of Ventricles

- The bad news comes from the fact that when the atria are fibrillating, they are not emptying the blood that is inside them. Think about what happens to blood when it just sits (as it does in AF). It will clot, right? Now that's a big problem because clots have a way of working themselves into places where they can cause a lot of damage. The clots in the atria are sometimes called mural thrombi and their most likely target is the brain. When there is a clot in the brain, the client has a stroke. Clients that have atrial fib are treated as soon as possible to try to prevent these clots from forming. Clot buster medications administered for stroke will be discussed in the Neuro chapter with Strokes.

Prominent U wave - Suspect HypoKalemia, Hypercalcemia or hyper thyroidism

EVALUATE PHARMACOLOGY

ANTICOAGULANTS

These drugs are administered to most clients that have AF. Keep in mind that anticoagulant drugs are used for many purposes (other than AF) such as DVT (Deep Vein Thrombosis), PE (Pulmonary Embolus), for clients who have an artificial heart valve, or to reduce the risk of heart attack or stroke. The most commonly prescribed anticoagulants are:

- **Warfarin (Coumadin)** is a "blood thinner" administered by mouth usually once a day with or without food. The dosage is monitored by a frequent blood test including PT and INR (International Normalized Ratio), which simply mean that the reporting of blood results will be the same all over the world. The normal INR for a client not taking an anticoagulant is 1. The higher the number, the longer it takes for the blood to clot. The target INR range for a client taking an anticoagulant is 2-3 times normal. An INR greater than 4 is an indication to notify the provider and hold the anticoagulant until further evaluation can be made. Needless to say, clients taking anticoagulants of all sorts are easier to bruise, may have bloody stools, bleeding in the gums, and uncontrolled bleeding after a cut or injury.

- **Drugs and Foods** also increase the INR, particularly when they are taken with Coumadin. These include aspirin, ibuprofen, some antibiotics, and birth control pills.

- **Vitamin K**, a natural blood-clotting factor, is the antidote for Coumadin and is found in common foods such as green leafy vegetables, asparagus, broccoli, cauliflower, and some meats, such as liver. For this reason, clients should be advised to use these foods sparingly or at least consistently, so that the Coumadin can be monitored.

- **Heparin**, used to decrease the blood's clotting ability, is administered subcutaneously (often in the abdomen) or intravenously. It is most often administered in a hospital setting and is often given concurrently with warfarin (Coumadin). Most clients are not discharged on heparin, but are likely to be given a prescription for Coumadin to take for weeks or months. The labs that monitor heparin are PTT and INR with reference ranges that vary if heparin is used alone or in combination with Coumadin. Most resources suggest reducing the drug and/or administering the antidote protamine sulfate if the INR goes to as high as 5. If the INR reaches 8, the heparin should be stopped and the antidote administered. In addition to being utilized for atrial fib, it is also given for venous thrombosis, mechanical heart valves, and prevention of thromboembolic disease. Aspirin and heparin is a very dangerous combination and should be monitored very closely for reducing the blood's ability to clot. All of these drugs are contraindicated for clients that have any blood dyscrasia such as hemophilia, conditions like ulcers that have a tendency to bleed, or anything that is causing active internal bleeding.

- **Low Molecular Weight Heparins (LMWH)** are easy to identify because their generic name ends in "**parin**"— dalte**parin** (Fragmin), enoxa**parin** (Lovenox), and tinza**parin** (Innohep). These drugs inhibit clotting, are given subcutaneously, and are used to treat thrombosis. They are commonly used for prophylactic treatment with clients who have heart condition such as unstable angina, invasive procedures such as cardiac catheterization, DVT (Deep Vein Thrombosis), and postoperative orthopedic surgery. Most clients do not have to be monitored while taking this drug as the bleeding risk is not as great as heparin and Coumadin. The blood test Anti-Factor Xa is currently the only reliable way to monitor these drugs. Watch for easy bruising.

- The good thing is that these drugs inhibit the ability of the blood to clot. The bad thing is that they do not dissolve clots that have already formed. This is the reason that the Clot Busters become so important as they DO dissolve the clots if administered within a very short period of time after stroke symptoms appear. Clot Busters (rt-PA) are discussed in the neurological chapter with stroke.

Other arrhythmias are likely to be more lethal than atrial fib.

VENTRICULAR TACHYCARDIA (VT) may be a death producing arrhythmia

Visit this link to see Ventricular Tachycardia on a cardiac monitor.
http://www.youtube.com/watch?v=UC-bu6_6zEA

If you saw this on a cardiac monitor, what would be the top nursing priority?

- Assess the client for consciousness

- Begin CPR if no equipment is available

- Defibrillate the client

This YouTube shows problems with the **qrs** sometimes labeled "funny looking beats." It is a rapid beat and is considered to be ventricular tachycardia. Most clients will experience palpitations with this arrhythmia. The client with VT at a slow rate may show no symptoms, but this can change quickly. The faster the VT, the closer to cardiac arrest. This is often an emergency death producing arrhythmia and should be treated immediately!

MEDICATIONS COMMONLY LISTED ON PROTOCOL TO SUPPRESS VENTRICULAR TACH INCLUDE:
- **amiodarone (Coradrone)**

- **lidocaine (Xylocaine)**

- **procainamide (Pronestyl)**

THESE DRUGS ARE USED FOR LIFE-THREATENING VENTRICULAR ARRHYTHMIAS. ACTIONS INCLUDE:

- Prolongs the action potential and refractory period

- Inhibits adrenergic stimulation

- Slows the sinus rate

- Increases PR and QT intervals on EKG

- Decreases peripheral vascular resistance (vasodilatation).

These drugs are used very cautiously for the failing heart!
When you cannot identify a qrs complex, you know that the client is in serious trouble!

VENTRICULAR FIBRILLATION (VF)

This YouTube link will show you what an ongoing VF looks like.
http://www.youtube.com/watch?v=oDvlb62Mrt4&feature=related

__Remember, it is not enough to identify the rhythm. In order to be safe, you have to document it and administer medications or other emergency treatment according to protocol.

Ventricular Fibrillation is a "fast death producing dysrhythmia" and screams for immediate action. Defibrillation is instantly called for if the equipment is available (and working). If not, CPR may be utilized to keep the vital organs perfused until medication or a defibrillator is available. This client is almost always unconscious.

CPR protocol changes often, but current American Heart Association (AHA) guidelines recommend immediate treatment with 30 chest compressions then 2 breaths, insert an airway, and continue until a defibrillator is available. A link has been inserted for you to determine the latest update from the American Heart Association. www.american heart.org

Medications for VF are commonly the same as for VT—amiodarone (Coradrone), lidocaine (Xylocaine), and procainamide (Pronestyl).

COMPLETE HEART BLOCK (CHB) is a lethal arrhythmia unless it is recognized .The electrical impulse between the atria and the ventricle is totally dissociated and each section of the heart is beating on its own. If you measure the **P waves** and the **qrs** complexes in this strip, you will find them regular, but they are not associated. For example, the **P waves** do not come before the **qrs**, as they normally should.

This shows Complete Heart Block on EKG http://www.youtube.com/watch?v=8z_Y5gTlnh4
This strip shows severe bradycardia, incompatible with life for much longer. This rhythm will lead to cardiac arrest shortly and can be considered a fatal arrhythmia. The client may complain of being tired, feeling dizzy, feeling faint, confused, have difficult breathing, and die suddenly. **This is an emergency situation and the client should receive immediate transcutaneous pacing if available, oxygen, continuous monitoring, and the crash cart should be close at hand.**

Atropine is sometimes administered for a slow bradycardia. It should be administered carefully, but may not be successful. Remember, complete heart block may be caused by an overdose of many drugs such as beta blockers, calcium channel blockers or Lanoxin. The prescribed drugs may have slowed the heart way too much.

Continuous monitoring by the nurse is vital in CHB.

This is an excellent YouTube showing how the heart's electrical system works and how a pacemaker is inserted. http://www.youtube.com/watch?v=a5HI2-AVQJs&feature=related

Watch this YouTube showing a cardiac pacemaker in action. http://www.mediscuss.org/ecg-18-cardiac-pacemaker-activity-video-783/ This video will show that the **qrs** has to be captured with a high enough velocity of electricity to cause the ventricle to beat, thus speeding the heart. On the video, the pacemaker is indicated by the straight line before the **qrs** wave.

This electrical current may hurt as it causes the chest wall to contract! It is important to assess the client's pain and administer analgesics to stop the pain. Once the cause of the CHB is determined, it may be necessary for the client to have a permanent pacemaker.

Cardiac strip for pacemaker captured. This strip indicates that a pacemaker is pacing both the atria and the ventricle and both are captured. This means there is a pacemaker artifact (line) that appears before both the **P wave** and the **qrs** complex. Monitoring is required until the pacemaker is captured.

This strip shows a pacemaker that is captured.

Many people require a permanent cardiac pacemaker if their heart block cannot be controlled with medication. A permanent pacemaker requires leads that go into the heart and a battery that provides the electrical signal needed for the heart to beat at a normal rate. The pacemaker battery is usually implanted in the upper chest and the leads threaded through a vein into the heart. This requires monitoring to assure the beats are captured. Feeling faint is a common symptom of a client who is having battery failure. The batteries have to be replaced depending on the type of battery and the length of time that it works.

You have seen these questions before. We can't emphasize them enough, so here is an example of the answers for pacemaker insertion.

There are 3 important questions that the nurse should be able to answer regarding any procedure.

1. **What should the client be taught prior to the procedure and what is the nursing priority?** As in any other surgery, the nurse should determine if the client is receiving Coumadin or any other drug that will prolong bleeding. Allergies should be determined. The client should understand if they are cognizant that they will have this pacemaker in their chest and it will be permanent. Vital signs should be obtained and recorded.

2. **What should the client be taught regarding the procedure itself and what is the nursing priority during the procedure?** This client will not be put under anesthesia, but will be given IV meds to make them drowsy. The procedure usually takes between 1-2 hours.

3. **What should the client be taught after the procedure is completed and what is the nursing priority?** The heart rhythm will be continually monitored and they will remain in a recovery area for 1-2 hours. There may be pain at the incision site and movement in the arm on the site of the insertion will be limited for around 24 hours. The client will be taught to monitor their pulse and to return for cardiac monitoring on a regular basis.

These are vital concepts to know and are often tested on *NCLEX*®.

Congestive Heart Failure

Congestive heart failure (CHF) occurs when the diseased heart is too weak to pump enough blood to the rest of the body. The cardiac output is decreased and bodily functions begin to fail. For example, the heart pumps blood into the kidney, but if it is unable to accomplish this, normal kidney function diminishes, output goes down, and metabolic acidosis occurs. Because of the weakened heart muscle, the blood in the heart begins to back up into other organs such as the lungs (pulmonary edema) and the liver (which will leak and cause acities). The fluid will also accumulate in the legs causing edema. Needless to say, if this condition is not treated, it will affect every organ and system in the body. An assessment for CHF is JVD (Jugular Venous Distention). Raise the head of the bed 30-45 degrees and stand on the client's right. Have them lie on their back and turn the head to the left. With a soft light, the jugular vein can be seen. If it is distended as high as the jaw angle, the client may have potential Congestive Heart Failure (CHF).

CHF should be further delineated by looking at **CHF left** and **CHF right**, because the client symptoms and clinical picture are somewhat different.

L Listen to lung sounds—fine crackles (rales) at posterior lower lobes	**R** Rapid or irregular heartbeat (listen for abnormal heart sounds)
E Edema (pulmonary) may see pink froth around the lips — cough	**I** Increased edema in feet, legs, abdomen, and liver
F Fluid overload (congestion) in the lungs causes shortness of breath	**G** Gained weight and distended neck veins
T Treat with nursing interventions	**H** Hard to breathe (SOB)
• Increase head of bed	**T** Treat with nursing interventions
• Decrease physical activity to tolerance	• Evaluate fluid overload and request an order for diuretics from provider
• Monitor I&O (watch for decreased urinary output)	• Evaluate and treat LEFT failure
• Medications for hypertension (found on page 5)	• Lifestyle changes of dietary (low salt), fluid restrictions, exercise
• Lanoxin may be ordered to slow the heart rate and increase cardiac output. Diuretics (see pages 5-6)	

Bottom line LEFT starts with an L and Lungs start with a L. This is the easiest way to remember. Eventually the entire heart will likely fail.

This 58 second YouTube demonstrates how the Swanz Ganz, flow directed, pulmonary artery (PA) catheter is inserted and the values measured. http://www.youtube.com/watch?v=EzWm0IJZ1_g

Hemodynamic monitoring of the PAP (Pulmonary Artery Pressure), CVP (Central Venous Pressure), and CO (Cardiac Output) are measured with this equipment. This allows for diagnosis and management of the client.

Hemodynamic monitoring devices have alarms that indicate the client's values are outside the normal. These alarms are indicators that nursing intervention is imminent! Evaluate any increase in Pulmonary Artery Wedge Pressure (PAWP). An increase may indicate fluid overload (possibly decrease IV rates)

Evaluate any increase in Pulmonary Artery Systolic/Diastolic Pressure. May indicate hypovolemia (possibly increase IV rates)

Be very careful increasing or decreasing IV rates for clients with Swanz Ganz catheters. The IVs may have medications in them.

EVALUATE PHARMACOLOGY

MEDICATIONS THAT COMMONLY AFFECT HEMODYNAMIC VALUES

Dopamine and dobutamine are commonly administered to clients with heart failure in intensive care settings. The desired outcome is to increase cardiac output. The heart rate and cardiac contractility is often increased as well.

Norepinephrine (Levophed) is often administered for acute hypotension and increases the heart rate and contractility. There is an old saying regarding this drug. It's called "Levophed, leave um dead." Much caution is advised when administering this drug. It may take time and careful monitoring to decrease or discontinue this vasoconstrictor.

These are nursing interventions that may be seen on protocol for a severely failing heart

It's time to GET MOVING!

G   Get vital signs and position for breathing (usually with head elevated). Shortness of breath is common.

E   Evaluate heart sounds. Can you hear them clearly or are they muffled? A good option from protocol for the pulmonary edema is to monitor lung sounds, I&O, and potassium levels. If there is no pulmonary edema, the IV rates should be increased to help with hypovolemia.

T   Try to keep the client comfortable and calm, use Morphine, or similar pain medications from protocol.

M   Monitor blood gases for acid base imbalance and electrolyte imbalance especially potassium.

O   Oxygen and possible pulmonary artery catheterization (PAC) hemodynamic monitoring with Swan-Ganz catheters (consent is needed for insertion and NPO is desirable, but not always possible due to emergency situation). Normal pulmonary wedge pressure is 4-12mm Hg. The insertion of any catheter through the skin becomes an issue in infection control. The best way to prevent infection is to use aseptic technique on insertion and with each dressing change. Clear dressings are preferred to allow observation of the site for signs of infection, drainage, edema, and erythema.

V   Various cardiac drugs such as amioderone are usually part of the protocol for this situation. Amiodarone strengthens the heart muscle and reduces afterload. Diuretics reduce the cardiac load.

I IVs must be balanced with fluid overload.

N Needs heroic intervention such as ventilator, possible stent placement, possible intra-aortic balloon pump or CABG, depending on the client's clinical picture.

G Get help! This is the time to call the provider in the middle of the night; the client may not make it until daylight. Much will be on protocol if the client is in a critical care unit. If not, the nurse does not have resources to deal with this client without help.

Many of these interventions come under the heading of intensive care units, so we are going to provide this guideline for clients that are of very high risk and are admitted to the intensive care unit.

INTENSIVE CARE UNIT (ICU)

S System specific focused assessment even though there is an assessment on the chart. The client has likely had serious changes since admission and the ICU RN is responsible for completing an assessment upon admission to the unit. This includes the client's positive ID as their sensorium may have changed. Heart sounds and lung sounds are imperative as well as renal function. Any sign of infection should be noted in the admitting remarks and a report to the provider if any complication is identified that has not been previously documented on the chart.

A Assessing for risk includes utilizing diagnostic testing and ICU equipment that may not have been utilized prior to admission to this unit. Common diagnostic testing in the ICU includes:

> SvO_2–an assessment of oxygen delivery versus oxygen consumption that determines tissue perfusion through a Pulmonary Artery Catheter (PAC). The normal is > 75%. The lower the reading, the more trouble the client is in with their oxygen consumption. A reading below 30% indicates that tissue perfusion is compromised to the point of lactic acidosis.
> Helping to decrease **stress.** (How can one get sleep in an ICU unless the nurse programs it?) Stress comes from being in the ICU itself. Other stressful factors include mechanical ventilation, severe pain and burns, multi-trauma, sepsis, and any condition that the client cannot handle. Medications are commonly on protocol to treat for the prevention of stress ulcers such as a proton pump inhibitor and H_2 antagonists.
> Providing **pain** medication in a timely fashion and recognizing when the standing order is no longer effective.
> Keeping the client **warm**. Shivering causes increased oxygen consumption
> Keeping the client **cool**. Hyperthermia utilizes more oxygen.
> Arterial blood gases
> Mechanical ventilator

F Find support for the client. This is a scary time for both client and family. Keep family informed to reduce their fear. Fear is catching; minimize it as much as possible.

E Evaluate and reevaluate the client This client can frequently "turn on a dime."

T Try to keep the client pain free and breathing easily.

Y Your management. The nurse is the client advocate. Remember ICU's may cause psychosis. Schedule rest periods. Three straight hours in 24 hours is needed for minimal rest. This does not happen if it is not put in the nursing plan and adhered to.

MEDICATIONS COMMONLY USED FOR CONGESTIVE HEART FAILURE
You will recognize these as most of them are also utilized to treat hypertension.
Ace Inhibitors, ARBs, Beta Blockers, Lanoxin, and Diuretics.

Clients may live many years with CHF and our description has been acute failure. If the CHF becomes chronic, there are life style changes that will be recommended to help control this debilitating disease.
- Reduce salt intake
- Reduce fluid intake
- Daily weights for monitoring
- Sleep with 2 pillows to help with breathing
- Restriction of alcohol
- Weight loss if a factor
- Cessation of smoking
- Exercise

Cardiogenic Shock

Cardiogenic shock is a physiologic state in which inadequate tissue perfusion results from decreased cardiac output most commonly following acute myocardial infarction (MI). An ST-elevation is found in most of the clients and is a clinical sign on the cardiac monitor that the client is going downhill fast. This lack of tissue perfusion causes a quiet fear among health professionals. The fear comes from the fact that most research studies indicate an 80-90% fatality rate with this condition, especially if the condition happens when the client is not in the hospital and around a 2/3 mortality rate even if the client is in the hospital.

The word **FEAR** will help you remember how to assess cardiogenic shock so that the client can be treated as soon as possible

F Fluid retention; the heart muscle is too weak to pump out venous return. This fluid retention will likely be heard in the lungs as this will lead to fluid overload and pulmonary edema. This piece of information is vital to the nurse who is monitoring this client. You hear pulmonary edema and you think **sit them up, slow the IV rate, administer oxygen, and call the provider for further orders**.

E End organ damage will take place because the heart muscle is not strong enough to get blood to the brain (leading to altered mental status and unconsciousness) and the kidney (leading to oliguria and renal failure). If there is no perfusion to the "vital organs," there sure won't be any to the periphery, so now we are feeling cold, clammy skin and likely seeing cyanosis.

A Acute pressure in the ventricles causes jugular vein distention as well as indicating a weak spot in the myocardial muscle due to an MI. A hole can blow out in the ventricles. At this point, there's not much we can do except to support the client's family and provide postmortem care with dignity and according to their religious standards.

R Raised heart rate is usually indicated by sinus tachycardia keeping us busy documenting frequent vital signs. The heart sounds may be muffled on assessment. **Keep the crash cart close.**

Cardiogenic shock is the leading cause of death of clients who have a myocardial infarction and there is minimum effective treatment for this dreaded diagnosis. The damaged heart is unable to perfuse the cardiac cells with oxygen and the blood pressure bottoms out. Extremities become cold and the client loses consciousness. There has been considerable controversy regarding treatment of this condition for many years. Some recent research indicates there may be a hyper-inflammatory process involved.

Drugs such as dopamine and norepinepherine (Levophed), and epinephrine are the usual drugs of choice in an attempt to keep the blood pressure elevated enough to perfuse the tissues. Ventricular assist devices or intra-aortic balloon pumps may also be used in a heroic effort to keep the vital organs perfused.

OTHER PRESCRIPTION AND STREET DRUGS AFFECTING THE HEART
These drugs are used to treat other medical conditions with the side effect of increasing the heart rate. Vital signs will change, but not due to a heart condition.
- Anti-Depressants—doxepin (Adapin, Silenor, Sinequan), amitriptyline (Elavil), desipramine(Norpramin), Fluoxetine (Prozac)
- Thyroid Medication—levothyroxine (Synthroid)
- Pseudoephedrine in over-the counter medications to treat sinus congestion and colds
- Attention deficit disorder in children—methlphenidate(Ritalin), amphetamine (Adderall)

SUBSTANCES USUALLY NON PRESCRIBED THAT INCREASE THE HEART RATE

- Alcohol in large amounts, Amphetamines, Caffeine, Cocaine, Crack
- Ecstasy, Herbal Ecstasy, Cloud 9, Rave Energy, Ultimate, Xphoria, and X,
- Heroin, Smack, Designer Drugs, Synthetic Heroin, Goodfella, LSD, Acid, Methamphetamines, Mushrooms, Inhalants, Marijuana, Nicotine, Tobacco, PCP.

These drugs as well as heart diseases can cause the heart to beat so fast that it will go into arrhythmias.

Commonalities that flow through client safety of every body system and are heavily weighted on the NCLEX® can be condensed into the following table on MANAGE.

These **NCLEX®** standards currently count for as much as **23%** of the total **NCLEX®** exam and are always a primary consideration for nursing.

PASS *NCLEX*®!

M	**Make sure of identity, accuracy of orders**
A	**Arrange privacy/confidentiality/consent/collaboration with other team**
N	**No injuries, falls, malfunctioning equipment or staff or hazards**
A	**Address errors, abuse, legalities, scope of practice—document**
G	**Give (delegate) orders to appropriate people**
E	**Establish priorities of clients and time**

There are questions on **NCLEX**® on every body system that reflects these standards. These examples on cardiology are offered to make you think about how you would answer. There are no answers to these in this book. We want you to think about these, because they may be asked on every body system. Remember, **management accounts for as much as 23% on *NCLEX*®!**

The client admitted with a myocardial infarction is unconscious. Which is the safest way to determine identity?

A person asks the nurse if the mayor has been admitted to the ED. What is the best response?

The client with CHF becomes confused at night. Which are priority interventions to keep this client safe? **Select all that apply.**

The client with the diagnosis of heart failure has a D5W IV flowing at the rate of 60 gtts/minute. What is the nursing priority?

Which nursing staff member should be assigned to care for a client who has been newly admitted with a myocardial infarction?

The EKG monitor is showing Ventricular Fibrillation. What is the nurse's first action?

Nurses have reported many unusual experiences that have happened to them during working with clients in cardiac arrest. Here is one such experience that confirms that you are not crazy if you experience something like this. It has happened to many of us.

MEMORABLE CARDIAC Client

I was a clinical instructor in a 500-bed hospital responsible for 10 senior nursing students who were four weeks away from graduation . These very competent students were assigned to MICU, SICU, CCU, and the Emergency Department (ED). While I was at lunch I heard the ambulance screaming into the ED, so I left my lunch and headed to the ED to make sure the students had my support. They were assessing a middle aged man who had collapsed on the street while he was watching a Dogwood Festival Parade. As I walked into the room, I knew we were all in trouble. The look in his eye that showed his fear and the odor of his body told me that he had suffered an acute MI. After so much experience, you can literally smell "it." You may not know exactly what "it" is, but you know that your client is not likely to survive.

The students and I were asked to transport the client from the emergency department to the coronary care unit. I was skeptical that he would make it up to the fourth floor so I asked the students to bring a crash cart with us. We passed floor two and he had a cardiac arrest. One of the students jumped on the gurney with him to do chest compressions and we were breathing him with the ambu bag. We hurried into the CCU where the cardiac residents and other nurses were ready to administer the cardiac arrest protocol that may save his life.

The students performed flawlessly with their part of the code. Suddenly, I saw the top half of the man's torso rise from his body to reach the ceiling and look down. He looked at me and I heard him ask, "What happened?" I said wordlessly, "You have had a heart attack and we are giving you medication." The defibrillator went off again and I watched as his "spirit" returned to his body and he said out loud, "Damn, that hurt!" The nurses told him that he had a heart attack and that he was going to be fine. He quickly arrested again. Again, I watched him float to the ceiling.

He looked at me and said, "Let me go." Amazingly, I felt calm, and had no doubt or fear of what I had seen and heard. The CPR, medication administration, etc. were still going on frantically with no results. I looked back at the ceiling and the client was not there. I said with calmness, "You know, it may be time to let him go." One of the docs said, "He is not ready yet." Half an hour later, he was pronounced dead.

I did not tell anyone about this experience for a long time. I thought they would think I was crazy, but when I did decide to talk about it, I quickly learned that many other nurses have had similar experiences. What an awesome experience to be a nurse!

Marshall Ganz, grassroots organizer, lecturer, and public policy maker writes, "Stories not only teach us how to act—they inspire us to act. Stories communicate our values through the language of the heart, our emotions. And it is what we feel—our hopes, our cares, our obligations—not simply what we know that can inspire us with the courage to act."

We hope our stories will encourage you to act.

ANEMIAS are considered to be the most common blood disorder. There are generally believed to be in the neighborhood of over 400 different types. You will be pleased to learn that we will not discuss them all, but will provide you the **"Bottom Line"** and a way to think about them.

Red blood cell (RBC) decrease-The RBCs carry oxygenated blood to all body tissues so we can't do without them The general range of RBCs for men is 4.7-6.1 million cells per microliter (cells/mcl). For women, the range is somewhat lower at 4.2-5.4 million cells/mcl. The hemoglobin and hematocrit is also determined at this time. Normal for male clients the range is from 13.8-17.2 gm/dL. The female client normally ranges from 12.1-15.1 gm/dL. These ranges vary somewhat from one laboratory to the next. Watch this brief YouTube to see an update on red blood cells and hemoglobin. **Remember exhaustion is the common sign in anemia.** http://www.youtube.com/watch?v=_ZV5140OykE

There are many causes for decreased RBCs including vitamin and mineral deficiencies (iron deficiency is the most common, but vitamin B-12 [pernicious anemia], B-6, copper, and folate should also be considered), heredity factors, kidney disease/hemodialysis, leukemia, malnutrition, chemotherapeutic agents, pregnancy, bone marrow disorders (Aplastic anemia), and hemorrhage. Recommend the aforementioned vitamins and minerals to the client.

SYSTEM SPECIFIC ASSESSMENT

The assessments for many types of anemia are fairly common and should include asking the client about being tired all of the time, being short of breath, weakness, being lightheaded, or fainting. Diagnostic testing for anemia is often as simple as evaluating a CBC (complete blood count) that includes an erythrocyte (RBC) count. Diagnosing the type of anemia may be a much more lengthy process and include a bone marrow analysis. This procedure requires a specific consent form. Possible risks include bleeding, infection, and pain.

ASSESS FOR RISK AND RESPOND

The use of NSAIDS, such as ibuprofen or aspirin, may be a cause of blood loss through bleeding. Assess for gastric ulcers that may cause internal bleeding. Assess for occult blood in the stool that may indicate bleeding. Perform diagnostic testing for occult blood. Assess for alcoholism. Clients may drink instead of eat. Risk includes dietary considerations and many clients need to learn to increase their RBCs by making changes in increasing the following foods:
- **Red** meats (especially organ meats) and **dark green** vegetables
- Dried beans, raisins
- Nuts
- Fortified or enriched bread, milk, and cereals

FIND, CHANGE, AND INTERVENE AS NEEDED

Clients with bleeding gums should be assessed. Soft toothbrushes may help. Exhaustion can undermine therapy. The nurse should plan for client rest and adequate nutrition. **Blood transfusions** are often administered to clients with anemia when an immediate change is needed. (Find the protocol for blood transfusions in the renal chapter.)

LEUKEMIA, "Cancer Of The Blood" While anemia is primarily an issue with RED blood cells (RBC), leukemia is an issue with WHITE blood cells (WBC). The bone marrow produces abnormal WBCs, which often proliferate crowding out all of the other cells in the blood including RBCs and Platelets. This crowding causes these cells to be unable to do their job. The incidence of leukemia is increasing as the population ages. Some leukemias are most common in children. **Remember, it's all about SAFETY**

SYSTEM SPECIFIC ASSESSMENT includes looking for the SCARE

- **S** Swollen lymph nodes
- **C** Chills and fever, especially night sweats
- **A** Abnormal weight loss
- **R** Really tired all of the time
- **E** Easy bleeding/bruising

Assessment may include bone marrow aspiration and/or biopsy. Most clients consider bone marrow biopsy painful. Watch for:
- Pain-control with PRN medications
- Infection—monitor vital signs and report elevated temperature
- Bleeding at the aspiration site
- Sedation medication issues, e.g. allergies, nausea, and arrhythmias

ASSESS FOR RISK AND RESPOND to the SCARE

- **S** Swollen lymph nodes may indicate an infection. Assign client to a private room to reduce the opportunity for infection.
- **C** Chills/fever/night sweats occur and make the client uncomfortable. Keep the client clean and dry at night, monitor vital signs for elevated temperature and administer medications as needed.
- **A** Abnormal weight loss calls for monitoring loss and providing appealing nutrition that will help with body healing.
- **R** Rest and relaxation is important. Plan nursing interventions so that the client gets sleep and rest.
- **E** Easy bleeding requires gentle handling. Watch IV medications; needle sticks may cause prolonged bleeding.

FIND CHANGES, TRENDS AND INTERVENE

Bleeding is a big risk. Gums may bleed. Soft toothbrushes may help. Risk for exhaustion should be assessed. Clients that refuse nutrition will be at higher risk.

EVALUATE PHARMACOLOGY

Chemotherapeutic agents are usually the preferred method of treatment although radiation, bone marrow transplant, and antibiotics may be used in combination. Chemo agents are often hazardous and the nurse should use protective equipment and procedures. The type of chemo depends on the type of leukemia.

If radiation is utilized be sure to:
- assess for skin breakdown at the radiation site and advise provider,
- assess for diarrhea, a common side effect,
- advise client that fresh fruits may cause diarrhea.
- have protamine sulfate and Vitamin K available.

TEACH CLIENT AND STAFF ABOUT INFECTION CONTROL, e.g., hand washing, exposure to ill persons

YOUR MANAGEMENT

- HIPAA—privacy and confidentiality
- OSHA—determine that equipment and staff are safe
- State Boards of Nursing—ethical, legal scope of practice
- TJC—document and report errors and client identification

PLATELET DISORDERS— platelets heal wounds and help the blood clot

Anemia is primarily an issue with RED blood cells (RBC); leukemia is an issue with WHITE blood cells (WBC). Bleeding disorders often have to do with another cell called Platelets or thrombocytes. The bone marrow also produces platelets, which are smaller in size than the other cells, but are vitally important to preventing bleeding by forming clots. The normal platelet count in a healthy person is usually between 150,000 and 450,000 per microliter of blood per liter. *Simply put , too few platelets put the client at risk for serious bleeding and too many platelets put the client at risk for blood clots.*

Too Few Platelets	Too Many Platelets
Common causes of too few platelets include: - Decreased production in the bone marrow - Infection - Drugs (especially chemotherapeutic agents) - Vitamin deficiency If the platelets become very low, a diagnosis of thrombocytopenia may be made. Examples of Platelet Disorders include: - **ITP,** Idiopathathic Thrombocythamia (platelet count of less than 150,000mm) - **vWD,** von Wilebrand's Disease (hereditary) - **TTP,** Thrombotic Thrombocytopenic Purpura	Common causes of too many platelets (thrombocytosis) include: - Increase of platelets in the bone marrow - Decreased function of the spleen to remove platelets - Infection - Drugs such as steroids - Cancer

Too Few Platelets	Too Many Platelets
Evaluate pharmacology Common drugs that may interfere with platelets that should be avoided include: • NSAIDS • Aspirin • Amitriptyline (Elavil) • Furosemide (Lasix) • Penicillins • Caffeine • Clot Busters (tPA) Drugs that may be administered depend on the type of platelet disorder and often include platelet transfusion or fresh plasma transfusion. Nursing is responsible for the following regarding safe transfusion: • Check identity of the client with another health professional • Check identity of the correct transfusion for the correct client with another health professional • Slow administration and constant monitoring of the client during the first 15 minutes • Monitoring client for transfusion reactions such as allergies, rash, difficulty breathing, or a feeling of doom. These indicate the transfusion should be discontinued and followed with normal saline to keep the vein open.	**Evaluate pharmacology** Common drugs that will interfere with platelet production that may be administered include: • NSAIDS • Aspirin • Anticoagulants (warfarin or Coumadin, heparin, and Lovenox) • Protamine sulfate • Clopidogrel (Plavix) • Amitriptyline (Elavil) • Furosemide (Lasix) • Penicillins • Caffeine • Clot Busters Nursing is responsible for monitoring clients carefully who are taking these drugs as they may cause bleeding.
Teach client and staff about infection control Include hand washing and exposure to persons who are ill. Infection control is vital when administering IV infusions.	**Teach client and staff about infection control** Include hand washing and exposure to persons who are ill. Infection control is vital when administering IV infusions. Utilize standard precaution.
Your management • **HIPAA**—privacy and confidentiality • **OSHA**—determine that equipment and staff are safe • **State Boards of Nursing**—ethical, legal scope of practice • **TJC**—document and report errors and client identity	**Your management** • **HIPAA**—privacy and confidentiality • **OSHA**—determine that equipment and staff are safe • **State Boards of Nursing**—ethical, legal scope of practice • **TJC**—document and report errors and client identity

Too Few Platelets	Too Many Platelets
Remember, it's all about SAFETY	Remember, it's all about SAFETY
System specific assessment includes looking for: • Bruising • Bleeding from mouth, nose, uterus, or intestine Assessment may include bone marrow aspiration and/or biopsy. Most clients consider bone marrow biopsy painful. Watch for: ▪ Pain—control with PRN medications ▪ Infection—monitor vital signs and report elevated temperature ▪ Bleeding at the aspiration site ▪ Sedation medication issues, e.g., allergies, nausea, and arrhythmias	**System specific assessment includes looking for:** • High platelet count (over 450,000mm/l) • Headache • DVT (Deep Vein Thrombosis) • TIA (Transient Ischemic Attack), mild strokes • Pulmonary embolism • X-ray, Bone Marrow Test, or CT scan of the abdomen
Assess for risk and respond • Avoid aspirin or medications affecting platelet function • Avoid activities or sports where there is a higher risk of injury • Female clients may need hormonal therapy to control heavy menstrual periods • Nosebleeds may lead to serious blood loss • Easy bleeding requires gentle handling. Watch for IV medications. The needle sticks may cause prolonged bleeding. • Assess for liver enzyme abnormality • Radiotherapy • Heparin, Coumadin, and other anticoagulants will likely be discontinued • Herbal remedies may interfere with anticoagulants by increasing bleeding	**Assess for risk and respond** • Any bone marrow disorder may lead to overproduction of platelets. Monitor platelet count and plan client exercise to prevent clots • Monitor hemoglobin and hematocrit as anemia may cause increased platelet production. Advise client on proper nutrition for anemia type • Determine recent history of myocardial infarction, pancreatitis, or spleenectomy which may cause reactive thrombocytosis • Assess for normal renal function • Assess hydration
Find change and prioritize Bleeding is a big risk. Hemorrhage must be stopped. Pressure points or blood transfusions may be required. Gums may bleed. Soft toothbrushes may help. Risk for exhaustion should be assessed. Clients who refuse close monitoring are at higher risk.	**Find change and prioritize** • Thrombosis is a big risk for an overabundance of platelets • Plan for client activity • Plan for client hydration • Dehydration is dangerous

Questions to make you think. (Answers provided at the end of the chapter.)

1. The client is admitted with chest pain and tachycardia. What is the priority nursing assessment?
   A. Vital signs
   B. Past medical history
   C. Auscultation of lung sounds
   D. Pain assessment

2. The client is admitted with chest pain and tachycardia. The physician orders 5mg Lopressor (Metroprolol) IV stat. Prior to administering this medication, what is the priority assessment? **Select all that apply**
   A. Respirations
   B. Blood pressure
   C. Heart Rate
   D. Oxygen Saturation
   E. Liver Enzymes

3. The client is receiving IV Potassium Chloride Replacement 40mEq. They are complaining of 10/10 pain burning at the IV insertion site. What is the priority nursing intervention?
   A. Stop the infusion
   B. Decrease the infusion rate
   C. Assess the IV site for redness and edema
   D. Remove the IV

4. The client is three days post admission for pneumonia. On assessment reveals unilateral 3+ Left lower leg edema and redness. The client states 7/10 pain in that area. What is the priority nursing action?
   A. Elevate the extremity
   B. Notify the physician
   C. Administer pain medication
   D. Ambulate the client

5. The client is admitted to the hospital with constipation. Which of the following nursing interventions are appropriate? **Select all that apply.**
   A. Ambulate the client
   B. Encourage fluids
   C. Administer narcotic pain medication
   D. Administer an enema
   E. Encourage a diet high in fiber

6. What tasks can be delegated to a Certified Nursing Assistant (CNA)? **Select all that apply.**
    A. Obtain vital signs
    B. Change a Foley Catheter
    C. Perform a central line dressing change.
    D. Administer medication
    E. Ambulate your client to the bathroom

7. Which nursing intervention must be delegated to a Registered Nurse (RN)?
    A. Obtaining your client's vital signs
    B. Feeding your client
    C. Performing a bed bath on your client
    D. Assessing your client's lung sounds

8. During the first 15 minutes of administration of Fresh Frozen Plasma (FFP), the client becomes diaphoretic, short of breath, and states, "I don't feel good." What is the priority nursing intervention?
    A. Assure the client that this is a normal reaction and that they will feel better after they get the Fresh Frozen Plasma (FFP)
    B. Immediately stop the transfusion and notify the physician
    C. Call the blood bank to report the reaction
    D. Increase the rate of the infusion to decrease the time of client discomfort

9. While caring for a client receiving prophylactic subcutaneous heparin injections for Deep Vein Thrombosis (DVT), assesment notes bruising on the abdomen. The client inquires why the shots make him bruise and bleed. What would the most appropriate response to the client be?
    A. Heparin thins the blood to prevent clots from forming. This sometimes causes bleeding and bruising at the injection site
    B. You must be allergic to the injections. I will notify the physician
    C. When you have a new nurse who is not experienced in administering injections, bruising and bleeding can occur
    D. The medication you have been given is too strong and is causing you to bleed. We will skip the next dose and restart this medication in the morning

10. The client is admitted with cellulitis around a pacemaker and is prescribed 4.5g piperacillin IV. It comes to you reconstituted in a 20 mL syringe. The order says to administer it over 30 minutes. What is the pump rate?
    _____mL/hr

11. The health care provider orders digoxin (Lanoxin) 2.5mg intravenously (IV) STAT. What is the appropriate nursing action?
    A. Administer the med as ordered
    B. Administer 0.25mg IV of digoxin (Lanoxin)
    C. Contact the ordering provider for clarification
    D. Contact the pharmacy to change the order

12. The client has an order for dobutamine (Dobutrex) intravenous infusion during daylight shift. The nurse arrives for the next shift and discovers dopamine is infusing. What are the most appropriate actions for the nurse to take? **Select all that apply.**
A. Discontinue the dopamine and hang dobutamine
B. Notify the physician of the error
C. Document the incident in the chart
D. Document the error on an incident report
E. Hang 1000 mL's of 0.9% NS at 10mL/hr

13. The client weighs 90 kg. The order states—Dopamine 400 mgm in 250mL of 0.9% normal saline to infuse at 5 mcg/kg/min. What is the infusion rate? _____

14. A client is to receive digoxin (Lanoxin) 0.125mg PO. What are the nursing priorities when administering this medication? **Select all that apply.**
A. Review current serum potassium level
B. Obtain apical pulse rate for one full minute
C. Review 24 hour intake and output (I&O)
D. Review most recent serum digoxin (Lanoxin) level

15. The client is admitted with a diagnosis of exacerbation of heart failure. How would the nurse assess the effectiveness of the diuretic therapy?
A. Client's daily weight
B. Client's troponin level
C. Client's heart rate
D. Client's blood pressure

16. The nurse is assessing the client who has suffered a myocardial infarction and has pulseless ventricular tachycardia. Which first line antiarrhythmic medication will be administered from protocol after CPR has been indicated?
A. Epinephrine
B. Lidocaine
C. Vasopressin
D. Atropine

17. The ambulating client complains of feeling dizzy, nauseated, and has chest pain. What are the appropriate nursing actions? **Select all that apply.**
A. Assist the client to his bed
B. Assess vital signs and pain
C. Permit the client to complete his task
D. Apply oxygen
E. Offer the client water

18. Which female client is priority for the registered nurse?
    A. A 65 year-old client complaining of a headache after her nitroglycerin patch is changed
    B. A 55 year-old client complaining of nausea after being given morning medications
    C. A 40 year-old client complaining of jaw and ear pain
    D. A 70 year-old client requesting information on Pradaxa

19. Following the administration of alteplase (t-PA) to a client with a myocardial infarction, what are the primary areas of assessment for the nurse? **Select all that apply.**
    A. Assess for change in level of consciousness
    B. Assess for signs of bleeding
    C. Assess for chest pain
    D. Assess for symptoms of fluid and volume deficit
    E. Assess for hypoglycemia

20. The client had a cardiac/respiratory arrest and is intubated and placed on a ventilator support. The plan of care for the client includes which of the following? **Select all that apply.**
    A. Turning the client every two hours
    B. Suctioning the client once a shift
    C. Performing mouth care every shift and as needed
    D. Prohibiting visitors
    E. Assessing the color, quality, and amount of endotracheal secretions

21. The charge nurse witnesses a staff member enter and quickly exit a contact isolation room without the proper isolation technique. What is the most appropriate action of the charge nurse?
    A. Immediately fire the nurse for breeching isolation protocol
    B. Ignore the action as the nurse was in the room briefly
    C. Remediate the nurse on facility isolation protocol immediately
    D. Report the nurse to the Centers for Disease Control (CDC)

22. The nurse making client rounds discovers a frayed electrical cord on an IV pump. What is the next action of the nurse?
    A. Call the biomedical department to inform them of the observation
    B. Remove the IV pump from service, place a tag on the pump, and report the issue to the biomedical department
    C. Unplug the IV pump and use electrical tape to correct the fraying portion
    D. No action is necessary as the electrical outlet is grounded

23. The health care provider explains the cardiac catheterization procedure to the client. Which of the following statements demonstrates client understanding?
    A. "A cardiac cath opens up the blocked vessels."
    B. "A cardiac cath looks at the blood flow to my heart."
    C. "I will have a pacemaker after the cath is over."
    D. "The doctor is putting a balloon in my aorta."

24. The client is soon to be discharged home. The client is very concerned about the cost of his medications. What are the most appropriate nursing actions? **Select all that apply.**
    A. Consult social service in an attempt to assist with Medicaid assistance application
    B. Give the client medication(s) from the floor stock
    C. Call the pharmacy and ask for a reduced rate on the medication
    D. Notify the prescribing physician
    E. Explain to the client that nothing can be done to assist him

25. The client is in critical condition following coronary artery bypass surgery. The nurse caring for this client notices his wife praying the rosary at the bedside. What is the appropriate action for the nurse?
    A. Call for a Catholic priest to come to the client's bedside
    B. Ask the spouse if she would like the priest notified
    C. Observe and wait for the client to ask
    D. Look at the information sheet to find out the client's religion

26. A client of Muslim belief is admitted to the hospital and dies. The nurse approaches the family by asking the following question. Select the appropriate response.
    A. "Will you please leave the room so we can perform the postmortem care?"
    B. "I am unfamiliar with Muslim law. Please let me know how to properly care for your family member."
    C. "I know nothing about this so let me know how to take care of the body."
    D. "What do I need to do to keep with the laws of your people?"

27. The client has been instructed to follow a low cholesterol diet. Which example best describes the prescribed diet?
    A. Hamburger, French fries, and a piece of pecan pie
    B. Liver and onions, a salad, and iced tea
    C. Grilled, skinless chicken breast, grilled squash, and fresh peas
    D. Baked ham, scalloped potatoes, and cauliflower

28. Which of the following elements should be included in the teaching plan of a client with severe mitral valve regurgitation? **Select all that apply.**
    A. Education on prescribed medications
    B. Education on dental care
    C. Education on general health maintenance practices
    D. Education on energy conservation
    E. Instruction on dietary and fluid restrictions

Answers and Rationale

1. **Answer A** because it provides data about the client's current health status which needs to be addressed now. B, C, and D are all important but are not the priority.

2. **Answers B and C** are the correct answers because metoprolol (Lopressor) is a beta-blocker that works by dilating blood vessels and slowing the client's heart rate and lower the BP. A baseline is needed. Other answers are inappropriate.

3. **Answer A** is correct because it should relieve the pain enough for you to assess what is actually causing the pain and determine your next action. Answers B, C, and D are follow-up actions that may be taken once you have relieved the pain and can gather more data.

4. **Answer B** is correct because this is a dramatic change that could indicate a Deep Vein Thrombosis (DVT) and needs to be evaluated by the physician. Answers A, C, and D are incorrect because, if it is a Deep Vein Thrombosis (DVT), there is risk dislodging the clot.

5. **Answers A, B, and E.** These actions are all known to encourage elimination. Answer C is known to contribute to constipation. Enemas need an order by the provider.

6. **Answers A and E** because they fall within the scope of practice of a CNA. Options B, C, and D all require a nursing license.

7. **Answer D.** It is a nursing action. The other actions can be delegated to another healthcare team member.

8. **Answer B.** The client is showing signs of a hemolytic reaction. The transfusion needs to be stopped and the physician notified so they can assess the client. Answers A and D are false and answer C will be done at a later time.

9. **Answer A.** It provides the client with a truthful explanation. Answer B is incorrect because the symptoms do not suggest allergy. Answer C is incorrect because the reaction is a result of the medication, not the administration. Answer D is incorrect because skipping a dose will not solve the problem or address the client's concern.

10. **Answer:** 40 mL/hr.

11. **Answer C.** Answer A is incorrect as the dose exceeds the safe parameters of dosage for digoxin (Lanoxin). Answer B is within the safe dosage range but the order is not for 0.25mg IV. Answer C is the correct answer because the physician must be notified that the medication was ordered in error. Answer D is incorrect. A pharmacist cannot change an order without physician approval.

12. **Answers A, B, and D.** Answer A must be done to complete the order. Answer B, the physician must be notified of the error immediately so as to attempt to counteract any potential problems. Answer C, medications errors are never documented in the chart but rather documented on an incident report. Answer D, there is no order to hang 0.9% Normal Saline.

13. **Answer:**

1. Convert mcg/kg/min into mg/hr. In the question, the dose would be 27 mg/hr.

$$\frac{(5mcg \times 90kg)}{1000} \times 60 = 27$$

2. Next, use the IV dose formula to finish the rest of the problem

$$\frac{27mg}{400mg} \times 250mL = 16.8 \text{ mL/hr}$$

14. **Answers A, B, and D.** Potassium is vital for optimal cardiac function. Additionally, low potassium may predispose the client to digoxin (Lanoxin) toxicity. Digoxin (Lanoxin) slows the heartrate; therefore, the accepted standard cutoff for giving Lanoxin is 60 beats/minute. The blood level of Lanoxin must be closely monitored to assess for toxicity. Intake and output (I&O) is a component in the care of the cardiac client but does not directly influence whether digoxin (Lanoxin) can safely be administered.

15. **Answer A.** Effective diuresis will remove fluid from the client. Of the choices, the best indicator of the effectiveness of diuretic therapy is monitoring the weight of the client. The troponin level monitors myocardial damage. While heart rate and blood pressure are influenced by the fluid status of the body, they are not consistently the best indicator of effective diuresis.

16. **Answer A.** The rhythm is identified as ventricular tachycardia. According to protocol, the first line drug to be administered is epinephrine. Answers B and C are considered second line drugs. Atropine is used for sinus bradycardia.

17. **Answers A, B, and D.** The client is in danger. He is demonstrating symptoms of instability. Option A is correct. By returning the client to bed, the nurse can assess the situation completely without fear of the client falling. Option B is the very first nursing action which should take place after getting the client to a safe position. Option D is also correct because the client is complaining of chest pain. The cause of cardiac chest pain is due to a lack of oxygen to the myocardium. Option C is incorrect as the client is demonstrating distress, which may be life threatening. Completing the client's grooming may not adversely affect his outcome in this situation. Option E is ineffective.

18. **Answer C.** Research indicates that females experiencing a cardiac event often present with atypical cardiac pain, e.g., jaw pain, ear pain. Answer C is the priority. Answer A is an expected outcome from the use of nitroglycerin-based preparations. Answer B is a commonplace occurrence with many medications when given by mouth. Answer D is lowest priority as the client is in no danger or discomfort.

19. **Answers A, B, and C.** The thrombolytic action of alteplase (t-PA) directly activates plasmogen to destroy fibrin which is present in clots. Through the lysis of the clot, coronary circulation is restored. Unfortunately, alteplase is not specific to coronary circulation and bleeding may occur from other sources, e.g., cerebral bleed, GI bleed, heavy menstrual bleeding, gingival bleeding, and epistaxis. By monitoring the neurological status of a client receiving alteplase (t-PA), the nurse can establish a baseline and note any changes in the neuro status. Assessing for chest pain is vital. There are times when the coronary artery may re-occlude following administration of alteplase (t-PA). A symptom of re-occlusion is chest pain.

20. **Answers A, C, and E.** In option A, the client is unable to reposition his/her self. In order to prevent skin breakdown, the nurse needs to place the client on a turning schedule. Option B is incorrect because suctioning of an endotracheal tube (ETT) must be done PRN to ensure patency of the tube and adequate oxygenation. Additionally, frequent suctioning assists in the reduction of ventilator-associated pneumonia. Good oral hygiene, option C, is necessary for the intubated client. By performing oral care, the nurse may significantly decrease the chance of ventilator-associated pneumonia. Option D is incorrect. Often intubated clients are sedated but they are aware of their surroundings. Visitors, who are there to support the client, may prove beneficial in the recovery process. Unless the visitors are disruptive or are infectious, they should be included as a support system for the client. By assessing the color, quality, and amount of secretions of the ETT, the nurse will recognize changes, which may indicate pulmonary edema (pink frothy sputum) or an evolving infection (green, brown, thick secretions). Early assessment and intervention may assist with improved client outcomes.

21. **Answer C.** While a violation of the institution isolation is a serious offense, the charge nurse does not have the ability to fire an individual. Option B is incorrect. Any breech in isolation places staff, clients, and visitors at risk. Option D is incorrect as this is not a mandated reportable offense. Option C is correct since the nurse demonstrates poor adherence to isolation practices.

22. **Answer B.** Any time an electrical cord of any type is frayed, this has great potential for electrical malfunction. Option B is correct. The pump must be removed from service so as to prevent injury. Additionally, the biomedical department should be notified and the IV pump should also be tagged so that no other individual will use the malfunctioning equipment. Option A does not remove the unsafe equipment from service. Option C is incorrect as the equipment remains at risk for malfunction. Option D is incorrect since a grounded outlet still is an active source of electricity.

23. **Answer B.** Option A is incorrect because a cardiac cath is purely a diagnostic, invasive procedure. During a cath, stent placement may occur in which the vessel will be opened. Option C is describing the insertion of a pacemaker. Option D describes the insertion of an intra-aortic balloon pump.

24. **Answers A and D.** Option A is correct because many facilities have indigent medication programs where the client is given medications at little or no cost for a brief period of time. Often Medicaid applications take some time to process but the client needs the medications when they are prescribed. Option B is incorrect. The nurse cannot dispense medications to a discharged client from floor stock. Option C is incorrect because hospital pharmacies often will not negotiate with prices. Option D is correct. Perhaps the provider has office samples, which may be distributed to the client. Option E is incorrect. The nurse's role in this situation is to act as an advocate for the client.

25. **Answer B.** In situations such as this, it is always best to ask if client or family would like clergy called. Option A is incorrect; perhaps the client does not share his wife's religious beliefs. Option C is incorrect. During times of stress, family does not want to inconvenience staff and will not ask for clergy to be called. Option D is incorrect. Often the religious information is not complete or is inaccurate so it is best to ask before calling.

26. **Answer B.** Most often, individuals of different cultures do understand that nurses are not experts on aspects of the different cultures. By asking for guidance, the nurse acts in a therapeutic manner toward the family as well as the deceased. For many, cultural and religious customs are essential components of their lives. Option A is wrong because Muslim law prohibits post mortem care. Options C and D are incorrect as the response indicates a non-therapeutic attitude toward the family and the deceased.

27. **Answer C.** Option A contains a high degree of fat. Option B is a good source of iron but organ meats also contain a high amount of cholesterol. Option D also contains a great deal of fat from the ham. Scalloped potatoes contain cheese, also a source of fat. Option C is the best choice for the cardiac client due to the low fat content of the skinless chicken and fresh vegetables.

28. **All of the answers are correct.** Every client taking a medication must be educated on dosage, side effects, and special considerations when taking the medication. Good dental care is important in the prevention of myocarditis, pericarditis, or endocarditis. General health maintenance practice is very important to the health of any individual. The client may be placed on a sodium and/or fluid restricted diet in order to reduce the workload of the heart.

The Pediatric CARDIOVASCULAR SYSTEM

Jessica Peck, DNP, RN, MSN, CPNP-PC, CNE
Edited by Sylvia Rayfield & Associates, Inc.

What is different about a child's heart?

CONGENITAL ANOMALIES ARE THE #1 CAUSE OF DEATH IN CHILDREN UNDER ONE YEAR OF AGE
AND CARDIAC ANOMALIES ARE #1 ON THE LIST!!!

KEY CONCEPTS TO REMEMBER:

- ❖ Congenital heart problems cause either impaired blood flow to the lungs or to the systemic circulation.
- ❖ Some defects will heal on their own, but others require surgery.
- ❖ Most of the time, cardiac anomalies will be diagnosed within the first year of life, but sometimes are not picked up until later.

You can remember some of the causes of babies being born with heart disease (congenital) by warning the mother of the **DANGER** to her unborn baby.

D—Diabetes

A—Alcohol

N—Non-prescription drugs (illicit, illegal)

G—Getting infections (toxoplasmosis, rubella, cytomegalovirus, etc.)

E—Extra small or extra large size (babies that are too large or too small have a higher risk)

R—Rx drugs

WHAT TO DO WHEN A BABY IS BORN WITH A CARDIAC DEFECT:

What do nurses do first? Assess!! Assess the infant using your ABC's.

ASSESSMENT	INTERVENTION
A- AIRWAY Airway should be open and patent. Babies have a tiny airway, so it can close quickly. Be alert!	Position the baby supine. For newborns, suction with bulb aspirator if necessary. Never instill saline in the nose or mouth and never suction the posterior pharynx, as this can cause profound bradycardia, apnea, and laryngospasm. ETT size for children is tiny! Follow this formula to estimate needed size: Uncuffed tube= age in years +4 4 Cuffed tube= age in years +3 4 The rule of thumb for neonates is to estimate the size of the outer diameter based on the size of the baby's pinky finger. **TRACHEAL SIZES 0.5MM SMALLER AND LARGER SHOULD ALWAYS BE READILY AVAILABLE AT THE BEDSIDE!!**
B- BREATHING Assess breathing effort. A normal newborn respiratory rate is 30-60 bpm.	If respiratory rate is >60, attach cardiopulmonary monitors, give oxygen, and notify provider. If baby is unresponsive to interventions, prepare for mechanical ventilation. **DO NOT FEED A BABY EXHIBITING SIGNS OF RESPIRATORY DISTRESS!! YOU WILL INCREASE THE RISK OF ASPIRATION.** **5 CARDINAL SIGNS OF RESPIRATORY DISTRESS:** 1. Tachypnea 2. Cyanosis 3. Grunting 4. Nasal flaring 5. Retractions **Stimulate:** If baby is not breathing, provide stimulation by slapping foot or rubbing vigorously with a towel. **Give oxygen:** Infants who are cyanotic or have signs of distress should receive supplemental oxygen. Oxyhood may be used. Administer initially @ 8-10 lpm via blow-by then mask, then ambu bag, then mechanical ventilation *(least invasive to most invasive).*

	If prolonged oxygen is needed in the immediate period, it may be given via nasal CPAP for babies, Bipap for older infants and younger children, and high flow nasal cannula for older children. O2 sats should be 92-96% for term infants and 88-92% for preterm infants.
C- CIRCULATION Circulation is measured in cardiac and renal output. If renal output is decreasing, this is a clue that cardiac output may be as well. Normal newborn COP is approximately 230 mL/minute/kg. The baby with obstructive defects, increased blood flow through extra openings in the heart, or transposition of great vessels may have decreased cardiac output.	Watch for decreased UOP! Normal UOP is **1mL/kg/hour.** You can measure UOP in diapers. 1g=1mL UOP. Also, assess for signs and symptoms of decreased cardiac output: - Peripheral edema may be present - Abnormal heart sounds possible (S3 &S4) - Tachycardia (normal pulse 150-180 bpm) - Poor perfusion - Color may be cyanotic, pale, or mottled - Weak peripheral pulses - Cool extremities - Capillary refill may be poor (< 3 seconds) - Murmur may be audible.... **Be concerned if pulses on upper extremities are bounding and lower extremities are diminished! It could be coarctation of the aorta or a cardiac problem** Where do you auscultate? Remember that **A**ll **P**oliticians **T**ake **M**oney. **A**ortic—centered @ the second right ICS and includes the suprasternal area, the neck, and the third left ICS. **P**ulmonic—second ICS @ left sternal border **T**ricuspid-fourth ICS and from left sternal edge to right of sternum **M**itral-the apex @ the fifth ICS at the mid-clavicular line, extending to the left sternal edge and laterally to the axillary region. **INITIATE COMPRESSIONS IF APICAL PULSE IS LESS THAN 60!!**
D- DECREASE COLD STRESS Infants who experience cold stress use more oxygen, which is very dangerous when experiencing	Normal newborn temp is 35.5-37.5 degrees Celsius Keep a warm environment. Use pre-warmed towels or blankets.

respiratory compromise from a cardiac defect.	Use an infant warmer.
	Monitor temp every 15 minutes until stabilized.
	Use warmed and humidified oxygen! (If you don't warm and humidify the O2, the baby will have to use energy to do it). For older babies and children, cool humidified O2 is acceptable.
E- ENERGY CONSERVATION Fatigue and activity intolerance is common but detrimental to conserving energy for growth. It is vital to avoid unnecessary stress and to allow for rest in order to decrease cardiac demands.	Keep a calm environment. Do not waste any of the baby's energy! That means, as much as possible, do not let the baby cry, be hungry, or be wet. This baby cannot handle any extra stressors! Bathe only as needed, and make it quick! Cluster care to minimize discomfort, anxiety, and crying. Maintain bedrest. (For babies, this means minimal playing, although babies still need to be touched, loved, sung to and talked to). Position in an infant seat at a 45-degree angle. Keep harness low or across the tummy. Nothing tight on the chest. Older children should maintain a semi-Fowler's or Fowler's position.
F- FLUID AND ELECTROLYE BALANCE Fluids are a very delicate and tricky thing for these babies. Volume is VERY small when in comparison to adults. Providers follow the 4-2-1 rule, which means: • 4cc/kg/hr/first ten kg • 2cc/kg/hr/next ten kg • 1cc/kg/hr each kg after You can see that FVO can occur quite easily. A KVO volume may be 1 cc/hr! We also use smaller needles for neonates, with an average 24 gauge IV (unless you are giving blood and then you must use a	Prepare for IV fluid therapy. Remember that if the baby is dyspneic, an NPO order will need to be established. Different IV's for babies may include scalp veins, umbilical arterial catheters (UAC) or umbilical venous catheters (UVC). Other routes common in babies with cardiac disease that require long-term therapy and support are PICC lines and CVC's. Maintain adequate hydration. (Dehydration causes tachycardia and stress!) Daily weight (Babies should be on track to double their birth weight by six months and triple it by one year). Strict I&O (output should be 1mL/kg/hour) Monitor serum electrolytes Maintain sodium and fluid restrictions if prescribed Administer potassium supplements if prescribed. Assess for adequate urination.

22g!)	
	Monitor for signs of **FLUID VOLUME OVERLOAD**: Peripheral edema, crackles in the lungs, bounding pulses, and irritability.
G- GROWTH AND DEVELOPMENT	Be sure to give all immunizations on time! These babies need extra protection from communicable disease! These babies are prone to FAILURE TO THRIVE. **FEEDING INTERVENTIONS:** Recognize early signs of hunger. Do not wait until baby is crying to feed. Feed small amounts frequently. A schedule of feeding every 3 hours is preferred. Use a preemie nipple or a nipple with enlarged hole to decrease sucking effort. Hold infant in semi-upright position for feeding. Allow for periods of rest during feeding. ***IF FEEDING LASTS FOR MORE THAN 30 MINUTES, GAVAGE FEED REMAINDER OF FORMULA OR BREASTMILK IN ORDER TO CONSERVE ENERGY.*** Use **30**kcal/oz formula instead of 20kcal/oz. Encourage breastfeeding mothers to alternate with high-density formula or fortified breastmilk.

Many times when a baby is born, the parents may not know he or she has a cardiac disease.

The clues that tell you something is wrong are not specific and the nurse should be alert to

clusters of these symptoms that cause **FEAR** in the hearts of parents:

F—Feeding poorly

E—Energy is low

A—Always fussy

R—Rapid respirations

Once **FEAR** is identified (usually by the parent), what does the nurse assess for?? See how many times you can spell **FEAR** with this baby's assessment findings.

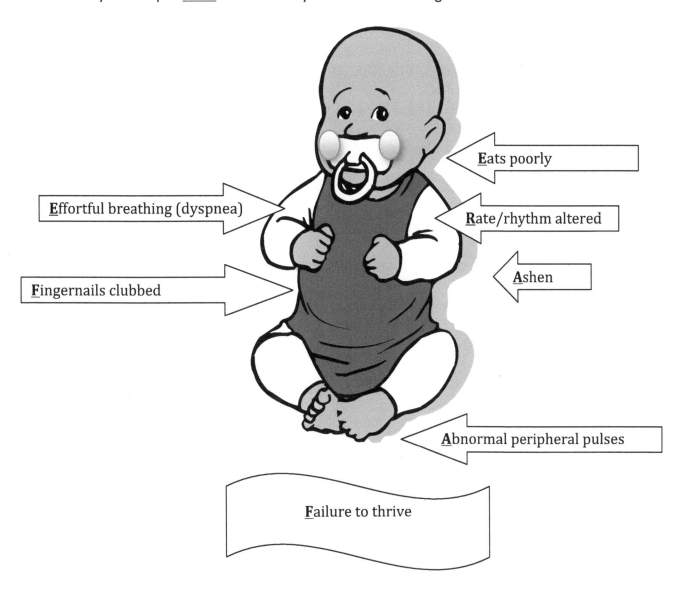

Eats poorly

Effortful breathing (dyspnea)

Rate/rhythm altered

Ashen

Fingernails clubbed

Abnormal peripheral pulses

Failure to thrive

What can you do to address the parent's **FEAR**?

F—Family coping skills, enhance them with nursing support.

E—Educate parents and provide resources to promote developmental growth in the child.

A—Activity—help parents to know appropriate guidelines for acceptable physical activity.

R—Reinforce the importance of adherence to prescribed nutrition requirements and medication.

DIAGNOSTIC TESTING FOR CONGENITAL CARDIAC DEFECTS:

What tests are done to confirm that a baby has suspected cardiac disease? Remember, most cardiac anomalies are anomalies of physical structures so you need a test that helps you to see the heart, but preferably non-invasive, because this is pediatrics! If you guessed an **echocardiogram**, then you are correct! An "echo" is an ultrasound of the heart. Sounds pretty easy, right? Well, not if you are a baby. To have a good ultrasound, you must be very still and sometimes babies don't listen when we tell them to stop moving.

WHAT MAKES AN ECHOCARDIOGRAM DIFFERENT FOR CHILDREN AND BABIES?

What makes this procedure different for babies and children is that, sometimes, mild sedation is required in order to make sure that children are still enough to get good pictures.

Care **BEFORE** the procedure	Care **DURING** the procedure	Care **AFTER** the procedure
NPO 4 hours prior to procedure. Administer mild sedation as ordered (usually an oral agent such as chloral hydrate) at the prescribed interval before the procedure.	Assist with positioning. Provide lots of distraction for children who have not been sedated! A movie or book usually works well.	Monitor for any reactions to sedation medication administered. Provide for child's safety, as they may be a little hung over! Don't let them fall and hurt themselves!

Visit here to see what a pediatric echocardiogram is like!

http://www.youtube.com/watch?v=Dhl8PivF2WQ

Sometimes once a cardiac defect is identified on the ultrasound, more invasive and specific testing must be done in order to determine a treatment plan. Sometimes the physicians can't tell how bad the condition really is until they see it directly for themselves. Do you know what other test is often done to evaluate cardiac conditions in children? Hopefully you guessed CARDIAC CATHETERIZATION.

WHAT MAKES *CARDIAC CATHETERIZATION* DIFFERENT FOR CHILDREN AND BABIES?

The nurse must have an emergency plan in place for this test! It is routinely done in children but you must be alert to potentially serious and fatal complications that can occur. Early intervention can save lives!! Remember all of these **"F"** words we are about to teach you, because if you don't remember them when giving care, you will be saying other **"F"** words and so will the providers around you!

***********THE FRIGHTFUL "F" WORDS*************

Care *BEFORE* the procedure	Care *AFTER* the procedure
FIND OUT if the patient is exhibiting any signs of any type of infection. Procedure cancelled!	**FREQUENTLY** take vital signs (every 15 minutes)
FIXATE on baseline vitals. These are important because they can indicate the severity of potential complications, such as hemorrhage.	**FREAK OUT** about low blood pressure (a potential sign of hemorrhage, always report if BP is lower than baseline to the provider)
FEATURE the dorsalispedis and posterior tibial pulses on both extremities to make them easy to find later. "X" marks the spot!	**FEMORAL** dressing should be **FREE** of blood
	FINGERFIRST on the hemorrhage (if the site starts bleeding, put your finger 1 inch above the insertion site, before you call the provider)
FORBID anything to be taken in by mouth. NPO!	**FEEL** skin temp of the affected extremity (it should not be pale or cold-emergency!)
FLAG any allergies to iodine or shellfish.	**FIND** the peripheral pulses (sometimes they can be a little diminished for a couple of hours, but they should strengthen, and should NOT be absent)
FACILITATE age appropriate teaching to child and parents.	

	FORCE the patient to keep their leg straight for at least **FOUR** hours
	FEED with **FLUIDS** (patients are NPO prior to procedure, the dyes have a diuretic effect, and they can lose blood during the procedure so give PO and IV fluids)

DIFFERENT TYPES OF CONGENITAL HEART DISEASE

What you need to know

http://www.youtube.com/watch?v=YzDNfr6y4P8

Visit here to watch some nursing students who made a really corny video about pediatric heart defects. Sadly, you won't forget it!

It is important to know which defects are cyanotic because this will affect your assessment and expectations of oxygenation and perfusion. Most important, you must know your patient's baseline oxygen saturations in order to maintain them.

<u>Cyanotic</u> **Heart Defects**:

Right to left shunt ➡ decreased pulmonary blood flow ➡ cyanosis/hypoxemia

It's all about the <u>"T's"</u>

These are pediatric heart defects, which cause cyanosis:

Truncus Arteriosus

Transposition of the Great Arteries

Tricuspid Atresia

Tetralogy of Fallot

Total Anomalous Pulmonary Venous Connection

Notice that they all start with "**T**" so there is a good chance that if it starts with "**T**" then it is a cyanotic defect. The *exception* is hypoplastic left heart syndrome, but this one is an *exception* because it causes the babies to be *exceptionally* blue. This is the "blue baby syndrome." Babies with this disorder often have oxygen saturations in the 70's and 80's! Know what their baseline oxygen saturation is and stick with it, whether it is 72% or 92%. This is one uncommon case in which oxygen can be detrimental to them. So stick to the baseline!

Remember that for *hypercyanotic spells*, also called "blue spells" or "tet spells," **IMMEDIATE** action is necessary. The infant will become acutely cyanotic and if action is not taken, profound cerebral hypoxic injury can occur. This is a baby that has a sudden and dramatic drop in oxygen saturations from baseline. You can remember what to do by thinking about a "SMURF!" Smurfs are blue. When your patient becomes a smurf, treat him like one!

S—Sit the baby immediately in a knee-chest position!

M—Morphine, give it IV if there is an existing line or SQ if there is not one

U—Use a calm and comforting approach

R— Rip open the oxygen and give it 100% "blow-by!"

F—Fluids, give IV fluid replacement and volume expansion if needed

http://www.youtube.com/watch?v=aPD-c96cZ0Q

Visit here to watch a series of videos on TOF from Children's Hospital of

Philadelphia. This is the first of six.

Acyanotic Heart Defects

Left to right shunt -- ⟹ increased pulmonary blood flow ⟹ s/sx of CHF

These disorders include: ASD, VSD, PDA, and AV Canal.

Obstructive defects: COA, Aortic Stenosis, Pulmonary Stenosis

These defects cause increased pressure load on the ventricle and decreased cardiac output.

Clinically, infants and children with obstructive defects will exhibit signs and symptoms of CHF.

Mixed Defects: (Transposition of Great Arteries/Vessels, Hypoplastic Left Heart Syndrome)

Multiple anomalies that cause a combination of cyanosis and CHF in variable degrees.

Speaking of oxygen, a quick word about **ventilators** and respiratory status**.**

Know how to do an initial assessment when receiving a patient on a vent. Investigate the size of the ETT, the level of the ETT, the prescribed settings of the vent, and auscultate breath sounds to establish a baseline. What do you do if the ET tube stops working or becomes dislodged?!? If this happens, don't be a **DOPE**!! Investigate the causes of tube dislodgement by thinking about looking for **DOPE**.

D—Displacement

O—Obstruction

P—Pneumothorax

E—Equipment failure

http://www.youtube.com/watch?v=BHgvn7O0eXM

If you don't feel great about ventilators, check out "Vent for Dummies!"

Other important things to know:

1. Early extubation within the first few hours after surgery is common.

2. Suctioning is limited to prevent laryngospasm and vagal stimulation, which can cause arrhythmias. Suction for no more than 5 seconds at a time to avoid oxygen depletion! During suctioning, observe for signs of **respiratory distress** and stop if they occur! Give supplemental oxygen via ambu bag before and after the procedure to prevent hypoxia. Position the child facing you so that you can closely monitor their response to the procedure.

3. For small babies who need frequent blood draws, be sure to keep track of the amount drawn. Many pediatric units have a policy on the maximum amount of blood that can be drawn in a 24-hour period. These babies cannot afford to lose a lot of blood. In adults, you may draw an initial blood sample equal to the volume in the catheter and then discard it before aspirating the sample to be tested. In babies and compromised children, do not discard the aspirated sample. Instead, return it to the patient in order to preserve adequate blood volume.

4. Chest tubes may be used to remove secretions and promote lung expansion. Chest tube drainage should be checked hourly. **CHEST TUBE DRAINAGE OF MORE THAN 3ML/KG/HR FOR MORE THAN 3 HOURS OR MORE THAN 5-10ML/KG IN ONE HOUR MAY INDICATE ACUTE HEMORRHAGE AND THE PROVIDER SHOULD BE NOTIFIED IMMEDIATELY!** Chest tubes are usually removed 1-3 days post-op. Medications such as morphine or other pain relief should be provided. The nurse must be vigilant to listen for decreased breath sounds that could indicate a pneumothorax.

MEDICATIONS COMMONLY USED FOR PEDIATRIC CARDIAC PATIENTS

MEDICATION	ACTION	NURSING CARE	EDUCATION	ALERTS
Digoxin (Lanoxin)	Improves contractility of the heart	**STOP!** This means YOU. **HOLD DOSE** if infant	Administer every 12 hours. If a dose is missed, do not give an extra dose or increase the next dose. If child	**CAUTION!** Always question an infant's dose if >1 mL!! Double check

		pulse **<90** or child pulse **<70**!	vomits, do not repeat dose.	with another nurse!
		  Monitor for **TOXICITY!** **_BAND_** **B**-Bradycardia **A**-Anorexia **N**-Nausea/Vomiting **D**-Dysrhythmias	Keep in a locked cabinet! Monitor for signs of toxicity.	Therapeutic level is 0.5-2 ng/mL, but dig levels cannot be solely depended on. Clinical signs and symptoms are just as critical!
		  Monitor **SERUM** digoxin levels. (0.8-2 ng/mL)	Give water to prevent tooth decay.	

MEDICATION	**ACTION**	**NURSING CARE**	**EDUCATION**	**ALERTS**
Captopril (Capoten) **Enalapril (Vasotec)**	ACE inhibitor Reduces afterload by causing vasodilation	 Watch for rapid drop in blood pressure!	Check blood pressure at home.	Block action of aldosterone, so potassium supplements are usually NOT needed!
	Decreased pulmonary and systemic vascular resistance	Monitor for signs of **HYPER**kalemia!	Normal blood pressures are based on ht/wt. Use a reference chart to find normal values.	ACE inhibitors can cause a cough as an adverse side effect.

MEDICATION	**ACTION**	**NURSING CARE**	**EDUCATION**	**ALERTS**
Furosemide (Lasix)	Potassium-WASTING Diuretic Removes excess fluid and sodium	Observe for side effects—remember it tastes bad and it can make you feel bad too! Watch for nausea, vomiting, and diarrhea.	Oral med can be mixed with juice... it tastes terrible! 	Observe for signs of **HYPO**kalemia! **H**—heart rate change (up or down) **Y**—yawning

				(drowsy)
				P—poor strength
				O—out of sorts (irritable)
		Monitor for signs of **HYPO**kalemia. Remember, we are WASTING the potassium.	Eat foods rich in potassium: bran, tomatoes, bananas, oranges, melons.	**HYPO**kalemia can enhance the effect of digoxin and increase the risk for toxicity!
		Monitor intake and output	Weigh daily!	

MEDICATION	ACTION	NURSING CARE	EDUCATION	ALERTS
Sildenafil (Viagra)	phosphodiesterase inhibitor Pulmonary vasodilation	Monitor BP closely The NICU can be a party place for cardiac babies! They take Viagra to lower their blood pressure and may also take caffeine to stimulate their heart rate and prevent apneic spells!		Not FDA approved in infants, but commonly given because efficacy being established in clinical trials.
MEDICATION	ACTION	NURSING CARE	EDUCATION	ALERTS
Milrinone **(Primacor)**	Inotropic, chronotropic, vasodilator Used to treat acute decompensated heart failure	Assess patient's perfusion closely. If patient's BP rapidly drops, slow or stop the infusion and call the provider!		May cause hypotension, and thrombocytopenia Patient must be on continuous EKG monitoring

MEDICATION	ACTION	NURSING CARE	EDUCATION	ALERTS
Prostaglandin E **(Alprostadil)**	Maintain patency of ductus arteriosus	Monitor for signs of apnea, fever, seizures, flushing, hypotension, and bradycardia	Prepare patient for impending cardiac surgery to repair defect	Monitor respiratory status throughout treatment! Neonates may experience profound apnea within first hour of infusion.

POSTOPERATIVE CARE

At some point, most children with congenital cardiac defects will have to undergo some kind of curative or palliative surgery. Immediate post-op care is usually given in an intensive care unit because of the invasive monitoring techniques that are used.

Vital Signs	• Always count pediatric respirations for one full minute! • Compare assessed vital signs to monitor readings. • Continuous EKG monitoring. • Monitor for hypothermia, common after surgery, and take corrective measures such as heated blanket, radiant warmer, etc. • Monitor intrarterial blood pressure; maintain a low-rate continuous infusion of heparinized saline to prevent clotting. • Maintain central venous pressure (CVP) line, usually placed in a neck vessel.
Provide Rest	• In the immediate post-operative period, provide sedation with agents such as lorazepam or Versed in order to reduce cardiac workload. • Progressively adjust activities based on signs of tolerance. Heart rate and respirations are evidence of the degree of cardiac demand.
Monitor Fluids	• Strict I&O • Watch for signs of renal failure (UOP <1mL/kg/hour) • Maintain fluid restrictions to prevent hypervolemia, which increases cardiac workload • Maintain NPO status while intubated. • Weigh daily, same time and same scale.
Pain	• Analgesics such as morphine, fentanyl, NSAIDS (Motrin and Ketorolac) are commonly administered. Monitor respiratory function with narcotic administration. • Perform treatments during peak of pain medication efficacy. • Decrease stress and stimulation.

Anticoagulants	• Administer anticoagulants as ordered after surgery in order to maintain patency of shunts and prevent clots around artificial valves, etc. (Heparin, Lovenox, ASA). • Monitor coagulation panels closely.

We have two more brief topics to cover, and then we will leave the cardiac section.

KAWASAKI DISEASE

Here is the down and dirty version of what you need to know:

1. KD is a systemic vasculitis with unknown etiology.

2. The symptoms are all about **red**ness: **red** eyes (conjunctivitis), **red** (and peeling) palms and soles, **red** lips, **red** strawberry tongue, **red** polymorphous rash, and red (irritable/angry) baby.

3. The worst things that can happen are coronary artery aneurysms and myocardial infarction.

4. This disease is treated with very high dose IV globulin and aspirin. **ALERT** ASPIRIN IS VERY RARELY GIVEN TO CHILDREN BECAUSE OF THE RISK OF REYES SYNDROME***THIS IS ONE RARE EXCEPTION!***

5. Because of the globulin administration, live vaccine administration should be deferred for one year.

Visit here to watch a parent's guide to Kawasaki Disease (KD)

http://www.youtube.com/watch?v=5knlkzlU2-4

RHEUMATIC FEVER

Rheumatic fever is an inflammatory heart condition caused by a case of strep throat that was partially treated or untreated. The symptoms usually present 2 to 6 weeks after the infection. Cardiac valve damage is the most significant complication.

*What are expected assessment findings for **RHEUMATIC** fever?*

R—RASH (appears on the trunk and inner surfaces of the extremities-erythema marginatum)

H—Heart problems (tachycardia, cardiomegaly, murmur, chest pain, muffled heart sounds)

E—Elevated inflammatory markers (ESR—sedimentation rate or CRP—C reactive protein)

U—Under the skin you will feel subcutaneous nodules

M—Most reliable lab test is elevated ASO titer

A—Arthritis & Arthralgia (large joints with painful swelling)

T—Tired all the time, too tired to eat

I—Irritability, behavior problems, poor concentration

C—CNS involvement (chorea, weakness, purposeless random movements)

What is the goal of nursing care for a child with rheumatic fever?

The goal is to cut the **CRAP** this family and child has to deal with.

C—*COMPLIANCE WITH MEDICATION!*

- Treatment is given until at least 5 years of age, and usually until 18 years of age

- Pencillin IM once a month -OR- twice a day PO

- If child is penicillin allergic (or allergic to cephalosporin because of cross-reactivity), erythromycin is an acceptable alternative.

R—*RECOVERY FROM ILLNESS*

- Rest and nutrition are very important. Activity restrictions should be followed.

- The nurse should monitor for altered heart rate/rhythm and murmurs.

A—*ABILITY TO COPE*

- Parents should be reassured that chorea is usually self-limiting.

- Education about the long-term nature of treatment should be given.

P—*PREVENT RECURRENCE*

- Watch for symptoms (fever, malaise, chest pain, poor appetite)

- Obtain prophylactic antibiotic therapy prior to dental work and invasive procedures

- Medical follow-up at least every five years

REVIEW QUESTIONS

1. A 3-month-old cardiac client suddenly turns blue and begins to have rapidly decreasing oxygen saturations. What are appropriate nursing actions to take? **Select all that apply.**

   1) Administer oxygen via nasal cannula
   2) Place the baby in a knee-chest position
   3) Give an IV dose of Morphine
   4) Stimulate the infant to increase breathing effort
   5) Call the provider

1. Options #2, #3, and #5 are correct. Option #1 is incorrect because oxygen should be given at a high rate, using blow-by or facemask. Option #4 is incorrect because the baby needs a calm, soothing approach to assist with recovery.

2. A 4-month-old client is awaiting surgery to repair a congenital cardiac defect. What is the best approach by the nurse to manage feedings?

   1) Administer larger feedings at less frequent intervals in order to conserve energy.
   2) Limit feeding sessions to less than 45 minutes to conserve energy.
   3) Gavage feed remaining formula after 30 minutes of feeding to conserve energy.
   4) Initiate feeding immediately when the infant cries in order to conserve energy.

2. Option #3 is correct. Options #1, #2, and #4 do not conserve energy. Smaller, frequent feedings are more efficient. Feeding sessions that last longer than 30 minutes consume more energy than they provide. Crying is a late sign of hunger and feeding should be initiated before the onset of crying.

3. In order to prevent infection following cardiac surgery, what is the best action to be taken by the nurse?

   1) Use meticulous handwashing technique
   2) Wear sterile gloves and gown when in contact with the infant
   3) Administer ordered antibiotics
   4) Avoid contact with the infant unless absolutely necessary

3. Option #1 is the best way to prevent infection. Option #2 is usually not necessary. Option #3 may be a good answer, but the best is handwashing. Option #4 is detrimental to the infant's need for attachment and could cause failure to thrive.

4. A 9-month-old patient with a history of congenital cardiac disease and congestive heart failure is admitted because of a 24-hour history of vomiting and diarrhea. The medications include digoxin (Lanoxin) and furosemide (Lasix). What assessment finding needs to be reported to the provider?
   1) Urine output of less than 1cc/kg/hr
   2) Potassium level of 3.9mEq/L
   3) A heart rate of 80 beats per minute
   4) Irritability

4. Option #3 is correct. Digoxin dosages should be withheld if the pulse rate is less than 90. Bradycardia is a sign of potential digoxin toxicity and should be reported immediately. Options #1 and #2 are normal values and option #4 would be expected in a hospitalized infant who is experiencing vomiting and diarrhea.

5. A nurse is assessing a 5-month-old infant at shift change. When the nurse looks at the cardiac monitor, a heart rate of 42 with an abnormal rhythm is detected. The infant is kicking and screaming. What should the nurse do first?

   1) Call the rapid response team
   2) Stimulate the baby with a foot tap
   3) Administer 2L O2 by nasal cannula
   4) Assess the cardiac lead placements

Option #4 is correct. An infant who is kicking and screaming should not have a heart rate of 42. Equipment is used to assist nurses, not replace them! Cardiac leads should be placed correctly: white on right, green on the ground, and black on the left (smoke over fire if red lead is used). It may be necessary to call rapid response or stimulate the baby if the heart rate is indeed 42. If the leads are correct, the nurse should assess the heart rate with a stethoscope to verify. None of the assessment findings warrant oxygen administration at this time.

6. A nurse is caring for a child post-op from a cardiac catheterization. The child complains of feeling wet and when the nurse lifts the sheet, blood has saturated the dressing and the bottom sheet. What is the priority action of the nurse?

   1) Call the physician immediately
   2) Call for rapid response
   3) Elevate the extremity and apply a tourniquet
   4) Apply direct pressure one inch above the insertion site

Option #4 is correct. You need to call the provider stat but not without applying pressure first! This patient is bleeding out! Stop the bleeding, then call. The extremity must be held straight and there is no way to apply a tourniquet proximal to the operative site.

7. A nurse is working in a neonatal intensive care unit with a premature infant. Upon assessment, the infant has mild perioral cyanosis and has an oxygen saturation of 91% and a respiratory rate of 44. What action should the nurse take?

    1) Increase the oxygen flow until the saturation improves
    2) Check to see what the infant's baseline saturation has been
    3) Call the code team
    4) Notify the provider

Option #2 is correct. Oxygen toxicity can cause retinopathy of prematurity (and potentially neonatal blindness). It is acceptable for some babies with cardiac defects, especially prior to surgery, to tolerate lower saturations if that is their established baseline.

8. A nurse is caring for a child with a congenital cardiac defect. The provider orders an ACE inhibitor and potassium supplements to be given IV. What is the appropriate course of action for the nurse?

    1) Question the provider about the order
    2) Start the potassium supplement prior to giving the ACE inhibitor
    3) Establish renal function before starting the potassium supplementation
    4) Draw a baseline potassium level before starting both medications

Option #1 is correct. ACE inhibitors block the action of aldosterone, therefore negating the need for potassium supplementation. Giving these meds together could cause hyperkalemia. Ordering a lab draw is not within the scope of practice for a registered nurse.

9. A nurse is caring for a toddler with a cardiac defect who is taking digitalis (digoxin). The most recent lab report indicates that the serum potassium is 3.2. What actions should the nurse take? **Select all that apply**.

    1) Notify the provider
    2) Hold the next dose of digoxin
    3) Implement sodium restrictions in the diet
    4) Recheck the lab in 4-6 hours
    5) Document the findings

Options #1 and #2 are correct. A decrease in serum potassium level enhances the effects of digitalis and conversely increases the risk of digitalis toxicity. This child's potassium level is already low, presenting a risk for toxicity. The provider should be notified so the hypokalemia can be corrected and a serum digitalis level can be drawn. Documentation of a result out of the norm may cause liability issues for the nurse.

10. A nurse is caring for a child with a cardiac defect who was weaned off oxygen the night before. The O2 saturations are 90% with a respiratory rate of 32 and signs of increased work of breathing. What is the appropriate action of the nurse at this time?

    1) Begin humidified oxygen administration at 10L/min by facemask
    2) Begin dehumidified oxygen administration at 2L by nasal cannula
    3) Notify the provider of the change in status
    4) Call for a consult with respiratory therapy.

Option #3 is correct. Oxygen is a drug and should only be administered with an appropriate order. Sometimes excess oxygen administration can be harmful. Oxygen should always be humidified. It is not within the scope of practice of a registered nurse to order a consult with respiratory therapy unless the provider has ordered such a service.

11. An infant has an order to start medication therapy with digitalis, or digoxin. The order is for 100mcg, which equates to a 2mL oral dose. What is the appropriate action of the nurse?

    1) Double check the calculation math with another nurse
    2) Administer the medication
    3) Notify the provider of a medication error
    4) Hold the dose until the provider makes rounds later that morning

Option #1 is correct. Any oral dose of digoxin over 1mL or 50mcg is a warning of an imminent medication error. This is too much!

12. A nurse is caring for a child experiencing intracardiac right to left blood shunting. The nurse is assessing the IV and finds several very small bubbles in the IV line. What is the appropriate action of the nurse? **Select all that apply**.

    1) Check the entire line for air bubbles
    2) "Bleed" the line by using a syringe to extract the bubbles
    3) Check to see if the IV has a filter in place
    4) Check each connection on the IV for air
    5) Flush the line with normal saline

Options #1, #3 and #4 are correct. This shunting allows air in the venous system to go directly to the brain, creating a risk for air embolism.

13. A nurse is suctioning a tracheostomy for an infant diagnosed with a cardiac defect. During the suctioning, which signs should alert the nurse to a possible problem? **Select all that apply**.

    1) Restlessness
    2) Use of accessory muscles
    3) Tachypnea
    4) Decreased O2 saturations

All four answers are correct. These are signs of respiratory distress and poor tolerance of suctioning and should be investigated.

14. A child has just undergone surgery to repair a cardiac defect and returns to the unit with a chest tube. The nurse assesses the output to be 3 mL/kg for the first hour, and 5mL/kg during the second hour. What action should the nurse take?

    1) Document the chest tube output in the daily I&O
    2) Assess the child's vital signs every 15 minutes
    3) Give IV replacement fluid therapy
    4) Notify the cardiac surgeon

Option #4 is correct. Any chest tube output of 3mL/kg for 3 hours or more or output of 5 to 10 mL/kg in one hour can indicate a hemorrhage and the surgeon should be notified to avoid the risk of developing cardiac tamponade.

15. A nurse is caring for a child with a cardiac defect who is awaiting surgery and notes a urine output of 1.5 mL/kg/hr, a BUN of 18mg/dL and a creatinine of 0.8 mg/dL. What is the appropriate action of the nurse?

    1) Notify the provider
    2) Check the child's vital signs
    3) Total the I&O from the last 8 hours
    4) Document the findings

Option #4 is correct. These are normal UOP and lab values.

16. A 16-year-old presents to the school nurse with complaints of headache, dizziness, and double vision. Which assessment is the priority at this time?

1) Pulse
2) Blood Pressure
3) Snellen
4) Temperature

Option #2 is correct. These are all signs of hypertension, which is becoming more prevalent in teenagers.

17. A child diagnosed with Kawasaki Disease (KD) is being discharged after a two-week hospital stay and therapy with aspirin and high dose immunoglobulins. The mother is crying and asks if it is true that the child may have suffered heart damage. What is the appropriate response of the nurse?

1) "The damage to her heart is reversible and will heal over time."
2) "I will give you the names of some support groups you may find helpful."
3) "I will be sure the doctor comes back in to talk with you."
4) "We will know more in 4-6 weeks time."

Option #4 is correct. The cardiac vessels do not reach a maximum diameter until 4-6 weeks after the onset of the disease and at that point sequelae can be better assessed. There is a risk of severe coronary artery damage.

18. A nurse is caring for a child who is post-operative for a cardiac defect. The nurse notes the child is irritable. BP is normal with narrowing pulse pressure. Slight tachycardia is noted. The child looks pale and complains of coldness of the feet. What is the appropriate action of the nurse at this time?

1) Notify the provider of the assessment
2) Administer ordered pain medication
3) Obtain a warmed blanket
4) Document the findings

Option #1 is correct. These are early signs of impending shock. Early identification allows for early intervention.

19. A provider orders an IM injection of penicillin for a child with strep throat. When the nurse inquires about allergies, the mother reports a past anaphylactic reaction to a cephalosporin. What is the appropriate action of the nurse?

1) Administer the injection as ordered
2) Monitor the patient's vital signs for one hour after injection
3) Notify the provider of the allergy history
4) Check the patient for a rash within 15 minutes of administration

Option #3 is correct. A child with history of an anaphylactic reaction to a cephalosporin should not receive a penicillin injection, as 30% of the population will cross-react.

20. A mother calls the pediatric clinic and reports to the triage nurse that her 5-year-old son is complaining of a sore throat and a fever for 2 days and now has a generalized rash with complaints of itching. What should the nurse advise her to do?

1) Try a bath with baking soda for itching
2) Come in to see the provider that day
3) Go to the nearest emergency room
4) Look online to see if it looks like chicken pox

Option #2 is correct. These are signs of possible scarlet fever.

The Pediatric HEMATOLOGY SYSTEM

Jessica Peck, DNP, RN, MSN, CPNP-PC, CNE
Edited by Sylvia Rayfield & Associates, Inc.

What is different about a childhood blood disorders?

LEUKEMIA IS THE MOST COMMON CHILDHOOD CANCER. LONG-TERM SURVIVAL FOR ACUTE LYMPHOID LEUKEMIA IS NEARLY 80%!!

KEY CONCEPTS TO REMEMBER:

- ❖ Iron deficiency anemia is the most common childhood form of anemia.
- ❖ Hemophilia is a genetic disorder that causes an impaired ability to control internal and external bleeding.
- ❖ Sickle Cell Anemia occurs when a recessive trait is inherited, resulting in RBC sickling, increased blood viscosity, obstructed blood flow, and tissue hypoxia.

HOW TO CARE FOR A CHILD WITH A HEMATOLOGICAL DISORDER:

What do nurses do first? Assess!! Assess the infant using your ABC's.

ASSESSMENT	INTERVENTION
A- AIRWAY Airway should be open and patent.	• Observe for signs of hypoxia.
B- BREATHING Assess breathing effort.	• Observe for shortness of breath and dyspnea.
C- CIRCULATION Circulation is measured in cardiac and renal output. If renal output is decreasing, this is a clue that cardiac output may be as well.	• Observe for tachycardia, systolic heart murmur, or signs of heart failure. • Follow protocol for blood transfusions. • Monitor cardiac rhythm. • Tissue hypoxia causes severe pain in the bones, joints, and abdomen during sickle cell crisis. The RBC's can actually be destroyed, releasing bilirubin and causing jaundice. • Signs of shock can occur during sickle cell sequestration. • Transcranial Doppler can be used to check intracranial

	blood flow, determining risk for CVA. This is an annual test for SCA patients. - Use passive ROM to decrease venous stasis. - Chemo can cause cardiotoxicity!
D- DECREASE BLEEDING	For children with hematologic disorders, we want to minimize blood loss. Bleeding can be internal or external! - Look for hematomas, bruising, epistaxis, gum bleeding, tarry stools, hematuria, obvious external bleeding. - Hemarthrosis- indicated by joint pain, stiffness, warmth, swelling, deformation, loss of joint mobility. - Intracranial bleeding: irritability, change in level of consciousness, headache, slurred speech. - Observe for prolonged partial thromboplastin time - Nosebleeds (epistaxis)—rarely serious!! Call rapid response if it lasts longer than 30 minutes!! Have child sit FORWARD (not lie down!!) and hold pressure for 10 minutes with ice across the bridge of the nose). - **AVOID RECTAL TEMPS** - **AVOID UNECESSARY PROCEDURES** - **APPLY PRESSURE FOR 5 MINUTES AFTER VENIPUNCTURE** - **REST AND IMMOBILIZE AFFECTED JOINTS** - **WATCH FOR SIGNS OF BLEEDING AND SHOCK!!** - **ADMINSTER BLOOD AS PRESCRIBED**
E- ENERGY CONSERVATION Fatigue and activity intolerance is common but detrimental to conserving energy for growth. It is vital to avoid unnecessary stress and to allow for rest in order to decrease cardiac demands.	Keep a calm environment. Cluster care to minimize discomfort, anxiety, and crying.
F- FOSTER GROWTH AND DEVELOPMENT	Prolonged untreated anemia or untreatable anemia can cause delayed growth and development. If babies are too tired to play, they are too tired to grow and learn! Encourage nutrition for adequate growth. Infants need iron-fortified cereal and formula. Breast is best! Diet should be high in protein, iron, vitamin C, and fiber. Be sure to give all immunizations on time! These babies need extra protection from communicable disease! Refer to available developmental services (occupational therapy, speech therapy, physical therapy).

G- GROWTH OF CANCER, METASTASIS	Observe for early signs of metastasis: - Constitutional signs—anemia, weight loss, fatigue, lymphadenopathy - Hepato/Splenomegaly - Periorbital swelling with or without ecchymosis - Nonspecific bone and joint pain - Paresthesias, neurological deficits - Respiratory Involvement—dyspnea, shortness of breath.		
H- HELP, HOPE AND HOSPICE	- Assess family coping - Offer support resources - Partner with family to create plan of care. - Be optimistic without giving false hope. - Allow parents to stay with the child as long as desired. - Accept that expressions of grief can be varied and unpredictable. - Encourage the family to share their memories. Pay special attention to the developmental level of siblings. - Remember that nurses can be very sad to lose patients they are close to. Find support for your grief.		

Know your <u>A-B-C's</u>	<u>Iron Deficiency Anemia</u>	<u>Hemophilia</u>	<u>Sickle Cell Anemia</u>
<u>A</u>sk about the history	Risk Factors: - Preemies - Poor Diet - Too much cow's milk, esp. <1yr! - Growth spurts - Chronic Disease **"TOMMY TOO TIRED"** ***Prolonged condition can cause developmental delay and growth arrest!*** *WORST CASE: <u>HEART FAILURE</u> because of increased demand on*	Risk Factors: - Severity differs depending on presence of clotting factors - X-linked recessive disorder ***Usually appears with excessive bruising after crawling begins in infancy*** *www.youtube.com/ watch?v=bWH2TMNN5 gs*	Risk Factors: - Family History - African Americans (also Mediterranean, Indian, & Middle Eastern ***Usually diagnosed on the newborn screen, but symptoms manifest after 6 months of age. Sickling cells lead to increased viscosity, obstructed blood flow,*

	the heart to oxygenate the tissues!!!	**Visit here to meet Drew**	tissue hypoxia and **PAIN**
B—Be aware of possible presenting symptoms you might detect on assessment www.youtube.com/ watch?v=kuNYgGjMlME **Visit here to see how Isaac lives every day with sickle cell anemia**	***The more severe the deficiency, the more severe the symptoms.*** This kid is "Tommy Too **TIRED**" and can't keep up with his peers. He is short of breath, dizzy, weak and pale. He may have tachycardia or a murmur. He is slow to heal and may have thin hair and clubbed nails. Poor **TIRED** Tommy!	Bleeding from: - Gums - Epistaxis - Hematuria - Tarry stools - Bruising - Hemarthrosis - SIGNS OF A BRAIN BLEED! (Change in LOC, slurred speech) www.youtube.com/ watch?v=MEPsKYUc6hE **Visit here to watch the Cowboy Hematologist**	This is "**PAIN**ful Precious." ***Precious will have many of the same symptoms that Tommy has. Pallor, fatigue, etc.*** The two most common crises that Precious Painful might face are: - Vaso-occlusive Acute: Severe PAIN Swollen joints/extremities Hematuria Jaundice Chronic: Blindness Renal Failure Liver Failure Seizures - Sequestration Hepato/Splenomegaly Tachycardia Shock
C—Care for the client until surgical repair is completed or condition resolves	This kid needs to take a tip from Popeye and eat his spinach (and other iron-rich green leafy veggies!)	- Place infant in padded crib - Ensure home environment is safe—no sharp corners and clutter-free. Encourage soft carpet flooring.	- MANAGE PAIN OTC vs. Opioids Warm packs to joints Interdisciplinary - HYDRATE I&O Fluid Support - OXYGENATE

	Breast is best for babies! Don't start cow's milk until after one year. Limit milk intake to <32 oz. **REST TOMMY, REST!!**	▪ No contact sports. ▪ Ensure child wears protective equipment while playing (helmets, joint pads, etc.). ▪ Encourage appropriate exercise. ▪ Medical identification bracelet. ▪ **ICE** and **REST** to affected joint during active bleeding!	Give oxygen if hypoxic. Provide rest. Passive ROM. ▪ BLOOD PRODUCTS Follow transfusion protocol. ****TRANSFUSIONS DO NOT CURE SCA**** ▪ INFECTION Oral prophylactic PCN until 6 years of age. Immunizations! Hand hygiene. Educate visitors. ALERT!! RISK FOR DEVELOPING **CVA** and **ACUTE CHEST SYNDROME**!! <u>REPORT A TEMP >101 IMMEDIATELY TO A HEALTHCARE PROVIDER!</u>

CARING FOR A CHILD WITH NEOPLASMS:

Know your <u>A-B-C</u>'s	Wilm's Tumor (Nephroblastoma)	Neuroblastoma	Leukemia
<u>A</u>sk about the history	Risk Factors: ▪ Toddler/Preschool Years ▪ Genetic Predisposition ****Metastasis is <u>RARE</u>!****	Risk Factors: ▪ Age <10years ▪ Genetic Predsiposition ****Metastasis is**	Risk Factors: ▪ Caucasian boys <1year ▪ Peak @ 2-5 years ▪ Trisomy 21 ****ALL (acute lymphoblastic**

		*COMMON***	*leukemia) is the most common form of childhood leukemia***
Know your <u>A-B-C</u>'s	**Wilm's Tumor (Nephroblastoma)**	**Neuroblastoma**	**Leukemia**
<u>B</u>—Be aware of possible presenting symptoms you might detect on assessment	▪ Unilateral, nontender abdominal mass ▪ Urinary symptoms if renal compression present ***NEVER PALPATE THE ABDOMEN IF THERE IS A SUSPECTED WILM'S TUMOR!!***	▪ Unilateral, nontender abdominal mass ▪ Urinary symptoms if renal compression present	▪ Early Fatigue, bruising, non-specific pains, headache, vomiting, anorexia. ▪ Late Severe pain, hematuria, enlarged kidneys, increased ICP
<u>C</u>—Care for the client until surgical repair is completed or condition resolves	Treatment: ▪ Shrink the tumor with chemo or radiation before surgical removal ▪ Follow-up chemo for 6-18 months ▪ Radiation for more severe or complicated cases www.youtube.com/watch?v=z2PQVWHjFro **Visit here to listen to Anna's parents make decisions about treatment for nephroblastoma**	Treatment: ▪ Immediate surgical removal ▪ Radiation prior if tumor is compressing spinal cord ▪ Palliative radiation to shrink tumors, for pain control and comfort measure. www.youtube.com/watch?v=KA1Cv9yR61M **Visit here to see Dylan. You won't forget him.**	Treatment: ▪ Induction— achieving <5% leukemic cells in the bone marrow ▪ CNS prophylactic therapy— prevent metastasis to the CNS, ***INTRATHECAL*** chemo given. ▪ Intensification— destroy any remaining and then resistant cells ▪ Maintenance- to sustain remission

MEDICATIONS COMMONLY USED FOR PEDIATRIC HEMATOLOGY PATIENTS

MEDICATION	ACTION	NURSING CARE	EDUCATION	ALERTS
Iron Supplements	Used to treat iron-deficiency anemia	**Don't make TIRED Tommy's tummy hurt!** Give this med on an empty stomach if you can, but after meals if necessary. Give 1hr before or 2hr after milk products. Give at regular intervals to optimize bone marrow supply!	Tummy troubles are typical at takeoff. This should get better over time. If Tommy's tummy trouble tarries, telephone the tender of care! Tell Tommy not to tremble when he sees his #2. It will be tenebrous! Therapy can take 3 months to increase Hgb levels!	Use a z-track injection method to avoid tinting Tommy's tegument! Store medication in a secure, childproof bottle in a locked cabinet. Use a straw for liquid preparations to avoid TARNISHING Tommy's teeth!!
Opioids **Codeine** **Morphine sulfate** **Hydrocodone** **Methadone**	Pain Management for vaso-occlusive crisis.	Oral or IV administration Give around the clock, not prn. Educate child on use of PCA.	Opioids can cause constipation. Ensure adequate fluid intake and high fiber diet.	Caution with ambulation!!
I-deamino-8-d-arginine vasopressin (DDAVP)	Vasopressor that increases plasma factor VII for hemophiliacs		Sometimes given as a prophylactic treatment for dental and surgical procedures.	**ONLY APPROPRIATE FOR MILD HEMOPHILIA**
Factor VIII	Prevents and treats hemorrhage with hemophilia	Administer by IV infusion.	Requires multiple treatment doses.	Block action of aldosterone, so potassium supplements are usually NOT needed!
Corticosteroids	Used to treat hemiarthrosis and hematuria	Monitor for signs of **INFECTION**!	Parents need to wash their hands well. Avoid illness, and crowded environments.	

CARE FOR CHILDREN RECEIVING CHEMOTHERAPY

Chemotherapeutic agents can be administered orally, intravenously, or intrathecally

STOP THE INFUSION IMMEDIATELY IF ANY SIGN OF ANAPHYLAXIS OR INFILTRATION OCCURS
Flush the IV line with saline and prepare an emergency crash cart. Monitor vitals closely!

Vital Signs	• Always count pediatric respirations for one full minute! • Compare assessed vital signs to monitor readings. • Report a temp >100 degrees F immediately to the provider! • Report changes in blood pressure.
Provide Rest	• Cluster care and maintain a calm environment. • Schedule specific rest periods, and limit visitors during that time.
Monitor Fluids	• Strict I&O • Watch for signs of renal failure (UOP <1mL/kg/hour) • Offer cool fluids to drink. • Weigh daily, same time and same scale.
Pain & Nausea	• Perform treatments during peak of pain medication efficacy. • Decrease stress and stimulation. • Give chemo early in the day. • Give anti-emetics prior to chemo treatments. Ondansetron (Zofran) is the preferred choice. • Allow different food choices of things the child prefers to eat. • Avoid strong odors and provide a happy place and time to eat. • Promote bowel health, observing for diarrhea or constipation.
Oral Care	• Observe the mouth frequently for signs of mucositis (mucosal ulcerations). • Use a soft toothbrush or oral swabs. • Lubricate the lips with lip balm. • Give soft bland foods with low salt content to avoid burning sensations. • Use mouthwash (1tsp baking soda with 1 qt water). • Use local anesthetic mouth rinses for pain control. • Use antifungal and antibacterial mouth rinses. • AVOID: viscous lidocaine (aspiration), lemon glycerin swabs (tissue ulceration), and hydrogen peroxide (can delay healing!). • Get regular dental care.
Infection Control	• Child will need a central venous access device (CVC, PICC or port-a-cath) for chemotherapy. Stringent aseptic technique is necessary. • Educate the family about immunizations, handwashing, avoiding crowds and keeping away people who are sick. • Avoid fresh fruits and vegetables. • Avoid invasive procedures.

	• Monitor for local and systemic signs of infection (sores, pulmonary congestion, IV sites, etc.). • Inspect skin frequently, reposition often.
Watch for signs of Bleeding	• No rectal temps, inspect rectal mucosa frequently. • Apply pressure to venipuncture sites for 5 minutes. • Gentle handling, careful repositioning
Hemorrhagic Cystitis	• Maintain adequate fluid intake. • Void frequently. • Give mesna (Mesnex) to protect bladder mucosa.

What is the goal of nursing care for a child with a hematology disorder?

The goal is to cut the **CRAP** this family and child has to deal with.

C—*COMPLIANCE WITH MEDICATION!*

- Treatments may go on for the duration of a lifetime.

- The number one reason children cannot continue their chemotherapy is because of the

   development of a secondary infection. Keep them infection free!!!

R—*RECOVERY FROM ILLNESS*

- Rest and nutrition are very important. Activity restrictions should be followed.

- Make sure the family has plenty of emotional and physical support.

A—*ABILITY TO COPE*

- Support groups, therapy providers, and hospice should be consulted.

P—*PREVENT RECURRENCE*

- Watch for symptoms (fever, malaise, chest pain, poor appetite).

- Medical follow-up at least every five years after remission

CHILDREN'S REACTIONS TO DEATH AND DYING

Infants & Toddlers (Birth-3 years)	Preschool (3-6 years)	School-Aged (6-12 years)	Adolescents (12-18years)
- They don't understand death. - They have profound separation and/or stranger anxiety. - They typically mirror the emotions of their parents. - They tend to have regressive behaviors. **They don't get it**	- They have magical thinking and may think they caused their death. - They don't understand the permanence of death. - They may see death as a punishment. **They kind of get it**	- They understand the facts. - They know death is permanent. - They are very afraid of pain. - It is hard for them to lose control. - It is common to be very curious about funerals. - They may be "difficult" in an effort to regain control. **They get it**	- They understand the concept. - It is very difficult to accept because of the invincibility factor. - They feel isolated from their peers. - Stressed more by the appearance of the illness than the actual illness. **They get it....and they HATE it.** Adolescents have the hardest time dealing with death.
Encourage family presence. Try to keep a normal routine.	Encourage family presence. Be HONEST (true blue!) with the child. Don't use big medical words.	Encourage self-care. Help child to plan the funeral service.	Be HONEST (true blue). Show respect. Encourage family and peer presence. Facilitate funeral planning.

Skylar's Story

I walked into my patient's room and was pleased to see a happy, vibrant beautiful little 5-year-old boy waving cheerfully at me as I entered. He was very pleased to see me. It was in this moment that I met Skylar. He had been diagnosed with leukemia the day before. His parents were overwhelmed but optimistic. They were the ultimate cheerleaders. I talked with them for a while; assuring them that Skylar was strong. He looked like a fighter! We talked about ways to give him the best chance he could have.

Over the next few weeks, Skylar's parents did everything they were asked to do. They researched, they read, they raised support, they raised awareness, they got to know everyone on the unit, and they prayed. Skylar began chemotherapy and remained his happy cherubic little self, although now he was a bald little fighter, but his parents laughingly told him he officially looked like a "real tough guy" now.

One day as they were nearing the very last of their treatments and were gleefully beginning to pack to go home, Skylar had a stroke.

The next day, Skylar died.

The entire unit was traumatized. It was unthinkable. It was cruel. It was wrong.

We missed his bubbly laugh. We missed his spunky spirit. It wasn't fair.

Many of the nurses attended Skylar's funeral, but as we entered we were told that the word funeral was not to be used. It was to be a Celebration of Life. Skylar's mom wore a Disney shirt with Skylar's favorite characters. There were balloons and a cheerful cake. It seemed irreverent at first, but then it dawned on me. Having a sad, mournful and dark service crying because

Skylar was gone would have been the epitome of irreverence. Skylar would not have wanted that. As I pondered these things as I left that day, I realized that all life is precious and sweet. Every day counts. Skylar had impacted more lives in his five short years than many would in an entire century. Children are just amazing little gifts that way.

REVIEW QUESTIONS

1. A nurse is administering IV chemotherapeutic agents to a 2-year-old patient with leukemia. The nurse notes that the child has developed an urticarial rash and minor wheezing. What is the appropriate first action of the nurse?

1) Administer oxygen via nasal cannula
2) Administer an emergency dose of epinephrine subcutaneously
3) Stop the infusion of medication and flush the line with saline
4) Monitor the child's vital signs every 5 minutes until the condition resolves

Option #3 is correct. Option #1 may be necessary but at this point there are no noted signs of hypoxia. Options #2 and #4 may also be necessary but #3 is more critical to complete first.

2. A 7-year-old experiencing hemarthosis in the left knee comes to the school nurse for attention. What is the best way for the nurse to manage the child's condition until his mother arrives to pick him up?

1) Immobilize the affected knee joint and elevate the leg.
2) Immobilize the affected knee joint with an applied warm compress.
3) Give the child 80mg aspirin and gently massage the joint.
4) Apply a warm compress and gently massage the joint.

Option #1 is correct. Options #2 and #4 are incorrect because ice should be applied. Option #4 is also incorrect because massage is contraindicated.

3. A 12-year-old is hospitalized to receive induction chemotherapy for Acute Lymphoid Leukemia and is battling severe neutropenia. She will be celebrating her birthday while hospitalized and her mother wishes to invite her friends to celebrate and cheer her up. What is the best response of the nurse?

1) "That is a great idea! Getting to see her friends will lift her spirits and aid her recovery."
2) "Perhaps you should consider just inviting some of the other children on the unit."
3) "We can do that but you will need to carefully consider food options to avoid making her nauseous."
4) "It would not be a good idea to have visitors, but perhaps we can arrange a "virtual party."

Option #4 is the best option at this time. Severe neutropenia means reverse isolation precautions. The other options all involve being around other children, which would be contraindicated for the safety of her health.

4. A 17-year-old girl with Sickle Cell Anemia is admitted with a vaso-occlusive crisis. Which of these nursing actions takes the highest priority?

1) Pain management
2) Recording intake and output
3) Antibiotic administration
4) Preparing for blood transfusion

Option #1 is correct. Pain is the most significant element of managing a vaso-occlusive crisis in SCA. Option #2 is important, but not as much as pain. Options #3 and #4 may or may not be necessary.

5. A nurse is educating a mother who is unable to breastfeed her 6-month-old (8kg) infant because of a blood pressure medication. She feels helpless about where to begin because the infant has been exclusively breastfed. What nutrition instructions should the nurse provide for this baby?

1) 24 ounces of cow's milk, 4 tablespoons of iron fortified rice cereal
2) 24-32 ounces soy formula, stage one vegetables and fruits
3) 28-32 ounces regular infant formula with DHA, 1-2 TBSP iron fortified rice cereal
4) 26-30 ounces lactose free formula, 1-tablespoon oatmeal cereal

Option #3 is correct. If infants younger than 12 months are given regular cow's milk, they can develop hemolytic anemia, a potentially life threatening disorder. Infants should start with rice cereal and progress to vegetables or fruits, introducing one new food every 3-4 days. Regular infant formula with DHA is recommended. DHA is an amino acid found in breastmilk that improves eye and brain development. The other formulas may be considered if regular formula is not tolerated.

6. Prioritize these nursing interventions for a patient just hospitalized with a crisis of sickle cell anemia.

1) Pain control
2) Hydration
3) Monitor for complications
4) Family support

The correct ordering is #2, #1, #3, and #4. Hydration is the most critical intervention to reverse the course of the crisis. Pain control is very important but hydration will help to relieve pain as well.

7. A nurse is caring for a 12-year-old patient who was admitted two days ago for an acute sickle cell anemia crisis. Upon assessment, the child is complaining of increasing discomfort and abdominal pain. Vital signs are: P- 142, BP-84/44, R-22, T-96.2, SpO2 94%. What is the appropriate action of the nurse at this time?

    1) Administer O2 by facemask at 10L/minute
    2) Administer an ordered dose of morphine
    3) Call the provider
    4) Encourage the child to drink more fluids

Option #3 is correct. These are ominous signs of possible splenic sequestration and impending shock. The provider needs to be contacted immediately.

8. A nurse is caring for a family with a 4-year-old child who has been newly diagnosed with sickle cell anemia. Which statement by the family indicates a poor understanding of the disease?

    1) We understand that a daily dose of oral penicillin will be required.
    2) It is very important for us to make sure that adequate hydration is a priority.
    3) It is possible that this disease can be cured after several blood transfusions.
    4) We must go to the emergency room if there is a fever >101 degrees F.

Option #3 is correct. While blood transfusions are used sometimes to treat sickle cell, it is not a curative therapy. Children under six years of age are particularly susceptible to sepsis as functional asplenics, thus the need for penicillin prophylaxis as well as emergency room visits for fever.

9. A 9-year-old patient with hemophilia has fallen on the playground and presents to the school nurse with hemearthrosis. What is the appropriate action to take at this time?

    1) Immobilize the joint and apply heat
    2) Call 911 for emergency medical support
    3) Apply ice and a compression bandage
    4) Allow the child to rest until the hemearthrosis resolves

Option #3 is correct. RICE is the appropriate course of action (Rest, Ice, Compression, Elevation). However, this does not negate the need for factor VIII administration. The mother should be notified so that arrangements to seek emergency medical care can be made.

10. The parents of a child newly diagnosed with hemophilia are feeling very overwhelmed. For which resources should the nurse advocate for at this time? **Select all that apply.**

    1) Interdisciplinary disease management approach
    2) Enrollment in a family support group
    3) Genetic counseling
    4) Professional psychological counseling
    5) Child Protective Services

Options #1, #2, and #3 are appropriate. Better outcomes can be achieved with collaboration between nurses, physicians, nurse practitioners, physical therapists, and social workers. A family support group is appropriate. Genetic counseling is important so decisions can be made about future childbearing. Professional counseling is not necessary at this point. It is normal for parents to feel overwhelmed with this initial diagnosis. They need time to cope.

11. A 5-year-old is undergoing treatment with chemotherapy for leukemia. She arrives at the primary care clinic for her regular check up. What approach should be taken for vaccination?

    1) Do not administer any vaccines at this time.
    2) Administer all recommended vaccines at this time.
    3) Administer only live vaccines at this time.
    4) Administer only inactivated vaccines at this time.

The correct option is #4. Live vaccines are contraindicated during chemotherapy treatment because the response is blunt and unpredictable. Live vaccines could cause illness. Inactivated vaccines may need to be repeated after chemotherapy is completed.

12. A nurse is administering IV chemotherapy to a child. During the infusion, the child begins to experience shortness of breath and a 20mmHg drop in systolic blood pressure. What is the appropriate action of the nurse at this time?

    1) Place the child on cardiopulmonary monitoring and check vital signs every 5 minutes
    2) Immediately stop the infusion and flush the IV tubing with saline
    3) Call the rapid response team to come immediately
    4) Elevate the child's legs above the heart and administer 2L O2 by face mask

The correct option is #2. This is an indication of an anaphylactic reaction. The infusion should be stopped immediately and emergency drugs and equipment should be kept ready close at hand.

13. A nurse is administering a chemotherapeutic agent through a child's peripheral IV line. The child complains that it hurts and stings. What is the appropriate action of the nurse?

    1) Stop the infusion immediately.
    2) Slow the rate of the infusion.
    3) Distract the child during the infusion.
    4) Give the child a prn ordered pain medication.

Option #1 is correct. The IV needs to be thoroughly checked for any signs of infiltration before proceeding. Chemotherapeutic agents can be extremely caustic to the veins.

14. A toddler undergoing treatments for cancer is experiencing severe mucositis. Which nursing interventions should be implemented? **Select all that apply.**

    1) Administer a clear liquid diet
    2) Use a soft toothbrush
    3) Provide frequent normal saline mouthwashes
    4) Administer viscous lidocaine solution as ordered
    5) Request an order for a nasogastric tube for fluid administration

Options #2 and #3 are correct. A clear liquid diet is insufficient for caloric intake. A soft, bland diet trying to incorporate all of the child's preferences as much as possible is best. Viscous lidocaine is not recommended for young children as it can depress the gag reflex and increase the risk of aspiration. Viscous lidocaine also carries a small risk of seizures. A nasogastric tube could potentially irritate mucosal ulcerations.

15. A child is undergoing chemotherapy treatments. Current lab values are: WBC 3,000; Hgb 5.8mg/dL; Hct 21.2%; and platelets 72,000. What are appropriate nursing interventions at this time? **Select all that apply.**

    1) Screen all visitors and staff entering the child's room.
    2) Minimize invasive procedures.
    3) Institute fall precautions.
    4) Ensure all vaccines are up to date.
    5) Administer granulocyte colony-stimulating factor as prescribed.

Options #1, #2, #3, and #5 are correct. Screening all visitors for signs of infection, minimizing invasive procedures and administering GCSF will help protect the patient from infection, especially considering the low WBC. The H&H and platelets are low, putting the child at risk for bleeding and necessitating fall precautions. Live vaccines are contraindicated.

16. A 17-year-old child undergoing chemotherapy treatments for cancer and has been hospitalized for 3 weeks with neutropenic precautions. The teen is lonely and exhibiting signs of depression. What is the appropriate response of the nurse?

1) Suggest to the mother they invite a group of friends from school to visit
2) Suggest a psych consult to evaluate the need for antidepressant medication
3) Help the teen with appropriate access online chat forums to connect with other teens who have cancer
4) Ask the nurses and staff on the floor to make cards and visit the teen

Option #3 is correct. #1 and #4 are incorrect because the child is on neutropenic precautions and visitors should be limited. #2 is probably not necessary at this time. It is normal to be discouraged in this situation. The teen needs contact with peers who will identify with having cancer.

17. A child is undergoing treatments for newly diagnosed leukemia and is currently receiving high doses of intravenous steroids and chemotherapy. The parents express concern because the child is combative, angry, and uncooperative. This is not like his usual personality and they ask the nurse for advice. What is the best response?

1) "This cancer can affect the central nervous system and temporarily change his behavior."
2) "He is angry about his diagnosis. You should let him express himself."
3) "This kind of behavior is unacceptable. He needs to have firm limits set despite his illness."
4) "Sometimes high doses of steroids can cause signs of aggression. We can talk to your provider about options to deal with this."

Option #4 is correct.

18. A nine-year-old is newly diagnosed with terminal cancer. Her parents do not want her to know that she is dying. When they leave, the child tells the nurse "I think my parents know something bad they are not telling me. What is going on?" What is the appropriate response of the nurse?

1) "You will need to talk to your parents about that."
2) "Yes, it is bad. You have a cancer that cannot be cured."
3) "Don't worry, the doctors here will take good care of you."
4) "What are you most worried about?"

Option #4 is correct. Assessing the child's concerns can assist the nurse in giving insight to the parents about how to best communicate about this difficult subject.

19. A child with terminal cancer has just passed away in the hospital. The parents have been in the room saying goodbye for several hours and refuse to leave. What is the best response of the nurse?

    1) Tell the parents gently but firmly that is time for them to go.
    2) Request a psychiatric consult to evaluate the parents.
    3) Call security to have them removed.
    4) Allow them to have as much time as they need to say goodbye.

Option #4 is correct. The parents must have the time they need to grieve.

20. A preschooler whose older sibling died six months ago from cancer still speaks about the sibling in the present tense. She frequently asks to set a place for her at the dinner table and talks to her as if she is an imaginary friend. The mother is concerned and asks the nurse for advice. What is the best response?

    1) "You should consider taking her to a child psychologist."
    2) "Preschoolers have a hard time understanding the permanence of death."
    3) "You should ignore this behavior and it will go away."
    4) "Taking her to the cemetery may help her understand that her sister is not coming back."

Option #2 is correct.

Nursing Management in Respiratory Disorders

Sylvia Rayfield, MN, RN, CNS
Edited by Sylvia Rayfield & Associates

"Breath is Spirit. The act of breathing is living."
Author unknown

Key Concepts:

- Asthma
- Bronchitis
- Chronic Obstructive Pulmonary Disease (COPD)
- Emphysema
- Fluid Overload (Pulmonary Edema)
- Infectious Disease: Pneumonia and Tuberculosis
- ARDS (Acute Respiratory Distress Syndrome)
- Pulmonary Embolism
- Trauma
- Practice Questions, Answers and Rationale

"I CAN'T BREATHE!"

No breath, no oxygen/carbon dioxide exchange in all body cells leads to death,
QUICKLY!

You won't even have to listen to the lungs of a client with a serious asthmatic attack or this YouTube for the 50 seconds until you know full well the panic the client is experiencing and the alarm that this panic and SOB produces in the health care provider.
http://www.youtube.com/watch?v=vFBFUauf5yA

Where to start in the midst of this panic of SOB (shortness of breath)?

Start with the abc's: airway, breathing, circulation.

Until the ABC's are stabilized, there is no time for anything else.

Airway Check for obstruction. O_2 does no good if the airway is not patent.

Breathing Look for the cause of SOB. Until the cause is established, medications cannot be utilized and may be harmful. The airway may need to be assisted by using intubation or mechanical ventilation. O_2 does no good if it is not breathed into the body to keep all cells alive. Sit the client up, begin oxygen at a low liter rate until diagnosed, and provide a calm atmosphere.

Circulation CPR may be necessary. This may not be a primary respiratory problem at all. It could be caused from a myocardial infarction (MI) or congestive heart failure (CHF). If this is the case, we can utilize respiratory intervention to no avail unless the underlying cause is determined and treated.

NOW IT'S TIME TO UTILIZE THE SAFETY ACRONYM FOR ORGANIZATION.

This important acronym allows for organization of:

- **Safe client care**

- **Study of heaviest weighted *NCLEX*® standards**

- **Study of all body systems for nursing exams**

PASS *NCLEX*®!

S   System specific assessment

A   Assess for risk and respond

F   Find change/trends and intervene

E   Evaluate pharmacology

T   Teach/practice infection control, health promotion

Y   Your management—legal/ethical/scope of practice, identity, errors, delegation, faulty equipment/staff, privacy, confidentiality, falls/ hazards

S   SYSTEM SPECIFIC ASSESSMENT

LOOK

➤   **Look** at vital signs.

➤   **Look** at the mouth and throat for obstruction or trauma,

➤   **Look** at the chest for trauma, uneven chest wall movements (paradoxical chest movements—part of the chest rises while part of the chest falls; the side damaged by trauma pushes in during inspiration while the rest of the chest rises during inspiration) called flail chest. This is caused from broken ribs and is life threatening. This condition is extremely painful which inhibits the client from breathing. Pain control, often through nerve blocks, may be utilized. Narcotics should be avoided if possible.

➤   **Look** for holes in the chest wall caused by knife wounds or impalement of obstacles from accidents or violence. The chest has a negative pressure (less than atmospheric air). If a hole is punched in the chest wall, outside air is sucked into the chest cavity causing the lungs to collapse. (Pneumothorax). Get ready for a chest tube!

➤   **Look** for the client's use of accessory muscles to breath, indicating stress.

➤   **Look** for a rash, itching, or anything that indicates that the client is having an allergic reaction.

➤ **Look** for cyanosis around the mouth and earlobes indicating decreased oxygen exchange. This may indicate heart disease or heart failure.

➤ **Look** for a barrel chest.

➤ **Look** at vital signs for increased heart /respiratory rate.

➤ **Look** for elevated temperature indicating infection (pneumonia).

➤ **Look** for pregnancy which may cause shortness of breath (SOB).

➤ **Look** for extreme obesity that may occlude the airway or place extensive pressure on the diaphragm.

LISTEN

Listen to the client's voice through the chest wall, which may be altered by consolidation such as fluid accumulation or mass. Place the stethoscope on the chest wall and ask the client to say the letter "eee" to determine vesicular breath sounds. Remember—clarity of sound means consolidation. Try again with the stethoscope on the chest and ask the client to say "99" to determine bronchophony. If the sound is indistinct or muffled, the client is OK. If you hear "99" clearly, there is consolidation.

➤ **Listen** to the history if the client is able of provide one. Ascertain alcohol or tobacco use (emphysema).

➤ **Listen** for occupational hazards such as fireman (smoke inhalation), construction worker (asbestos inhalation), or other environmental hazards.

➤ Ascertain current prescription drugs that may cause an undesirable effect (Beta Blockers with a client history of COPD), environmental allergies, or in the case of Ace Inhibitors, cough.

➤ **Listen** for history of COUGH which may indicate fluid buildup in the lungs. Assess SPUTUM consistency (bloody— possible pulmonary edema, pulmonary embolism, or tuberculosis; pus colored—possible infection)

➤ **Listen** for WHEEZING (possible asthma) OR CHEST PAIN (possibly heart related).

➤ **Listen** to sounds surrounding palpation to determine if the tissue is filled with fluid, air, or solid sounds (crackles with palpation indicates trauma to the lungs with air under the skin).

➤ **Listen** to breath sounds. These YouTube videos are very useful to review the different sounds in the lungs.

This YouTube video on breath sounds will refresh your memory. Remember, Pearson Vue provides earphones for you to identify sounds and make a decision about the nursing intervention. http://www.youtube.com/watch?v=yFWWSIGB6-0

Remember these words **side to side, top to bottom, back and front** and you will know how to listen to breath sounds.

DIAGNOSTIC TESTS FOR RESPIRATORY ASSESSMENT

NCLEX® testing often includes what the nurse should provide before, during, and after the diagnostic tests.

Spirometry
Measures airflow or breath.

Before	During	After
Advise against eating heavy meal Ban smoking for six hours May be required to withhold inhalers	Compliance with instructions affects outcomes Possible nose clips/tight fitting mouthpiece	Possible lightheadedness Document results on client record

Sputum culture

Before	During	After
Schedule for A.M. Rinse mouth before exam	Take deep breaths Cough/spit into sterile cup	No usual effects Carefully label specimen and transport to lab

Bronchoscopy
May be useful in the indication for infection, tumor, airway obstruction, bleeding, excess mucus.

Before	During	After
Need informed consent NPO 6–12 hours prior to procedure	Sedation Biopsy of tissue Possible SOB	No driving Sore throat Cough up blood Carefully label specimen

X-RAY

Before	During	After
Explain to client	Maintain safety from falls	Notify provider of results
Determine allergies if dye is used	Maintain confidentiality and privacy	

CT SCAN
Non-invasive diagnostic test used to visualize internal injuries with or without dye. The test visualizes cross sections of the area.

Before	During	After
Explain to client non-invasive nature	Maintain safety from falls	Monitor vital signs if dye was used
Determine if client is claustrophobic	Sedation may be required	Notify provider of results
Determine allergies if dye is used	Maintain confidentiality and privacy	Push fluids to clear dye if needed
Review BUN and creatinine reports		

OXYGEN SATURATION
An excellent way to quickly determine changes in the client's condition

PULSE OX

Looks like a clothespin on the end of the finger, toe, or earlobe that measures oxygen saturation in a client's blood. Pulse ox monitors may vary, but the normal reading of a healthy client is approximately 90-100%. Older clients or clients with COPD (Chronic Obstructive Pulmonary Disease) may range from 88-94% on pulse oximeter. A quick, easy, non-invasive way to assess the client with suspected heart disease or oxygen perfusion issues.

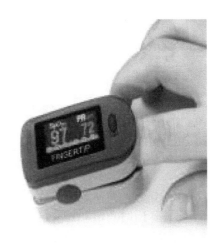

A   ASSESS FOR RISK AND RESPOND

- Assess for sputum in airway
- Teach to avoid allergens, considering them triggers to future attacks.
- Begin teaching the need for smoking cessation and help them find a program.
- Teach to wear appropriate filter masks or ventilators in hazardous occupations
- Recommend tuberculin skin testing.
- Initiate breathing exercises (may include incentive spirometer).
- Teach the correlation between obesity and SOB and begin weight loss program if needed.
- Advise client to carry emergency medications on person.

F   FIND TRENDS AND CHANGES IN CLIENT CONDITION AND INTERVENE APPROPRIATELY

BLOOD GASES ARE AN EXCELLENT WAY TO FIND CHANGE IN THE RESPIRATORY SYSTEM.

The respiratory system regulates pH by hypoventilation (retaining CO_2) or hyperventilation (blowing off CO_2); the kidneys regulate pH by excreting/retaining hydrogen ions or bicarbonate. This can be determined by assessing ABG's (Arterial Blood Gases).
Normal ranges include:

pH = 7.35-7.45
A pH < 7.35 indicates acidosis, > 7.45 indicates alkalosis
$PaCO_2$ = 35-45
Bicarbonate = 22-26
Normal PaO_2 at sea level is 80-100; normal oxygen saturation is 90-100%

Easy way to remember those all important normal blood gases:
Think about it this way. I like my oxygen at 100%, but if I can't have that I will take 90-100%.

PaO_2	90-100
$PaCO_2$ (1/2 the O_2)	45
HCO_3 (1/2 of CO_2)	23

Note: Clients with COPD have a lower PaO_2.

An easy way to think about acidosis includes remembering that CO_2 is ACID. If the CO_2 is being retained inside the body due to occluded airway (sputum) or the inability of the lungs to breathe it out, then the acid is staying inside the body—ACIDOSIS. This means we've got to get them suctioned and/or utilize postural drainage to open the airway or ventilation to help the failed lungs function.

Conversely, if the client is breathing fast (hyperventilating), then the CO_2 (ACID) is being blown out of the body which means they have ALKALOSIS. Now it may be time to get out the paper bag. If the client breathes into the bag, they will retain CO_2 back into the body and re-balance the acid-base.

One way to determine the type of acid-base imbalance is the mnemonic **R-O-M-E**
RESPIRATORY OPPOSITE/ METABOLIC EQUAL (Used with Permission of Creative Nurse Educators)

Respiratory Acidosis: decreased pH, increased $PaCO_2$

This is due to **hypoventilation and respiratory failure.** Place in High-Fowler's position, encourage incentive spirometer, and decrease narcotics. These clients may need respiratory support by intubating and placing on a ventilator. If on a ventilator, then the client may need an increase in tidal volume. If naloxone (Narcan) is given to reverse narcotics, be aware the client will wake suddenly and be very restless; blood pressure and heart rate will be elevated. **Naloxone (Narcan) is only effective for a few minutes, so be prepared to support ventilations if needed.**

Respiratory Alkalosis: increased pH, decreased $PaCO_2$

This is due to **hyperventilation.** May be indicated by lightheadedness, tingling in the hands feet or lips. Causes include pain, anxiety/panic attack, hypoxia, and pulmonary emboli. Place in High Fowler's. Treat pain or anxiety that is present with pharmacological and non-pharmacological interventions. If the client is on a ventilator, the tidal volume may need to be decreased. Monitor pulse ox and apply oxygen as needed.

Metabolic Acidosis: decreased pH, decreased HCO_3

This is seen in severe **diarrhea, diabetic ketoacidosis, renal failure, shock, and lactic acidosis.** Treatment should be aimed at correcting the metabolic condition. Some examples include: evaluating cause and stopping the diarrhea, correcting the blood sugar, or treating for shock. Administration of sodium bicarbonate may be given.

Metabolic Alkalosis: increased pH, increased HCO_3

This is seen with excessive **vomiting, NG suctioning, or excessive use of diuretics.** The client needs to be supported and symptoms treated. Hold diuretics, try and clamp NG tube, or give anti-emetics.

PARTIAL COMPENSATION

The body strives to return the pH to normal—again, it is respiratory opposite/metabolic same. When partial compensation occurs, the pH is still outside normal limits, but the CO_2 and HCO_3 are responding and moving the pH towards normal. To compensate for respiratory acidosis, HCO_3 is retained. In respiratory alkalosis, HCO_3 is excreted. To compensate for metabolic acidosis, CO_2 is blown off and decreased. Think Kussmaul's respirations. To compensate for metabolic alkalosis, CO_2 is retained (hypoventilation).

COMPENSATED

Finally the pH is within normal limits, however, pH trends near either the acidotic or alkalotic side. CO_2 and HCO_3 are outside normal limits showing that compensation has taken place.
Examples:
Compensated respiratory acidosis   pH 7.36, PCO_2 48, HCO_3 28
Compensated respiratory alkalosis   pH 7.44, PCO_2 32, HCO_3 20
Compensated metabolic acidosis   pH 7.36, PCO_2 32, HCO_3 20
Compensated metabolic alkalosis   pH 7.44, PCO_2 48, HCO_3 28

When thinking about acid-base balance, it is not enough to be able to recognize the imbalance, but you must also be aware of interventions to correct the imbalance.

E   EVALUATE PHARMACOLOGY

It is as important to know which medication NOT to administer, as well as which medication to administer. Remember, beta-blockers can be lethal to clients with asthma and COPD because they cause bronchoconstriction. Always check the accuracy of the order and reconciliation prior to administering a Beta-blocker to these clients! The literature indicates that using cardioselective beta-blockers in mild COPD may be useful; however, vital signs must be monitored, including breath sounds. Prior to administering any drug, the nurse must be **CAREFUL!** This acronym will assist you in remembering the *NCLEX* ® standards on medication administration.

PASS *NCLEX*®!

C	**Calculate correctly**
A	**Assess for allergies**
R	**Rights of administration**
E	**Evaluate response**
F	**Feel free to call provider if intuition alerts**
U	**Utilize assessments in determining ordered parameters**
L	**Lab data pertinence**

Asthma

ASTHMA is an inflammatory condition caused by allergens (foods, exercise, smoke, other illness) that make the airways become too narrow for air to pass. Early symptoms of asthma include frequent cough especially at night, shortness of breath, feeling tired or weak with exertion, wheezing or coughing after exertion, or signs of a cold or allergies (sneezing, runny nose, nasal congestion, sore throat). These early changes may happen just before or at the very beginning of an asthma attack. Wheezing, coughing, shortness of breath, chest tightness, and extreme anxiety are common with a full asthma attack.

Pharmacological interventions for asthma are available in many forms including inhaled, tablet, liquid, or injection. The inhaler Beta 2 Agonist is often preferred. The more central the administration of medications (IV or oral as compared to inhaler), the more opportunity there is for undesirable effects of the medication with the client.

Beta Agonists (short acting RESCUE bronchodilators)

Nursing Implication	Drug	Action	Evaluation
Identify/avoid triggers Teach the possibility of shaky hands and nervousness when using these drugs	Albuterol (Proventil) Ipratropium (Atrovent, Ventolin) Pirbuterol (Max Air)	Relieves bronchospasm Relaxes smooth muscle in lung Fast acting	Breathing easier Attack averted Increased heart rate Weakness, upset stomach, muscle aches, cramps, insomnia, arrhythmias

Long Acting Bronchodilators
Chronic Asthma
Used in combination with inhaled steroids

Nursing Implication	Drug	Action	Evaluation
Teach medication spacing	Salmeterol (Advair, Serevent) Formoterol (Foradil, Symbicort)	Long acting Maintains airflow Reduces exacerbations in clients	May increase death from asthma Should be used with inhaled steroid Evaluate for rash, swelling of face and mouth Evaluate vital signs Evaluate for nervousness

Long Acting Steroid Inhalers

Nursing Implication	Drug	Action	Evaluation
Teach NOT to use for prolonged periods Edema For asthma attacks Use bronchodilator BEFORE steroid inhaler. Allow 2-3 minutes between inhalers (spacing) Rinse mouth Gargle Taper off gradually	Flunisolide (Aerobid) Mometasone (Asmanex) Triamcinolone (Azamacort) Fluticasone (Flovent) Budesonide (Pulmicort) Beclomethasone (Qvar)	Anti-inflammatory Action improves lung function for clients with asthma	Watch for decreased respiratory activity Watch for thrush in mouth and throat Watch for wheezing or fast heart beat

Leukotriene receptor antagonist (LTRAs)

Nursing Implication	Drug	Action	Evaluation
Take drug in evening Avoid aspirin/NSAIDS Chronic treatment of asthma Ineffective for acute attack	Montelukast (Singulair) Zafirlukast (Accolate)	Non-steroidal Anti-inflammatory inhalers Blocks chemical action leading to inflammation in airways	Watch for decreased effect of rifampin and phenobarbital Increased effect of Couomadin Dizzyness

Xolair
Allergic asthma poorly controlled

Nursing Implication	Drug	Action	Evaluation
Do not administer to children under 12. Is not utilized as rescue drug Expensive injection Keep EpiPen® available	Omalizumab (Xolair)	Improved lung function	Watch for rash Determine vital signs, especially elevated temperature Evaluate for anaphylaxis

Bronchitis

Bronchitis is an inflammatory process in the main airways of the lungs causing cough, increased mucus production, and shortness of breath. Often the treatment is uncomplicated as in getting rest, drinking lots of fluids, and avoiding noxious inhalants (smoke, etc). Bronchitis may be acute, chronic, or infectious.

Drugs that treat Bronchitis

Nursing Implication	Drug	Action	Evaluation
Assess for cough, mucus, fatigue, fever, SOB, and wheezing Determine ABG's, Pulse Ox Collect sputum sample prior to administering any antibiotic Start smoking cessation program Encourage drinking lots of liquids, rest Teach to use humidifier/steam May become infectious. Be sure to apply principles of infection control (e.g., hand hygiene, isolation, and universal precautions)	➤ Acetaminophen (Tylenol)	Reduces fever Deleterious effect on the liver	Evaluate vital signs and liver function
	Beta Agonists — Short acting rescue bronchodilators ➤ Albuterol (Proventil) ➤ Ipratropium (Atrovent, Ventolin) ➤ Pirbuterol (Max Air)	Relieve bronchospasm Relaxes smooth muscle in lung Fast acting	Breathing easier Attack averted Increased heart rate Weakness, upset stomach, muscle aches, cramps, insomnia, arrhythmias
	Long acting bronchodilators, used in combination with inhaled steroids ➤ Salmeterol (Advair, Serevent) ➤ Formoterol (Foradil, Symbicort)	Long acting Maintains airflow Reduces exacerbations in clients	May increase death from asthma Should be used with inhaled steroid Evaluate for rash, swelling of face and mouth Evaluate vital signs Evaluate for nervousness

Antibiotics

Antibiotics are utilized when there is an infectious bacterial process but are not effective in the treatment of viral bronchitis. These are some of the antibiotics utilized in treating bacterial bronchitis.

Nursing Implication	Drug	Action	Evaluation
Watch for elevated temperature Determine allergies to drug or penicillin Caution with renal or liver impairment Determine other medications that may interact If client is taking antacids, they should be taken two hours prior to or after these medications.	**Antibiotics** Cephalosporins: ➤ Cefazolin (Ancef) ➤ Cefuroxime (Ceftin) ➤ Cefprozil (Cefzil) ➤ Cefadroxil (Duricef) ➤ Ceftriaxone (Rocephin) ➤ Cefixime (Suprax) **Penicillins** ➤ Amoxil ➤ Augmentin	Anti-infective Reduces temperature	Evaluate for cough GI symptoms — nausea/vomiting Itching, skin rash, difficulty breathing or swallowing Monitor Blood Urea Nitrogen (BUN) and Creatinine levels Fainting Decreased temperature

Cough suppressants are not recommended as the productive cough helps the lungs get rid of excess mucus.

Chronic Bronchitis over time can lead to Chronic Obstructive Pulmonary Disease (COPD).

Chronic Obstructive Pulmonary Disease (COPD)

Chronic obstructive pulmonary disease is a lung disease that makes it hard to breathe caused by damage to the lungs over many years. It is often diagnosed through spirometry and is one of the most common lung diseases. **Spirometry** is a simple test used to measure lung function by making the client breathe in and out through a spirometer. The results are compared to a standardized set of values based on the client's age sex, height, and weight.

Clinical manifestations include SOB, wheezing, fatigue, cough (with or without mucus), and multiple respiratory infections. COPD gets worse over time. Damage from long-term lung disease can't be cured, but we can take steps to prevent more damage and to make the client feel better. As COPD progresses, the client may experience flare-ups when symptoms exacerbate. When this happens, care is essential and is likely to include low flow oxygen, part or all of the time

Drugs used to allay symptoms and treat COPD

Nursing Implication	Drug	Action	Evaluation
Determine if there is a history of smoking (the most common cause) and counsel client to stop. It is never too late Look for physical signs —prolonged expiration phase, barrel chest, clubbing of the fingertips, and accessory muscle use with breathing	**Inhalers**	Bronchodilators	Evaluate vital signs for increased heart rate, as arrhythmias are fairly common Evaluate the medication effect by listening to lung sounds for decreased wheezing. Evaluate nervousness and trembling a common side effect
Listen to breath sounds and evaluate for wheezing in lung sounds Assess arterial blood gases Assess physical ability for ADL (activities of daily living)	**Beta Agonists —** Short acting rescue bronchodilators ➢ Albuterol (Proventil) ➢ Ipratropium (Atrovent, Ventolin) ➢ Pirbuterol (Max Air)	Relieve bronchospasm Relaxes smooth muscle in lung Fast acting	The client should be breathing easier and the attack averted Evaluate for weakness, upset stomach, muscle aches, cramps, insomnia
	Long acting bronchodilators, used in combination with inhaled steroids ➢ Salmeterol (Advair, Serevent) ➢ Formoterol (Foradil, Symbicort)	Long acting Maintains airflow Reduces exacerbations in clients	May increase death from asthma Should be used with inhaled steroid Evaluate for rash, swelling of face and mouth Evaluate vital signs Evaluate for nervousness

Long Acting Steroid Inhalers for COPD

Nursing Implication	Drug	Action	Evaluation
Steroids may be given orally, by inhalation, or intravenously Evaluate for SOB from COPD and asthma	➢ Methylprednisolone (Medrol) ➢ Prednisolone (Prevone) ➢ Prednisone ➢ Beclomethasone (Qvar) ➢ Flunisolide (Aerobid) ➢ Fluticasone (Flovent) ➢ Budesonide (Symbicort) ➢ Fluticasone/ salmeteraol(Advair)	Reduces swelling and inflammation in the lungs, allowing better air exchange	Watch for improved breathing, improved blood gases, improved O_2 saturation Prolonged steroid use may cause osteoporosis, cataracts, diabetes, and hypertension Weight gain is a side effect in oral steroids Assess for sore throat, thrush, cataracts, and fragile skin

Leukotriene receptor antagonist (LTRAs)

Nursing Implication	Drug	Action	Evaluation
Take drug in evening Avoid aspirin/NSAIDS Chronic treatment of asthma Ineffective for acute attack	➢ Montelukast (Singulair) ➢ Zafirlukast (Accolate)	Non-steroidal Anti-inflammatory inhalers Blocks chemical action leading to inflammation in airways	Watch for decreased effect of rifampin and phenobarbital Increased effect of Couomadin Dizzyness

Oxygen Therapy
Oxygen is often necessary 24/7 at a low dose (around 2L/minute). Oxygen at a high dose diminishes the breathing reflex.

Emphysema

Emphysema is a type of COPD and is the inability of the lungs to eliminate CO_2. Smoking is most often the cause of this preventable disease. The SOB, mucus production, and wheezing is real, progressive, and chronic. Dyspnea occurs first with exercise and progresses to include SOB at rest.

Teach the client self care:
- Exercise to build lung capacity
- Avoid walking when short of breath
- Avoid very cold air or second hand smoke (including fireplace)
- Utilize purse lip breathing to empty lungs prior to the next breath
- Prop up in bed at night for easier breathing.

Medications are the same as with COPD.

Fluid Overload

Fluid overload (hypervolemia) may be caused by a cardiac event or hypertension leading to an inability of the heart to pump adequate cardiac output This will lead to fluid in the lung sounds and SOB. The pharmacology for this is entirely different from the other respiratory processes as it is likely to include treatment for the underlying cardiac condition as well as the volume overload.

With fluid volume overload the treatment of choice is diuretics and the expected outcome would be a decreasing trend in the central venous pressure (CVP) or pulmonary capillary wedge pressure (PCWP). You would expect to see increased urinary output, clearing lung sounds, decrease in BP, decreasing edema, and weight loss. Clients are at risk for dehydration and must be monitored. Remember, you must know the potassium level prior to giving a loop diuretic such as furosemide (Lasix).

Nursing Implication	Drug	Action	Evaluation
Educate for daily weights, foods, or drugs that will not interfere with this medication	**Diuretics:** These are just a few of the common diuretics ➤ Furosemide (Lasix) ➤ Bumetanide (Bumex) ➤ Torsemide (Demadex) ➤ Hydrochlorothiazide (Hydrodiuril)	Reduce volume through diuresis Assess for client allergies, especially to sulfa	Dry mouth especially on the first dose Hypokalemia Tinnitus, hearing loss, ototoxicity Hyponatremia I&O, daily weights

Nursing Implication	Drug	Action	Evaluation
		Diuretic side effects can be summed up with these 6 issues: ► Dehydration ► Hypotension ► Diuresis ► Electrolyte imbalance ► Allergy to sulfa ► Tinnitus (except with Thiazides)	Hypocalcemia Evaluate muscle cramps and weakness Evaluate for hives, swelling of lips, tongue, and difficult breathing
Check K+ Levels Education for frequent K+ checks Educate for GI upsets	**Common K+ sparing diuretics:** ➢ Spironolactone (Aldactone) ➢ Amiloride (Midamor)		Hyperkalemia Evaluate for nausea and vomiting Peptic ulcer

Infectious Diseases of the Lungs

Pneumonia is a common lung infection of the alveoli caused by bacteria, a virus, or fungi. Cough, fever, rapid breathing and chest pain are common symptoms. Pneumonia is most often treated with rest, increased pulmonary hygiene, and antibiotics. Assess the type of bacteria to determine if the pneumonia is contagious and if isolation is needed.

Tuberculosis (TB) is the second most common cause of death due to infectious disease and has often been defined as being a progressive pneumonia. It is an infectious disease often starting in the lungs that spreads to other parts of the body and to other people. Cough, fever, night sweats, weight loss, chest pain, and blood-tinged sputum are hallmarks of this disease. TB is spread through aerosol droplets and newly diagnosed clients should be isolated. **Masks** should be utilized (n95 fit mask). Appropriate medication for approximately two weeks usually renders the client noncontagious. Full recommendations on treatment and isolation are available at www.cdc.gov/tb/.

The first issue to be discussed is TB screening which includes the Mantoux tuberculin test. The medication is inserted by intradermal injection on the forearm and is evaluated 24-72 hours later for a response. A positive result is a measurement of 5mm or more of the induration (raised area). This test indicates the need for further evaluation and does not necessarily suggest active disease.

History and Chest X-ray can be helpful and could raise suspicion as to a disease cause, but culturing sputum and obtaining Mycobacterium tuberculosis bacteria can be the only way to confirm TB.

Medications for tuberculosis are unique in that they usually are administered over a period of months and sometimes longer. The most common ones are listed below.

Nursing Implication	Drug	Action	Evaluation
Educate for abstinence of alcohol consumption with this drug Educate to avoid other drugs that affect the liver, such as Tylenol Assess for alchoholism Assess liver function Assess for jaundice or other symptoms of hepatitis	➤ Isoniazid (INH, Laniazid, Nydrazid)	An anti-infective	Assess for diarrhea, eye pain, vision problems, skin rash, sore throat
Assess for allergies that may cause hives, rash, and swelling of the lips, difficult breathing Assess liver function prior to administering Educate that this drug turns body fluids orange: tears, saliva, sputum, urine	➤ Rifampicin/rifampin (Rifadin, Rimactane)	Bactericidal antibiotic	Assess for GI upsets including cramps and diarrhea May lead to muscle weakness Evaluate for thrush
Often used in combination with INH or rifampicin	➤ Pyrazinamide (generic)	This drug reduces the amount of time that other TBC drugs have to be administered	Evaluate for joint pain Evaluate for durg induced hepatitis Evaluate for hives, swelling of lips, tongue, and difficult breathing

Nursing Implication	Drug	Action	Evaluation
Assess for allergies that may cause hives, rash, and swelling of the lips, difficult breating Assess renal function Educate for blurred vision and loss of red-green vision leading to color discrimination	➤ Ethambutol (Myambutol)	Anti-infective	Evaluate for decreased renal function Evaluate for hepatic side effects

Acute Respiratory Distress Syndrome (ARDS)

ARDS is a severe shortness of breath causing hypoxemia that often results in multiple organ failure. It often occurs within 2 days of a severe injury or illness such as trauma, drug/alcohol abuse, burns, sepsis, shock, or other life threatening illnesses. Fluid builds in the alveoli and furosemide (Lasix) may be utilized to help remove the fluid. Careful intake and output should be recorded.

The SOB is so severe that the majority of these clients must be placed on mechanical ventilation. Positive end-expiratory pressure (PEEP) is used to improve oxygenation.

Appropriate antibiotics are administered **after** cultures are obtained.

This is such a life threatening disease that new graduates should have the support and expertise of medical providers.

Oxygen Delivery Systems

1. **Nasal cannula**—two soft prongs that arise from oxygen supply tubing that delivers oxygen at low flow (2-5 liters/minute). O_2 concentration (FiO_2) is 22-45% dependent upon flow. The advantages include that it is low cost, is readily available, is easy to set up, and is well tolerated by the client. The client can eat, drink, and talk with good mobility. The disadvantages include low accuracy of O_2 measurement with higher flows. O_2 concentrations do not increase significantly with increase in liters delivered and there is a drying and irritation of the nasal mucosa. Humidified air is required with higher flows.

2. **Simple mask**—a tight fitting mask with oxygen supply tubing attached delivering 6-10 liters/minute low flow. Advantages include a greater rate of delivery and increased FiO_2 concentration from 25-60%. Disadvantages include that a tight seal of the mask must be obtained. Some clients feel hot and confined and this appears impractical for long-term use. *Note: a minimum of 6 liters is required for all makes to flush expired breath and prevent re-breathing CO_2. Please see the following YouTube for both nasal cannula and oxygen mask: http://www.youtube.com/watch?v=uV7Wfa2cLQc

3. **Partial non-rebreather**—a tight fitting mask system with a reservoir bag and oxygen supply tubing attached that delivers 8-12 liters/minute low flow O_2 with FiO_2 concentrations from 35-60%. The advantages to this system include flaps on the side of the mask that stay open and allow expired CO_2 to leave the mask. The disadvantages include the need for a tight seal, the reservoir bag must stay inflated at all times, and the mask is impractical for long-term use.

4. **Non-rebreather**—delivers the highest possible oxygen concentration without intubation. This system has a facemask with reservoir bag and oxygen supply tubing. The low flow rate is from 10-15 liters per minute and it delivers an O_2 concentration of 80-95%. The disadvantages include the need for a tight seal on the mask, the reservoir bag must remain inflated at all times, and the mask appears impractical for long-term use. This YouTube video will provide a review: http://www.youtube.com/watch?v=VV5w4qerBDg

5. **Venturi Mask** is a high-flow oxygen delivery system that delivers fixed concentrations of oxygen regardless of the inspiratory flow or the client's breathing pattern. A colored valve connected to the base of the mask regulates its flow and it delivers FiO_2 concentration from 24-60%. Please see this YouTube video for further instructions. http://www.youtube.com/watch?v=zdIXQVVuLs4

VENTILATORS

In quick review, respiration is the exchange of gases between the lungs and the pulmonary blood vessels. Oxygen and carbon dioxide move from one area to the other due to pressure gradients. The systemic levels of CO_2 and O_2 can be measured, and influence the depth and rate of the client's ventilation. Ventilators are indicated when a client's spontaneous ventilation is inadequate to maintain life. The goals of mechanical ventilation include decreasing the work of breathing, maintaining ABG values within normal range, and improving gas distribution. A ventilator may be short or long-term depending on the problem.

Positive pressure ventilators require an artificial airway (endotracheal or tracheostomy tube) and use positive pressure to force gas into the client's lungs. Inspiration can be triggered either by the client or the machine. There are two major types of positive-pressure ventilators:

1. **Volume-cycled ventilators** deliver a preset tidal volume, then allows passive expiration. This is ideal for clients with ARDS or bronchospasm as the same tidal volume is delivered regardless of the airway resistance. This is the most commonly used ventilator in critical care environments.

2. **Pressure-cycled ventilators** deliver gases at a present pressure, then allows passive expiration. The benefit of this type is a decreased risk of lung damage from high pressures.

Ventilator settings are ordered by a health care provider and are individualized for the client. The settings include respiratory rate (number of breaths/time period), tidal volume (the volume of gas the ventilator will deliver in each breath), and oxygen concentration (range from room air to 100%).

With alarms, it is a priority to assess you client's condition first, but remember to say to yourself, "High dry...Low leak!"

The pressure limit regulates the amount of pressure the ventilator can generate to deliver the present tidal volume. If this limit is reached, the **high alarm** will sound. This indicates the client's airway is obstructed with mucus and is usually resolved with suctioning. Other causes can be the client coughing, biting on the tubing, breathing against the ventilator, or by a kink in the ventilator tubing.

The **low alarm** indicates a leak in the closed system of a ventilator. Consider checking to see if the tracheostomy is still in place, if the cuff on the tubing is inflated, if all connections are snug, and if any "port holes" are partially open (such as the type that would be used for delivering aerosol therapy).

Pulmonary Embolism (PE)

Pulmonary embolism is described as sudden onset SOB, rapid breathing, and chest pain due to obstruction of the airway by a blood clot, air embolus, or fat embolus. Since blood clots are the most common cause of PE, nursing should do all possible to prevent these clots from forming. The clots often originate in the legs after a period of bed rest.

Sample Medications used to treat Pulmonary Embolism, the most common type. Clients diagnosed with fat embolus and air embolus do not ordinarily receive blood thinners.

- **Low Molecular Weight Heparins (LMWH)** are easy to identify because their generic name ends in "parin"— dalteparin (Fragmin), enoxaparin (Lovenox), and tinzaparin (Innohep). These drugs inhibit clotting, are given subcutaneously, and are used to treat thrombosis. They are commonly used for prophylactic treatment with clients who have a heart condition such as unstable angina, invasive procedures such as cardiac catheterization, DVT (Deep Vein Thrombosis), and postoperative orthopedic surgery. Most clients do not have to be monitored while taking this drug as the bleeding risk is not as great as heparin and Coumadin. The blood test Anti-Factor Xa is currently the only reliable way to monitor these drugs. Watch for easy bruising.

- **Warfarin (Coumadin)** is a "blood thinner" administered by mouth usually once a day with or without food. The dosage is monitored by a frequent blood test including PT and INR (International Normalized Ratio), which simply means that the reporting of blood results will be the same all over the world. The normal INR for a client not taking an anticoagulant is 1. The higher the number, the longer it takes for the blood to clot. The target INR range for a client taking an anticoagulant is 2-3 times normal. An INR greater than 4 is an indication to notify the provider and hold the anticoagulant until further evaluation can be made. Needless to say, clients taking anticoagulants of all sorts are easier to bruise, may have bloody stools, bleeding in the gums, and uncontrolled bleeding after a cut or injury.

- **Drugs and Foods** also increase the INR particularly when they are taken with Coumadin. These include aspirin, ibuprofen, and some antibiotics. Foods include dark green vegetables.

- **Vitamin K**, a natural blood-clotting factor, is the antidote for Coumadin and is found in common foods such as green leafy vegetables, asparagus, broccoli, cauliflower, and some meats, such as liver. For this reason, clients should be advised to use these foods sparingly or at least consistently so that the Coumadin can be normalized.

- **Heparin**, used to decrease the blood's clotting ability, is administered subcutaneously (often in the abdomen) or intravenously. It is most often administered in a hospital setting and is often given concurrently with warfarin (Coumadin). Most clients are not discharged on heparin, but are likely to be given a prescription for Coumadin to take for weeks or months. The labs that monitor heparin are PTT and INR with reference ranges that vary if heparin is used alone or in combination with Coumadin. Most resources suggest reducing the drug and/or administering the **antidote protamine sulfate** if the INR goes to as high as 5. If the INR reaches 8, the heparin should be stopped and the antidote administered. In addition to being utilized for Atrial Fib, it is also given for venous thrombosis, mechanical heart valves, and prevention of thromboembolic disease. Aspirin and heparin is a very dangerous combination and should be monitored very closely for reducing the blood's ability to clot. All of these drugs are contraindicated for clients who have any blood dyscrasia such as hemophilia, conditions like ulcers that have a tendency to bleed, or anything that is causing active internal bleeding

- The good thing is that these drugs inhibit the ability of the blood to clot. The bad thing is that they do not dissolve clots that have already formed. This is the reason that the Clot Busters become so important as they will dissolve the clots if administered within a very short period of time after stroke symptoms appear (golden standard within 3 hours). Clot Busters are discussed in the Neurological chapter with stroke.

Trauma

This section is a review of any trauma or surgery that causes collapse of the lung with need for Pleur-evac chest drain systems. Think about it this way: the thoracic cavity that houses the lungs has a negative pressure. This means that the lungs function in a space whose pressure is less than atmospheric air. Because of this fact, anytime there is an opening in this space whether due to surgery, automobile accident, or a spear, the outside air will rush into the lung space and cause the lung to collapse. Talk about SOB! People do not do well with collapsed lungs.

Bring on the chest drainage system!

The main objective of the chest drainage system is to allow the lung to expand and be useful. Returning negative pressure to the thoracic space may be accomplished by:
- Placing one end of a chest tube into the chest where the lung is collapsed.
- Placing the other end of this chest tube under water into a system (be it glass [bottle] or plastic [Pleur-evac]). The level of the water in the system will fluctuate with the client's inspiration and expiration. If it does not fluctuate, it may be occluded. Check it!

The underwater tube must ALWAYS be kept under water. If it is allowed to come out of the water then the atmospheric air rushes back into the chest and the lungs collapse again!

- For this reason, it is imperative that the client's chest position is higher than the Pleur-evac. If the collecting system is higher that the chest, the water for the water seal can drain back into the lungs and drown the client we are trying to keep alive.
- It is also imperative to note the fluctuation on the medical record, which will prove (if you need it) that you are evaluating the system.

- Drainage such as blood or serous fluid in the lungs can be drained through the chest tube into a second bottle or another section of the Pleur-evac. This tube will likely have suction added to help drain this extra fluid. The drainage must also be checked, emptied, and recorded. The provider of care sets the amount of suction to be utilized. Make sure that the suction matches the provider's orders and record. As the air comes out of the chest cavity and the lung inflates, the air will bubble in the water seal area a little at the time. **If the air bubbles fast (big time) then there is an air leak in the system and it is time to call the provider for further orders. Air leaks render the chest drainage system ineffective!**

Remember to listen to lung sounds to determine if the chest drainage system is working!

T   TEACH AND PRACTICE INFECTION CONTROL

Many of the respiratory diseases are infectious. All should be treated "as positive" until ruled out.
- Help visitors understand infectious diseases.
- Teach infection control measures to the staff to prevent further spread.
- Teach the client how to prevent spread of the infection.
- Match the isolation process to the disease process.
- Watch for infection around wounds in the chest and the chest tubes.

Y   YOUR MANAGEMENT

Commonalities that flow through client safety of every body system and are heavily weighted on the *NCLEX®* can be condensed into the following table on manage.

These standards currently count for as much as 23% of the total **NCLEX®** exam and are always a primary consideration for nursing.

	PASS *NCLEX®*!
M	Make sure of identity, accuracy of orders
A	Arrange privacy/confidentiality/consent/collaboration with other team
N	No injuries, falls, malfunctioning equipment or staff or hazards
A	Address errors, abuse, legalities, scope of practice—document
G	Give (delegate) orders to appropriate people, report when they are unsafe
E	Establish priorities of clients and time

1. Which would be the best management decision regarding delegation of care of a client with a chest tube?
    A. Delegate to a new graduate as they have had recent experience.
    B. Assess current staff members for their experience in caring for a client of this nature.
    C. Provide a demonstration for all staff so that everyone can care for this client.
    D. Care for the client yourself.

2. The client with staph pneumonia has a medication order for Vancomycin IV. What are the priority actions prior to administering this drug? **Select all that apply**
    A. Complete a culture and sensitivity for the lab.
    B. Teach the client the side effects of the drug.
    C. Determine if the client is allergic to penicillin.
    D. Review the lab data on the client's kidney prior to administering.
    E. Review the lab data on the client's liver prior to administering.

3. Discharge teaching to the family of an elderly client following hospitalization with pneumonia should include which of the following? **Select all that apply.**
    A. Assure that the client receives a pneumonia vaccination every year.
    B. Asses for changes in client's mental status.
    C. Provide 6-8 glasses of fluid to drink every day.
    D. Arrange for a follow up chest x-ray once a month.
    E. Arrange a suction machine for home use.

4. The assessment determines that the client is in brochospasms. Which is the priority nursing action.
    A. Notify the provider of the client's difficulty.
    B. Utilize an albuterol (Proventil) inhaler per protocol.
    C. Administer salmeterol (Serevent) inhaler per protocol.
    D. Sit the client up and give them a glass of water.

5. The high pressure alarm is going off on the client's ventilator. What is the nursing priority?
    A. Turn the alarm off so that it does not disturb everyone.
    B. Increase the pressure on the ventilator.
    C. Listen to lung sounds.
    D. Suction the client's airway

6. Which discharge planning will best assist the client with asthma? **Select all that apply.**
    A. Teach the client about "triggers."
    B. Emphasize the need for rescue inhaler availability.
    C. Warn the client to avoid acetaminophen (Tylenol).
    D. Encourage daily rest times.
    E. Encourage the client to eat a high protein diet.

7. Following change of shift report in an intensive care unit, which client should be assessed first?
    A. The child with a head injury.
    B. A client with a diagnosis of bronchitis.
    C. The client with atrial fibrillation.
    D. A client receiving an antibiotic IV.

8. The charge nurse notes a respiratory therapist aide utilizing a suction catheter that was left in the room from the last shift. What is the most priority action?
    A. Notify the Respiratory Therapy department head and ask for assistance.
    B. Stop the suctioning and provide a new suction catheter to the aide.
    C. Notify the house supervisor of the situation.
    D. Complete an incident report regarding the facts.

9. The client is admitted to the ED with shortness of breath. Assessment indicates rales in the lungs and swollen limbs. Which medication from protocol should be administered?
    A. Prednisone 5mg P.O.
    B. EpiPen®
    C. Furesomide (Lasix) 20mg IV
    D. Albuterol (Proventil) inhaler.

10. The client is admitted with SOB, nasal oxygen, and a diagnosis of emphysema. What is priority to include in the teaching plan?
    A. Begin a smoking cessation program.
    B. Begin an exercise program.
    C. Advise a high fiber diet.
    D. Teach to use bronchodilator inhalers prior to steroid inhalers.

11. The client had been admitted to the unit with cough, bloody sputum, and night sweats. Which is the nursing priority?
    A. Place the client is isolation until the client can be further assessed.
    B. Arrange for a sputum culture.
    C. Encourage family visitors to prevent anxiety.
    D. Delegate care to a new graduate.

12. The client admitted for chest surgery two days ago suddenly complains of chest pain and acute shortness of breath, Rapid respirations are noted. What is the nursing priority?
    A. Notify the provider of the symptoms stat.
    B. Sit the client into Fowler's position and begin oxygen.
    C. Administer furesomide (Lasix)according to protocol.
    D. Draw arterial blood for gases.

13. The client with status asthmaticus has been admitted with the following orders. Which of these orders should be questioned?
    A. Albuterol (Proventil) 2.5mg every 4 hours.
    B. Methylprednisolone sodium succinate (Solu-medrol) inhaler Q6h.
    C. NaCL 0.9 solution IV to keep the vein open.
    D. Suction airway every hour.

14. A young client is admitted by ambulance to the ED with severe SOB and inability to talk. What is the best way to determine the identity and age of this client prior to beginning treatment?
    A. Look for identity on the client such as a wallet, purse or backpack.
    B. Question family or friends regarding client's identity.
    C. Begin treatment immediately without waiting for identity or age indication.
    D. Question the EMT personnel who brought the client in.

15. The client is admitted to the ED with SOB. Which is priority assessment for this client?
    A. Determine open airway.
    B. Determine the type of lung sounds.
    C. Check vital signs.
    D. Draw blood gases.

16. The client's pulse ox is 80%. What is the nursing priority?
    A. Begin emergency ventilation.
    B. Notify the provider of care.
    C. Draw blood gases.
    D. Administer oxygen.

17. The pulse ox reads 0%. What is the next step?
    A. Reposition the pulse ox and read it again.
    B. Determine if the client is breathing.
    C. Utilize new pulse oximeter equipment as equipment may be faulty.
    D. Begin CPR.

18. Which will be best in promoting comfort for the client who is short of breath?
    A. Lay them in a prone position.
    B. Sit them in Fowler's position.
    C. Allow them to assume the position most comfortable for them.
    D. Place them in Sim's position for better oxygenation.

19. The client with tuberculosis has been on isonizaid (INH) for 3 weeks and is ready to return to work. Which is the best information for the home health nurse to provide?
    A. Advise the client to wear a mask for one month as a precautionary measure.
    B. Advise the client to wash hands frequently after using the bathroom.
    C. Teach cough and sneeze precautions.
    D. Teach immaculate skin and mouth care.

20. The client with a new diagnosis of tuberculosis expresses concern about his newborn. What is priority teaching?
    A. Continue isolation techniques until tuberculosis drugs have been taken for 2-3 weeks.
    B. Advise him that infants have immunity to this kind of infection.
    C. Notify the child's pediatrician regarding this issue.
    D. It is acceptable to hold the newborn, but not to feed the infant.

21. The client in the ED is admitted with respirations of 20/minute. Within 15 minutes the respirations are noted at 40/minute. What is the next step?
    A. Assess the client for pain.
    B. Determine additional vital signs.
    C. Prepare for emergency ventilation.
    D. Document the findings.

Answers and Rationale

1. **Answer B** is the best answer. Start with an experienced person if you have one. Answer C is the next best answer. This action would educate the staff and provide back up. Answer D is the worst answer. In management we have to learn to delegate, otherwise we will be doing everything all the time.

2. **Answers A and D**. A culture and sensitivity should be completed prior to drug administration. Vancomycin is known to damage kidneys so renal function should be determined prior to administration. Answers B, C, and E are not needed for this client.

3. **Answers. B and C**. The elderly often have changes in mental status such as confusion before they have other symptoms. The fluids will help liquefy the secretions and decrease the opportunity for pneumonia infection. Answer A, the pneumonia vaccination is usually administered every 5 years. Answer D, a chest x-ray every month is inappropriate and, Answer E, a suction machine is ordinarily not needed.

4. **Answer B** is the only option for a bronchodilator that will assist this client to breathe. Serevent is a long -term treatment for asthma not utilized for acute bronchospasms. Be careful offering water to any client with dyspnea as they may aspirate.

5. **Answer D**. The high pressure alarm is often an indicator that the pressure is building with no place to go due to an airway obstruction. The client should first be suctioned. Answer A, turning the alarm off, is not priority. The client has first priority and increased pressure may be harmful. It's fine to assess the lung sounds but this comes later. Intervention comes first.

6. **Answers A and B** will be the most useful. Tylenol is ordinarily not an issue with the other asthma meds and daily rest times are not usually required. There is no known reason to require a high protein diet.

7. **Answer A**. Head injury is likely to make a change. Trends should be documented. Answer B, the client with bronchitis would likely be next. Unless a change has been reported in shift report, the clients with atrial fib and IV antibiotic can be seen later.

8. **Answer B** is the safest for the client. Then notify the RT department head. Follow agency protocol regarding incident report of errors.

9. **Answer C**. Not all SOB is lung originated. The signs and symptoms may be the same, but the underlying cause must be addressed in order for the client to breathe. Answers A, B and D will be unlikely treatments in this case.

10. **Answer B**. Treat the client first so they can breathe! They are likely smokers as this is the highest risk in clients with emphysema; however, if they can't breathe, they cannot listen to lectures on smoking, exercises, or diet.

11. **Answer A**. These symptoms may indicate tuberculosis and the client should be isolated until a sputum culture rules out a contagious disease.

12. **Answer A**. These are the symptoms of a pulmonary embolus and the provider must be notified. These symptoms are life threatening. Answers B and D may be useful and are secondary. Lasix is not likely to help in this situation.

13. **Answer D**. Suction of a client with status asthmaticus is risky behavior and can exacerbate the situation. Suction should only be used if deemed necessary. All other orders are common for this situation.

14. **Answer. C**. Clients admitted to the ED may legally be treated as "John/Jane Doe" until their identity and age can be determined. Family/friends or wallet are ways to verify identity. EMTs are probably the last to know the name if they are unaccompanied.

15. **Answer A**. No airway, no lung sounds, decreasing vital signs. Don't take time to draw blood gases until the airway is open.

16. **Answer A**. With pulse ox this low, enhanced ventilation is likely needed. All other options are secondary.

17. **Answer B**. Is the client alive? If so, there is an issue with the placement of the equipment or the equipment itself. Always rely on the client's clinical picture rather than the equipment.

18. **Answer C**. Even children will fight to be in the position that allows them to breathe. Never restrain a client that is having SOB if possible.

19. **Answer C**. As tuberculosis is spread through droplets, this will help prevent further contamination. Usually after 2 weeks on tuberculosis drugs, the client is no longer at risk for spreading the disease.

20. **Answer A** is first and **Answer C** is second. Tuberculosis is contagious until the client has been in compliance with medication protocols for at least 2 weeks.

21. **Answer A**. Without knowing anything else about this client, pain may be an issue and should be assessed. The other options are secondary.

The Pediatric RESPIRATORY SYSTEM

Jessica Peck, DNP, RN, MSN, CPNP-PC, CNE
Edited by Sylvia Rayfield & Associates, Inc.

What is different about the way children breathe?

CHILDREN ARE MUCH MORE LIKLELY TO EXPERIENCE RESPIRATORY ARREST THAN CARDIAC ARREST. REMEMBER THAT THEIR HEARTS ARE YOUNG AND STRONG BUT THEIR LUNGS ARE SMALL AND VULNERABLE. IF YOU FIND A CHILD WHO HAS ARRESTED, THINK AIRWAY FIRST!

KEY CONCEPTS TO REMEMBER:

- ❖ The goals of managing a respiratory emergency are to (1) maximize oxygen delivery, (2) correct ABG imbalances, (3) treat underlying cause, (4) minimize organ failure, and (5) anticipate complications.
- ❖ Prompt action can prevent cardiac arrest, which has a poor outcome.

WHAT TO DO WHEN A CHILD SHOWS SIGNS OF RESPIRATORY SYMPTOMS OR DISTRESS:

What do nurses do first? Assess!! Assess the infant using your ABC's.

ASSESSMENT	INTERVENTION
A- AIRWAY Airway should be open and patent. Babies have a tiny airway, so it can close quickly. Be alert! All the respiratory structures are physically close to each other. Infection can spread easily and quickly.	Croup and epiglottitis can cause rapid airway obstruction. If respiratory arrest is imminent or occurs, position baby supine with chin elevated, but not hyperextended. **NEVER EXAMINE THE THROAT OF A BABY IN RESPIRATORY DISTRESS!!! NEVER DO A BLIND FINGER SWEEP!!** **If child is drooling, in tripod position, and cyanotic, CALL RAPID RESPONSE AND PREPARE FOR EMERGENCY AIRWAY! Position child for COMFORT! You do not want this kid to cry! Keep in mama's lap, or wherever he is not crying. Crying increases risk of respiratory compromise.

Ages 6 months to 3 years are most likely to react more severely to infection. Alert! Risk for respiratory distress, arrest, and invasive disease!	**CARDINAL SIGNS OF IMPENDING ARREST:** **RESTLESSNESS** **TACHYPNEA** **TACHYCARDIA** **DIAPHORESIS** (**R**ALLY **T**HE **T**ROOPS **D**OUBLETIME!)
B- BREATHING Assess breathing effort. Respiratory rates >60 in any age infant or child should cause immediate concern. Ventilation is MOST important for kids. Give SMALL puffs of air (enough to make the chest rise and fall) but not too much or you could give them a pneumothorax). www.youtube.com/watch?v=sJLHiTaXrtc **Visit here to see respiratory distress in a child.**	If respiratory rate is >60, attach cardiopulmonary monitors, give oxygen, and notify provider. If baby is unresponsive to interventions, prepare for mechanical ventilation. **DO NOT FEED A BABY EXHIBITING SIGNS OF RESPIRATORY DISTRESS!! YOU WILL INCREASE THE RISK OF ASPIRATION.** **5 CARDINAL SIGNS OF RESPIRATORY DISTRESS:** 1. Tachypnea 2. Cyanosis 3. Grunting 4. Nasal flaring 5. Retractions **CPR GUIDELINES CHANGED IN 2005. YOU DO NOT CODE A KID THE SAME WAY YOU CODE AN ADULT.** Remember that most children will arrest because of respiratory causes. If they are not breathing, you need to help them quickly before they experience cardiac arrest. If you find a child who is unresponsive and you didn't see what happened, you need to do 5 cycles of CPR **BEFORE** calling EMS!! You don't know how long their brain has been without oxygen and seconds matter! If you see them collapse, then call EMS FIRST and **THEN** do CPR. You know you have a few seconds to spare because you know exactly what time they went down. **HCP CPR is:** 1. Head-tilt chin lift 2. Two initial rescue breaths 3. If you are the lone HCP, do 5 cycles of CPR. Ratio 30:2 3a. If you have help, do 5 cycles with a ratio of 15:2 ALL babies and children should have a compression rate of about 100/minute.

| | 4. Check for breathing and pulse after 5 cycles. |
| | |
	5. Breaths should be about every 6 seconds. Children under 8 about every 3-5 seconds.
C- CIRCULATION Babies have short, fat necks. Don't waste your time trying to find the carotid pulse! Go for the BRACHIAL or FEMORAL pulse. Use the carotid pulse in children>8 years. **www.youtube.com/watch?v=1K6o Ui8cTWA** **Visit here to review use of AEDs.**	**INITIATE COMPRESSIONS FOR INFANTS IF APICAL PULSE IS LESS THAN 60!!** Just because a baby has a pulse does not mean it is adequate to maintain organ perfusion. If pulse is <60 for infants, begin compressions. Don't wait until they completely arrest! **A WORD ABOUT AEDs (Automated External Defibrillator):** 1. AEDs are not approved for use in infants <1 year of age. There is no data to either support or refute their use. 2. Children ages 1-8 should get pediatric pads. >8 years will get adult pads. 3. Initiate AED in the hospital within 5 minutes, within 3 minutes in the community. Just remember that an AED is NOT the first thing you get during a code. AIRWAY is first for kids!!
D- DECREASE STRESS A calm environment is key to decreasing respiratory distress. 	Allow parents to stay with the child, EVEN DURING RESUSCITATION EFFORTS! Studies show that family presence alleviates anxiety, decreases anger, minimizes doubts about whether the best treatment was given, and ultimately can facilitate the grieving process in negative outcomes. If parents cannot remain with the child, a caregiver should remain with the parents at all times. Do whatever you can to keep the child calm. This is not the time to insist on a rectal temperature because it is "THE POLICY!"
E- EASE RESPIRATORY SYMPTOMS If symptoms show that child is not in distress or in danger of impending respiratory failure, focus on making the child more comfortable and alleviating symptoms.	Provide humidified mist for therapeutic relief. Promote rest. If a child refuses to stay in bed but is playing quietly or ambulating peacefully without exacerbating symptoms, LET IT GO!! Pediatric nurses must be flexible and go with what works based on the individual child! Saline drops to the nose with bulb suction. Reduce fever, which increases respiratory rate. It also can cause

	dehydration. Give antipyretics as prescribed. Promote hydration. High calorie fluids are encouraged, as children with respiratory symptoms are often anorexic. Avoid caffeinated drinks, as they can speed dehydration with diuresis. Assess hydration status frequently. Allow children to eat what they want when they want. Forcing foods can cause nausea, vomiting, and food aversion.
F- FIGHT THE SPREAD OF DISEASE!	Many pediatric respiratory diseases are highly contagious. It is critical to prevent germ spread! The BEST thing you can do is wash your hands frequently and encourage all who come in contact with the patient to do the same thing. Toddlers are messy with their snot. It goes everywhere! Use tissues to cough and sneeze into and throw them away! Teach kids to cough into their "yucky armpit" where germs belong. Think about your patient assignments. Do not care for a child with RSV (respiratory syncytial virus) if you have an immunocompromised patient next door!! Do not allow children with different contagious infections to room together. Administer antibiotics as prescribed for bacterial infections and counsel parents about the importance of completing prescribed regimen to decrease the risk of bacterial resistance. Be sure to protect babies <3 months from contagious disease. They are most likely to experience life-threatening complications with respiratory disease. Be sure immunizations are up to date!
G- GUARD AGAINST COMPLICATIONS	Be aware that babies and children are at high risk for developing secondary complications and infections. Just because a disease is diagnosed as viral, such as RSV, does not mean they could not develop a secondary bacterial infection such as otitis media, pneumonia, sepsis, or meningitis. The younger the child, the greater the risk, and the faster it happens.

A WORD ABOUT OXYGEN:

O2 Sats: Acceptable limits range from 91%-100%. Lower is acceptable for preemies and some cardiac babies, so don't freak out if a preemie's O2 sat limits are set at 88%. Be sure to ask about the baby's normal sats. If the sat is reading low, the first thing you should do is to check the sensor probe! Make sure it is on good and make sure your machine is working. If the sat says 72% and the baby is pink, smiling and breathing, the sat is wrong. Don't forget to look at your patient!

ACUTE RESPIRATORY INFECTIONS

KEY CONCEPT TO REMEMBER:

❖ Most of these infections also occur in adults. The key here is: "What makes nursing management different for children?"

1. THE MOST COMMON, THE COMMON COLD

The most common respiratory problem children and babies experience is a cold (Upper

Respiratory Infection or URI). Management is very simple, yet important.

C—Comfort symptoms

O—Offer fluids

L—Look for complications

D—Decrease spread of disease

2. STREP THROAT (GABHS PHARYNGITIS)

S- —Symptoms to watch out for: sore throat, fever, and LAD (lymphadenopathy)

T—Tummy aches are common. Sometimes kids only complain of N/V.

R—RED throat. White spots/exudate are usually not associated with strep! Think more like raw hamburger meat.

E—Emphasize the importance of antibiotics! This is treated with PCN, either po or IM.

P—Prevent the risk of rheumatic heart disease by promoting early detection and complying with abx.

2. TONSILLITIS

T—Tonsils in kids are NORMALLY very large! They atrophy as we age.

O—Often viral in nature.

N—Nasty mouth breathing. Adenoids are often enlarged, making it difficult for air to pass from the nose to the mouth. Mouth breathing + buffalo breath +snoring= Adenoid evaluation!

S—Surgery is sometimes done to remove tonsils or adenoids or both. However, surgery can be risky and should only be done if clinical symptoms have severity to warrant it.

I—Intense post-op care (simple surgery, but potentially fatal complications)

L—Let them play normally about 1-2 weeks post-op.

POST-OP CARE FOR T&A

Vital Signs	• Always count pediatric respirations for one full minute! • Monitor for hypothermia, common after surgery, and take corrective measures such as heated blanket, radiant warmer, etc. • Monitor for tachycardia and hypotension, signs of potential hemorrhage

Provide Rest	• Position on side to minimize aspiration. HOB up when fully awake and alert.
	• Avoid suctioning. If you have to do it, be CAREFUL!
	• Avoid coughing, blowing nose, laughing or crying (This is accomplished with sedation and narcotics!)
Monitor Fluids	• Expect a LITTLE bit of blood—some old, some new, but prepare the parents
	• Antiemetics as necessary to avoid vomiting (ondansetron/Zofran).
	• Clear liquids after gag reflex returns.
	• AVOID RED FLUIDS (so if they vomit blood you won't be confused) AND MILK PRODUCTS (it makes them clear their throat too much). Contrary to popular belief, you do NOT get an ice cream diet after a T&A.
	• Advance diet with soft, bland foods.
Pain	• Ice collar is helpful but poorly tolerated.
	• **PAIN MEDS SHOULD BE GIVEN ROUND THE CLOCK!** (Think codeine and acetaminophen or both).
	• Decrease stress and stimulation.
ALERT	• WATCH FOR FREQUENT SWALLOWING, TACHYCARDIA, PALLOR, AND RESTLESSNESS. THESE ARE POTENTIAL SIGNS OF HEMHORRAGE! THIS CAN OCCUR UP TO TEN DAYS POST-OP!!

3. INFLUENZA

Flu is more deadly for kids. Children < 2years are more likely to experience severe consequences and to be hospitalized. ALL **KIDS 6 MONTHS AND UP NEED TO BE VACCINATED!** If children are <9 years old and it is their first flu shot, they will need a booster 30 days later. Children 6 months—3 years get a half dose (0.25cc).

3. OTITIS MEDIA

Children < 7years have shorter eustachian tubes, which allows pathogens to enter the middle ear more easily. Chronic otitis can lead to hearing loss and speech impairment. The two most important identifiable risk factors are (1) socioeconomic status—the lower the status the higher the risk, (2) exposure to other kids—daycare = lots of exposure to illnesses which create risk for developing OM. It is critical to take all antibiotics as prescribed. Children can get pressure-equalization tubes (PET) if OM is persistent. If PET are present, no swimming in river or lake water and try to keep bathwater out as well.

NURSE IN ACTION: PREVENTION

1. GET ALL VACCINES ON TIME! (Pneumococcal vaccine especially helps).

2. NO SMOKING!

3. AVOID DAYCARE IF POSSIBLE. (Lots of kids = lots of germs = lots of risk).

4. BREASTFEED AT LEAST ONE YEAR!

5. DON'T PROP BOTTLES! SIT UPRIGHT FOR FEEDINGS.

CROUP SYNDROMES

Know your A-B-C's	Acute Epiglottitis	Acute Laryngotracheobronchitis (Croup)	BACTERIAL TRACHEITIS
Ask about the history www.youtube.com/ watch?v=UFIFqFzulcg **Visit here to learn more about croup**	Risk Factors: ▪ Age 2-8 years ▪ Lack of immunization ▪ Usually *h. influenza* **A serious and deadly form of croup*	Risk Factors: ▪ <5 years of age ▪ URI ▪ RSV ▪ Influenza **Most common form of croup*	Etiology: ▪ Bacterial **Can lead to ARDS, respiratory failure, and organ failure.*
	Acute Epiglottitis	**Acute Laryngotracheobronchitis (Croup)**	**BACTERIAL TRACHEITIS**
B—Be aware of possible presenting symptoms you might detect on assessment	▪ ABRUPT ONSET ▪ Rapidly progresses to resp. distress. ▪ **CLASSIC SX: TRIPOD SIT**	▪ "Barking cough" ▪ Gradual onset of sx ▪ STRIDOR & RETRACTIONS ▪ AWAKES WITH	▪ FEVER ▪ Symptoms similar to epiglottitis

	DROOLING AGITATION LACK OF COUGH	SYMPTOMS IN THE MIDDLE OF THE NIGHT	
C—Care for the client until need for respiratory support or condition resolves	Don't look in the throat! Get the provider right away! Avoid x-ray and transport (increases anxiety). Prepare to intubate. STAY CALM!!	Racemic epinephrine Humidified oxygen Corticosteroids IM or IV Albuterol and antibiotics do not help! STAY CALM!!!	In case you have forgotten, **DO NOT LOOK IN THE THROAT!!** **EARLY** signs of impending respiratory failure are: tachycardia, tachypnea, retractions, nasal flaring, and restlessness.

LOWER RESPIRATORY INFECTIONS

Know your **A— B—C's**	**RSV** **Respiratory Syncytial Virus**	**Pneumonia**	**Pertussis**
Ask about the history	Risk Factors: • < 3 years of age • Winter & Spring • RSV before age one increases risk of developing asthma • Daycare • Smoke exposure **Most premature babies should be vaccinated for RSV with synagis/palivizumab*	Risk Factors: • Bacterial or viral • Abrupt onset • Appears very ill *School-aged children can have a viral pneumonia that is usually managed at home.*	Risk Factors: • Not up to date with vaccines • Very deadly in infants <1year • Spring & summer *Resurgence in the U.S. is happening at an epidemic rate. Vaccine boosters for pertussis are now recommended for preteens and up.*
B—Be aware of possible presenting symptoms you might detect on assessment	• Apnea may be the first sign in infants • Wheezing • Dyspnea/Retractions • Tachypnea	• Pain often referred to abd. • Fever • Dyspnea	• Typical "whoop" cough • Infants have atypical presentation, apnea

C—Care for the client until need for respiratory support or condition resolves	Remember, RR >60 in any age is a sign of impending respiratory failure! Humidified oxygen IV fluid support Infection control—don't spread this on the unit! Saline drops and bulb suction to the nose. Monitor pulse ox closely.	Antibiotics May need chest tube for purulent drainage Encourage fluid intake Monitor pulse ox. May need postural drainage or CPT. May benefit from bronchodilators.	Treat with antibiotics Humidified oxygen Maintain hydration Infants <6 mos. may need intubation and ventilator support. Pneumonia is the most common complication that can lead to death.

WHAT MAKES ASTHMA DIFFERENT FOR CHILDREN AND BABIES?

Assessment	• Watch for signs of impending respiratory failure (**R**ally **T**he **T**roops **D**oubletime!) • Look for retractions. • Sometimes breath sounds can be diminished and then WORSEN after a breathing treatment. This means the kid was worse than you thought because the child wasn't moving any air prior to the treatment. • ABSENT BREATH SOUNDS WITH TACHYPNEA INDICATE IMPENDING RESPIRATORY FAILURE!
Complications	• Children are more likely to develop secondary complications, such as pneumonia, hypoxemia, hypo/hypercapnia, or respiratory failure. • Children can "crump" (meaning decompensate) much more quickly than adults!
Parent Instructions	• Asthma often associated with allergies. Treating both is ideal for optimal outcome. • Child needs to learn to manage their therapy and self-administer medications. • Be vigilant for signs of infection. • Exercise is a good part of asthma therapy regime, especially swimming. • Get a flu shot, every year!
Inhalers	• Most children cannot adequately manage an inhaler used directly. • Treatments may be administered via nebulization. • Inhalers may be used with a spacer and mask.
ALERT	• Never put an inhaler in water to see if it is full. Water inactivates the propellant in many cases and makes the inhaler useless. • Parents must count the number of actuations and keep track. An inhaler can be empty and parents are using it to treat symptoms with no relief.

Medications are the most critical component of asthma management. Prevention of attacks is the goal of therapy and this can only be done with medications, augmented by environmental desensitization (removing allergens from the home and getting allergy treatment).

MEDICATION	ACTION	NURSING CARE	EDUCATION	ALERTS
Corticosteroids Inhaled corticosteroids are first line asthma therapy in children >5yrs of age.	Decreases inflammation in the lungs. Inhaled-preventive PO—burst therapy for exacerbations IV—for severe exacerbations	STOP! This means YOU. **Rinse mouth with water after each use!** Never use a corticosteroid inhaler without a spacer. Doing these two things can prevent oral candidiasis.	Long-term use does not affect the child's linear growth! Report unexpected sudden weight gain. Report frequent infections.	CAUTION! Monitor by PCP every 3-6 months for long term side effects.
Beta Adrenergic Agonists Levalbuteral (Xopenex) Albuterol	Relaxes muscles in the airway	This medicine can give you the SHAKES! Other side effects include nausea, anxiety, tachycardia and tachypnea.	This is a RESCUE medication for acute symptoms. Parents should report increased need for usage.	Do not take more than 4 times per day! If symptoms are persistent and unrelieved, contact the provider!
Long-Acting Beta 2 Agonists Salmeterol (Serevent)	Anti-inflammatory	Rinse mouth after use.	Do NOT use to treat acute symptoms!	Do NOT use more than prescribed!

CYSTIC FIBROSIS

KEY CONCEPTS TO REMEMBER:

❖ An inherited, autosomal recessive trait
❖ Median survival age 37.4 years
❖ Number one goal of all therapy is to prevent infection. Infection reduces life expectancy. Number two is to provide adequate nutrition.
❖ Diagnosis is made with sweat chloride test. Most babies diagnosed before one year and most states now offering newborn screening.

ASSESSMENT FINDINGS:

❖ GI: foul, fatty, frothy, foracious stools; frightfully thin; failure to thrive; funny looking (sallow) skin; fetid mucous; fat-soluble vitamin deficiencies.
❖ Resp: wheezing, cough and dyspnea progresses to cyanosis, barrel-chest, clubbing, and recurrent bronchitis and pneumonia.
❖ Meconium ileus in 10% of patients.
❖ Hyperglycemia related to insulin resistance

NURSING CARE:

❖ CPT is the mainstay of therapy! Do it one hour before or 2 hours after meal to preserve appetite. You would not want to cough up all kinds of secretions and then be able to eat your lunch.
❖ Be compliant with respiratory treatments such as bronchodilators.
❖ Use oxygen cautiously to prevent narcosis.
❖ Monitor blood glucose.
❖ Take all antibiotics as prescribed.
❖ Give pancreatic enzymes with food. Can be swallowed whole or sprinkled on.
❖ HIGH calorie diet with lots of protein.
❖ Give water-soluble fat vitamins.
❖ Coordinate interdisciplinary care (PT, RT, OT, social services, dieticians).
❖ Encourage regular PCP visits and compliance with immunizations.
❖ Teach to recognize early symptoms of infection.
❖ Connect family with a support group.
❖ Promote physical exercise.

What is the goal of nursing care for a child with cystic fibrosis?

The goal is to cut the **CRAP** this family and child has to deal with.

C—*COMPLIANCE WITH MEDICATION!*

- Often prophylactic antibiotics are given.

- Respiratory treatments, nebulizers and inhalers

- CPT and breathing exercises immediately after inhalers (bronchodilators).

R—*RECOVERY FROM ILLNESS*

- Give three daily meals and three daily snacks.

- Provide foods from home whenever possible.

A—*ABILITY TO COPE*

- Offer respite care.

- Encourage normalcy with developmentally appropriate activities with peers.

- Expect grief and anger; encourage family counseling.

- CF patients often have infertility. Make sure they understand the difference between infertility and impotence or ability to engage in sexual behavior.

- Encourage independence as much as possible.

- Make preparations for end-of-life care.

P—*PREVENT RECURRENCE*

- Watch for symptoms (fever, malaise, chest pain, poor appetite)

- Comply with prophylactic antibiotic therapy

- Recognize early signs of infection and see healthcare provider frequently.

http://www.youtube.com/watch?v=Dn0grhu9h4g

Visit here to see what a day in the life of a teenager with CF is like.

A Lesson On Pediatric Tracheostomies

When pediatric patients get tracheostomies, it can seem pretty traumatic to the family. However, this is often used for chronically ill children (especially preemies) as a step down from endotracheal intubation. Complications of the surgery include aspiration, hemorrhage, edema, and accidental decannulation. Nursing care is centered around maintaining a patent airway, giving humidified O2 to prevent drying of the mucosa, preventing infection, and monitoring for hemorrhage. Often times the child's hands must be restrained in order to prevent them from pulling out the tube. Post-op we call this a "fresh trach" meaning, "This is fragile! Be careful and don't screw it up!"

Many times parents are very afraid to learn how to suction but once they do learn, they are often more expert than the nurses are! If you think about it, they do it multiple times a day every day of their lives for someone they love and cherish! I often advise my students who are nervous about trach suctioning to ask the parent for a demonstration. This gives the parent a huge boost in confidence and the student will usually see expert technique!

When suctioning, make sure you have your equipment ready! Suction should be set at 40-60mmHG for preemies and 60-100mmHg for bigger babies and children. The suction catheter should be about half the size of the tracheostomy tube. If it doesn't fit, don't force it! The catheter is inserted to the end of the tracheostomy tube. NO SALINE REQUIRED! The use of saline is not backed by the evidence. SUCTION LESS THAN 5 SECONDS!! Hyperventilation before and after is recommended.

IF O2 SATS DROP, TACHYCARDIA OCCURS, OR CYANOSIS OR DYSPNEA IS NOTED, STOP SUCTIONING IMMEDIATELY!

You should always keep a tracheostomy tube one size smaller taped to the bedside in case of emergency. I didn't realize how important this was until one day when I was at the outpatient clinic. One of our chronically ill patients came in for fever. It looked like he was septic, which was a reoccurring event for this particular 3-year-old boy. He was very agitated and before we knew it he yanked out his trach! I instinctively reached for the trach that was a size smaller to reinsert but then remembered we were in the clinic and it was not there! Remember that kids need to breathe! If they yank out their trach tube, you need to put it back in! Back to the patient, I realized we did not have a tracheostomy tube in the clinic that would work. We prepared for oral intubation but lo and behold when we opened the child's mouth and looked at his throat we realized he had swallowed his trach button and it was lodged in the posterior pharynx! We had called an ambulance for transport to the hospital but the ambulance was lost and could not find the clinic. The physician and I told the child's caregiver to run and get the car, as we were only 3 blocks from the hospital. The physician and I grabbed an oxygen tank and jumped in the back of the pick-up truck and raced to the hospital. The child thankfully made a full recovery! You can bet though that we went back and ordered TWO of every trach size! Remember, if it falls out, put it back in!

REVIEW QUESTIONS

1. An 18-month-old child is being treated in the emergency room for acute laryngotracheobronchitis. The nurse needs to reassess the child's respiratory status after a nebulizer treatment of racemic epinephrine. What action by the nurse is the most appropriate?

    1) Ask the mother how she feels the child is doing.
    2) Address the mother's guilt about smoking around the toddler.
    3) Allow the child to remain on the mother's lap for the assessment.
    4) Lay the child supine on the exam table to do a thorough assessment.

Option #3 is correct. Options #1 and #2 are appropriate nursing interventions but not the most appropriate way to assess the child's respiratory status at the time. This child needs to stay calm to prevent exacerbation of stridor and remaining on the mother's lap is the best way to accomplish that.

2. A nurse is caring for an 8-year-old child with an acute asthma exacerbation. Which assessment finding should the nurse immediately report to the provider?

    1)   The child's mother confesses to the nurse that she is not very good about giving her child his corticosteroid inhaler every day.
    2)   Physical assessment reveals diminished breath sounds bilaterally.
    3)   The child's respiratory rate is now 26 breaths/minute.
    4)   Recent blood gas analysis reveals an oxygen saturation of 95%.

Option #2 is correct. This is a sign of impending respiratory failure. The other signs are things to be considered and observed carefully, but the most emergent finding is #2.

3. A 7-year-old child has just returned to the post-anesthesia care unit to after undergoing a tonsillectomy. The nurse observes the child swallowing frequently. What is an appropriate nursing intervention for this child?

    1)   Apply warm wet compresses to the neck
    2)   Check the child's pulse and blood pressure
    3)   Encourage the child to cough up any drainage
    4)   Place the child in a supine position with head and neck flat

Option #2 is important because frequent swallowing is an early sign of hemorrhage following a tonsillectomy. Option #1 is not an appropriate intervention as ice collars are recommended. Coughing is discouraged because it could rupture the surgical site. The child should be placed in a side-lying position to prevent aspiration.

4. A 2-year-old girl is brought to the emergency room by EMS from her provider's clinic. She has a strange croaking sound on inspiration, is agitated, and is drooling. The nurse tries to

have her lie down for examination but the child struggles to sit upright with legs extended and arms pushing down on the table. What action should the nurse take?

1) Allow her to sit upright and finish the rest of the assessment.
2) Ask the girl's mother for assistance in getting her to cooperate with examination.
3) Call the provider immediately prepare for endotracheal intubation.
4) Examine her oropharynx for a possible foreign body.

Option #3 is correct. This child is exhibiting symptoms of epiglottitis and respiratory failure is impending. It is CONTRAINDICATED to examine the oropharynx when these symptoms are present. The exam could exacerbate the airway inflammation. When these symptoms are present, the nurse should stop whatever they are doing and make preparations for an emergency.

5. A mother calls the nurse to inquire about giving her toddler an over-the-counter cold medicine. She wants to know if it is acceptable to give acetaminophen for fever concurrently with the cold medicine. What is the best response by the nurse?

1) Ask the mother to list the ingredients in the cold medication.
2) Tell the mother it is safe to give both medications concurrently.
3) Advise the mother not to give both medications concurrently.
4) Recommend a call to the local pharmacist.

Option #1 is correct. Many cold medicines are combination medications that contain acetaminophen. It is important to calculate the dosages to avoid overmedicating.

6. A nurse is giving home care instructions the mother of a child diagnosed with strep throat. Which information is incorrect and should not be included?

1) Replace the child's toothbrush after 72 hours
2) The child may return to school after 24 hours on antibiotics
3) It is important to finish all of the medication as prescribed.
4) Force the child to drink at least 24 ounces of fluid per day.

Option #4 should not be included. You cannot force children to do anything. They may be reluctant to eat or drink because of pain, so pain should be addressed.

7. A nurse is completing a health history for a nine-month old-infant. Which of the following should the nurse identify as risk factors for otitis media? **Select all that apply.**

1) Secondhand smoke exposure
2) Propping bottles for feedings
3) Daycare attendance
4) Low socioeconomic status

All of these items are risk factors for OM. The two most significant identifiable risk factors are degree of exposure to other children and family socioeconomic status.

8. A nurse is providing home care instructions for a teenager just diagnosed with infectious mononucleosis. Which of the following symptoms should the family report immediately to their provider? **Select all that apply.**

1) Abdominal pain
2) Difficulty swallowing
3) Extreme fatigue
4) Difficulty breathing
5) Temperature >102 F

Options #1, #2, and #4 are correct. Mono can cause splenic enlargement so abdominal pain can be an ominous sign. #2 and #4 indicate throat swelling. #3 and #5 are not uncommon symptoms in patients with mono.

9. A provider orders a throat culture for a 4-year-old patient in the emergency department. The nurse enters the room and finds the patient agitated, drooling, and sitting up leaning on her arms. What is the appropriate action of the nurse at this time?

1) Notify the provider
2) Continue with the procedure and notify the provider
3) Auscultate the patient's lungs
4) Take the child's vital signs

Option #1 is correct. This is a sign of possible epiglottitis and impending airway failure. The provider needs to be notified immediately and preparations for an emergency airway should be taken.

10. Which of the following symptoms are early signs of impending airway obstruction? **Select all that apply.**

1) Tachypnea
2) Tachycardia
3) Decorticate posturing
4) Restlessness
5) Cyanosis

Options #1, #2, and #4 are correct. #3 is a sign of a neurological deficit. #5 is a late sign.

11. What is the most effective way to promote infection control when caring for a hospitalized patient with RSV?

1) Meticulous handwashing
2) Restrict visitors
3) Contact precautions
4) Grouping RSV patients together

Option #1 is correct. The other options will all help prevent infection, but the best measure that will do the most good is handwashing!

12. A 10-year-old child is admitted for treatment of bacterial pneumonia. Upon assessment, the child's vital signs are: T-101.2, R-34, P-122, and BP 110/72. SpO2 95%. Lung auscultation reveals crackles at the bases bi-laterally. What is the priority action of the nurse at this time?

1) Administer an antipyretic.
2) Administer antibiotics.
3) Administer oxygen.
4) Call the provider.

Option #2 is correct. This child has bacterial pneumonia and needs antibiotics to clear the infection and relieve symptoms. An antipyretic is appropriate, but not more important than the antibiotic. Oxygen is not necessary at this time. All of these symptoms are expected for a child hospitalized with pneumonia and there is no need to call the provider at this time.

13. A nurse is called emergently to the hospital playroom and finds a 2-year-old child who is cyanotic, cannot speak, and collapses in front of the nurse. What is the appropriate immediate action of the nurse?

1) Begin CPR with chest compressions
2) Begin 5 cycles of back blows and chest thrusts
3) Administer oxygen by mask
4) Call the code team

Option #2 is correct. This child is 2-yrs-old and in the playroom with sudden onset. He is likely choking. For a witnessed collapse, the nurse should do 5 cycles of CPR or back blows/chest thrusts before calling the code team. Administering oxygen will not help if the airway is obstructed.

14. An adolescent comes to the school nurse's office with complaints of an asthma exacerbation and severe shortness of breath. Upon assessment, the nurse auscultates but hears no breath sounds despite a respiratory rate of 56. What action should the nurse take?

> 1) Administer the teen's albuterol inhaler immediately
> 2) Administer oxygen by facemask at 10L
> 3) Call 911
> 4) Have the teen breathe into a paper bag

Option #3 is correct. Absent breath sounds, SOB and tachypnea creates a very ominous picture of impending respiratory failure and imminent respiratory arrest.

15. A nurse is caring for a child hospitalized with asthma. The nurse enters the room and assesses VS: P-146, T-97.2, R-26, BP 96/24, SpO2 94%. The child is agitated, shaking and crying. What is the appropriate initial action of the nurse at this time?

> 1) Check the medical record to note the time of the last breathing treatment
> 2) Call the provider
> 3) Request an order for Benadryl to be given as a sedative
> 4) Discuss possible reasons for agitation with the child's mother

Option #1 is correct. Bronchodilators such as albuterol can cause tachycardia, jitteriness, and agitation. If a recent breathing treatment was given, that would explain the adverse effects.

16. How should the nurse advise a family about the best way to see if their metered-dose-inhaler is full?

> 1) Count each actuation and keep track of cumulative use
> 2) Place the inhaler in water to see if it floats
> 3) Test with one actuation in the air to see if vapor appears
> 4) Shake the inhaler to see if liquid is heard

Option #1 is correct. This is the only accurate way to track inhaler usage. Some inhalers have counters on them. Placing the inhaler in water can destroy the propellant and render it useless. Even if an inhaler seems full, it could be propellant remaining and not medication.

17. A child is hospitalized for asthma for the third time in a year. Which questions should the nurse ask the family? **Select all that apply.**

1) Tell me about the daily use of your inhaler.
2) What is your asthma rescue plan?
3) How do you plan to come for follow up care?
4) What do you think is causing the need for repeated hospital visits?
5) What is the most difficult part of your asthma management plan?

All of these questions are appropriate. The family may be using expired medications. They may be using preventive meds as rescue meds and they may not understand the rescue plan. Their perception of the challenges is critical. Is the burden financial, time, or other?

18. What is the priority nursing goal when caring for a patient with cystic fibrosis?

1) Preventing infection
2) Prolonging life
3) Promoting adequate nutrition
4) Optimizing development

Option #1 is correct. The most critical element of CF treatment is prevention of infection, which can cause scar tissue in the lungs, decreasing elasiticity, and declining lung function, which ultimately accelerates the arrival of death. Prolonging life may not be the patient's wish. Nutrition is important, but mostly to assist in preventing infection.

19. A 16-year-old patient has just undergone his second lung transplant for cystic fibrosis and is currently in rejection of the newly implanted organ. He is placed in critical care and is a top priority to receive another lung for a third transplant. The teen tells the nurse he wants to refuse the transplant but his parents will not permit it. What is the appropriate action of the nurse at this time?

1) Help the teen to accept his parents' decision
2) Tell the parents about the teen's wishes and ask them to comply
3) Have an interdisciplinary team meeting with the teen and parents to discuss options and prognosis
4) Ask the hospital's legal department about medical emancipation

The correct option is #3. This is the best initial way to reach a consensus on treatment.

20. A 9-year-old has a unilateral chest tube placed after a traumatic pneumothorax. Which of the following constitutes appropriate chest tube management?

1) Administration of opioids for pain
2) Enforce strict bed rest
3) Maintain integrity of the dressing over the site
4) Adjust the vacuum setting as needed

Option #3 is correct. Opioids are not usually necessary for chest tube pain. Acetaminophen is usually adequate. Children may ambulate with a chest tube. Vacuum settings should be maintained exactly as prescribed. If a change is needed, the nurse must call the provider.

Nursing Management in Renal and Urinary Tract Disorders

Judy Duvall, EdD, RN, MSN

Edited by Sylvia Rayfield & Associates, Inc.

Keeping your body healthy is an expression of gratitude to the whole cosmos-the trees, the clouds, everything.

Thich Nhat Hanh

Key Concepts:

- ♪ **System Specific Physiology**
- ♪ **Diagnostic Testing**
- ♪ **Nephrotoxins**
- ♪ **Medications for Renal Disorders**
- ♪ **Urinary Catheters**
- ♪ **Acute Kidney Injury(AKI)/Acute Renal Failure(ARF)**
- ♪ **Chronic Kidney Disease(CKD)/Chronic Renal Failure(CRF)**
- ♪ **Kidney Filter Functioning**
- ♪ **Practice Questions, Answers and Rationale**

The kidneys are amazing organs. They receive about 20-25% of the cardiac output. There is a direct correlation between the amount of cardiac output and renal output. Here is an easy way to think about this connection.

- 🍂 *6L of cardiac output = 60 mL of urine per hour*
- 🍂 *5L of cardiac output = 50 mL of urine per hour*
- 🍂 *4L of cardiac output = 40 mL of urine per hour*
- 🍂 *3L of cardiac output = 30 mL of urine per hour (This low output is a red flag).*
- 🍂 *2L of cardiac output = 20 mL of urine per hour*
- 🍂 *1L of cardiac output = 10 mL of urine per hour*
- 🍂 *0L of cardiac output = 0 mL of urine per hour*

From this, it can be determined that even though there may be no renal disease, if there is heart disease that affects cardiac output, the kidneys will be affected. This can be labeled as **PRE RENAL.**

Most people are born with two kidneys but can function with one. The functions of the kidneys include producing urine; however, that is a small role. The kidneys remove toxins and wastes from the body through the process of excretion. They regulate the amount of water and sodium in the blood, which helps control fluid balance. The kidneys play a large role in the regulation of blood pressure by producing the enzyme renin. They regulate the pH of the blood by excreting hydrogen ions or bicarbonate. They produce a hormone called erythropoietin, which simulates the production of red blood cells. And the kidneys are also activate Vitamin D, which stimulates bone development.

When trying to remember nursing intervention for clients with urinary tract disorders, ask yourself if the kidney is functioning as a filter or not. If the filter is damaged, like in acute or chronic renal failure and glomerulonephritis, the nursing intervention changes to restricting fluids. This can be labeled as **INTRA RENAL.** If there is no intrarenal problem, the filter is working well. Common conditions surrounding the kidney but not involving the filter system include bladder and kidney infections, kidney stones, after a TURP, urinary tract trauma, neoplasm, or where there is bleeding. This may be labeled as **POST RENAL.** In this case, the nursing intervention is to flush the urinary tract. Push fluids, either orally, IV, or both.

As a person ages, it is normal to lose kidney tissue. There is a decrease in the number of functioning nephrons, which results in a decreased glomerular filtration rate (GFR), increased serum creatinine, and increased blood urea nitrogen (BUN). This is known as CRI (chronic renal insufficiency). The geriatric client experiences decreased excretion of drugs, which can lead to toxicity and an inability to excrete medications. There is a decreased ability to concentrate urine, which can result in nocturia.

It's all about SAFETY!

WE WILL USE THE ACRONYM SAFETY FOR ORGANIZATION OF CONCEPTS TO HELP SIMPLIFY YOUR LEARNING.

PASS *NCLEX®*!

S   System specific assessment

A   Assess for risk and respond

F   Find change/trends and intervene

E   Evaluate pharmacology

T   Teach/practice infection control, health promotion

Y   Your management—legal/ethical/scope of practice, identity, errors, delegation, faulty equipment/staff, privacy, confidentiality, falls/ hazards

---

Increased Weight Gain, Elevated Blood Pressure, and Edema

- A gain of 1kg = a fluid gain of 1000 mL. Daily weights are a noninvasive, inexpensive tool to assess fluid balance. Weight should be performed at the same time, on the same scale, and with the same clothing.

- Elevated blood pressure may indicate fluid overload. Renin-Angiotensin-Aldosterone System is a natural protector. If the kidneys sense a decrease in blood flow they release renin. Renin causes the release of angiotensin I. Angiotensin converting enzyme (angiotensinogen) converts angiotensin I to angiotensin II, which is a very potent vasoconstrictor. This results in an increase in blood pressure. Renin also stimulates the adrenal glands to release aldosterone, which causes the retention of sodium and water. This increases the blood volume and therefore the blood pressure. The kidneys are very sensitive to blood pressure/blood flow. If the mean arterial pressure (MAP) decreases below 60-65 mmHg, blood flow to the kidneys is compromised. A lack of blood flow to the kidneys results in ischemia and kidney failure.

$$MAP = \frac{1 \text{ systolic} + 2 \text{ diastolic pressures}}{3}$$

- Periorbital edema occurs in glomerulonephritis and preeclampsia. Pedal edema is swelling of the feet and legs. Pedal edema can be pitting when an indentation remains. Pitting edema can also be found in the sacral area. You may see pitting edema classified as 1+-4+, but this is a subjective finding. Nonpitting edema occurs in lymphedema and myxedema. Anasarca is generalized edema.

Urinary Output

Normal urinary output is 0.5 mL/kg/hr for an adult. Some sources consider a urinary output of 30 mL/hr as a normal output; however, this is the lowest possible number of normal and is based on a body weight of 60 kg. As we all know, the population of the United States has gotten heavier, therefore calculating urinary output based on weight is more accurate. Causes of low output can include both decreased cardiac output as discussed earlier or renal disease. Nursing interventions to increase renal output should ideally begin before the client's output reaches the minimum normal number of 30 mL/hr. Normal output is 0.5-1 mL/kg/hr for a child and 2 mL/kg/hr for an infant or toddler.

Diagnostic Testing

Urinalysis -normal color should be pale yellow-amber, clear, and nearly odorless.

- Color and odor are strong indicators of abnormalities.
    - Pink, red or dark smoky color - hematuria (think UTI, kidney stone, tumor, glomerulonephritis, anticoagulants)
    - Yellow-brown to olive green - excess bilirubin (think liver disease)
    - Orange-red - drug effect (think Pyridium, rifampin)
    - Green - drug or food effect (Vitamin B, Propofol, dyes)
    - Cloudy - infection
    - Foul odor- infection
    - Ammonia smell – urine allowed to stand too long
    - Colorless – excess fluid intake, renal failure, or diabetes insipidus

- Protein (random dipstick) normally 0-Trace; 24-hour urine <150 mg/day Persistent proteinuria is characteristic of acute or chronic renal failure, glomerulonephritis, and heart failure. In absence of disease, think strenuous exercise, high protein diet, stress, or fever.

- Glucose normally is not present. If it is, think diabetes mellitus (normal renal threshold is 180 mg/dl).

- Ketones are not normally present. Think diabetic ketoacidosis, starvation, and dehydration.

- Bilirubin is normally not present. Think liver disease. Bilirubin may appear in urine before jaundice appears.

- Specific gravity- 1.003-1.030
    If < 1.003, think overhydration, excessive diuresis, or diabetes insipidus.
    If >1.030, think dehydration, proteinuria, or glycosuria.
    If fixed ~1.010, think end stage renal disease, kidneys unable to concentrate urine.

- RBCs normally <4/hpf. If >4/hpf, think cystitis, renal calculi, cancer, glomerulonephritis, post-kidney biopsy, trauma, or tuberculosis.

- WBCs 0-5/hpf. If > 5/hpf, think urinary tract infection or inflammation.

- pH 4.0-8.0 (average 6.0).
    If > 8.0, think urinary tract infection or urine allowed to stand too long.
    If < 4.0 think respiratory or metabolic acidosis.

Urine can also be collected to measure specific elements such as electrolytes, glucose, protein, catecholamines, creatinine, and 17 ketosteroids. Specimen collection time can range from 2-24 hours. Urine culture to confirm suspected urinary tract infection. Use sterile container and instruct the client to only touch the outside of the container. Cleanse the meatus using three antiseptic wipes (from front to back on females, have males retract foreskin and cleanse glans). Instruct the client to begin to urinate and then to "catch" urine in the sterile container. Urine is normally sterile, but bacteria are present in the urethra. In order to confirm a UTI, a bacterial colony count of $>10^5$/mL must be present.

- **Creatinine Clearance**

    The 24-hour creatinine clearance is the "gold standard" of evaluation of kidney function. The creatinine clearance is a reflection of the GFR. Normal GFR is 85-125 mL/min. As the nephrons begin to fail, the GFR decreases. A GFR of < 15 mL/min is usually indicative of renal failure. The creatinine clearance is a 24-hour urine collection. Nursing responsibility includes discarding the first specimen when the test is started and then collecting all urine for the next 24 hours. It is also necessary to obtain a serum creatinine at some point during the 24-hour period.

    Creatinine clearance = Urine creatinine (mg/dl) x Urine volume (mL/min)
    Serum creatinine (mg/dl)
    Normal creatinine clearance is 80-135 mL/min

Renal Labs

Test	Normal Level	Important Points
BUN: Blood Urea Nitrogen	6–20 mg/dl	Other factors can cause an elevated BUN—think dehydration, GI bleeding, trauma, infections, high protein diet, steroids
Creatinine	0.5–1.5 mg/dl	Levels >2 are a cause for concern. Creatinine is more reliable than BUN for renal function.
BUN/Creatinine Ratio	10–20:1	>20:1 Think prerenal problem <10:1 Think intrarenal problem

Diagnostic Procedures

Test	Purpose	Nursing Responsibility
KUB (x-ray of abdomen and pelvis)	To determine size, shape, and location of kidneys; stones and foreign bodies can be seen.	Noninvasive. May need bowel prep.
IVP (intravenous pyelogram)	Injection of contrast to visualize urinary tract. Tumors, lesions, cysts, and obstruction can be seen as distortions in the normal shape of kidney, ureter, or bladder.	Bowel prep is needed. Inquire about allergy to x-ray contrast, shellfish, or iodine. Evaluate renal labs. Hold metformin 24 hours before and 48 hours after test.
Renal Arteriogram	Visualizes renal blood vessels. Can diagnose renal artery stenosis, abnormalities of blood vessels; help differentiate between cysts and tumors. Also used to evaluate blood flow for potential kidney donors	Same as above. Requires informed consent. Entry is via femoral artery. Post-procedure, observe for bleeding, hematoma formation, assess pedal pulses, vital signs, and maintain bed rest with procedural leg straight for prescribed period
Renal Ultrasound	Used to detect masses and obstructions.	Noninvasive. No bowel prep required. No exposure to x-ray or contrast.
CT Scan	Kidneys well visualized. Tumors, cysts, abscesses, and stones can be seen. Adrenal glands are also visualized.	May or may not need contrast. Ask about allergies to shellfish, iodine, or x-ray dye. The client must be able to lie very still during the procedure.
MRI	Kidneys are visualized. Tumors, cysts can be seen but stones are not visualized.	Ask client if he is claustrophobic (may need sedation) or has any metal implants. Contraindicated in those with an implanted pacemaker, Implantable Cardioverter Defibrillator (AICD), magnetic implants, etc.

Test	Purpose	Nursing Responsibility
Cystoscopy	Inside of bladder is examined using a scope. Ureteral catheters can be inserted, stones removed, biopsies taken, and bleeding lesions can be treated.	May or may not need general anesthesia. Informed consent required. After procedure urine may be pink tinged. There may be mild burning, urgency, and frequency after the procedure.
Renal Biopsy	Tissue is obtained to determine the type of renal disease or to follow the progression of the disease. Usually done percutaneously by a needle inserted into the lower lobe of the kidney with CT or ultrasound guidance.	Absolute contraindications include bleeding disorders, uncontrolled hypertension, or one kidney. Pre-procedure: CBC, PT/INR, and bleeding/clotting time. May need type and crossmatch. Anticoagulants and antiplatelet meds must be held. After procedure, a pressure dressing is applied. Keep client on affected side for 30–60 minutes; bed rest for 24 hours. Routine post-op VS. Observe for bleeding, flank pain, hypotension. No lifting for about one week post-procedure.

Nephrotoxins

FIND CHANGE AND INTERVENE

If your client has Chronic Renal Insufficiency (CRI), question orders for potentially nephrotoxic drugs. These include aminoglycoside antibiotics (gentamycin, streptomycin, tobramycin, neomycin) as well as other antibiotics, such as vancomycin, cephalosporins, levofloxacin (requires lower dosing), and rifampin. Other nephrotoxic drugs include NSAIDS, aspirin, chemotherapy, heroin, cocaine, and lithium.

X-ray contrast can also be nephrotoxic. If your client has an elevated creatinine prior to receiving contrast, be certain he is receiving IV fluids before and after the procedure. Often acetylcysteine is ordered to be given one day prior to the procedure and 1-2 days after. This is also given to clients who have been on metformin. Acetylcysteine is available in a liquid form that smells strongly of sulfur. Dilute in small amount of juice and encourage client to swallow it quickly. It may be helpful to have the client hold his nose to avoid smelling the drug.

Monitor intake and output to determine if the renal function is sufficient.

EVALUATE PHARMACOLOGY These *NCLEX*® Standards are for administration of every type of drug in every system.

Common Medications For Renal Disorders

Medication	Prior to Administration	Nursing Actions/ Education	Alerts
ACE Inhibitors Angiotensin Converting Enzyme The **"pril"** drugs Benaze**pril** (Lotensin) Capto**pril** (Capoten) Enala**pril** (Vasotec) Lisino**pril** (Zestril) Moexi**pril** (Univasc) Rami**pril** (Altace)	Determine baseline BP. Caution with renal or liver impairment. Determine other medications that may interact. Determine allergies.	ACE Inhibitors are contraindicated in clients who have renal artery stenosis and are not effective in those with End Stage Renal Disease (ESRD). However, they can be nephroprotective in clients with diabetic nephropathy. They are also the antihypertensive of choice in those with acute glomerulonephritis. Evaluate for first dose drop. Report headache, weakness, diarrhea, dizziness, and rash.	Verify orders due to some contraindications. Hypotension A tendency to cough. Renal failure Liver failure Angioedema Decrease in WBC's

Medication	Prior to Administration	Nursing Actions/ Education	Alerts
"ARBS" Angiotensin II Receptor Blockers, also called "sartans" Lo**sartin** (Cozaar) Telmi**sartan** (Micardis) Cande**sartan** (Atacand) Epro**sartan** (Teveten) Val**sartan** (Diovan) Olme**sartan** (Benecar)	Determine other medications that may interact such as Lasix or Lithium. Determine allergies. Caution with renal or liver impairment.	ARBS are contraindicated in clients who have renal artery stenosis and are not effective in those with End Stage Renal Disease (ESRD). However, they can be nephroprotective in clients with diabetic nephropathy. Report headache, weakness, diarrhea, dizziness, and rash May cause birth defects in pregnant women. Decongestants increase BP. Micardis may interact with Lanoxin.	Hypotension Possible erectile dysfunction.

Antibiotics
 	
Cephalosporins:
  Cefazolin (Ancef)
  Cefuroxime (Ceftin)
  Cefprozil (Cefzil)
  Cefadroxil (Duricef)
  Ceftriaxone
    (Rocephin)
  Cefixime (Suprax)
	Watch for elevated temperature.
	
	Determine allergies to drug or penicillin.
	
	Caution with renal or liver impairment.
	
	Determine other medications that may interact.
		If client is taking antacids, the antacids should be taken 2 hours prior to or after these medications.
		
		Evaluate for cough.
			GI symptoms
			Nausea/vomiting
			
			Itching, skin rash, difficulty with breathing or swallowing.
			
			Monitor Blood Urea Nitrogen and Creatinine levels.
			
			Fainting

Sulfa Drugs Sulfamethoxazole (Bactrim) (Septra)	Determine allergies to sulfa drugs including past reactions.	Educate the client in increasing fluid intake to help the drugs reach and clear the kidneys	Itching, skin rash, difficulty with breathing or swallowing.

Medication	Prior to Administration	Nursing Actions/ Education	Alerts
Calcium Channel Blockers relax and enlarge blood vessels causing a decrease in BP. Many of these drugs end in "**pine**". Amlodi**pine** (Norvasc) Amlodi**pine** with Atorvastatin (Caduet) Amlodi**pine** with Benazepril (Lotrel) Amlodi**pine** with Valsartan (Exforge) Felodi**pine** (Plendil) Nicardi**pine** (Cardene) Nisoldi**pine** (Sular) Verapamil (Calan)	Determine baseline vital signs. Note that the combination drugs must be treated as giving both drugs. Since Caduet is given with a statin, the liver enzymes should be determined. If given with a "**pril**," allergies to this med or tendency to cough should be determined.	Educate client to keep personal BP/pulse record. Educate for dizziness or lightheadedness, flushing, or feeling warm. Monitor heart rate. This drug slows the heart rate. Peripheral edema is a very common side effect.	Hypotension Dizziness Weakness Fainting
Drugs that lower the BP often are given in combination with each other or with diuretics. Diuretics work by excreting salt and water through the kidney causing a volume loss.	Determine allergies to sulfa drugs. Check renal function. Determine baseline vital signs.	Administer during day as urinary frequency will occur. Measure I&O Weigh daily Educate to eat foods that are high in potassium. Avoid foods high in sodium.	**Side effects and adverse reactions to these meds:** Too much fluid may be excreted causing dizziness and lightheadedness, and hypotension. Causes loss of potassium which can affect the electrical conduction in the heart, hypokalemia. Dehydration.

Medication	Prior to Administration	Nursing Actions/ Education	Alerts
Diuretics These are just a few of the common diuretics. Furosemide (Lasix) Bumetanide (Bumex) Torsemide (Demadex) Hydrochlorothiazide (Hydrodiuril)	Assess for client allergies especially to sulfa	Educate for daily weights, foods, or drugs that will not interfere with this medication. Educate to eat foods high in potassium Watch for muscle cramps and thirst. Monitor for low potassium	Hypokalemia Hyponatremia Tinnitus, hearing loss, ototoxicity except with hydrochlorothiazide Hypocalcemia except with hydrochlorothiazide
Common K+ sparing diuretics Spironolactone (Aldactone) Amioloride (Midamor)	Check K+ levels.	Educate for frequent K+ checks. Educate for GI upsets.	Hyperkalemia GI upsets and peptic ulcer.

		Diuretic side effects can be summed up with these 6 issues
		    Dehydration
		    Hypotension
		    Diuresis
		    Electrolyte imbalance
		    Allergy to Sulfa
		    Tinnitus (except with
		        Thiazides)
			Dry mouth especially on the first dose.
			
			I&O, daily weights
			
			Evaluate muscle cramps and weakness.
			
			Evaluate for hives, swelling of lips, tongue, and difficulty breathing.

TEACH INFECTION CONTROL

Urinary Catheters

Inserting and maintaining ureteral catheters is a nursing responsibility. Catheter-associated urinary tract infection (CAUTI) is the leading nosocomial infection in the urinary system. Urinary catheters should only be used when it is absolutely necessary. This would include clients who must have accurate output measurements such as those who are critically ill; relief of urinary retention due to obstruction, paralysis or inability to void; during and immediately after abdominal or pelvic surgery, as well as surgery on the urinary tract; those with Stage 3-4 pressure sores that can be contaminated with urine that impedes healing; and those who are terminally ill or suffer from severe pain that makes positioning and changing extremely painful. Infection control is vital when working with client's catheters.

If your client has an indwelling catheter, ask about removal as soon as possible. If the client spikes a fever, obtain a culture and remove the catheter. Question the necessity of reinserting it. Intermittent catheterization is associated with a decreased risk of infection. External catheters may also be used to decrease risk of infection.

Decrease in urinary output and MAP

In order to avoid acute kidney injury, fluids are given to increase MAP > 65 mmHg. The initial fluid of choice is either 0.9% normal saline or Lactated Ringers (isotonic crystalloid). Often there is an order to administer a fluid bolus (250-500 mL) rapidly. Monitor vital signs closely and assess for signs of fluid volume overload. If the client has a CVP or pulmonary artery catheter in place, monitor for increases or decreases in CVP, right atrial pressure or PCWP. Observing for changes in trends is crucial and can avoid acute renal failure.

Accuracy of Assignments

Assign the client with the most unpredictable outcome to the RN who has the most experience and skill. Avoid assigning clients who require teaching, IV medications, frequent assessments, and changes in the plan of care, or evaluation of labs to the LPN.

It is acceptable to have the CNA measure output and assist with vital sign monitoring; however, it is the RN's responsibility to evaluate the findings.

.

Analysis Of Priority Nursing Interventions And Concepts

Acute Kidney Injury(AKI)/Acute Renal Failure(ARF)

Prerenal: This is the result of factors outside of the kidney. A decrease in systemic circulation due to hemorrhage, shock, burns, or decreased cardiac output results in decreased renal blood flow. The Renin-Angiotensin-Aldosterone system is stimulated, causing vasoconstriction and increasing volume by retaining sodium and water. The pituitary gland releases ADH and increases the blood volume by retaining water. The oliguria associated with prerenal problems is usually reversible. If the underlying pathology is not rapidly reversed, it can lead to intrarenal problems as the kidneys lose their ability to compensate and glomeruli are damaged.

Intrarenal: This is the result of direct damage to the kidney tissue that causes destruction of nephrons. Causes include prolonged ischemia, nephrotoxins, hemolysis, or rhabdomyolysis (breakdown of muscle cells), which can block the filter. Primary kidney diseases such as acute glomerulonephritis or autoimmune diseases can also cause intrarenal failure. The most common form of intrarenal failure is Acute Tubular Necrosis (ATN). This is most often due to ischemia, sepsis, or nephrotoxins. ATN is responsible for about 90% of AKI.

Postrenal: This is caused by an obstruction below the kidneys. This would include BPH, bladder cancer, stones, strictures, spinal cord injury, neuromuscular disorders, and trauma. If the flow of urine is obstructed, urine refluxes into the renal pelvis and results in hydronephrosis. If the obstruction is unilateral, it rarely results in azotemia. Bilateral obstruction that can be relieved within 48 hours often results in complete recovery.

Nursing Interventions ARF
- **Assess for fluid volume overload**
    - VS, daily weight, intake/output, evaluate for edema, auscultate lung sounds
    - Follow ordered fluid restriction during oliguric phase.
- **Assess for electrolyte imbalances**
    - Monitor for dysrhythmias due to hyperkalemia or hypocalcemia.
    - Restrict potassium intake, sodium intake, and phosphate intake
    - Increase calcium intake or give phosphate-binding agents (Renagel, NuPhos)
    - Assess for and treat metabolic acidosis
- **Nutrition**
    - Adequate protein intake and calories
    - May need enteral nutrition or TPN

- **Assess for fatigue due to anemia**
  - Monitor Hgb/Hct
  - GI prophylaxis
  - May need blood replacement
  - Give erythropoietin (Epogen, Procrit)
  - Provide rest periods
  - Oxygen to maintain $SPO_2 > 90\text{-}92\%$
- **Avoid complications of bedrest**
  - DVT prophylaxis
  - Stool softeners
  - Passive and active range of motion
  - Turn, cough, deep breath, incentive spirometer
- **Avoid infection**
  - If on dialysis, observe access site for signs of infection and observe vital signs.
  - Dialysis pulls off large amounts of fluid and electrolytes and can cause hypovolemic shock.
  - Monitor for increased temperature
- **Emotional support for client/family**

Goals of treatment
- Recovery of kidney function
- Normal fluid and electrolyte balance
- Avoid complications

Chronic Kidney Disease(CKD)/Chronic Renal Failure(CRF)

Incidence
Over 26 million Americans have been diagnosed with CKD. CKD has five stages. Stage 5 requires renal replacement therapy (hemodialysis, peritoneal dialysis, or transplant) to maintain life. About 90,000 die each year from CKD.

Risk factors
Hypertension, diabetes, history of kidney disease, family history of kidney disease, frequent UTIs. African-Americans, Native-Americans, and Hispanics are at higher risk of developing CKD than Caucasians.

Nursing Interventions

- ◆ **Monitor for electrolyte imbalances ($K+$, $Ca++$, PO_4, $Na+$)**
- ◆ **Monitor for anemia and bleeding**
  - Need blood transfusions
  - Erythropoetin replacement—Procrit, Epogen
- ◆ **High risk for CAD, dysrhythmias**
- ◆ **Monitor Respiratory status**
  - May have Kussmaul's respirations due to metabolic acidosis
  - May have dyspnea from fluid overload/pulmonary edema
  - Predisposition to pulmonary infection
- ◆ **Monitor GI status**
  - Anorexia, nausea, vomiting develop
  - Malnutrition and weight loss may occur
  - Stomatitis with ulcerations is common
  - Metallic taste in the mouth
  - Constipation
  - May have GI bleeding
- ◆ **Monitor for neurological changes**
  - Can be due to electrolyte imbalance, increased waste products in the blood, or metabolic acidosis
  - CNS can be depressed
  - Seizures may occur
- ◆ **Monitor for pruritis, bruising**
  - Provide good skin care
  - Observe for the development of infection due to scratching
- ◆ **Monitor dialysis access site**
  - Peritoneal-catheter inserted through the abdominal wall
    - Exit site infection-observe for redness, tenderness and exudates
    - Peritonitis-observe for cloudy return of dialysate
    - Send cloudy fluid for culture
    - Weight is the best gauge of fluid removal
    - Assess lung sounds for fluid overload
  - Hemodialysis access sites
  - AV fistula/graft
    - Takes 2-4 weeks to mature
    - Assess for bruit and thrill
    - No BP, IV starts, lab draws in arm with the fistula
  - Temporary Vascular Access
    - Inserted percutaneously in internal jugular (IJ), subclavian or femoral vein.
    - Femoral access can remain in place for 1 week; IJ or subclavian for 3 weeks.
    - Do not use for IV access or blood draws. Only the dialysis nurse can access

- **Long term-cuffed catheters**
  - Tip is in the right atrium
  - Inserted surgically; exits on upper chest wall
  - Can be used for long-term access
  - Meticulous care to avoid infection
  - Do not use for IV access or lab draws. Only the dialysis nurse can access
- **Complications of hemodialysis**
  - Hypotension, muscle cramping, hepatitis, infection, disequilibrium syndrome, cardiovascular disease, and exsanguinations. Watch these YouTubes for further learning:
  - http://www.youtube.com/watch?v=jpQtnVC47iI&feature=related
  - http://www.youtube.com/watch?v=JXQb-0aDSrc&feature=related

Kidney transplantation

Even though renal transplantation is the best treatment option for most people with End Stage Renal Disease (ESRD) < 5% receive an organ. There is a tremendous demand for organs; however, a short supply. About 75% of kidney transplants use a cadaver kidney, the remaining 25% are live donors.

- Clients receiving transplants receive large doses of steroids to prevent rejection. This renders them extremely immunosuppressed.
- Infection control is vital. Visitors may be limited. Client and family education is extremely important.

SAVE A LIFE. SIGN YOUR ORGAN DONATION CARD

Blood Transfusions

Administering blood products is a frequent nursing function in all areas of the hospital and in the outpatient setting. Patients with ESRD need frequent transfusions due to the lack of erythropoietin.

Prior to administering a transfusion there must be consent to receive blood. There is a risk of transmitting blood borne pathogens through a blood transfusion and some religions prohibit the acceptance of blood or blood products.

There must be a type and cross-match completed prior to administering blood. Two RNs must check the patient and the unit of blood at the bedside prior to beginning the transfusion. Blood must be administered through an IV access that is at least a 20 gauge. Normal saline is the only solution that can be given with blood. And blood must be administered using special tubing with a filter. Vital signs, including temperature, are accessed prior to beginning the transfusion. The RN must stay in the client's room for the first 15 minutes that the transfusion is running. Vital signs are repeated at 15 minutes and hourly thereafter with a final set being obtained after the transfusion is complete.

Blood must be started within 30 minutes of removal from the blood bank, so be certain that IV site is functioning well. The transfusion must be completed within 4 hours.

Transfusion reactions range from very severe and life threatening to mild itching and hives. Acute hemolytic transfusion reaction can be life threatening. The urine darkens due to destroyed red blood cells, there is severe back pain, and the client can have circulatory collapse. Clients can also suffer an anaphylactic reaction. There can be a febrile reaction or itching and hives. If a transfusion reaction is suspected, immediately stop the transfusion and infuse normal saline with new tubing through the line. Assess and treat the client. Notify the Health Care Provider and the blood bank. A urine sample will need to be sent to the lab and the blood unit with the tubing attached will be returned to the blood bank. Finally, an occurrence report must be completed.

You can usually anticipate an increase of 1-2 grams of hemoglobin for each unit administered. Remember sodium citrate is an anticoagulant/preservative used in blood and that combines with calcium and that can result in hypocalcemia. Think "Skinny Cat" and observe for Chvostek or Trousseau's sign.

Acute Post-streptococcal Glomerulonephritis (APSGN)

Most commonly occurs in children but all age groups can be affected. APSGN develops 1-3 weeks after a strep infection. Antigen-antibody complexes form and are deposited in the glomeruli. The classic symptom is "coca-cola" colored urine, edema, hypertension, and proteinuria. Edema initially is periorbital but can progress to generalized. Treatment is symptomatic. Bed rest is recommended until hematuria, proteinuria, and hypertension are resolved. Hypertension is treated by fluid/sodium restriction and diuretics. ACE inhibitors can also be given to treat hypertension. Antibiotics are only given if there is still an active strep infection. About 95% of those with APSGN recover completely with management of symptoms; however, 5% develop chronic glomerulonephritis, which slowly progresses to renal failure.

Nursing Interventions
- Monitor blood pressure closely, intake/output, daily weights, fluid restriction and maintain bed rest.
- Patient/family education focuses on the importance of completing the entire course of antibiotics.

UTI, Pyelonephritis, Kidney Stone
Nursing Interventions
- Force fluids orally. If unable to tolerate oral fluids may need IV.
- For infection, antibiotics are given.
- Pain can be an issue—assess and treat pain**—major issue with calculi.
- Strain urine for calculi
- I&O, daily weight, VS

TURP or Other Conditions with Bleeding/Clots
Nursing Interventions
- Maintain continuous bladder irrigation to keep urine pink with minimal small clots.
- Assess and treat pain.
- If client C/O bladder spasm, assess that urine is free flowing. May have medication ordered to treat bladder spasms.
- Keep track of irrigant instilled and calculate urine output.
- Notify surgeon immediately if catheter becomes occluded with clots.
- I&O, daily weight, VS

Urinary Diversions
Ileal Conduit
- Ureters are implanted into a portion of resected ileum or colon and an abdominal stoma is created.
- External appliance is necessary. It is normal to have mucus in the urine.
- Monitor post-op output and vital signs closely.
- Meticulous skin care is necessary.
- Observe stoma—it should be pink and moist.
- Educate client/family regarding stoma care and appliance changes.

Nephrostomy (catheter inserted into renal pelvis and brought to skin) or Ureterostomy (Ureters brought through abdominal wall)
- Monitor output and VS closely post-procedure..
- External appliances are required.
- There is a high risk for infection.
- Never clamp a nephrostomy tube.

FIND RISK AND PRIORITIZE—especially in emergencies
- Monitor and treat cardiac dysrhythmias
- Maintain fluid balance—fluids for hypotension, diuretics for fluid overload
- Observe for and treat bleeding
- Assess and treat electrolyte abnormalities
- Assess and treat infection before it becomes sepsis
- Maintain a safe environment—fall and seizure precautions

Expected outcomes

- **AKI** (ARF): Return of normal kidney function, maintenance of fluid and electrolyte balance, and avoidance of complications.
- **CKD** (CRF): Avoidance of complications, maintenance of dialysis access, maintenance of fluid/electrolyte balance
- **APSGN:** Maintenance of kidney function, control of blood pressure, lack of edema, clear yellow urine.
- **Cystitis:** Relief of burning, urgency, frequency. Complete full antibiotic course,(compliance is crucial). Repeat culture negative.
- **Pyelonephritis:** Relief of symptoms and negative urine and blood culture.
- **Calculi:** Passage of stone and understanding of prevention.

Trends

- Observe for decreasing or increasing urinary output.
- Observe for weight gain/loss.
- Observe for changes in vital signs.
- Observe for increasing BUN/creatinine, decreased pH, and hyperkalemia.

Cover your assets

- Make appropriate assignments.
- Notify Health Care Provider of changes in condition.
- Keep environment as safe as possible. Use fall and seizure precautions as appropriate.
- Question drugs that are nephrotoxic for clients with CRI.

The kidneys are amazing and very forgiving. Good nursing assessments and watching for subtle changes can allow the nurse to identify decreased renal blood flow before acute kidney injury occurs. It is estimated that about 20% of clients in a critical care unit at any given time have acute renal failure. Good nursing can definitely save a kidney!

YOUR MANAGEMENT

Commonalities that flow through client **SAFETY** of every body system and are heavily weighted on the **NCLEX®** can be condensed into the following table on **MANAGE.**

These standards currently count for as much as 23% of the total *NCLEX®* exam and are always a primary consideration for nursing.

PASS *NCLEX®*!

M   **Make sure of identity, accuracy of orders**

A   **Arrange privacy/confidentiality/consent/collaboration with other team**

N   **No injuries, falls, malfunctioning equipment or staff or hazards**

A   **Address errors, abuse, legalities, scope of practice—document**

G   **Give (delegate) orders to appropriate people**

E   **Evaluate priorities/response to treatment**

Questions to make you think. (Answers provided at the end of the chapter.)

1. A client with a urinary tract infection has an order for furosemide (Lasix). What is the nursing priority prior to administration?
    A. Determine the client's potassium level prior to administration
    B. Assess skin turgor
    C. Determine the accuracy of the order
    D. Teach the client the action and side effects of the drug

2. Which health care partner should be assigned for basic care and comfort to a client with chronic renal failure?
    A. An RN
    B. The LPN
    C. The CNA
    D. A Certified Nurse Practitioner

3. Which initial nursing assessments should be made for the client with renal failure? **Select ALL that apply.**
    A. Daily weights
    B. Intake and output
    C. Vital signs
    D. PSA testing
    E. Pitting edema

4. What is the priority nursing assessment prior to administering a blood transfusion?
    A. A signed consent form
    B. Determine the client's identity
    C. Determine the client's religion
    D. Determine client allergies

5. What size needle is needed for administration of a blood transfusion? Fill in the blank.

    _____

6. Assessment of a client with renal disease indicates the blood potassium level has changed from 4.5 to 6.0 over the last week. What is the nursing priority?
    A. Repeat the blood test tomorrow to make certain there is no mistake
    B. Notify the health care provider regarding this change
    C. Determine the client's vital signs
    D. Assess for additional symptoms

7. Which is the best assessment to determine an infant's urinary output?
    A. Daily weights
    B. Vital signs
    C. Number of wet diapers
    D. Assessment of skin turgor

8. The client has had a Foley catheter for 3 days and complains of burning around the catheter. Which action is priority?
    A. Inspect the area where client is burning
    B. Request a complete blood count
    C. Replace the Foley with a sterile catheter
    D. Determine the output for the last 24 hours

9. The client is to receive phenazopyridine (Pyridium). What is the priority teaching?
    A. The urine must be acidic before this drug can be utilized
    B. This drug turns the urine orange
    C. Clients allergic to penicillin should not take this drug
    D. The drug should be taken prior to bedtime

10. An 89-year old client is receiving medication that causes frequent urination. Which should be included in the teaching plan? **Select ALL that apply**
    A. Side effects of the medication
    B. Fall protocol
    C. Drinking several glasses of water
    D. Eating foods that are high in sodium
    E. To report cloudy or murky urine

11. An RN observes an LPN inserting a Foley catheter into the wrong orifice. Which is an appropriate nursing action?
    A. Tell the LPN immediately that she is inserting the catheter in the wrong orifice
    B. Write an error report regarding this matter
    C. Offer to help the LPN and get a sterile catheter
    D. Report the incident to the charge nurse

12. A client with renal calculi is taking ibuprofen (Advil). What is priority teaching?
    A. Drink 8 glasses of water a day with this drug
    B. Eat prior to taking the medication
    C. This medication will turn the urine red
    D. Clients allergic to penicillin should not take Advil

13. The client receiving peritoneal dialysis has 800mL intake and 700mL output from the dialysis catheter. What is the priority nursing action?
    A. Notify the health care provider
    B. Determine vital signs
    C. Reposition the client for better drainage
    D. Irrigate the dialysis catheter

14. The client is one hour post-op of a hemodialysis fistula in the left arm. Which nursing measures are most important? **Select ALL that apply.**
    A. Take blood pressure reading in the right arm
    B. Begin IV's in the fistula
    C. Check pulse in the right arm
    D. Place heat on the fistula
    E. Observe the fistula area for redness and heat

15. The client is crying after being told that hemodialysis must be initiated. What is the best nursing action?
    A. Reassure the client that everything will be good after the dialysis
    B. Listen to the client's concerns
    C. Notify the health provider to return for further explanation
    D. Leave the client alone to process the diagnosis

16. The client is scheduled for an MRI with contrast to examine the kidney. Which is the highest nursing priority prior to the exam?
    A. Determine an accurate identity of the client
    B. Remove all metal, eyeglasses, and jewelry
    C. Determine client's hemoglobin count
    D. Assess client for allergies

17. What is included in the teaching plan of a young school-age female client with a urinary tract infection?
    A. Lubricate the meatus with Vasoline
    B. Limit the time the child sits in the bathtub
    C. Provide scheduled times for bladder emptying
    D. Provide urine sticks to test urine at home

18. The client diagnosed with renal calculi has been discharged to "see if the stone will pass." What is priority teaching? **Select ALL that apply.**
    A. Recommend 8 glasses of water a day
    B. Recommend walking as much as possible
    C. Suggest taking aspirin for pain
    D. Ask client to call the provider for severe pain
    E. Ask client to return to the clinic within 2 weeks

19. During the insertion of an indwelling catheter, the tip of the device touches the underside of the sterile field. Which nursing action is priority?
    A. Cleanse the catheter tip with an antiseptic solution prior to re-insertion
    B. Obtain a new catheter and new gloves
    C. Back flush the catheter with an antibiotic solution after insertion
    D. Notify the provider to prescribe an antibiotic

20. Which is the best method to collect a urine sample from an infant? **Select ALL that apply.**
    A. Utilize the urine in a wet diaper
    B. Utilize a plastic collection bag
    C. Wash the area around the uretha
    D. Sit the infant on the potty for the collection
    E. Take the infant to the clinic for catheterization

21. Which are priorities when inserting an indwelling urinary catheter. **Select all that apply**
    A. Explaining the procedure to the client if conscious
    B. Utilize appropriate hand washing technique
    C. Utilize aseptic technique|
    D. Instill water into the balloon
    E. Anchoring the catheter to the bed linens.

Answers and Rationale

1. **Answer C.** The client may be receiving the Lasix for an unknown reason but the accuracy should be checked with the health care provider. A, B, and D are important but not priority.

2. **Answer C.** There is no reason that a certified nursing assistant cannot care for this client for basic care and comfort.

3. **Answer A, B, C, E.** All are vital assessments of renal disease. PSA testing is not a vital initial assessment that should be made by the nurse.

4. **Answer A.** If there is no consent, the other options do not matter. B and D would be next in priority.

5. **Answer: 20 gauge** is needed for blood viscosity.

6. **Answer B.** This potassium level is reaching a dangerous level and the provider should be notified immediately.

7. **Answer C.** The assessment of an infant's output is not as easy as I&O for an adult. Diapers are the preferred assessment.

8. **Answer A.** When the client complains, it is time to look and see what is happening. B, C, and D are all options but **A** is priority.

9. **Answer B.** This drug will turn the urine orange and may stain clothes but it is a wonderful numbing agent when there is a urinary tract infection. The other options are incorrect.

10. **Answers A**, **B**, and **E.** Clients should always be taught side effects of the medication and to report cloudy or murky urine as this may be a sign of infection. An 89-year old is likely to require fall protocol. We do not know enough about the medication to determine that we should automatically teach to replace with water or sodium.

11. **Answer C.** By offering to help and bring another sterile catheter, the nurse may avoid upsetting the client. Answering **A** would certainly advise the client that there is a problem. Reports may be later, but first things first.

12. **Answer B.** NSAIDS are likely to cause stomach ulcers if they are continually taken on an empty stomach. The other options are inappropriate for NSAIDS.

13. **Answer C.** The I&O indicates that 100mL is being retained which can place the client in fluid overload. Reposition first, keep an eye on vital signs, and notify the health provider if the repositioning does not work.

14. **Answers A, C,** and **E** are correct. IV's should be started in the opposite arm. Heat should not be applied to a new fistula.

15. **Answer B.** Listening and being with the client is always appropriate. Reassurance at this point may seem superficial since outcomes are unknown. C and D are not useful at this time.

16. **Answer D.** Allergies of contrast are priority. Other answers are good but not priority.

17. **Answer B.** A little girl's urethra is small and short. The longer she sits in the bathtub (especially with milk bath or other bath crystals), the greater the opportunity of a UTI. All other answers are inappropriate.

18. **Answers A** and **D.** Forcing fluids may assist the movement of the stone. The client should have access to pain medication for their comfort. Anyone who has experienced a kidney stone will assure the fact that they are not capable of walking very much. Aspirin may cause bleeding as the stone is passed. Two weeks is too long for this client to be re-assessed.

19. **Answer B.** Always prevent infection. All other answers will allow for the infection and then try to fix it!

20. **Answers B** and **D.** Collection bags for urine specimens are commonly used. The area is washed to provide for the removal of contaminants. Other answers are inappropriate.

21. **Answers A, B,** and **C** are all most priority. Sterile technique should be utilized to prevent infection. Sterile water should be instilled into the balloon and the catheter should NOT be anchored to the bed linens.

The Pediatric GENITOURINARY SYSTEM

Jessica Peck, DNP, RN, MSN, CPNP-PC, CNE
Edited by Sylvia Rayfield & Associates, Inc.

THE GREATEST RISK TO A CHILD'S GENITOURINARY SYSTEM IS CONGENTIAL DEFECT.

KEY CONCEPTS TO REMEMBER:

- ❖ Differentiate acute glomerulonephritis (AGN), acute post-streptococcal glomerulonephritis (APSGN) and nephrotic syndrome.
- ❖ Structural disorders of the genitourinary tract
- ❖ Urinary tract infections and enuresis

RENAL DISORDERS

What are the priorities in focused assessment?

Know your A-B-C's	Acute Post-Streptococcal Glomerulonephritis (APSGN)	Nephrotic Syndrome (NS)
Ask about the history	• AGN can happen for unknown reasons or can be an antibody-antigen response to a number of viruses • APSGN is what happens when a case of strep throat causes injury to the kidneys • Renal symptoms show up 10-21 days after the initial infection **Peak incidence 6-7 years of age.*	• NS occurs when alterations in the glomerular membrane causes proteins to flood out through the urine. • Cause is unknown. Can be congenital or acquired. • It is not a disease, but a group of symptoms, just as you see this group of kidneys below. **Peak incidence 2-7 years of age.*
	Risk Factors:	Risk Factors:

	• Recent viral or bacterial infection	• History of glomerular damage

B—Be aware of possible presenting symptoms you might detect on assessment	APSGN is all about **BLOOD**! The disease *attacks* the kidney and when you are attacked there is **blood**. It elevates **BLOOD** PRESSURE and causes hematuria (**BLOOD** in the urine).
	
	B—Bulging/edema around eyes (periorbital), **B**LOOD PRESSURE HIGH!!
	
	L—Lousy appetite, **L**ungs with crackles, **L**ooks really sick
	
	O—**O**liguria, **O**rthopnea
	
	O—**O**ut of sorts (very cranky!)
	
	D—**D**eathly pale, **D**yspnea, **D**istended neck veins
	
	LABS:
	
	• Throat Cx to look for strep
	• UA—BLOOD in urine, tea-colored, proteinuria, elevated specific gravity
	• Elevated BUN and creatinine
	• ASO titer- + means recent strep infection
	• CXR—look for pulmonary edema, cardiomegaly, and pleural effusions.
		NS is all about **PROTEIN**!! There is usually no hypertension and usually no hematuria.
		
		P—PROTEINURIA
		
		   • > 3.5g in 24 hours
		   • >3+ or 4+
		
		R—Really cranky and tired
		
		O—Oliguria, urine is dark and frothy
		
		T—Terrible appetite, N/V/D
		
		E—EDEMA
		
		   • worse in the morning
		   • improves during day
		   • dependent edema
		   • labia, scrotum, legs, ankles
		   • ASCITES
		
		I—Increased weight gain
		
		N—Normal or slightly elevated BP
		
		LABS:
		
		HYPOalbuminemia (protein in blood is low because it is all being excreted through kidneys)
		
		HYPERlipidemia
		
		HEMOconcentration

C—Care for the client until condition resolves	• Goals of therapy are to prevent complications from fluid volume overload and hypertension and ultimately preserve renal function • Prognosis varies depending on cause • Recovery is spontaneous • Recurrence is not common	• Therapy goals are to reduce protein excretion, reduce fluid retention, prevent infection, and preserve renal function • Treatment is primarily with steroids given for several weeks • Relapse is common, occurs in 2/3 children • Parents are taught to monitor urine

▪ Follow-up is weekly for several months and then monthly until resolved.	at home for protein to afford early intervention

ASSESSMENT	INTERVENTION
▪ **AIRWAY**	▪ Monitor for patent airway
▪ **BREATHING**	▪ Monitor for adventitious lung sounds that could indicate pulmonary infection, pulmonary edema, or pleural effusion
▪ **CIRCULATION**	▪ Monitor vital signs
▪ **DIET**	▪ Restrict high sodium foods!! ▪ If oliguria present, restrict foods high in potassium ▪ Small frequent meals of child's favorite foods are best because they have a lousy appetite ▪ NS: Encourage HIGH PROTEIN foods for replacement
▪ **EDEMA**	▪ Monitor strict I&O ▪ Daily weight, same scale, same time ▪ Elevate edematous extremities ▪ Assess degree of pitting, color and texture ▪ NS: Measure abdominal girth daily to evaluate for ascites.
▪ **FLUIDS**	▪ Restrict fluids if edema or HTN present ▪ Monitor for HYPOkalemia
▪ **GUARD THE PATIENT AGAINST INJURY**	▪ Monitor skin integrity and reposition to prevent bedsores ▪ Provide for frequent rest periods ▪ Cluster care ▪ Report fever immediately so potential infection can be treated promptly ▪ Turn, cough, and deep-breathe to prevent pulmonary infection ▪ NS: PREVENT INFECTION that can be caused by long-term high-dose steroid use. Make sure patient is up-to-date on immunizations! Patients can also develop peritonitis, pneumonia, and cellulitis.
▪ **HYPERTENSION** **HTN** is most commonly found in **APSGN**. In NS, it is much more uncommon and usually	▪ Neurologic checks (HTN can cause neuro dysfunction) ▪ Watch neuro status closely in children with HTN, hematuria and edema ▪ Implement seizure precautions if necessary

	less severe if present.	▪ Treat with diuretics and antihypertensives as prescribed

STRUCTURAL DISORDERS

	Ask about the history	B—Be aware of possible presenting symptoms you might detect on assessment	C—Care for the client with goal to prevent complications of condition
Hypospadias & Epispadius	Risk Factors: Genetics	Hypo- meatal opening is on the ventral side of the penis. May be associated with chordee (curvature of the penis) Epi- meatal opening is on the dorsal side of the penis	***CRITICAL—DO NOT CIRCUMCISE THESE BABIES. THE EXTRA FORESKIN IS USED IN SURGICAL REPAIR OF THE MEATUS***
Phimosis	Narrowing of the opening on the foreskin that prevents the foreskin from retracting over the glans	Difficulty retracting foreskin Adhesions	Mild- manual retraction and cleansing Severe-surgical circumcision
Cryptorchidism	Failure of one or both testicles to descend into the inguinal canal	Testicles not palpable in scrotum	***Failure to surgically correct (orchipexy) after one year of age is associated with a higher risk of testicular cancer and sterility.**
Hydrocele	Collection of fluid in the testicular sac.	***Transilluminates with a pen light***	May come and go, surgical repair if unresolved by one year.
Bladder Exstrophy	Protrusion of the bladder wall through the abdomen		Surgery to preserve renal function, attain urinary control, and improve body image and sexual function
Ambiguous Genitalia	Risk Factors:	Congenital malformation that makes it difficult to	Gender assignment is usually dependent on

	Congenital Adrenal Hyperplasia	visually distinguish the sex of the baby.	predominant characteristics. Family support is essential!

KEY CONCEPTS TO REMEMBER ABOUT STRUCTURAL DEFECTS:

- ❖ The goal of most repairs is to preserve or create normal urinary and sexual function
- ❖ **EARLY INTERVENTION IS CRITICAL TO PRESERVE NORMAL BODY IMAGE AND REDUCE EMOTIONAL TRAUMA!**
- ❖ Defects should ideally be corrected before potty training age.
- ❖ Family emotional support is a key portion of care.
- ❖ Explain defects to child on a developmentally appropriate level.
- ❖ Ensure that child understands that surgery is not a punishment.
- ❖ It is VERY important to watch for signs of post-operative infection such as fever, lethargy, blood in urine.
- ❖ Use play therapy to help children cope with disease process.

URINARY TRACT INFECTIONS AND ENURESIS

Know your <u>A</u>-<u>B</u>-<u>C</u>'s	<u>Urinary Tract Infections</u>	<u>Enuresis</u>
<u>A</u>sk about the history	▪ An organism can be present anywhere in the kidneys, urinary tract or bladder. ▪ **Untreated UTI's can cause sepsis, permanent renal scarring, and death.** ****ANY CHILD UNDER THE AGE OF 2 WITH A UTI SHOULD BE EVALUATED FOR A STRUCTURAL DEFECT, ESPECIALLY BOYS!!**.**	▪ Having urinary accidents after potty training is achieved ▪ Can be diurnal or nocturnal ▪ Must occur >2x's/week x at least 3 months ▪ Diagnosed after age 5 years ▪ More common in males ***Peak incidence 2-7 years of age.*

	Risk Factors:	Risk Factors:
	<ul><li>Urinary tract anomalies</li><li>Vesicoureteral reflux</li><li>Girls are more likely to develop a UTI because of close proximity of the urethra to the rectum, but boys are more likely to have a structural defect if diagnosed with a UTI</li><li>Constipation</li><li>Toilet Training</li><li>Tight underwear and wet bathing suits</li><li>Sexually active adolescents</li></ul>	<ul><li>Family history</li><li>Associated bladder disease/dysfunction</li><li>Emotional Issues</li></ul>
B—Be aware of possible presenting symptoms you might detect on assessment	<ul><li>Frequency</li><li>Urgency with small amounts</li><li>Dysuria/Nocturia</li><li>Abdominal or back pain</li><li>Enuresis</li><li>Fever</li><li>INFANTS HAVE NON-SPECIFC SYMPTOMS SUCH AS IRRITABILITY, ANOREXIA, VOMITING, AND MALAISE!</li></ul>**LABS**:<ul><li>Urinalysis (Sterile straight catheter for patients <2 years, clean catch for >2years and toilet trained).</li><li>Don't make the child drink a lot before collection, as it may dilute the bacteria and alter the culture result.</li><li>Send UA to lab immediately</li><li>Definitive diagnosis is urine culture with >100,000 count identified bacteria.</li><li>UA- dark or cloudy urine, +WBC, +protein, +RBC</li></ul>	<ul><li>History of family disruptions</li><li>Excessive fluid intake in the evening</li><li>History of chronic illness</li></ul>

| C—Care for the client until condition resolves | ▪ Diagnostic Imaging to evaluate for structural defect: cytoscopy, intravenous pyelogram, or voiding cystourerthrogram. Young children and infants may require sedation.
▪ Encourage frequent voiding
▪ Encourage fluid intake
▪ Give medications as indicated (make sure all antibiotics are completely taken)
▪ Teach hygiene care—wipe front to back, retract and clean foreskin, keep underwear dry, use cotton underwear, drink fluids, avoid bubble baths, prevent constipation, void after intercourse. | ▪ Treat with evening fluid restrictions, bladder retraining, and medications
▪ Pelvic muscle exercises
▪ Evaluate self-esteem
▪ Support coping strategies
▪ Assess family coping
▪ Affirm that child should not be punished
▪ Medication therapies may help short-term but are not a cure. |

MEDICATIONS COMMONLY USED FOR RENAL PATIENTS

MEDICATION	ACTION	NURSING CARE	EDUCATION	ALERTS
Corticosteroids	Anti-inflammatory		Avoid large crowds or persons with known infections	High doses and prolonged use can cause weight gain (especially in the face) and mood swings
Furosemide (Lasix)	Loop diuretic	Monitor signs of altered electrolytes	Eat foods high in potassium	Give with caution in impaired renal function!
25% albumin	Increases plasma volume and decreases edema	Monitor I&O		Watch for signs of anaphylaxis!
Cyclophosphamide (Cytotoxan)	For children who are resistant to steroid therapy or have multiple relapses			

DDAVP (Desmopressin Acetate)	Anti-diuretic; reduces urine volume in the bladder	Observe for possible adverse effects: headache, nausea, flushing, fluid retention.	Administer at bedtime Keep nasal spray refrigerated	
Tricyclic antidepressants		Observe for adverse side effects: dry mouth, constipation, anxiety, insomnia	Administer one hour before bedtime	
Oxybutynin chloride (Ditropan)	Reduces bladder spasm	Observe for the following side effects: dry mouth, nausea, drowsiness.		
Antibiotics for urinary tract infection	Sulfa drugs Penicillin Cephalosporin Nitrofurantoin	Patient should have a follow-up urine culture 10 days after antibiotics are completed to ensure infection is eradicated.	Ensure all 10 days of medications are taken, even if symptoms resolve.	There is a potential cross-reaction allergy between penicillin and cephalosporins! Any patient who is allergic to one may be allergic to both!

An Unforgettable Renal Patient

On this particularly unforgettable day, I was a clinical instructor for a pediatric course and I had a group of ten students placed at a very large children's hospital. I was beginning my morning rounds on the renal floor and came across three of my students conferencing in the hallway. They looked very animated and were speaking earnestly and urgently to one another. I approached them and asked them to share with me their discussion. They told me to come quickly, that one of them was having a terrible problem with her patient and she was at a loss as to what to do. They began literally pushing me around the corner and when I walked toward the patient's room I saw a group of several nurses gathered in the hallway in a circle. As I began to walk up to the nurses they stepped aside and I could see a girl who seemed to be about 5 years old sitting in a little push car. The problem was that she weighed over 120 pounds and she was very much stuck in the car and could not get out. My mind immediately pictured poor little Winnie the Pooh, stuck in Rabbit's hole because he had eaten too much honey. My face must have asked the question because the nurses told me that this poor little girl had end-stage renal failure and the mother did not have the heart to put any limits or restrictions on her and so she spent her days eating enormous amounts of fast food and watching TV, as well as demanding and receiving multiple gifts. The nurses asked me if I had any ideas and I suggested getting some hand soap to see if we could get her out of the car. The students looked at me as if I had completely lost my mind but ran to get the soap. We poured soap all down the insides of the car. Four nurses held the car steady and the students and I did our best to pull her out of the car. Nothing happened. She didn't even budge. My next suggestion was to call the orthopedic surgeons. They came, as orthopedic surgeons are always ready for an adventure that requires power tools. Those physicians cut open that poor little car like they had the jaws-of-life. I should tell you the little girl and her mother were quite unaffected by the whole fiasco. They were enjoying the spotlight of the floor. When she was finally free, I saw that she was wearing a diaper because the mother did not want to stress her out with potty training, and she had 4 pacifiers pinned to her gown. She smelled so bad, I was quite taken aback, but the mother said she did not like baths at all and she did not want to force the issue. This mother really and truly thought she was doing what was best for her daughter. She had been told not to stress her out and to conserve her energy. The mother thought that by treating her as she did, it might prolong her life and allow her to live until an organ donation became available. It taught me that the art of nursing is about much more than the physical aspect. These nurses had facilitated the little girl's dialysis, given all her meds, adhered to her fluid restrictions, and all the other physical things. But those interventions were harmed by not attending to the whole picture. Nursing is holistic and requires an artisan's touch.

REVIEW QUESTIONS

1. What is the most appropriate primary nursing intervention for a child with nephrotic syndrome?

1) Administer antihypertensives to control blood pressure
2) Monitor urine frequently for hematuria
3) Encourage consumption of foods rich in potassium to replace losses
4) Weigh the patient daily at the same time on the same scale

1. Option #4 is correct. Options #1 and #2 are interventions for AGN. Option #3 may be a good choice if the patient is on potassium sparing diuretics, but #4 is the most important because the degree of edema and fluid retention help to indicate the severity of the disease. Weight loss is often one of the first signs of improvement.

2. The nurse is caring for a 5-year-old male patient with acute post-streptococcal glomerulonephritis. Which of the following assessment data requires immediate attention?

1) A blood pressure of 132/80.
2) Gross hematuria
3) Severe periorbital edema
4) Mild crackles bi-lateral lower lung fields

2. Option #1 is correct. Hypertension is potentially deadly and can cause neurological alterations such as seizures. This should be addressed immediately. Options #2 and #3 are expected findings with AGN and while they should be monitored, they do not need immediate intervention. Option #4 also needs further assessment, but is also a common finding with this disease and it is not as critical as the hypertension.

3. A 3-month-old male is 24 hours post-op from a hypospadius repair. Which of the following items should the nurse report to the healthcare provider?

1) A urine specific gravity of 1.010
2) > 5 WBC per microscopic field on UA
3) 4 RBC per microscopic field on UA
4) Urine pH of 6.2

3. Option #2 should be reported as it may indicate the development of a post-operative infection. #3 is an expected finding after a surgical procedure on the urinary tract and # 1 and #4 are normal UA findings.

4. The mother of a 6-year-old boy tells you during his well child visit that he has been wetting the bed at night. The mother is completely frustrated because of having to change his sheets and clothes each night. She has "tried everything" including spanking him, but nothing is working. How should the nurse respond?

1) Call CPS to report abusive behavior
2) Tell the mother that this is a normal occurrence and that he should not be punished
3) Suggest that the mother limit his fluid intake at night
4) Obtain more information about the symptoms and psychosocial situation

4. Option #4 is correct. This client needs a full assessment before determining any options for therapy. Option #1 is not appropriate without more information. Option #2 is incorrect because this is not a normal occurrence, and even though he should not be punished, further evaluation is necessary before telling the mother not to worry. Option #3 is appropriate in the therapeutic management of nocturnal enuresis, but not enough data has been gathered to know that this is the problem.

5. Surgical repairs of the genitourinary tract are performed as early as possible for which of the following reasons?

1) The baby will not remember the surgery
2) There will be fewer post-operative complications
3) There will be improved body image
4) Hospitalization will not be as traumatic

5. Option #3 is correct. Surgical repairs are optimally completed before toilet training age so that normal body image and acceptance can be optimized. Options # 1 and # 4 are incorrect. The fact that the baby will not remember the surgery is not a decisive factor, although a nice benefit. Long-term memory begins to emerge at 18 months. Option #2 is incorrect as younger babies typically experience increased morbidity following surgery.

6. Which of the following symptoms can be indicative of a urinary tract infection in an infant?

Select all that apply.

1) Irritability

2) Poor appetite

3) Fever

4) Urgency

5) Crying with urination

6) Foul smelling urine

All options except #4 are correct. An infant cannot adequately convey urinary urgency.

7. A nurse is caring for a 15-year-old patient who was admitted for a febrile urinary tract infection. The mother conveys concern and tells the nurse she suspects her daughter may be sexually active and asks the nurse to talk to the daughter about it and report back the conversation. What is the most appropriate response of the nurse?

1) "Your daughter's health is at risk if she is sexually active. I will see what I can find out."
2) "I cannot discuss this with you because of patient privacy regulations."
3) " It would be best for you two to discuss privately."
4) "Let's set aside some time to discuss ways that it might be best to talk about this with your daughter."

Option #4 is best. It does not dismiss the mother or violate any privacy issues. It is a good opportunity to explore methods of therapeutic communication and building a stronger bond with her daughter. Many parents do not feel comfortable talking to their adolescents about sexual health and need guidance on effective ways to do so.

8. A toddler is admitted for nephrotic syndrome and has orders for daily urine protein checks with a dipstick. The toddler wears diapers and cannot urinate on demand. How should the nurse collect the urine sample?

1) Place cotton balls in the diaper
2) Perform a straight catheterization
3) Adhere a urine bag (u-bag)
4) Use a syringe to extract urine from the diaper

Option #1 is correct. Checking for protein does not require sterile technique (straight cath). Diapers are so absorbent that it is impossible to extract urine with a syringe. A u-bag is more uncomfortable and unnecessary for such a small amount of urine.

9. A school nurse has a 9-year-old student who has been in her office frequently complaining of malaise. The nurse observes that the child has gained 6 pounds in the last 4 weeks and his clothes appear to be too tight. He looks pale and withdrawn. His parents have recently divorced and he has just started this school 3 months ago. What is the next step the nurse should take?

    1) Establish a rapport with the child and encourage him to open up about his feelings
    2) Call CPS to report possible abuse
    3) Speak to the school counselor about evaluation for depression
    4) Advise the mother to make an appointment with a provider as soon as possible.

Option #4 is correct. This child is exhibiting signs of nephrotic syndrome. It is important not to overlook a physical disorder when there are multiple variables. Never make assumptions. Seek to rule out a physical cause first.

10. A 5-year-old patient is admitted with a Wilm's tumor and is being prepared for a nephrectomy. What is the priority nursing intervention?

    1) Consult with child life to help prepare the child for the surgical procedure
    2) Post a sign above the child's bed that reads "DO NOT PALPATE ABDOMEN."
    3) Restrict activities and minimize the need for bathing and handling.
    4) Strictly monitor intake and output.

Option #2 is correct. Palpating the tumor can cause dissemination and subsequent metastasis to other sites in the body. Activities should be restricted to minimize the risk for trauma, but the priority intervention is not to palpate the abdomen.

11. A newborn is newly diagnosed in the newborn nursery with hypospadias. What is the priority nursing intervention?

    1) Place an indwelling catheter to keep the meatus patent
    2) Ensure that a circumcision not be done
    3) Measure strict I&O
    4) Administer pain medication

Option #2 is correct. The foreskin is used during corrective surgery so it is essential that a circumcision not be done. A catheter is placed after surgical correction. Pain medication is not necessary until post-op.

12. What nursing actions are appropriate for a child with nephrotic syndrome? **Select all that apply.**

   1) Administration of antihypertensives
   2) Strict monitoring of intake and output
   3) Weighing the patient daily
   4) Frequent repositioning
   5) Encourage high protein foods

Options #2-#5 are correct. Nephrotic Syndrome does not usually cause hypertension. I&O and daily weights help monitor disease progression, severe edema can cause risk for impaired skin integrity (thus the need for repositioning), and high protein foods can help replace losses.

13. A 12-year-old male has just undergone a nephrectomy for Wilm's Tumor. The nurse is giving discharge instructions. Which is the most critical instruction at this time?

   1) Avoid contact sports
   2) Report fever immediately
   3) Enroll in a support group
   4) Enforce bed rest for 2 weeks

Option #2 is correct. This child has had a major surgery and is at risk for infection. Early intervention is key to protect his remaining kidney. Children post-nephrectomy should generally not play contact sports but this child is not likely to do this immediately post-op, so the priority is not as high. A support group would likely be beneficial but an infection can be life threatening. Bed rest is not necessary.

14. The mother of a three-year-old child expresses concern to the nurse at her well child visit because she "is always touching herself down there." The mother thinks she may have a urinary tract infection. What is the best response by the nurse?

   1) "That is definitely not normal. Have you recently divorced?"
   2) "Don't worry about it. That's normal."
   3) "We will be sure to talk with the provider about your concerns today."
   4) "Do you let her watch inappropriate television at home?"

Option #3 is correct. It is not within the scope of practice to tell the mother the child does not have a urinary tract infection. However, she may be reluctant to talk about it to the provider. It is good for the nurse to validate her concern and encourage her to discuss it with the provider.

15. A 7-year-old has had recurrent urinary tract infections. The medical work-up is negative for any structural defect. The nurse is providing the mother with information on prevention. Which interventions are effective at prevention? **Select all that apply.**

    1) Void frequently, at least every 2-3 hours.
    2) Drink 6 ounces of cranberry juice daily.
    3) Wear cotton underwear.
    4) Use only child-approved products for bubble bath
    5) Encourage fluid intake

Options #1, #3, and #5 are correct. Cranberry juice does not affect urine pH and is not an effective prevention measure for UTIs. No bubble baths should be done, period. Adequate fluid intake and frequent voiding prevents bacteria proliferation and helps urine to be flushed out of the bladder.

16. A newborn was delivered 2 days ago with ambiguous genitalia. The mother has refused to see the baby since delivery and has been crying continuously in her room. What is the most appropriate course of action for the nurse to take?

    1) Request a psychiatric consult
    2) Request a sedative
    3) Suggest adoption
    4) Allow the mother to grieve

Option #4 is correct. It can be very distressing to parents when their baby is born with ambiguous genitalia. They do not know if they have a boy or a girl or what to do about a name. The family must be supported during the grieving process. Usually the parents will make a decision but surgical options are usually reserved until the time the child is old enough to make those decisions.

17. A mother of a baby diagnosed with hypospadias has just been told surgical repair will take place when the baby is one year of age. The mother wants to wait longer, until she can explain things to the child better. What is the best response of the nurse?

    1) "It is best to have the repair early so he won't remember it."
    2) "He will feel better about himself if he can stand up to pee like your husband does."
    3) "This condition can worsen and needs to be corrected as soon as possible."
    4) "This condition can put your child at risk for a urinary tract infection."

Option #1 is correct. Between 3-6 years of age, children have "magical thinking" which means they have trouble knowing what is real and what is not real. They have intense fears, especially of bodily harm. Gender identification begins at 3 years. It is best for surgeries to be completed between 6-15 months before fears emerge, before long-term memory sets in (@18 months), and to minimize psychological trauma from anesthesia and surgery.

18. Which of the following are goals of treatment for nephrotic syndrome? **Select all that apply**:

      1) Preventing infection
      2) Reducing edema
      3) Decreasing urinary protein excretion
      4) Minimizing therapy complications
      5) Maintaining a low-potassium diet

Options #1-#4 are correct. Treatment is high-dose (sometimes long term) corticosteroids, which can cause immunosuppression and increase the risk for infection. A low-sodium diet is indicated.

19. A 7-year-old is admitted for acute post-streptococcal glomerulonephritis. Prioritize the following nursing interventions from most important to least important.

      1) Monitor daily weight
      2) Check blood pressure
      3) Enforce fluid restrictions
      4) Maintain no-added salt diet

The correct order is #2, #3, #1, #4. Hypertension can occur with this disorder. It is critical to carefully monitor the blood pressure. Daily weight check is the most effective way to monitor fluid balance.

20. A 12-year-old is admitted with acute post-streptococcal glomerulonephritis. He is permitted to have 18 ounces of fluid per day. What is the best way to enforce this fluid restriction?

      1) Require a parent or guardian to be present at all times.
      2) Carefully measure and personally administer all fluids
      3) Restrict access to the playroom and lock the bathroom.
      4) Allow the child to create a plan for daily fluid consumption.

Option #4 is correct. At 12 years old, he is old enough to participate in his care and may be more likely to comply if given autonomy and power of choice.

Nursing Management in the Gastrointestinal System

Jessica Roberts , MSN, RN
Edited by Sylvia Rayfield & Associates Inc.

The digestive canal represents a tube passing through the entire organism and communicating with the external world, i.e., as it were the external surface of the body, but turned inwards and thus hidden in the organism.

Ivan Pavlov

MOST COMMON TYPES OF GASTROINTESTINAL DISORDERS

Key Concepts:
- ৡ **Aspiration and Perforation**
- ৡ **Tubes**
- ৡ **Gastroesophageal Reflux Disease (GERD) and Ulcers**
- ৡ **Food Intolerances**
- ৡ **Chronic Inflammation of the Bowel**
- ৡ **Emergency Surgery of the Bowel**
- ৡ **Hepatic Disease/Six Ways to Pass a Test on the Liver**
- ৡ **Practice Questions, Answers and Rationale**

Our approach to easy learning and remembering is to provide the acronym **SAFETY** as a powerful tool . Utilize this tool every time you walk into a client's room or answer an *NCLEX*® question. All of these are standards tested on the current *NCLEX*® exam.

PASS *NCLEX*®!

S   **System specific assessment**

A   **Assess for risk and respond**

F   **Find change/trends and intervene**

E   **Evaluate pharmacology**

T   **Teach/practice infection control, health promotion**

Y   **Your management—legal/ethical/scope of practice, identity, errors, delegation, faulty equipment/staff, privacy, confidentiality, falls/ hazards**

As Ivan Pavlov has said, the gastrointestinal system is a series of complex digestive organs with several nervous system innervations that act to fuel the body for everyday function. It sounds complicated, but it can be made insanely easy by just thinking of it as a pipe that runs from the mouth to the anus. Enzymes and such flow into the tube and nutrients from food flow out, but in the end what goes in must come out!

Aspiration and Perforation

SYSTEM SPECIFIC ASSESSMENT

Digestion begins in the mouth as food is entered into the body and broken down by digestive enzymes. This is an important step, as food that is not broken down properly can cause problems. Common problems include aspiration (food takes an unscheduled exit from the pipe into the lungs), obstruction (chew that steak before you swallow), and perforation (what slides in smoothly may not always slide out). The safe nurse knows how to prevent these problems from getting out of hand. First, assess the client's ability to swallow. This is important especially if a stroke has left a client debilitated. If swallowing is impaired due to hemi-paralysis then thickening liquids may be important. Food consistency can play a big part in caring for your client through the lifespan. When caring for children we know to avoid small hard foods that get stuck. Only foods small enough to pass through the tube should go in the mouth. For the adult this may also be important if the tube, or esophagus, has become narrow or developed a stricture. Food objects may become lodged in this now narrow tube. Peristalsis decreases as a client ages. Perforation can also occur as pressure from the bolus can over expand the tube. Our psychiatric clients should be watched for perforations as well. If you swallow a straight pin you may not get it back, Ouch!

All of these problems bring us to our first procedures of the GI tract. As the nurse caring for these individuals going through a procedure, it is important to know the:

HOW, WHY, WHEN, WHERE, and WHAT'S NEXT?

HOW?

How will the foreign object be removed? Often this is done by retrieving the object under sedation. Sometimes the object may be allowed to pass naturally or given a little help, but that depends on the size and safety of the object. If allowed to pass naturally, sometimes medications can be given to support the process. Did you know Glucagon also dilates the esophagus? As a safe nurse it's always important to know all the uses of medications.

These NCLEX® standards are for administration of every type of drug in every system.

PASS NCLEX®!

C	**Calculate correctly**
A	**Assess for allergies**
R	**Rights of administration**
E	**Evaluate response**
F	**Feel free to call provider if intuition alerts**
U	**Utilize assessments in determining ordered parameters**
L	**Lab data pertinence**

Tubes

How will your client get nutrients if they are unable to swallow? This can be done by artificial means. Tubes may be placed to help support nutrition. The location of the tube placement is based on how long the tube will need to be in place. Nasogastric (NG) tubes may be placed to help support in the short term and peg tubes are used for the long term.

NG tubes work great both ways! We can take contents out of the GI tract as well as put nutrients in with a nasogastric tube. This can be useful when an object gets stuck as it can relieve the pressure behind it. Just add a little suction and remove the pressure. Just be careful these tubes always stay in place, otherwise you can have big problems including aspiration!

How will the perforation be fixed? New exits from the tube can cause major problems as what is in the tube is not designed to be out of the GI tract unless its processed first. The food we put in the GI tube is not sterile. In fact, we have bacteria throughout our GI tract that helps the process of digestion. If this is allowed to escape into the sterile cavities of the body, our clients can have major problems. This type of client will be looking at extensive surgery and antibiotic treatments with a long recovery.

WHY?

Why is removing the object important? Any object that is not small enough to pass through the GI tract can cause problems. If it gets stuck, food and digestive secretions can build up behind the object causing large amounts of pressure. This pressure can expand the tube so much that it bursts, spilling all sorts of non-sterile material into the body in areas where it should not be. These obstructions can be very dangerous.

The object may also slide into areas it should not go. For instance a coin swallowed by a child may slip into the wind pipe and block the flow of the respiratory system. Smaller objects that slip into the respiratory system may not cause obstruction but can cause bacteria to grow. Remember the GI tract it not sterile (duh, poop) but the rest of the body is and we want it to stay that way!

Why do we need to supplement nutrients? Well, that's an easy question. We know that the body requires nutrients to function properly. Nutrients help the body to heal and fight infection A better question may be, why do we place a tube in the nose vs the mouth, stomach, or intestines? This boils down to how long the tube is needed or are other options not available. A tube in the mouth is ideally not going to stay in place as long as one in the nose but if the nose is not available, the mouth may be the best option. Oral gastric tubes are used less commonly now as we have found better alternatives and they can cause so many problems. Often an OG tube is used in the case of gastric lavage (cleaning out the stomach) in cases of overdose. Lavage is dangerous because of high aspiration risk and is only used in rarely. NG tubes are much more comfortable for your conscious client and can be placed at the bedside by skilled, trained individuals.

WHEN?

The when of these upper GI procedures can be answered in a quick question: If this is not done immediately will it threaten the life of the client? In the case of an obstruction causing perforation, the answer is YES! If a tube is not placed in a client with a full obstruction, pressure can cause a perforation. If the client has already experienced a perforation and they are not taken to surgery quickly, the bacteria from the GI system can invade the body causing sepsis. Tubes placed for nutrition may be put off a little longer as long as IV hydration is being maintained.

WHERE?

Where a tube is placed is important only in how it works. Nasogastric tubes require food to be processed through the entire GI tact which means more opportunity to absorb nutrients. Tubes placed lower in the

GI tract such as GJ tubes (gastrojenumal feeding tube) do not have as much opportunity for nutrient absorption. Care for all the tubes is essentially the same. Tubes that enter the GI tract via surgery are a little different as they must be placed in a sterile environment but once placed, they can be handled with aseptic technique. All these tubes have several things in common regardless of where the tubes are placed.

> First, the tubes work better with gravity. Tubes that are draining can be below the area that is draining but if you are putting stuff in the body, it's best to keep the tubes high. This way the feedings or medications are going in at a more natural rate that the body can handle. If you are required to force fluid in with a lot of pressure, something may be wrong with the tube.

> Placement of the tube is important regardless of where the tube lies. Even a gastric tube originally placed in surgery can become displaced so always check placement before using. This can be done in several was: expressing gastric secretions, radiography, or air bolus (NG/OG only).

> Finally all these tubes should be treated like a mouth without teeth. Which means, aseptic technique may be used not sterile, and only liquids or dissolved pills may be used in the tube.

WHAT'S NEXT?

The provider may order a CT scan with contrast. This diagnostic test is used to take pictures of body organs for diagnosis. The contrast (usually iodine) is utilized to provide a better view. Now is the time to determine if the client is allergic to shellfish or other iodine preparations, as the tests should not be given with this contrast.

Ensure proper identification of client when providing care. Nurses are responsible for making certain that the right client receives the CT scan.

As the nurse, it is your responsibility to ensure that the client remains stable after the procedures are complete. If the client has had surgery, you want to make sure your assessments of the client are more frequent immediately after surgery. Assess and re-assess. Bowel sound assessments are especially important with these types of procedures as sedation can decrease peristalsis. If the gut stops moving and the client eats, they can end up with an obstruction because the gut is too sleepy to keep the food moving along.

Interesting that tubes are the most utilized instruments to diagnose the GI Tube!
- **Endoscopy (EGD)**—a flexible tube allowing the provider to look and diagnose and cauterize bleeding
- **Colonoscopy**—a flexible tube allowing the provider to see polyps, growth, ulcers and cancer
- **Sigmoidoscopy**—a flexible tube allowing the provider to see growths/obstructions in the sigmoid
- **Enteroscopy**—a flexible tube allowing the provider to see the small bowel to determine diagnosis including GI bleeding malabsorbtion.

There are 3 important questions that the nurse should be able to answer regarding any diagnostic test.

1. What should the client be taught prior to the exam and what is the nursing priority? Verify that the client comprehends and consents to procedures, including procedures requiring informed consent.

2. What should the client be taught regarding the procedure itself and what is the nursing priority during the procedure? Many providers utilize sedation so that the client never knows that they have undergone the procedure. (Information for the nurse: puncture of the GI tube by the instrument tube is possible. Material spilled from the non-sterile GI tract into the sterile body is likely to cause massive infection. Aspiration is possible.)

3. What should the client be taught after the procedure is completed and what is the nursing priority? Fever is possible. If the client "feels bad," call the provider. They may bleed internally from a biopsy or rupture.

THESE ARE VITAL CONCEPTS TO KNOW AND ARE OFTEN TESTED ON NCLEX®.

Gastroesophageal Reflux Disease (GERD) and Ulcers

The **stomach** works to process foods for nutrition and may take 2-3 hours for this process. The process may take longer than normal if the meal is especially large. This can strain the stomach and make it work harder to digest the food. Continued strain can reduce the effectiveness of the esophageal sphincter allowing food and gastric enzymes to reflux up into the esophagus. The highly acidic nature of the gastric contents can damage the lining of the esophagus. Continued damage can cause the cells to change so much that a malignant mutation can occur. This is called Barrett's esophagus and can lead to esophageal cancer. Reflux has also been linked to chronic coughs and irritation of reactive airway diseases. Large meals and meals that are hard to digest increase reflux as the pressure in the stomach increases. Avoiding these two things can reduce the symptoms of GERD but, if that fails, we have medications that can reduce the gastric secretions.

COMMON MEDICATIONS USED TO TREAT GERD AND ULCERS

Medications also cause these symptoms. One of the most common causes of mucosal ulceration is NSAIDS (non-steroidal anti-inflammatory drugs). Steroids, aspirin, and other anti-inflammatory drugs such as Advil may also **cause** ulcers.

The following facts should be included in the teaching plan of clients who are taking these OTC drugs:
- Take with food.
- Minimize the dosage to treat the symptoms.
- Do not take together unless specifically prescribed.
- Watch for bleeding (in stomach and bowel contents).

Dumping syndrome occurs if the stomach releases its contents into the small intestine too quickly. This causes a sudden shift in fluid from the vascular system into the intestines to help move the large bolus along. A drop in vascular fluid causes a drop in total plasma volume, which can cause signs of hypovolemia such as weakness, pallor, hypotension, tachycardia, and diaphoresis. Rapid distention of the intestines by this unprepared food bolus can cause cramping, nausea, vomiting, and diarrhea. Dumping syndrome more commonly occurs when the structure of the stomach has been changed, such as with gastrectomy or pyloroplasty. It can also be related to a cholesectomy or bowel disease but this is less common.

Breaks in the stomach lining can cause ulcerations and inflammation. The breaks are often caused by nicotine exposure (increases acid production), alcohol, NSAIDs (inhibit prostaglandins), H.pylori (stimulates acid and pepsin), chronic GERD, or ischemia.

Common medications administered for H. pylori are effective for almost 90% of the clients with this type of inflammation.

- Metronidazole/clarithromycin, 4 times/day
- Tetracycline/amoxicillin, 4 times/day
- Bismuth subsalicylate (PeptoBismol), 4 times/day
- These medications often cause a bad taste in the mouth and an issue with compliance. Reiterate to client the need to take all of the medication for 2 weeks for optimum results

FIND CHANGE, TRENDS AND INTERVENE

Stress, either from illness or emotional, can also cause ulcers. Ulcers are dangerous as they can cause a great deal of pain and, if allowed, to extend into the blood vessels or create gastric bleeds. This is a life-threatening emergency. Gastric bleeds go unnoticed until a large amount of blood loss occurs. Fecal occult blood test and gastro-occults can identify gastric bleeding in the early stages. Large amounts of blood in the stomach are irritating, causing severe nausea, vomiting, and diarrhea. If the GI bleed is high in the GI tract, the placement of an NG tube can reduce these symptoms as it pulls the irritating blood off the stomach. The NG tube will also allow for the nurse to identify the quantity of blood loss that is occurring. In the client with a blood loss of greater than 1000mL, the nurse would expect to see tachycardia, postural hypotension, and dizziness. As the blood loss continues, the client will go into shock as indicated by decreased perfusion to the kidneys (low to no urine output), pale skin, altered levels of consciousness, and eventually death. Often these clients need emergency transfusions and surgical procedures to stop the source of bleeding.

Blood transfusions are high on the list of errors in hospitals.
Important aspects to remember include:
- **Right blood right client.** Be able to prove this by checking the client's identity with another nurse.
- **Utilize the correct equipment** for the type of blood product involved, including the correct size needle. A needle too small (less than 20ga.) may lyse the cells and negate the transfusion.
- **Blood products often cause allergic reactions.** Administer the blood slowly and monitor the client closely. Any breathing difficulty, pain, or rash indicates stopping the transfusion immediately and keeping the vein open with D5W.
- **Never discontinue the line into the vein**, as this client may be in real trouble and another vein may not be available.

GI bleeds can also occur lower in the GI tract from polyps, inflammatory disease, cancer, or hemorrhoids. Assessment of the bleeding can help to determine the site of bleeding. New blood is normally red where old blood normally takes on a dark appearance. So, if a client is vomiting bright red blood, we know this is an upper GI bleed that is fresh. Ruptured esophageal varices often present like this as the blood does not have an opportunity to digest. Dark, grainy coffee-ground type emesis indicates a certain level of digestion. Bright red blood from the rectum normally indicates a fresh wound such as a bleeding hemorrhoid whereas most rectal bleeding is presented by dark, tarry, foul-smelling stool (melena).

Food Intolerances

Each area of the **intestine** is responsible for certain digestion. The proximal area is responsible for breakdown of carbohydrates, proteins, and fat emulsion. The proximal area is assisted with breakdown by pancreatic enzymes, intestinal enzymes, and bile salts. Several problems can occur in this area if the enzymes are lacking. Lactase deficiency inhibits the breakdown of milk sugar; bile salt deficiency decreases ability to digest and absorb fat; and pancreatic enzyme insufficiency causes maldigestion of all nutrients (carbs, fats, and proteins). As the safe nurse caring for these clients, it is important to understand the care of clients with special dietary concerns. Clients with lactose intolerance will need to avoid milk products. If not, the undigested lactose can cause bacteria to ferment which produces gas formation. This gas formation irritates the intestines and is characterized by flatulence, bloating, cramping, and diarrhea. There is a strong correlation between lactose intolerance and gluten allergies. Gluten sensitive clients should steer away from barley, rye, oats, and wheat or suffer the same symptoms as lactose intolerance but to a higher degree.

Nutrient absorption is also a high concern with individuals with bowel disorders. The bowels utilize several fat soluble vitamins such as A,D, E, and K. These are absorbed in the intestinal tract. Water-soluble vitamins, such as thiamine, riboflavin, niacin, folic acid, biotin, and vitamins B and C, are also absorbed from the intestinal tract. If the body does not receive these vitamins, several severe health issues could occur. Alterations in the integrity of the bowels can produce severe deficiency such as in the case of alcoholism. In chronic alcoholism the lining of the intestines becomes damaged so that the important vitamins are not absorbed. Lack of these vitamins can lead to Wernicke's encephalopathy, chronic anemia, bleeding disorders, and Korsakoff's syndrome. Alcoholism is not the only disorder that causes a lack of absorption; any disorder that changes the integrity of the bowel places a client at risk. Other examples would be cancer, malnutrition, inflammatory bowel disease, excessive vomiting, or nasogastric use.

Chronic Inflammation of the Bowel

Chronic inflammation of the bowels can be caused by **Crohn's disease**. This is a disease of the gastrointestinal tract that can result in swelling deep into the layers of the gastric mucosa. It can affect anywhere in the GI tract from the mouth to the anus. Crohn's is random in its pattern causing skip lesions where one side of the intestine may be affected and not the other. These lesions cause fistula with a characteristic cobblestone granuloma. **You can remember that because both Crohn's and Cobblestone begin with C. You can also remember the characteristics of Crohn's since it affects the Complete intestines whereas its counterpart, ulcerative colitis, affects the rectum first than spreads. The U of ulcerative colitis is at the end of the alphabet and reminds us that ulcerative colitis begins at the end of the GI tract.** Crohn's and **ulcerative colitis** have very similar symptoms. Both cause an irritable bowel most often presented as diarrhea with mucus or blood passage. Chronic inflammation causes changes of the cells which may lead to cancer. Diarrhea is a cardinal symptom of these clients.

Fluids containing sodium and potassium are necessary to fight the dehydration that goes with diarrhea!

Additional dietary changes include **avoiding** the **SAC**.

S   spicy foods including black pepper

A   alcohol

C   carbonated, caffeine drinks, and chocolate.

There are many others but these are easy to remember.

EVALUATE PHARMACOLOGY

Remember, when administering medications we must be CAREFUL!

Common Drugs utilized for diarrhea include: acidophilis, probiotics, loperamide (Imodium), atropine/diphenoxylate (Lomotil), and psyllium (Metamucil). All except the Lomotil are OTC (over the counter without prescription) drugs. One of the most important teaching points involving these drugs is that they should never be taken with a stomach ache that does not include diarrhea! Drugs used for chronic diarrhea such as Crohn's include, but are not limited to:

- Sulfasalazine (Azulfadine)—a sulfa drug (watch for sulfa allergies)
- Corticosteroids—Take with food, may cause elevated blood pressure, weight gain, Cushinoid symptoms
- Adalimumab (Humira)—used when other drugs fail. May have a risk of infection such as tuberculosis
- Metronidazole (Flagyl)—teach dangers of taking while drinking alcohol, fainting is a side effect
- Ciprofloxacin (Cipro)—antibiotic with gastrointestinal side effects.

The more the client knows about their medication, the more likely they are to be compliant.

TEACH AND PRACTICE INFECTION CONTROL

Surgical management is used more often in ulcerative colitis because cutting out the offending bowel is much easier than with the skip lesions of Crohn's. Often surgery leaves the client with a new rectum formed by placing an artificial opening, or stoma, on the outside of the body called a colostomy or ileostomy. The type of stool and level of functioning that the new rectum is capable of is based on at what level the new opening occurs. The lower the opening the more formed the stool will be and the more absorption the intestines will be capable of performing. A formed stool has the ability to be trained as to when it should be passed. Loose stool cannot be trained. This means the higher the stoma, the more lifestyle changes the stoma will cause. Leaking feces causes embarrassment due to odors and noise production. It will cause irritation to the skin and may lead to skin breakdown with possible infections. These types of stomas require vigilant care and upkeep.

The nurse should know proper skin care and bag replacement methods to ensure the client has as few complications as possible. Use precautions to prevent injury and/or complications associated with a procedure or diagnosis.

- Assess the stoma after surgery as it can become swollen and necrosed. Determine color and size.
- If the stoma is low, teach bowel retraining utilizing irrigations.
- If the stoma is high, teach appropriate utilization of a bag, solutions used to adhere the bag to the skin, cleanliness of the bag (soap and water usually works best).
- Psychosocial issues must be heard and addressed or the client will not care if the bag is clean.

CLOSTRIDIUM DIFFICILE (C. DIFF)

This bacteria is highlighted since it causes severe diarrhea at a whole new deathly level! Fever, dehydration, decreased blood pressure.

It is highly contagious and usually transmitted "hand to mouth." It is important to apply principles of infection control (hand washing, room assignment, isolation, aseptic/sterile technique, universal/standard precautions) and to perform skin assessment and implement measures to maintain skin integrity and prevent skin breakdown

- ▶ **Wash your hands!**
- ▶ C.diff is located on many surfaces including toilet seats, bed pans, stethoscopes, linens, floors, diaper pails, infants, and pets.
- ▶ Commonly found in hospitals, nursing homes, and extended care facilities.
- ▶ Determined by stool specimen, culture, and flexible sigmoidoscopy.
- ▶ Most likely caused by prescribed antibiotics that kill off the good flora in the gut.
- ▶ May be quickly deadly especially with weakened or older people.

Common drugs used to treat C.diff include:

Vancomycin (Vancocin) is a high-powered antibiotic that is known to be nephrotoxic and ototoxic. Determine kidney lab values prior to administering. Watch for "Red Man Syndrome" within 4 minutes of administering this drug. Flushing and rash may occur. Antihistamines from protocol may be useful in this situation.

Fidaxomicin (Dificid) Serious side effects include GI bleeding and intestinal obstruction. This drug is known to react to cyclosporine, an immunosuppressant commonly administered to transplant clients to prevent rejection

Emergency Surgery of the Bowel

Attached to the cecum is the appendix, which has little function except evidently to get infected and give people a reason to have surgery. Appendicitis is the most common surgical emergency of the large gastrointestinal tract. If the appendix becomes inflamed and is allowed to progress then it can become gangrenous and cause perforation. As we talked about earlier, poop outside the shoot is bad! Appendicitis can present with vague symptoms early on and progress to intense pain, vomiting, and fever. Often children describe pain in their umbilical region as they are not able to localize pain easily. If a child is too sick to jump up and down, the nurse needs to think about inflammation as a cause even if the child doesn't have a fever. For the adult client, the pain can normally be localized with one finger to the RLQ (Right Lower Quadrant). The tenderness is more pronounced on the rebound than the compression. For the nurse preparing a client for emergency surgery, certain things need to be ascertained to maintain **safety**. First, determine the last time the client ate. This will insure proper maintenance of the airway. A person may aspirate when sedated if they have eaten too recently. Does this mean we delay surgery to allow the stomach to empty? Not normally. In an emergency situation, an NG tube may be placed to remove the contents of the stomach before surgery. Also, allergies need to be checked. There are many medications, including antibiotics, that are given during surgery so ensuring that the proper allergies are listed for the client is important.

Antibiotics commonly given for ruptured bowel include.
- **Amoxicillin (Amoxil)**, a penicillin-like antibiotic. Evaluate for renal disease. Administer all prescribed
- **Clindamycin (Cleocin) Warning**, assess for diarrhea and C.difficile.
- **Gentamycin (Garamycin, Cidomycin, Septopal)** Evaluate for renal disease
- **Metronidazole (Flagyl)** May interfere with blood thinners. **Avoid alcohol.**

Also, anything that will promote bacterial growth needs to be removed prior to the client going to surgery. This includes any jewelry or false parts (legs, eyes, and such). Dental bridges need to be removed for anesthesia safety as well. The safety concerns are not over once the client has come out of surgery. Abdominal surgery can cause major complications such as atelectasis, constipation, pain, pneumonia, and blood clots. The safe nurse knows how to recognize these problems and prevent them. We now know how important it is to get clients up and out of bed after operations as this decreases the complications of immobility. Teaching a client how to splint encourages proper movement and lung expansion. When abdominal surgery is preformed, holes must be poked or cut through the muscles that contain the abdominal organs or viscera. These holes decrease the integrity of the muscle and can make it very painful to do even simple things like rising from bed. By teaching the client to splint while moving or coughing, the nurse will reduce the client's pain significantly.

Sylvia Rayfield MN, RN and Loretta Manning MSN, RN, GNP
All images are used with the permission of I CAN Publishing®, Inc.
www.icanpublishing.com
These and many more fun images that help learning and retention can be found in
Nursing Made Insanely Easy, and *Pharmacology Made Insanely Easy.*

The liver is such a vital organ with so many functions and processes that it is important to find a way to organize your thinking. This book is written to give you a way to think about this material, pass your nursing test on these concepts, **Pass NCLEX® Questions**, and utilize this material in your nursing practice.

The remarkable acronym **SAFETY** is going to be your guideline to help you pass your test.

> ➤ The word **SAFETY** has 6 letters and by using this word, you will have a way to think about a client with liver disease and six ways to pass your test!
> ➤ We will add images to help you remember. The images are funny and you will never forget them.
> ➤ We will also provide some high difficulty level test items similar to the questions used on *NCLEX®*. Practice on these test items with the provided rationale will add to your learning.

Let's begin with the first letter in safety, the S. (The first way to pass.)

S   SYSTEM SPECIFIC ASSESSMENT OF THE LIVER

Every nursing decision is based on the clinical assessment and reassessment that you make on your client. Put your stethoscope on your liver. Can you hear it? No. Can you smell it? No. Can you see it? No. Can you feel it? No, unless it is larger than normal.

When it is tucked up under the ribs on the right side of the body, what would make us feel it? We would feel it if it were enlarged. A normal liver may hold as much as 300mL of fluid, but no more. If blood becomes congested in the liver, as in congestive heart failure, the blood backs up and enlarges the liver. Now we can feel it below the rib line. With this much fluid, the liver capsule will leak. Leak what? On a normal day the liver synthesizes protein. If the liver is engorged and the capsule leaks, the protein would leak into the abdominal cavity causing ascites. All of this fluid will make the abdomen swell and enlarge, giving us a way to assess the liver by measuring the abdominal girth, which will now be larger than normal.
Now, here's the question: What is normal? The only way that we would know that is to look at the medical record and compare the last measurement. What if there is no last measurement? We now know the importance of a good assessment on admission as this will be our way to assess the amount of swelling in a liver that is engorged.

Since the protein is leaking out into the abdomen, the colloid osmotic pressure will decrease. The COP not only holds fluid in the liver, but in the blood vessels. If fluid is not in liver and blood vessels, where would it be? It may leak everywhere causing edema along with the ascities. The edema can be assessed and gives us another way to determine liver function. This client is going to need at least 1g/kg protein in his diet daily to help make up for this loss.

The liver metabolizes protein that we eat. Spell the word protein. It ends in an N and nitrogen begins and ends with an N. If the liver is not working, the end products of nitrogen collect in the brain eventually causing hepatic coma. This condition will likely give us an unconscious client. Another way to see decreased liver function.

One of the easiest non-invasive ways that the health care provider has to assess the liver is by looking at the liver enzymes in blood work. The AST (Aspartate Transferase) and ALT (Alanine Transferase) are one way to determine if liver cells are dying. The AST (SGOT) normal is 5-40 u/l and the AST (SGPT) is 7-56 u/l. An elevated level enzyme indicates liver damage, but not to what extent the liver is damaged.

ELEVATED LIVER ENZYMES

Remember, elevated liver enzymes
are as easy as **ABC**

Alcoholism (ast, alt)

Biliary obstruction (alp)
"plugged up Paul"

Cirrhosis (ast, alt)

The bottom line—even though we could not see, hear, smell or feel the liver. We now have made a really good assessment to give us a way to think about it when something goes wrong. The answer to these questions will also give us more insight into a better assessment.

> ### We can add to our assessment by asking leading questions such as:
> - When did you have your last drink of alcohol?
> - What medications are you taking?
> - Are you sharing needles with anyone?
> - Have you ever had yellow skin or eyes?
> - Are you taking any supplements from the health food store?

The provider will go further in the medical assessment by utilizing a **liver biopsy** to determine the extent of damage in the liver. To remove a piece of tissue from an organ that is already at risk for **bleeding** is precarious at best and requires the nurse to be very attentive to this client. A close monitoring of vital signs to determine hemorrhage and applying pressure to the biopsy site (right side) are the primary nursing responsibilities. This situation requires frequent reassessment. Watch this for further learning: http://www.youtube.com/watch?v=mnHPx5XEvfQ

The liver performs over 1000 biochemical processes. You will be happy to know we will not discuss all of them here, but let's look at a few more that are likely to be on your nursing test.

The liver stores Vitamin K. This substance coagulates the blood and prevents hemorrhage. If our client is bleeding too long after an injection or blood withdrawal or has a prolonged prothrombin time, this may indicate decreased liver function. This would be a reason for us to be extra vigilant about adding pressure to an injection site.

The liver is lined with Kupffer cells. They remind me of the little Dow chemical brushes that clean the bathtubs on the TV commercials. These guys phagocytize bacteria in the body. Decreased Kupfer cells equal a decreased immune system equals a much better chance of **infection**. We can get an indication of infection through assessments such as increased body temperature and increased white cell count. As always, the best activity is one of prevention. These clients have a decreased immune system and need to be advised that immunizations should be up-to-date, especially flu and pneumonia injections.

The liver detoxifies over 70% of the drugs that we give clients. Decreased liver function may cause drug overdose and symptoms indicating prolonged drug effects.

The liver has a dual blood supply. Blood is pumped in from the hepatic artery and from the portal vein. This is great as long as the liver is soft and receiving a lot of blood. Here is a way to think about this process. Put a chicken liver in alcohol and it gets hard. A hard "hobnailed" liver is called **cirrhosis**. This process causes blood to back into the portal vein causing portal hypertension. The backup will not stop there; it will go around the splenic vein and up to the esophageal veins. Now we give our client a breakfast of hot coffee and bacon. The hot coffee dilates the esophageal veins, the bacon scratches them, and now we have **bleeding espohogeal varicies.** Endoscopy is an important tool to assess the presence of varicies.

The liver manufactures a substance called **bile**. This is an explanation of how that happens. The kidney manufactures erythropoietin which stimulates the bone marrow to produce red blood cells that live for about 45 days. Then they break apart and are eliminated except for the hemoglobin which can be recycled. An imaginary recycle truck from the liver comes and picks up the old hemoglobin and takes it back to the liver, dumps it (conjugates it), and uses it to make bilirubin. The liver makes lots of bilirubin; so much that it can't stay in the liver because there is no room, so it goes down the biliary tract to the gallbladder where it is stored and concentrated as bile.

Bile digests fats. Our client eats a fatty meal, the gut calls for help to digest it, the brain sends a message to the gallbladder to send bile. Bile emulsifies the fatty meal, which goes on down the colon and comes out in a brown stool; the brown is from the characteristic color of that old hemoglobin. If the stool is not brown, we likely have a gallbladder issue or a biliary stop up. The gall bladder is located just under the liver. The other problem is that, if the liver or gall bladder is diseased, this billirubin/bile backs up into the body. A condition called jaundice. Where is the first place we can see it? In the sclera of the eyes and in the yellow color of the skin (jaundice). Now again, we can see effects of the liver and have yet another way to assess liver function.

Even though you thought you could not see, hear, smell or touch the liver, there are lots of ways to assess it.

Keep on Going!

The second way to pass your tests and the second letter in safety stands for ACCURACY OF ORDERS. (Just because they order it, does not mean that we give it.)

A   We, as nurses, must determine the accuracy of orders from other health care professionals such as providers, provider assistants, and nurse practitioners. We must also make sure the client's room assignment is safe.

What if we have an order to administer several intramuscular injections to our client with liver disease and we know that these injections are likely to cause bleeding due to Vitamin K decrease? We may suggest to the provider that the medications may need to be administered by another method.

What if our liver client is assigned to be in a hospital room with a client that has a severe infection? We have to remember that Kupffer cells are decreased and this client should not be exposed to infection. We should arrange a different room assignment.

If a regular diet is ordered, it should be questioned as this client tends to retain salt and likely should have a sodium restricted diet. The all-American **HOT DOG** is your way to remember foods that are high in salt and should be avoided by clients with liver disease. If you're going to have a HOT DOG what is the first thing you need? A wiener which, of course, is processed meat. Think of all the other processed meats that this represents like Spam®, salami, bologna, pepperoni, and pressed ham. Next, we need a bun for our dog. The bun contains baking soda and soda is salt. Ketchup is processed tomatoes. The tomatoes are not high in salt, but the processing increases the salt level. The same process goes with pickles. Cucumbers are placed into brine (salt water). The chili comes mostly from cans and normal canned food is high in salt. So, to remember those foods high in sodium all you have to do is remember HOT DOG and you can safely advise your client.

FOODS HIGH IN SODIUM

If the client has a problem with sodium retention; Mary will show you how the client gets edema.

FLUID SHIFTS

"Mary had a little lamb and everywhere Mary went the lamb was sure to go."

As you can see, Mary is the sodium and the lamb is water. Where there is sodium retention there is fluid accumulation. Keep this image in mind when considering edema formation.

Remembering the role of protein is tricky, because with early liver disease the client needs high protein to help the liver damage repair and provide the client with the proper nutrition. After progression to hepatic encephalopathy, the protein must be restricted, due to accumulation in the brain.
This image of high protein foods will give you a way to remember which foods should be encouraged or avoided.

Foods high in protein can easily be remembered if you recall the jingle *Happy To Consume My Calories Sanely*. **See in the picture**

HAPPY	hamburger
TO	tuna
CONSUME	chicken
MY	milk
CALORIES	cottage cheese
SANELY	soy beans

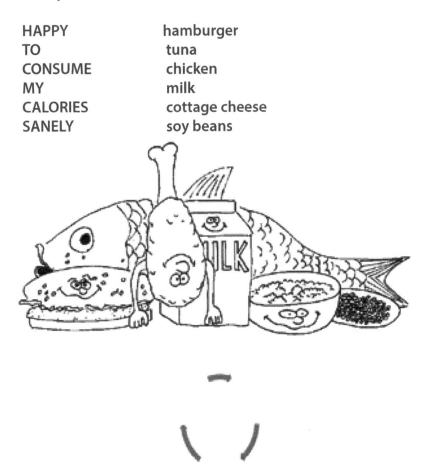

The third way to pass your tests and the third letter in safety stands for First. Priorities have to be determined.

F   **We determine which action to take FIRST. We have to set priorities with this client as well as all of our clients.**

If we had 4 clients to see, would our client with liver dysfunction be our first priority? Probably not. Liver disease is often very slow to progress. Many of these clients are admitted into the hospital over and over again as their disease progresses; sometimes over the course of 40-50 years. Re-assessment can change our priorities.

The fourth way to pass your tests and the fourth letter in safety stands for Evaluate pharmacology

E **We must evaluate pharmacology,** meaning the drugs that are ordered or already being taken or should be taken.

We should assess liver enzyme tests before administering drugs that are detoxified in the liver. Watch any drugs given to a client with liver dysfunction. Remember over 70% of drugs are detoxified in the liver. What if the client has a high cholesterol level (cholesterol is manufactured in the liver)? Would we want to administer any of the "statin" drug group? At least give a provider the opportunity to share their rationale for administering these and other similar drugs.

This image will help you remember the importance of the "statins".

Officer "L.L. Statin" has stopped the liver mobile and its driver, Cholesterol. These drugs lower cholesterol, but can be highly toxic to the liver. Drugs that are in this group end in "statin."

What if our client has a headache? Would we want to administer the over the counter drug Tylenol? Look at this picture and remember forever that Tylenol beats the heck out of the liver.

TYLENOL OVERDOSE

Why beat something that already has a decreased function? ALL **NSAIDs** should be questioned as they make bleeding more likely and cause further liver damage.

Determine if the client has had current adult immunizations? This is the time to remind clients of the importance these that may save their life. Common infections such as flu and pneumonia may increase death in clients with liver disease by as much as 20%. Encourage flu and pneumonia shots.

Clients are often taking non-prescription alternative substances that should also be evaluated. Evidence exists that Milk Thistle may be useful in the treatment of liver damage by coating the liver with protection, enhancing protein uptake and providing anti-inflammatory effects as seen in this image.

MILK THISTLE

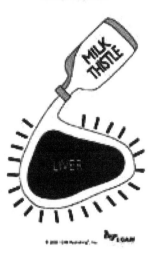

Milk Thistle is sold at the health food stores as a substance that alters the outer liver cells so that toxins cannot enter the cell. Nurses should determine if the client is taking Milk Thistle and document and report it to the health care provider. This substance is sold without prescription but has serious implications for nursing assessment. Liver functions tests should be monitored when this substance is taken.

Kava-Kava and Valerian have been documented to cause liver damage . These supplements should definitely be avoided in liver disease.

There may be dangerous drug/drug interactions with psychiatric medications such as Haldol and phenothiazines. Other drugs that cause reactions are Dilantin, Tylenol and some types of anesthesia. If the order reads Heparin, Coumadin, Lovenox, Aspirin, Plavix or similar substance affecting the clotting of the blood, the order should be questioned and clearly understood before administering.

Abstinence from alcohol is imperative for the client with liver disease.
We can say this to our clients, but our experience indicates that it does not usually happen.

The fifth way to pass your test and the fifth letter in safety is the T for teach and practice infection control.

T   **It is imperative that we teach and practice infection control.**

Hepatitis is inflammation of the liver that causes fatigue, itching, nausea, vomiting, low grade fever and dark urine; yet another way to assess.

> Here is a likely story. Some restaurant cook goes to the potty and does not wash his hands. Remember A is for anal and this is where Hepatitis A comes from. To protect ourselves and our other clients, we must wash our hands when caring for this client. Counsel the client to go to clean restaurants and avoid infected family members and friends.

> B stands for blood and can help you remember where Hepatitis B comes from. We do not want our own liver to be infected just because we have not worn gloves while caring for the client with Hepatitis B.

> Hepatitis C is the most common cause of cirrhosis and in these clients hepatocellular carcinoma is a leading cause of death. Wear gloves

> **The key to practicing universal precautions is to remember the importance of safely handling blood and body secretions. This image will help.**

GLOVES

G loves

L ather up

O rifices

V ery special handling

E veryone may be infected

S harps

GLOVES

Infection Control • 35

A major problem in hospitals today is nosocomial infections. GLOVES will help you remember how to decrease these infections.

G Gloves—wear them

L Lather up—hand-washing is the single best technique to prevent infections

O Orifices in the body secrete body fluids. Handle carefully.

V Very special handling of used equipment, needles, linen will decrease infections

E Everyone may be infected and should be suspect

S Sharps controlled are vitally important so that one does not get stuck with infected needles

The sixth way to pass your test and the sixth letter in safety is the Y for cYa.

Y **Sixth and the last way to pass is called our cYa group and stands for cover your management assets.**

This group of concepts is greatly significant as it appears in the **MANAGEMENT SECTION** of the National Council of State Boards of Nursing for *NCLEX*®.

There is no question; if you do not cYa, then you have a MESS! This image will help you remember the importance of preventing a MESS.

CYA

M edication errors
M anage restraints

E nsure confidentiality, and identity

S afe equipment (prevent falls)

S afe staff
S afe delegation

Errors in medication and treatment are always dangerous and nurses must accept their responsibility to admit errors made and take subsequent actions.

▪ *Verifying the identity prior to administering medications or treatments* of the client is life saving and career saving for the nurse.

▪ *Fall Protocol* is a particularly important intervention. If this client has progressed to a clouded sensorium of pre-hepatic coma, he is likely to be susceptible to falls.

▪ *Safe equipment and safe staff* is a right for any client, especially one who cannot metabolize medications or fight infection. Faulty equipment or faulty staff must be avoided by being proactive. If equipment is going to be used, test it prior to using it on the client. If it breaks while using it, report it instantly so that you have documentation regarding the incident and the equipment can be repaired prior to using it again. Faulty staff is a scary situation. The person may be taking drugs, be intoxicated, and/or so depressed that they cannot function safely or they may be too incompetent to care for this complex client. In any case, it is your responsibility as a nurse manager to protect the client.

Confidentiality must be provided to this client. He may be a government official that does not want anyone to learn that he has liver dysfunction especially if it is caused from alcohol, Hepatits A, or whatever. HIPAA laws as indicated by the Hippo image will help you remember the confidentiality issue.

HIPAA

©2008 I CAN Publishing, Inc.

H ow to release information to health care workers that "need to know"

I mpermissible uses and disclosures result in lawsuits

P rotect privacy of individually identifiable health information

A rrange for sharing information with families in a discreet manner

A ccess by clients to medical records including the right to see and copy

Repetition is the "mother of learning" so we suggest reviewing this image of Larry Leak liver to bring all of this information together for you.

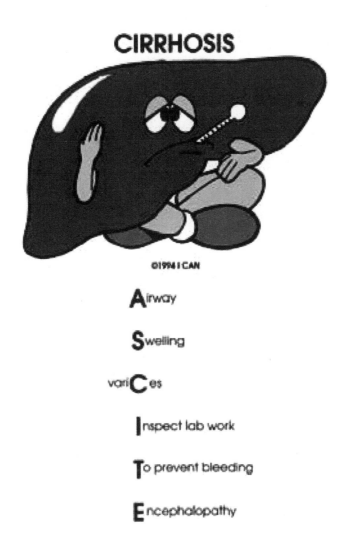

CIRRHOSIS

©1994 I CAN

Airway

Swelling

vari**C**es

Inspect lab work

To prevent bleeding

Encephalopathy

Commonalities that flow through client safety of every body system and are heavily weighted on the **NCLEX**® can be condensed into the following table on MANAGE.

These standards currently count for as much as 23% of the total **NCLEX**® exam and are always a primary consideration for nursing.

PASS *NCLEX*®!	
M	**Make sure of identity, accuracy of orders**
A	**Arrange privacy/confidentiality/consent/collaboration with other team**
N	**No injuries, falls, malfunctioning equipment or staff or hazards**
A	**Address errors, abuse, legalities, scope of practice—document**
G	**Give (delegate) orders to appropriate people**
E	**Establish priorities of clients and time**

Practice Questions, Answers and Rationale

Answers and rationale follow at the end of the questions. We recommend answering all questions prior to looking at any of the answers.

1. A client is admitted from the emergency service with a diagnosis of drunkeness and spitting up blood. A proirity assessment would include: (**Select all that apply**)
   A. Vital signs, abdominal assessment and neuro checks
   B. Seek provider order for liver enzymes and complete blood count
   C. Complete head to toe physical assessment
   D. Determine current medications and alternative medications
   E. Seek order for liver biopsy and blood alcohol level

2. Which is the highest management priority in the next 4 hours for the client with a diagnosis of drunkeness and spitting up blood?
   A. Provide privacy and confidentiality for the client
   B. Establish fall protocol
   C. Determine the staff member best equipped to care for this client
   D. Evaluate the equipment that is in the client's room

3. The client with a diagnosis of cirrhosis of the liver reports that he is taking milk thistle from the health food store. Which prescription drug should be questioned if ordered? **Select all that apply.**
   A. Compazine for nausea
   B. Thorazine for the second diagnosis of a mental illness
   C. Aspirin or Tylenol for headaches
   D. Penicillin for an infection

4. The client with hepatitis A has asked if he can return to his job at McDonald's. What is the priority teaching for this client ?
   A. The importance of weekly blood drawn for liver enzymes
   B. Hand washing techniques and compliance with his employer's standards
   C. Keeping the appointment for an EGD to determine esophageal varicies
   D. Continuing the administration of Coumadin

5. The nurse is changing a dressing on an infected abdomen after a liver biopsy and notices a large amount of purulent drainage. What is the best way to perform this procedure?
    A. Obtain clean gloves and dressings, remove the soiled dressing and use another pair of clean gloves to dress the wound
    B. Use clean gloves to remove the soiled dressings, change to sterile gloves and use sterile dressings to cover the wound
    C. Use sterile gloves to remove the dressing, obtain clean gloves and sterile dressing to reapply to the wound
    D. Initiate protective isolation; utilize sterile gloves when removing the dressing and reapply using sterile technique

6. To maintain client safety, which should be determined prior to performing a paracentesis for ascities? **Select all that apply.**
    A. If the client is taking Tylenol
    B. If the client is taking Coumadin for stroke prevention
    C. If the client is taking Aspirin to prevent heart attacks
    D. If the client is allergic to local anesthetics as used in the dentist office
    E. If the client has a urinary tract infection

7. During the insertion of a paracentesis needle, the tip of the needle brushes the underside of the sterile field. Which nursing action is most appropriate?
    A. Wipe the tip with alcohol before insertion
    B. Bring this to the attention of the provider performing the insertion so that a new needle can be obtained
    C. Notify the provider to order antibiotics after the procedure is completed
    D. Monitor the WBC count for 3 days after the test is complete

8. A client with hepatic cancer is admitted to the hospital with neutropenia. Which signs and symptoms are most important for the nurse to report to the next shift?
    A. Arthralgia and stiffness
    B. Vertigo and headache
    C. Jaundice and pain
    D. Temperature elevation and lethargy

9. Which of these clients would be most appropriate for the RN to assign to the LPN/LVN?
    A. A 33- year old client who has been admitted for a blood transfusion
    B. A 43-year old client with cirrhosis and is taking antibiotics
    C. A 53-year old client with pyelonephritis presenting with acute pain
    D. A 78-year old client with urinary incontinence starting bladder training

10. The client admitted with liver failure shares some very confidential information with the nurse. The nurse demonstrates appropriate management with this information when he:
    A. Discusses this information with his colleagues
    B. Documents the information on the client's flow sheet
    C. Reviews the information with those staff involved in the plan of care
    D. Keeps the client's confidence and shares the information with no one

11. The client is admitted for an EGD (esophagogastrodudenoscopy). Which are important prior to the client's having the procedure? **Select all that apply.**
    A. Determine that the client has been NPO for at least 4 hours
    B. Determine if the client is allergic to shrimp
    C. Have an informed consent signed by the client
    D. Explain that the client will have general anesthesia
    E. List all current medications the client is taking on the chart

12. The client has diagnoses of osteoporosis and GERD. Which of these medications should be questioned in the teaching plan?
    A. Tums
    B. Rolaids
    C. Prilosec
    D. Maalox

13. The client is admitted to the ED with severe diarrhea. What are the nursing priorities? **Select all that apply**
    A. Determine vital signs
    B. Asses for dehydration
    C. Determine if the client has visited foreign countries
    D. Determine if other family members have diarrhea
    E. Call provider for anti-diarrheal drug

14. The client has an order for a colonoscopy. Which is priority teaching prior to this procedure?
    A. Explain the procedure and what the client should expect
    B. Clarify the bowel preparation for this procedure
    C. Explain that a 3- day recovery time is necessary
    D. Provide the provider's contact information
    E. Ask the client to hold all NSAIDS and Aspirin

15. The Girl Scout camp nurse has been advised of an outbreak or nausea, vomiting and diarrhea. What is priority teaching for the campers?
    A. Hand washing technique
    B. Eliminating food brought from home
    C. Boil the camp water
    D. Reduce high-energy activities

16. The client admitted from the ED smelling strongly of alcohol has asked repeatedly for his bottle. Which is the best response to his demands?
    A. Listen to his concerns with empathy
    B. Advise him that alcohol cannot be consumed in the hospital setting
    C. Ask him what the alcohol means to him
    D. Administer a PRN drug from protocol to make him comfortable

17. Several clients are admitted to the ED with symptoms of food poisoning. Which of these will be useful in determining the source?
    A. Ask clients if they have traveled to foreign countries
    B. Determine hand hygiene of clients
    C. Determine where clients have eaten within the last 24 hours
    D. Get a full diet history on the clients

18. The client with extensive gastrointestinal surgery is returning home after 6 days in the hospital. Which should be included in the discharge planning?
    A. Educate the client on home safety issues
    B. Provide a full list of approved foods and liquids.
    C. Recommend that the client cease smoking
    D. Advise the client to refrain from alcohol

19. The client's naso-gastric tube has stopped draining at 3pm. At 1pm the I&O indicates an N/G tube output of 75mL. Which nursing action would prevent complications?
    A. Turn the client and ask them to breathe deeply
    B. Walk the client in the hall
    C. Reposition the N/G tube and re-evaluate
    D. Ask the provider to order an x-ray to determine placement

20. Which assessment is priority with the client who is admitted to the ED with nausea, vomiting, diarrhea, muscle weakness and EKG changes? **Select all that apply**
    A. Assess for signs and symptoms of dehydration
    B. Determine hand hygiene
    C. Assess the client's diet for the last 24 hours
    D. Determine medications that the client is taking
    E. From protocol, order an electrolyte panel.

21. Client's bowel sounds are assessed at 3-4 per minute. Which is nursing priority?
    A. Evaluate the amount of fluid the client has ingested in the last 24 hours.
    B. Document normal bowel signs.
    C. Ask the client to turn and re-evaluate
    D. Notify the provider and ask for further orders.

22. The client is admitted to the ED with bleeding from the mouth and rectum and heavy bruising of the skin. Initial assessment indicates a smell of alcohol. What is priority assessment?
    A. Determine the volume of bleeding
    B. Assess vital signs
    C. Determine the time of the last ETOH intake
    D. Determine the client's identity

23. Fidaxomicin (Dificid) is ordered for the client with severe diarrhea. Which assessment should be determined prior to administering this drug?
    A. Level of consciousness
    B. Kidney lab values
    C. GI bleeding
    D. Other drugs client is receiving

24. The family has asked not to be notified if the client is admitted smelling of alcohol. Which action is most useful?
    A. Notify the family if the client is admitted
    B. Establish a therapeutic relationship with the client
    C. Provide end-of–life counseling for the client
    D. Plan interventions that will include the family.

25. The elderly client with nausea, vomiting, and diarrhea is admitted from a nursing home partially unresponsive and showing signs of dehydration. Which assessment is vital after emergency measures are completed?
    A. Assess and plan for the client's emotional needs
    B. Plan a therapeutic relationship with the client's family
    C. Facilitate client/family coping
    D. Assess the potential for abuse or neglect

Answers and rationale

1. **Answers A, B, and C** are all needed for an initial assessment. Answer D may be premature at this point at least until the liver enzymes studies are reported.

2. **Answer B** has the highest priority due to the current assessment of the client. All of the rest are important, but Answer B has priority.

3. **Answers A, B, and C** are contraindicated with the client taking Milk Thistle. Answer D is an acceptable drug as long as allergies have been established.

4. **Answer B** has the highest priority. Non compliance with the hand washing standard is the likely cause of the Hepatitis A. Answer A is not necessary. Answer C may be premature. Answer D, the nurse would not advise a client with hepatitis to take Coumadin without clarifying the provider's order.

5. **Answer B** is the best answer. Sterile gloves and dressings are used in the application of dressings to wounds. Answer D is incorrect because protective isolation is not appropriate for this client. Sterile gloves are not necessary for removing the soiled dressings.

6. **Answers B, C, and D** are correct. Coumadin and aspirin will thin the blood and cause more bleeding during the procedure. Local anesthetics are used to deaden the entrance of the needle used for paracentesis. Tylenol and a urinary tract infection are not likely to affect the test.

7. The best answer is **Answer B**. All others are not legal or ethical.

8. **Answer D.** With a low WBC (neutropenia), the client is at risk for the development of infection This could be best determined by the client's temperature. Answer C could be experienced due to the client's condition, but does not indicate an infection. #a and b are incorrect.

9. **Answer B** is most stable of this group of clients. LPN's do not administer blood without additional education, The client with acute pain needs assessment and the 78-year old requires new teaching.

10. **Answer C** is the best answer. This information must be respected and remain confidential, but should be shared with the staff caring for the client. Answer D does not benefit the client.

11. **Answers A and C** are vital. Iodine is not used in this procedure and rarely do clients receive general anesthesia . Current meds are nice to know, but not vital.

12. **Answer C.** Prilosec is known to increase the risk for bone fractures. The other medications are likely safe for this client.

13. **Answers A and B** are top priorities. The client may have hypotension or an accelerated heart rate due to severe dehydration. All other options are good but not as high priority.

14. Answers A, B and E have the highest priority. The client should know what to expect to reduce anxiety and promote cooperation. The bowel prep is crucial to a successful colonoscopy. Since biopsy are common during colonoscopy all drugs that reduce blood clotting should be avoided for several days prior to the procedure.

15. Answer A. Hand washing has the highest priority.

16. Answer B. While all of the answers may be appropriate, setting limits may be the first place to start.

17. Answer C. While all of the answers may be useful, the priority is to determine the source of poisoning so that it may be contained.

18. Answer B takes priority over all very good options.

19. Answer C is the best. Answers A and B may also work and Answer D is last resort.

20. Answers A, D, E. These symptoms may indicate a high potassium level. This could be confirmed from the electrolyte report. The other options are appropriate, but not priority.

21. Answer C. This should be re-evaluated prior to notifying the provider.

22. Answer B Although all are important, vital signs come first even if the client is unconscious with no identification available.

23. Answer D is correct, as Dificid is known to react strongly to some immunosuppressant drugs. Other answers are secondary.

24. Answer B. Obviously the client does not have the support of the family. Being non-judgmental is crucial. If the client is of age, family notification may be denying confidentiality and privacy.

25. Answer D. Abuse and neglect may be overlooked in the emergent situation. If not corrected, the client will likely return with diminished health.

The Pediatric GASTROINTESTINAL SYSTEM

Jessica Peck, DNP, RN, MSN, CPNP-PC, CNE
Edited by Sylvia Rayfield & Associates, Inc.

What is different about fluid and electrolyte balance for kids?

IN DEVELOPING COUNTRIES, 24% OF ALL CHILD DEATHS ARE FROM DIARRHEA AND DEHYDRATION!! IN THE U.S. THERE ARE MORE THAN 200,000 CHILDREN HOSPITALIZED PER YEAR WITH DIARRHEA AND DEHYDRATION.

KEY CONCEPT TO REMEMBER—WHAT PUTS INFANTS AND CHILDREN MORE AT RISK FOR DEHYDRATION?

- ❖ Infants ingest and excrete more fluid per body weight
- ❖ Body is slower to respond with corrective measures when disturbances occur.
- ❖ Infants <2years have more than 50% extracellular fluid. This is 2-5 times greater than adults!
- ❖ Higher metabolic rate
- ❖ Immature kidney function
- ❖ GI VIRUSES AND INTESTINAL DISORDERS CAN CAUSE CHILDREN TO BECOME DEHYDRATED VERY QUICKLY. **IT IS CRITICAL TO RECOGNIZE EARLY SIGNS OF FLUID AND ELECTROLYTE IMBALANCE AND TO ACT QUICKLY TO REVERSE IT!**

WHAT TO DO WHEN A CHILD SHOWS SIGNS OF GI ILLNESS OR DEHYDRATION:

What do nurses do first? Assess!! Assess the infant using your ABC's.

ASSESSMENT	INTERVENTION
A- AIRWAY Airway should be open and patent. Babies have a tiny airway, so it can close quickly. Be alert!	Position for comfort if not in distress.
B- BREATHING Assess breathing effort. Respiratory rates >60 in any	Monitor for tachypnea, a sign of dehydration. The more rapid the rate, the more severe the fluid loss. Tachypnea also speeds fluid loss.

age infant or child should cause immediate concern.	If respiratory rate is >60, attach cardiopulmonary monitors, give oxygen, and notify provider.		

C- CIRCULATION

Babies have short, fat necks. Don't waste your time trying to find the carotid pulse! Go for the BRACHIAL or FEMORAL pulse. Use the carotid pulse in children>8 years.

Tachycardia is a sign of dehydration. The more rapid the rate, the more severe the case. Blood pressure will be low and continue to lower while heart rate continues to increase as hypovolemic **shock** sets in.

Pulse

BP

D- DEHYDRATION SIGNS

Identifying early signs of dehydration enhances the possibility of a positive outcome.

	MILD	MODERATE	SEVERE
Wt loss	3-5%	5-10%	>10%
Resp Rate	Normal	30-60	>60
Pulse	Normal	Slight increase	Marked increase
Activity	Normal	Irritable	Lethargic
Anterior Fontanel	Normal	Normal or sunken	Sunken
Skin	Cap refill <2sec.	Decreased skin turgor, cap refill >3 seconds	Mottling Acrocyanosis Tenting Cool
Sp. gravity	>1.020	>1.020	Oliguria/anuria

2 or more abnormal findings should point to dehydration >5%

E- EVALUATE I&O

Daily weight, same time, same scale, naked!

Assess every drop of fluid that comes from every pore and orifice of the body:
FREQUENCY, COLOR, CONSISTENCY, VOLUME, ODOR

	Diarrheal stools burn the booty! Avoid wipes, air dry, use petroleum ointment, and don't do rectal temps. Ouch!
	Remember that 1g diaper weight=1mL output!
ASSESS THESE FLUIDS:	Sweat Urine Stool Emesis NG suction Wound Drainage
F- FLUIDS TO REHYDRATE!  **DO NOT GIVE:** **Fruit Juice** **Carbonated Drinks** **Jello** **(High carbs, low electrolytes)** **Caffeine** **(Diuretic)** **Broth** **(High Sodium)** 	*ALERT* ORAL REHYDRATION IS THE FIRST CHOICE OF TREATMENT FOR DEHYDRATION**NOT**IV FLUID THERAPY!! IT IS SAFER, WORKS BETTER, IS PAIN FREE AND COSTS LESS!! Oral Rehydration Solutions (ORS) are first line therapy. Give 50-100mL/kg over 3-4 hours for mild cases. Give 1 tsp every 5-10 minutes. Give 10mL/kg for each loose stool. ONLY STOP ORT IF VOMITING IS SEVERE!! AVOID NPO STATUS TO PREVENT CHANGES IN INTESTINAL PERMEABILITY. IF VOMITING, POSITION SIDE-LYING TO AVOID ASPIRATION. *ALERT* THE BRATT DIET IS AN OUTDATED PRACTICE!!! NEVER RECOMMEND THE BRATT DIET!!! IT IS LOW IN ENERGY AND PROTEIN, HIGH IN CARBS AND LOW IN CALORIES. THE AMERICAN ACADEMY OF PEDIATRICS DOES NOT SUPPORT THIS PRACTICE!* Early reintroduction of food is optimal. Breastfeeding should never stop unless absolutely necessary. Do NOT dilute formula. Milk and regular diet can generally be resumed after oral rehydration is achieved (usually 3-4 hours). FEED THESE BABIES!! Warn parents they might have more diarrhea with feeding, but overall this is better than lack of ingested nutrients. *ALERT* IF THE CHILD IS SEVERELY DEHYDRATED, SHOWING SIGNS OF SHOCK, HAS PERSISTENT VOMITING OR IS UNABLE TO CONSUME LIQUIDS BY MOUTH, IV FLUID THERAPY MUST BE STARTED IMMEDIATELY.* IV SOLUTIONS: Usually normal saline or lactated ringers is appropriate for volume replacement. Maintenance fluids may be D5 1/4 NS with KCL 20mEq/L. Watch for acidosis! *ALERT* WATCH THE IV SITE CAREFULLY!! INFILTRATION OF A FLOWING BOLUS CAN CAUSE PERMANENT DEFORMITY. WATCH

	FOR SIGNS OF FLUID VOLUME OVERLOAD, WHICH CAN OCCUR WITH RAPID REHYDRATION. IF YOU SEE EDEMA, HEAR CRACKLES, OR FEEL BOUNDING PULSES, THEN SLOW YOUR FLUID TKO (1-2cc/hour) AND CALL THE PROVIDER!!*
G- GUARD AGAINST COMPLICATIONS	(1) Maintain fluid and electrolyte balance (2) Rehydrate to correct fluid losses (3) Maintain appropriate fluid therapy until recovered (4) Reintroduce regular diet
H- HELP PREVENT SPREAD OF INFECTION!!	Designate a space for dirty diapers (not on the bedside table!). Discard soiled linens promptly. Change clothes and undies often. HANDWASHING!! Food safety- no raw meat, store food @ proper temperatures. Travel safety—boiled or bottled water, no unwashed or raw fruits/veggies.

A WORD ABOUT CONSTIPATION:

Constipation is not defined by frequency but by CONSISTENCY. If the baby poops once a week but it is soft, that is not constipation! If the baby poops little hard rocks three times a day that is constipation! In pediatrics, constipation can be caused by a congenital malformation or disorder such as Hirschprung's, spina bifida, hypothyroidism, or strictures. However, for most kids constipation is idiopathic and can be managed with a high fiber diet and adequate fluid intake.

INFECTIOUS GI DISEASES

Germ	The nurse watches for signs of.................
Rotavirus	DEHYDRATION
Escherichia coli	HEMOLYTIC UREMIC SYNDROME
Salmonella	SEPSIS or MENINGITIS
Clostridium	PSEUDOMEMBRANOUS COLITIS
Enterobius Vermicularis	PERIANAL ITCHING—DO A TAPE TEST TO LOOK FOR WORMS
Giardia Lamblia	GREASY, PALE, FOUL STOOLS

WHAT IS THE DIFFERENCE BETWEEN GERD AND PYLORIC STENOSIS??

I Feel.........	SICK	MAD
Diagnosis:	**GERD**	**PYLORIC STENOSIS**
Risk Factors:	Preemies Cystic Fibrosis Cerebral Palsy Esophageal Disorders	Genetic Component More common in first born males
Infant Symptoms:	Spitting up A LOT! FORCEFUL spit up (hits the wall!) Hematemesis Classic Back Arching ALTE (Apparent life-threatening event) Apnea Recurrent aspiration pneumonia	HUNGRY!!! Vomits 30-60min after feeding FTT (Failure to Thrive) Dehydration Olive-shaped mass on RUQ (Right Upper Quadrant)
KEY FACT:	Vomiting is intermittent and does not worsen progressively over time. This baby feels **SICK** because he is vomiting/refluxing all the time. Weird but true—babies with diagnosed severe GERD can sleep prone to prevent aspiration. Parents should be cautioned not to use soft bedding.	Vomiting starts in first few weeks of life and progressively gets worse and worse, usually peaking @ 6 weeks. This baby feels **MAD** because she is so hungry and she works so hard to eat but her tummy is never full.
Child Symptoms:	Chronic Cough Heartburn Difficulty swallowing Abdominal Pain	None. This happens in infancy.

Lab changes:	Hyponatremia Hypokalemia METABOLIC ALKALOSIS	Hyponatremia Hypokalemia METABOLIC ALKALOSIS
I Feel.........	 **SICK**	 **MAD**
Diagnosis:	Upper GI (rule out structural anomaly) 24 hour pH probe (gold standard) Endoscopy (to rule out strictures)	Abdominal Ultrasound (r/o sausage-shaped mass and elongated pylorus)
Treatment:	No treatment needed for thriving infants. May thicken feedings with 1tsp of rice cereal per ounce of formula. Elevate HOB 30 degrees for 30-60 minutes after feedings. May need ranitidine (Zantac), famotudine (Pepcid), pantroprazole (Protonix), or omeprazole (Prilosec). If FTT, recurrent aspiration, esophageal erosion, or failure to respond to pharmacological agents, should consider surgical repair.	The only option for treatment is surgical repair.
Repair:	Usually resolves before one year of age. If unresolved and affecting growth, Nissen fundoplication indicated.	Surgery is emergent- pylorotomy. Surgical incision into the pyloric sphincter.

Know your A-B-C's	APPENDICITIS	HIRSCHPRING'S DISEASE	INTUSSUSCEPTION
	Danger!		
Ask about the history	Risk Factors: • Average age 10 years • Lack of immunization • Usually diagnosed in infants **Inflammation of the appendix caused by an obstruction of some sort **Most common emergency pediatric abdominal surgery in the U.S.	Risk Factors: • Acute or chronic ** Stool accumulates because of non-innervated area in the intestine that causes peristalsis	Risk Factors: • Usually occurs <5 years of age • Most common in 5-9 mos of age • Seen with cystic fibrosis **Telescoping of the intestine into itself.
B—Be aware of possible presenting symptoms you might detect on assessment	• ABRUPT ONSET • Pain starts @ peri-umbilical and then moves to RLQ • Rigid abdomen • Pain with movement • Vomiting • Anorexia • Pallor • Lethargy • Tachycardia • Fever	• Newborn: Failure to pass meconium, bilious vomiting, abd. distention • Infant: GI sx (vomiting, diarrhea, constipation), FTT and abd distention • Child: ribbon-like stool, constipation, abd distention, fecal mass	• This baby will be absolutely fine and then scream its head off. The pain is cyclical with peristalsis. • Palpable mass in RUQ • Distended abdomen • **CLASSIC WARNING SIGN IS CURRANT JELLY STOOL- STOOL MIXED WITH MUCOUS AND BLOOD**

		palpable, undernourish-ed appearance	■ If baby passes a normal stool, it is critical to notify the provider. The intussusception may have corrected itself and the provider may change treatment course
	■ Leukocytosis **ONSET IS ACUTE!! THE PAIN WILL WORSEN OVER A PERIOD OF A FEW HOURS AND INCREASE IN INTENSITY. IF YOUR PATIENT ALL OF A SUDDEN "FEELS SO MUCH BETTER!" THEN WATCH OUT! WARNING!! RED ALERT!!! THE APPENDIX MAY HAVE PERFORATED, TEMPORARILY RELIEVING PRESSURE AND PAIN. THIS CAN OCCUR WITHIN 48 HOURS OF ONSET OF SX. LOOK FOR SIGNS OF SEPSIS!!**		
<u>C</u>—Care for the client until surgical repair is completed.	NO SUPPOSITORIES! NO LAXATIVES! NO ENEMAS! NO RECTAL TEMPS! THIS INCREASES BOWEL MOTILITY AND INCREASES RISK OF PERFORATION! Surgery to remove the appendix is indicated. This is done via open or laparoscopic incision.	Dx is established with rectal biopsy. Repair is accomplished via removal of the aganglionic portion of the colon. The baby may require a temporary (sometimes permanent) colostomy.	Dx is established with ultrasound and/or barium enema. Repair is attempted with an air or barium enema. If unsuccessful, surgical reduction is indicated.

POST-OPERATIVE CARE

	APPENDICITIS	HIRSCHPRUNG'S DISEASE
COMPLICATIONS:	*Peritonitis*	*Enterocolitis*
TIME FRAME:	▪ Usually occurs within 48 hours of onset of illness	▪ Can occur at any time in a child with this disease
ASSESS FOR:	▪ Temperature >101 ▪ Leukocytosis ▪ Increasing or unmanageable pain ▪ Rigid abdomen ▪ No bowel sounds ▪ Be alert for symptoms of sepsis and shock!	▪ HORRIBLE diarrhea! ▪ Measure abd. girth daily @ umbilicus with paper tape measure ▪ Be alert for symptoms of sepsis and shock! ▪ Administer abx as ordered.
INTERVENTIONS	▪ Manage NGT with suction ▪ Maintain fluid and electrolyte balance ▪ Possible JP drains ▪ Pain management ▪ Listen for bowel sounds- this is the cue to begin PO fluids.	

CLEFT LIP AND PALATE

KEY CONCEPT TO REMEMBER:

- ❖ Babies can have a cleft lip AND/OR a cleft palate. It can be unilateral OR bilateral.
- ❖ Palatoplasty is done after the palate has developed, and may be done in stages.

Know your **A-B-C's**	**Cleft Lip and/or Palate**

Ask about the history	Risk Factors:
	
	- Heredity
	
	- Teratogens
	
	    • ***Maternal history of taking phenytoin (Dilantin)***
	
	    • *Maternal smoking*
	
	    • *Family history of cleft lip/palate*

B—Be aware of possible presenting symptoms you might detect on assessment	- Cleft lip is visible upon assessment - Cleft palate may not be visible, need to palpate the palate with a gloved finger.
C—Care for the client until surgical repair	- Assess baby's ability to suck. - Daily weight. - Encourage breastfeeding if desired. Educate moms about pumping. - Parents need lots of support. Promote bonding! Promote coping! - Encourage healthy self-esteem - Coordinate interdisciplinary care with ENT, plastic surgeon, orthodontist, Child Life/play therapy, OT, speech therapy, nutrition, and social services, support groups. - USE AN ENLARGED NIPPLE FOR FEEDINGS, STIMULATE SUCK REFLEX, AND WATCH FOR CHOKING. LIMIT FEEDINGS TO LESS THAN 30 MINUTES TO PREVENT FATIGUE. ASSIST PARENTS WITH ALTERNATIVE FEEDING DEVICES IF NEEDED. BURP MORE FREQUENTLY.

Vital Signs	• Always count pediatric respirations for one full minute! • Monitor for hypothermia, common after surgery, and take corrective measures such as heated blanket, radiant warmer, etc. • Provide gentle oral and nasal suction to prevent aspiration. Observe respiratory effort closely.
Prevent Infection	• Assess operative site for erythema or drainage. • Cleanse site with sterile cotton swab and sterile saline. • Apply antibiotic ointment as prescribed. • Position upright, on back or side. No prone position for lip repair! If palate repair, baby can lie prone. Change positions often. • Use elbow or jacket restraints as necessary to prevent damaging the repair site. These restraints may have to be used for 4-6 weeks!!! • Assess packing used in palate repair, typically remove 2-3 days post-op. • Don't put anything in baby's mouth! (thermometer, pacifier, etc.).
Monitor Fluids	• Strict I&O and daily weight. • IV fluids until NPO status lifted. • Gradually advance to soft foods and fluids, preferably with no utensils.
Pain	• Use an age-appropriate pain scale. • Manage pain aggressively to prevent crying and rupturing sutures!

Visit to watch Allison's Journey with Cleft Lip and Palate

http://www.youtube.com/watch?v=QwldFDSx3vw

Visit to watch Paul's journey with Cleft Lip and Cleft Palate

http://www.youtube.com/watch?v=wgUcRifwXsU

What is the goal of nursing care for a child with cleft lip or palate?

The goal is to cut the **CRAP** this family and child has to deal with.

C—*COMPLIANCE WITH MEDICATION!*

- Take prophylactic antibiotics post-op as prescribed.

R—*RECOVERY FROM ILLNESS*

- Watch for signs of aspiration.

- Watch for signs of ear infection and encourage early intervention.

- Advise parents that speech and language delays are common. Encourage early

  intervention.

- Advise parents that child may experience long-term dental problems. Seek early dental

  care.

A—*ABILITY TO COPE*

- Encourage bonding.

- Educate about positive outcomes of surgeries.

- Utilize interdisciplinary resources.

P—*PREVENT RECURRENCE*

- Early dental care can prevent complications.

- Early intervention for language can help prevent speech delays.

SOME THINGS TO THINK ABOUT HEPATITIS A:

Facts	• The most common form of acute viral hepatitis in the whole world! • MOST COMMONLY AFFECTS CHILDREN <15 YEARS OF AGE! It is often misdiagnosed as a GI virus because GI bugs are very common and children tend to be more resilient. To complicate things, children don't typically become jaundiced with Hep A. However, when they give this to Mama and Daddy, they don't take it so well!
Contagion	• Average incubation period is ~30 days. Hep A can live without a human host this long! Yuck! • Transmitted by fecal-oral route.
Treatment	• Hepatitis A Vaccine is very effective in prevention • If known exposure, give Hep A vaccine AND Hep A IgG. • Handwashing is the best way to prevent infection!!

MEDICATION	ACTION	NURSING CARE	EDUCATION	ALERTS
Antiemetics **Ondansetron (Zofran)** **Phenergan**	Used to stop vomiting.	**May be given as ODT (orally dissolving tablets) or IV**	Can be used to augment ORT to avoid need for IV.	 Phenergan – contraindicated in < 2 year old
Antidiarrheals	Stops diarrhea, duh.	 STOP! This means YOU. NOT RECOMMENDED FOR CHILDREN!!!	Don't give to children at home. The med slows the intestine and can prolong the illness.	DID WE MENTION THESE ARE NOT RECOMMENDED FOR CHILDREN?
Antibiotics	Anti-infectives	Generally NOT given for bacterial diarrheas as		Bloody frequent diarrhea after

		most are self-limiting and can actually prolong the carrier period (for salmonella).		antibiotic use should be reported to rule out clostridium.
Mebendezole (Vermox)	Treats pinworms	Take one now and one in 2 weeks.		
Metronidazole (Flagyl)	Treats c-diff and giardia		Report any GI upset.	

A GI STORY

This is a story about my 5-year-old daughter. One morning while she was getting ready for kindergarten, she told me that her tummy hurt really bad. I decided to keep her home, not knowing what might come of it. Shortly after that, she started having violent diarrhea. After one hour had passed and she had not gotten off the potty, I knew we were going in. On the way to the clinic, she started trembling, she got tunnel vision, and she told me she was scared and she felt like she was going to die. She kept saying "Mommy, help me, please!" I was completely panicking on the inside. I ran into the clinic carrying Savannah, threw my keys at the receptionist and asked her to please go get my other children. The pediatrician took one look at us and told his nurse to start an IV while he went for the car. The nurse squeezed in a bolus while I carried her to the car and we drove half a mile to the hospital, running up to the floor. She was going into-hypovolemic shock. She had clostridium, courtesy of an antibiotic for an ear infection. Thankfully, she has fully recovered. Always in my pediatric classes before I had emphasized to my students that "kids can get real sick, real fast, you gotta stay on your toes" but now when I tell them I can't do it without tears in my eyes and a lump in my throat.

REVIEW QUESTIONS

1. A 9-month-old child is brought in to the emergency room for vomiting and diarrhea. The nurse performs an assessment. The infant's pulse is 168, respiratory rate is 40, temp is 101.1, blood pressure is 74/42, skin is cool to the touch and there is tenting of the skin on the abdomen. What action should the nurse take at this time?

1) Ask the mother to voice her concerns.
2) Prepare an IV fluid bolus and administer immediately.
3) Notify the provider of possible impending hypovolemic shock.
4) Encourage the mother to breastfeed to orally rehydrate the infant.

Option #3 is correct. The physical assessment findings indicate impending shock. Options #1 and #4 may be appropriate nursing interventions but not at this time during possible impending emergency. A nurse cannot administer an IV fluid bolus without a provider order.

2. A nurse is caring for an 8-year-old child with severe abdominal pain that began approximately 8 hours ago. Suddenly the patient reports that she feels much better. She sits up and asks for something to eat. What action should the nurse take at this time?

1) Offer small sips of clear fluids, ~5cc every 10 minutes as tolerated.
2) Call the provider immediately.
3) Order a tray from the cafeteria with BRATT diet foods.
4) Check the patient's vital signs

Option #2 is correct. This is a sign of possible rupture of the appendix. Offering clear fluids may not be contraindicated and checking the patient's vital signs is not inappropriate but it is more critical to notify the provider. The BRATT diet is no longer recommended.

3. A 6-month-old infant is being admitted from the ER for dehydration. Upon initial assessment the nurse notes bounding peripheral pulses, periorbital edema, and crackles in both lungs with increased work of breathing. What is the appropriate nursing intervention?

1) Increase oral fluid intake
2) Weigh the baby and compare to ER admission weight
3) Administer blow-by oxygen until work of breathing decreases
4) Notify the provider of impending hypovolemic shock

Option #2 is important because overhydration may have occurred. Infants can easily be given too large of a bolus, causing fluid volume overload. Options #1 and #4 are not appropriate because the infant is experiencing signs of fluid volume overload. Option #3 may be a necessary intervention but the most critical element is to evaluate for FVO and take corrective action.

4. An 18-month-old has just had surgery to correct a cleft lip and palate and is now 4 hours post-op. The nurse notes a small amount of serous bloody drainage coming from the side of the patient's mouth. What is an appropriate intervention for this patient?

   1) Use a tongue depressor and a penlight to gently inspect the surgical site.
   2) Use sterile cotton swabs to gently cleanse the inside of the oral cavity.
   3) Use gentle suction to remove the secretions.
   4) Call the provider to report the secretions.

Option #3 is correct. This is an appropriate intervention. It is CONTRAINDICATED to insert anything into the mouth following cleft palate repair. A small amount of drainage is to be expected post-op and at this point would not be necessary to report to the provider.

5. A nurse is giving the mother of a 2-month-old infant anticipatory guidance regarding health promotion. The mother is exclusively breastfeeding and asks if any supplements are necessary for the baby. Which of the following is appropriate advice?

   1) Suggest over-the-counter iron drops to be given daily
   2) Advise the mother to discuss vitamin D supplementation with the provider
   3) Advise the mother to obtain a prescription for calcium supplementation
   4) Suggest 2 ounces per day of citrus juice for vitamin C

Option #2 is correct. 400IU of Vitamin D is recommended for infants who are exclusively breastfed. Iron from breastmilk is very efficiently absorbed and no additional supplementation is needed until 4-6months, when maternal iron stores begin to decrease. Iron fortified cereal is usually adequate. Calcium supplements are not recommended for infants and they should not have citrus juice until 12 months of age.

6. A 7-year-old with a history of a peanut allergy comes to the school nurse during lunchtime complaining of itching and tightness in her throat. She sounds mildly hoarse. Her vital signs are all normal.   What action should the nurse take at this time?

   1) Administer the child's epi pen and call 911.
   2) Administer one dose of oral Benadryl.
   3) Call 911
   4) Call the child's mother for guidance

Option #1 is correct. These are early signs of anaphylaxis and need to be treated before the symptoms progress to a life-threatening state. This child has a history of allergies, has an epi-pen, and was in the lunchroom at the time of the exposure.

7. A 13-month-old (10kg) infant was admitted with dehydration and has been fully rehydrated in the Emergency Department. The provider on the floor writes an order to administer lactated ringers at 92 cc/hour. What is the appropriate action of the nurse?

    1) Question the provider about the rate
    2) Adjust the rate to 4cc/hour
    3) Adminster the fluid as ordered
    4) Question the provider about the fluid

Option #1 is correct. Maintenance fluid is calculated as 100mL for first 10kg, 50mL for the second 10kg, and 20mL for the remainder of weight in kg. Divide the total by 24hours. Using this formula, the baby should receive 4cc/ hour for maintenance, which makes a rate of 92 potentially life threatening. An RN cannot adjust the IV rate without provider orders.

8. A 2-year-old toddler has been hospitalized for severe diarrhea and dehydration. The provider orders a clear liquid diet. Which of the following are appropriate choices to offer? **Select all that apply.**

    1) Apple juice
    2) Lemon-lime soda
    3) Chicken or beef broth
    4) Flat cola
    5) Gelatin

This is a trick question! None of these options are correct. Apple juice and lemon-lime soda are high in carbohydrates and low in electrolytes. Chicken and beef broth have excessive sodium and inadequate carbohydrates. Cola contains caffeine, which acts as a diuretic. Oral Rehydration Solutions (ORS) are the drink of choice.

9. The mother of a 1-year-old child tells a nurse that the child occasionally experiences constipation. The mother would like advice about foods that are high in fiber. What is the best advice to give?

        1) Peanuts, seeds, legumes and popcorn
        2) Raw vegetables such as broccoli and cauliflower
        3) Raw fruits with skins or seeds
        4) Whole-grain cereals or breads

Option #4 is correct. While all of these foods are high in fiber, the first three present possible choking hazards for an infant.

10. The nurse is caring for an infant who has just had an ileostomy placed as a treatment for Hirschprung's Disease. The nurse assesses the ostomy bag and finds it very tight and full of air. The bag appears as though it is about to burst. What is the appropriate action to take at this time?

        1) Notify the provider immediately
        2) Use a syringe with a small gauge needle to extract the air from the bag
        3) Remove the bag and replace it with a new one
        4) Open the clamp to push the air out of the bag.

Option #4 is correct. You have to "burp the bag." Gas escapes into the bag and must be released or the bag may rupture. There is certainly no need to call the provider to report the baby has gas! A syringe will poke a hole and take away the integrity of the bag. Replacing the bag is within the nurse's scope of practice but certainly not necessary!

11. A nurse is caring for a 3-month-old who has been hospitalized for gastroesophageal reflux (GER). The provider tells the mother to keep the baby on "reflux precautions." The mother asks the nurse what this means? Which of the following should be included in the explanation? **Select all that apply.**

        1) Feed the baby larger amounts at less frequent intervals
        2) Feed the baby smaller amounts at more frequent intervals
        3) Keep the baby upright for at least 30 minutes after feedings
        4) Keep the baby supine for at least 30 minutes after feedings
        5) Avoid rocking the baby immediately after feedings
        6) Raise the baby's mattress 60 degrees

Options #2, #3, and #5 are correct. Rocking or jostling can cause reflux episodes. The mattress should be elevated 30 degrees or six inches.

12. A nurse is caring for a 15-year-old with severe abdominal pain. The teen suspects she is having severe menstrual cramps but is waiting to go to ultrasound to rule out appendicitis. Which intervention could be especially harmful at this time?

      1) Offer the teen a heating pad for comfort
      2) Administer an ordered dose of morphine
      3) Place the teen in a side-lying position
      4) Allow the teen to have bathroom privileges

Option #1 is correct. Heat to the abdomen can stimulate bowel motility and increase the risk of perforation of the appendix. Laxatives and suppositories are also contraindicated.

13. A 3-year-old child has been diagnosed with Hepatitis A. Which question to the mother is most important at this time?

      1) Have all household members been vaccinated for Hepatitis A?
      2) Which daycare does the child attend?
      3) Have you notified your place of employment about this illness?
      4) Have you traveled out of the country recently?

Option #1 is correct. The priority is to ensure all family members have been vaccinated. The vaccine is recommended for post-exposure prophylaxis. Family members may also get an injection of immunoglobulin. The health department will need to be notified and it is their responsibility to work with the daycare. The mother may also informally notify them. Traveling out of the country is a risk factor for Hepatitis A, but it is no longer critically relevant because diagnosis has been established.

14. A 3-month-old infant has just undergone cleft lip and palate repair. Which of the following is appropriate to include in her post-operative care?

      1) Suction secretions to minimize contamination of the sutures with saliva
      2) Use a pacifier for comfort to prevent crying
      3) Maintain elbow restraints for 4-6 weeks
      4) Encourage mom to pump breastmilk and feed by syringe until healed

Option #3 is correct. Elbow restraints are critical to prevent permanent damage and scarring to the surgical site. Pacifiers, suction, tongue depressors or any other objects in the mouth are not allowed. Infants may breastfeed once fully awake from surgery.

15. A nurse is assisting a new mother to breastfeed her newborn. After the second feeding, the baby has small amounts of frothy saliva. After the third feeding, the baby experiences a transient episode of cyanosis and increased secretions. What action should the nurse take at this time?

       1) Call the provider
       2) Put the baby on cardiopulmonary monitoring in the nursery
       3) Administer oxygen via blow-by
       4) Suction the secretions and deliver oxygen by face mask

The correct option is #1. This baby is experiencing signs of esophageal atresia or a tracheoesophageal fistula, which are both medical emergencies.

16. A 4-month-old infant has been admitted for suspected intussusception and is in the procedure room awaiting a therapeutic enema. The nurse notes that the infant has passed a formed brown stool while waiting. What action should the nurse take at this time?

       1) Postpone the procedure until bowel preparation can be completed.
       2) Notify the provider of the stool passage
       3) Continue the procedure as planned
       4) Administer a suppository before doing the procedure.

The correct option is #2. This indicates the intussusception may have reduced itself and the provider may choose to alter the treatment plan after reevaluation.

17. A 3-year-old with acute lead toxicity is admitted for chelation therapy. What is an appropriate action to be taken prior to medication administration of Calcium EDTA?

       1) Establish adequate urine output
       2) Perform a baseline neurological assessment
       3) Ensure that child has been NPO for at least 4-6 hours
       4) Place the child on cardiopulmonary monitoring

The correct option is #1. EDTA (as well as lead) can be toxic to the kidneys so monitoring and preserving renal function are critical. Acute lead poisoning can impact the neurological system, but it is not related to the EDTA administration. The child does not have to be NPO or on cardiopulmonary monitoring for the administration.

18. Which measures can the nurse recommend to parents who live in a house built prior to 1960 to help prevent lead poisoning? **Select all that apply.**

      1) Wash toys and pacifiers frequently
      2) Wet mop floors and window sills at least once per week
      3) Use only hot water from the tap
      4) Give the children regular meals and frequent snacks
      5) Place rugs and carpets throughout the home to cover the floors.

Options #1, #2, and #4 are correct. Hot water dissolves lead more easily so only cold water should be used for consumption purposes. Flush the pipes by letting the water run for at least 30 seconds before consumption. This removes water with higher concentrations of lead that have been sitting in the pipes. Rugs and carpets require vacuuming, which stirs up dust. Hard floor surfaces that can be wet-mopped are preferred. Lead is also best absorbed on an empty stomach so frequent snacks can be helpful.

19. The nurse is caring for a 4-year-old child with clostridium difficile. Which measures should be implemented to help prevent the spread of infection? **Select all that apply.**

      1) Wash hands before and after each patient contact
      2) Use alcohol gel after washing hands with soap
      3) Strictly enforce droplet precautions
      4) Place the child in a private room
      5) Require visitors to adhere to isolation precautions

Options #1, #4, and #5 are correct. Alcohol gel does not kill clostridium spores. Correct handwashing technique is critical. Contact precautions are appropriate.

20. A nurse is caring for a 3-year-old who has gotten into some medications that were in the grandmother's purse during a hospital visit. There were three different medications and the family is unsure which ones were ingested. The child begins to vomit. What actions should the nurse take at this time? **Select all that apply.**

      1) Request an order for ipecac syrup
      2) Lie the child supine in the bed with side rails up
      3) Suction secretions
      4) Call the provider
      5) Establish baseline vital signs

Options #3, #4, and #5 are correct. The child should be placed in the recovery position on his side to prevent aspiration. Suctioning is a good way to collect a specimen that can be analyzed for drug ingestion. Ipecac is no longer recommended because it can cause excessive vomiting.

Nursing Management in Fluids, Electrolytes, and Acid Base

IT'S NOT ROCKET SCIENCE!!!

Judy Duvall, EdD, MSN, RN

If you do not know how many miles are in a kilometer, you won't know how long it will take to get there!

Mention **Fluid and Electrolytes (F&E)** or acid-base balance and the new graduate's eyes often glaze over and pallor sets in. The bottom line with F&E/acid-base is there is a need to do some memorization, but there is also a need to have understanding of the concepts. Our bodies are amazing mechanisms that seek to remain in homeostasis or balance. When these things are out of balance, it can often be life-threatening, so it is crucial that the practitioner recognizes critical levels and understand how they are treated.

Let's start with fluid balance. About 60% of our total body weight is water, 40% is intracellular, and 20% is extracellular. Extracellular fluid is further broken down—15% is interstitial and 5% is intravascular. The total percentages are less in the elderly and infants, so these folks become dehydrated much more readily. The two nursing diagnoses are **Fluid Volume Deficit (FVD) and Fluid Volume Overload (FVO).**

To assess for **FVD**, daily weight is one of the nurse's best tools. A loss of 1 kg (2.2 pounds) equals a loss of one liter of fluid. Other assessments would include blood pressure, increased heart rate, increased respiratory rate, dry mucous membranes, and decreased urinary output. Skin turgor is a poor assessment, especially in the geriatric client who has lost elasticity of the skin. FVD is treated with fluid administration.

To assess for **FVO**, again, daily weight is one of the best tools. Auscultation of lungs may demonstrate crackles. There may be hypertension, tachycardia, edema, and neck vein distention. Fluid volume overload is treated medically with diuretics. Nurses should position the client sitting up so they can breathe better. They may be taught to sleep on two pillows or raise the head of the bed. They also may be taught fluid restrictions.

With fluid volume overload the medical treatment of choice is diuretics and the expected outcome would be a decreasing trend in CVP or PCWP. You would expect to see increased urinary output, clearing lung sounds, decreasing edema, and weight loss. Remember, you must know the potassium level prior to giving a loop diuretic such as furosemide (Lasix). Lasix will deplete potassium and cause cardiac arrhythmias.

Types of Dehydration

Isotonic Dehydration

If there is isotonic dehydration the client is losing water and sodium equally. This results in intravascular volume depletion and can be medically treated initially by the administration of isotonic IV fluids (0.9% NS or Lactated Ringers). Isotonic solutions "fill up the tank" or the vascular space. If the client has a CVP (central venous pressure) or PA(pulmonary artery) catheter in place as you are treating FVD, the expected outcome would be an increase in the CVP (norms 2-6 mmHg or 6-12 cm H_2O) or PCWP (pulmonary capillary wedge pressure—norm 8-12 mmHg). The specific number is not as important as the trend. If it is rising, things are moving in the right direction. You would also anticipate an increase in BP and urinary output, as well as weight. Recognize trends and changes in client condition.

Hypertonic Dehydration

If a client has hypertonic dehydration, the osmolality of the blood is elevated. You might see this in diabetic ketoacidosis where the glucose and ketones are making the blood very "syrupy." In order to maintain homeostasis, fluid is drawn into the vascular space from the interstitial spaces and the cells. This results in cellular dehydration. To rehydrate the cells, hypotonic IV solution is administered. This would be 0.45% NS or 0.225% NS. If the provider orders other types of fluids, determine the accuracy of the order.

Hypotonic Dehydration

If the client has a low serum osmolality, such as might be seen in hypoalbuminemia, hyponatremia, or SIADH, fluid leaks from the vascular space into the interstitial spaces and the cells. The cells begin to swell and the client has edema, ascites, and change in level of consciousness. Recognize trends and changes in client condition.

The brain is especially sensitive to swollen or shrinking cells. Initial treatment would include fluid restrictions and diuretics from protocol. Hypertonic IV solutions include 3% NS, which can be administered very cautiously with close monitoring for fluid volume overload as fluid gets pulled into the vascular space. Close observation of neurological status is crucial when administering this solution.

Other hypertonic solutions include TPN, 10% DW, Hespan, and albumin. Close attention must be paid to fluid volume balance when administering these solutions. This includes daily weights, close monitoring of vital signs, and focused cardiac, respiratory, and neuro assessments.

Hypovolemic and Distributive Shock Including Fluids and Medications

MEDICATION ADMINISTRATION ALERT

Remember, nurses must be CAREFUL prior to administering medications.

PASS *NCLEX*®!

C	Calculate correctly
A	Assess for allergies
R	Rights of administration
E	Evaluate response
F	Feel free to call provider if intuition alerts
U	Utilize assessments in determining ordered parameters
L	Lab data pertinence

Type of Shock	Shock	Rescue	Fall Out
Hypovolemic	**Causes:** trauma, hemorrhage, burns, large draining wounds, excessive vomiting/diarrhea	Lower head to flat or 10 degrees, raise legs to increase blood volume to vital organs.	Acute renal failure (pre-renal) Lactic acidosis
	Early symptoms: anxiety, tachycardia, tachypnea, widening pulse pressure	Insert at least 2 large bore IVs. May need central line and arterial line insertion.	Multi-organ dysfunction syndrome (MODS)
	Late symptoms: decreased blood pressure, tachycardia, tachypnea, cool/clammy skin, decreased urinary output, decreased level of consciousness	Administer crystalloid solutions initially: 0.9% NS or Lactated Ringers, may need colloids (albumin, Hespan, blood, and blood products) Insert indwelling catheter and monitor urinary output every hour. Monitor vital signs and CVP (if available) every 15 minutes until stable. May need to be intubated and placed on ventilator to assist with tissue oxygenation. Trauma clients and those with hemorrhage may need to go to surgery. Vasopressors used if fluid resuscitation not effective.	Death

TYPE OF SHOCK	SHOCK	RESCUE	FALL OUT
Septic	**SIRS:** heart > 90, temp < 96.8 or > 100.4; Respiratory rate > 20 or $PaCO_2$ < 32; WBC > 12,000 or < 4,000 or with > 10% bands. If caused by infection, this is sepsis. **Septic shock** is the presence of sepsis and hypotension. **Early:** Massive vasodilation, skin warm and flushed, hypotension, tachycardia, tachypnea, decreased urinary output **Late:** MODS, anuria, cold/clammy, decreased LOC; DIC Death	Fluid resuscitation: monitor CVP, VS, and urinary output. Prepare to assist with arterial monitoring or PA monitoring. Will most likely be intubated and placed on mechanical ventilator. Obtain cultures prior to beginning antibiotics. Administer antibiotics within one hour of order. Vasopressors: norepinephrine (Levophed) or dopamine—titrate to maintain MAP>65 mmHg. Vasopressin (anti-diuretic hormone) @ 0.01-0.04 units/min. Do not titrate. Consider Xigris (activated protein C) if high risk of death. Monitor for bleeding. Monitor platelets, PT, PTT. Maintain glucose level < 150 mg/dl.	Early recognition and treatment is the key to improving mortality rates. Most hospitals now use sepsis screening and sepsis bundles to better identify and treat clients early. DIC is a frequent outcome of sepsis, along with multi-system organ failure and death. Vasopressors should be administered through a central line to avoid necrosis of tissue due to extravasation from peripheral line. Glycemic control has been linked to improved survival.

TYPE OF SHOCK	SHOCK	RESCUE	FALL OUT
Neurogenic	If due to spinal shock, stabilization of the spinal cord is priority. Symptoms include hypotension due to loss of sympathetic tone and bradycardia. This results in relative hypovolemia.	Close monitoring of VS. Will need to be intubated and ventilated. Cautious fluid resuscitation. Vasopressors to increase sympathetic tone (phenyephrine [Neosynephrine]) and improve BP and organ perfusion. Atropine to treat bradycardia. Monitor for hypothermia.	**MODS,** circulatory collapse, death

INSERTION AND CARE OF CENTRAL LINES AND PICC LINES

Central and PICC lines provide a means of administering large amounts of fluid, irritating medication, parenteral nutrition, obtain blood specimens and monitor central venous pressure. In spite of these benefits, central lines are a leading cause of blood stream infections. To reduce this risk, most hospitals have adopted central line bundles which are based on the latest evidence.

When a decision is made to insert a central line, it is the RNs role to assist with the insertion. A consent form must be obtained and the nurse will gather the equipment and explain the procedure to the client. The client is positioned in Trendelenburg to decrease the risk of an air emboli and to engorge the internal jugular vein. The client needs to be informed that his/her face will be covered during the procedure but that he/she will be able to breathe. A local anesthetic (1% lidocaine) is used.

In addition to assisting the HCP with equipment during the insertion, the nurse must also provide emotional support to the client and observe for **any** break in sterile technique. Following insertion, it is generally the nurse who cleans the site with chlorhexadine and applies a transparent dressing. A portable chest x-ray is obtained immediately after insertion to look for correct placement and for a pneumothorax, which is a complication of the procedure.

PICC lines are usually inserted by a specially trained nurse or technician. The PICC line is inserted using ultrasound and is typically inserted above the brachial vein. A gauze dressing is placed over the site and it is covered with a transparent dressing. This procedure also requires meticulous sterile technique. Apply principles of infection control. Again, a portable chest x-ray is recommended to check placement.

Most facilities now require a sterile dressing change 24 hours after insertion and then every 7 days thereafter. A Biopatch® is placed at the insertion site. This has been shown to decrease the incidence of infection. A mask is applied on the client and he/she is asked to turn their face away from the site. The following is a link demonstrating central line care:

http://www.youtube.com/watch?v=-2FHgk9GCgs&feature=related

If the client has a PICC line, **avoid blood pressure on the affected arm**. The upper arm circumference is measured daily.

Arterial Monitoring When clients have decreased blood pressure or peripheral perfusion, need frequent arterial blood samples, or are receiving vasoactive drugs that require close monitoring of vital signs, an arterial line is frequently inserted. The presence of an arterial line requires, for monitoring, that the client be in the critical care unit. The radial artery is the most common site to place an arterial catheter; however, if the client is gravely ill, it may be necessary to use the femoral artery. If a decision is made to insert an arterial line, a consent form must be obtained. Equipment includes a pressure bag, a bag of normal saline with pressure tubing and transducer, a bedside monitor with pressure cable, and the arterial catheter. Chlorhexadine is the recommended prep and sterile barriers should be used. Below is a link that shows the insertion procedure. http://www.youtube.com/watch?v=RYf1ZSBjymk

Nursing care for the client with an arterial line includes maintaining the monitoring system and careful assessment of the site for compromised circulation to the hand. An arm board is frequently used to prevent flexion of the wrist. The insertion site is covered with a sterile transparent dressing. The pressure bag needs to be inflated to 300mm Hg. Continuously observe the arterial waveform and keep the alarm set at all times. If there should be a disconnection in the tubing, a client could bleed to death. The arterial line should be removed as soon as it is no longer necessary. To remove the line, perform hand hygiene and apply clean gloves. Sutures will need to be cut if present. Place a folded 4x4 gauze pad at the insertion and remove the catheter. Observe the catheter to be certain it is intact. Apply firm pressure to the arterial insertion site for a minimum of 10-15 minutes and/or until hemostasis is achieved. Apply a pressure dressing to the site and observe frequently for bleeding or hematoma development.

ELECTROLTYES

These need to be memorized. Electrolyte balance is critical.

HYPONATREMIA
Serum sodium < 135 mEq/L
- **Critical Level** < 120 mEq/L

Serum osmolality < 280 mOsm/kg
- **Critical Level** < 250 mOsm/kg

Causes:
- Excess sodium loss
- Water gains
- SIADH
- Excessive hypotonic fluid
- Eating disorders
- Psychogenic water intoxication

Symptoms:
- Anorexia, N&V, abdominal cramping, diarrhea
- Headache
- Muscle cramps, weakness, tremors
- Seizures and coma

Nursing Interventions
- I&O
- Daily weights
- VS assessment
- Neuro assessment/seizure precautions
- Fall precautions
- Fluid restriction
- Increase Na intake/ loop diuretics

HYPERNATREMIA
Na level > 145 mEq
- Critical Level > 160 mEq/L
- May be present in fluid volume deficit or fluid volume excess—think Cushing's disease
- Hypernatremia almost never occurs in clients with an intact thirst mechanism
  Think geriatric clients, infants, those in a coma, clients on enteral nutrition

Symptoms
- CV: tachycardia, HTN, decreased contractility
- Skin: dry, sticky mucous membranes, rough, dry tongue, flushed skin
- Neuromuscular: twitching, tremor, hyperreflexia, seizures, coma
- GI: watery diarrhea, nausea, thirst

Nursing Interventions
- If fluid deficit: hypotonic IVFs
- If fluid and sodium loss: isotonic IVFs

- If poor renal excretion: diuretics
- Adequate water intake and sodium restriction
- If on tube feedings, add free water
- I&O
- VS monitoring/ neuro assessment
- Daily weight
- Safety: fall and seizure precautions
- Sodium restriction

HYPOKALEMIA

Serum potassium < 3.5
Critical value < 2.5
Causes

- Excess GI losses
- Renal losses
- Inadequate intake
- Shift into cells (alkalosis)
- Eating disorders

Since 98% of potassium is inside the cell, minor changes in extracellular potassium levels can cause major problems

- Occurs when serum potassium is >3.5 mEq/L
- Hypokalemia can be life threatening
- Severity of problems is dependent upon how rapidly it drops

Symptoms

- Musculoskeletal: muscle weakness, weak grasp, hyporeflexia
- Respiratory: weakens muscles needed for breathing resulting in shallow respirations
- Cardiovascular: weak, thready pulse, EKG abnormalities (flat T waves, U wave, PVCs)
- Neurologic: changes in mental status, irritability, anxiety followed by lethargy, confusion, and coma
- GI: decreased peristalsis, hypoactive bowel sounds
- Psychosocial: behavioral changes can occur quickly, obtain baseline data

Nursing Interventions

- Potassium supplements: given IV for severe hypokalemia
- Recommended infusion rate 5-10 mEq/hr—never exceed 20 mEq/hr via central line—must be on cardiac monitor
- Severe tissue irritant—**never** give IM or Sub Q
- Oral potassium supplements (K-Dur, Micro-K,)
- Encourage high potassium foods
- Safety: fall precautions due to muscle weakness
- Monitor respiratory status-rate and pulse ox every hour at a minimum; evaluate ABGs for hypoxemia and hypercapnea
- Cardiac monitoring

It was the middle of the night in a small hospital decades ago. I was a relatively new nurse working in the critical care unit. I was caring for a client who had had surgery for a ruptured abdominal aortic aneurysm and who was not stable. My co-worker was caring for three clients in the room next door. Two were routine post-op clients and the third was admitted about 11 pm with diabetic ketoacidosis. He was a 19 year old male whose admitting glucose level was > 500 mg/dl. His attending provider was a general practitioner who had practiced for decades in the community.

The client was on an insulin drip and the blood glucose was coming down nicely. He was receiving fluid replacement at 200 mL/hr and his output was increasing and vital signs were stabilizing. Glucose levels were being measured hourly but other labs were not being monitored. The client was becoming unresponsive and my colleague notified the provider. She received an order for STAT electrolytes and the doctor came in. As he arrived, I answered a phone call from the lab who reported a critical potassium level of 1.9 mEq/L. When I went into the room to report the lab value, the client was in cardiac arrest. In spite of prolonged resuscitation efforts, he passed away.

As a result of this experience, the relationship between glucose, potassium, and bicarbonate is deeply etched in my brain. Insulin is the "key" that unlocks the cell and carries glucose into the cell. This decreases serum potassium levels. As acidosis is resolving, the serum potassium level also decreases. I feel in my heart that this young man did not have to die. If his electrolytes were monitored every two hours, hypokalemia would have been apparent before it was life-threatening. Looking back on the telemetry strips, it was apparent that the T wave was flattening and a U wave developed. I can comfort myself with the thought that he wasn't my client but that does not relieve my responsibility. I carry him in my heart to this day and I know what I learned that night has helped save other clients.

HYPERKALEMIA

Serum potassium > 5.0
Critical value > 6.5
Causes

- Renal failure
- Potassium sparing diuretics
- Excess potassium intake
- Aged blood
- Cell and tissue damage
- Acidosis

Symptoms

- Muscle twitches, cramps, parathesias
- EKG changes-tall peaked T-wave, widened QRS, prolonged PR interval, dysrhythmias
- Abdominal cramping, diarrhea
- Irritability and restlessness
- Decreased BP

Interventions for critical levels
- Insulin/50% Dextrose/ Sodium bicarbonate to move potassium into the cell
- Calcium Gluconate for cardiac effects
- Kayexalate and sorbitol-binds with potassium in the large intestine-eliminated through stool
- Emergent dialysis
- Administration of loop duiretics

Nursing Interventions
- I&O
- Monitor Serum K + and EKG
- Client education
- Low potassium diet
- No salt substitutes

POTASSIUM

Hyperkalemia   Mount T (t-wave) Tall t-waves

Skier at top (Hyper)--NVD, numbness, muscle twitches, irregular heart beat (bradycardia), tremors

Wrecks at bottom of hill and has massive tissue injury

Hypokalemia   Flat t-waves

Skier gets wobbly (Lethargy), cannot hold on to poles (hyporeflexia), confusion

Credit: Dr. Melissa Geist

HYPOCALCEMIA

"skinny cat"

Ca^{++} t who is hungry (low milk supply)
>   On edge
>   Muscle irritability (Tetany)
>   hyperreflexia
Bradycardia
>   Prolonged QT interval
>   Prolonged ST segment
Calcium = 4-5 meq/L
OR 9-10 mg/dl

Credit: Dr. Melissa Geist

HYPOCALCEMIA=SKINNY CAT
Chovstek and Trousseau's Sign

- over stimulation
- muscle spasms
- decreased pulse
- hypotension
- anxiety
- psychosis
- hyperreflexic
- cardiac dysrhythmias, especially Torsades des pointes V.Tach

Causes of hypocalcemia
- Hypoparathyroidism
- Hypomagnesemia; hyperphosphatemia
- Alkalosis
- Multiple blood transfusions
- Acute Pancreatitis
- AcuteRenal Failure
- Alcoholism
- Malnutrition
- Sepsis
- Burns

Interventions
- Drugs: calcium replacement, muscle relaxants
- High calcium diet
- Seizure precautions
- Injury prevention/fall precautions
- Cardiac monitoring

- ## HYPERCALCEMIA
"Fat Cat"
- Ca++ t with belly full of milk (calcium)
- Slows down
- Drowsy
- CNS depression
Shortened QT interval

Credit: Dr. Melissa Geist

HYPERCALCEMIA=FAT CAT
Causes
- Hyperparathyroidism
- Some cancers
- Prolonged bedrest
- Excess intake
- Chronic renal failure associated with hyperparathyroidism

Interventions
- I&O
- Seizure precautions
- Fall precautions
- Low calcium diet
- VS and Neuro sign assessment
- Drugs: 0.9% NS IV fluids to promote excretion, Lasix, NSAIDs—prevent Ca++ from leaving bone
- Calcitonin or plicamycin
- Dialysis
- Cardiac Monitoring

HYPOMAGNESEMIA
Serum magnesium < 1.6 mg/dl
Critical value < 1.2 mg/dl
Causes
- Alcoholism
- GI losses
- Impaired absorption
- Inadequate replacement
- Increased excretion
- Eating disorders

Symptoms
- CV: SVT, ventricular dysrhythmias, increased susceptibility to Dig toxicity, P and T waves that are broad, flat and inverted, ST depression, prolonged QT
- Neuromuscular: twitching, tremors, hyperreflexia, mood changes, seizures
- Laryngeal stridor
- GI: hypoactive bowel sounds, distention

Interventions
- D/C drugs that decrease magnesium (diuretics, aminoglycosides, phosphorus)
- Drugs: magnesium containing antacids, Mag-oxide
- Replace Magnesium Sulfate IV (1-2 Gms over 1 hour)
- Diet: Increase magnesium rich foods
- Seizure and fall precautions
- Cardiac monitoring

MAGNESIUM RICH FOODS

- o Green, leafy vegetables
- o Seafood
- o Meat
- o Milk
- o Bananas
- o Oranges
- o Chocolate
- o Molasses
- o Coconut

HYPERMAGNESEMIA
Serum magnesium > 2.6 mg/dl
   Critical value > 4.7 mg/dl
Causes
- Renal insufficiency or failure
- Excess intake of antacids, laxatives
- Excess magnesium administration

Interventions
- Decrease magnesium intake
- Diuretics if stable renal function
- Close monitoring
- Emergent treatment: IV calcium gluconate or dialysis
- Fall precautions

ACID-BASE BALANCE
The body strives to maintain homeostasis in acid-base balance. The respiratory system regulates pH by hypo- or hyperventilating; the kidneys regulate pH by excreting/retaining hydrogen ions or bicarbonate

NORMALS
pH 7.35-7.45.   A pH < 7.35 indicates **acidosis**, > 7.45 indicates **alkalosis**

$PaCO_2$ 35-45

Bicarbonate 22-26

Normal PaO_2 at sea level is **80-100. Normal oxygen saturation** is **90-100%**

> I like my oxygen at 100%—but if I can't have that I will take 90-100%. If I have COPD, an oxygen saturation of 87% may be acceptable

PaO_2 90-100

$PaCO_2$ (1/2 0f that) 45

HCO_3 (1/2 of that) 23

One way to determine the type of acid-base imbalance is the mnemonic **R-O-M-E**
Respiratory Opposite/Metabolic Same (Used with permission of Creative Nurse Educators)

Respiratory Acidosis: decreased pH, increased $PaCO_2$
This is due to **hypoventilation and respiratory failure**. Place in High-Fowler's position, encourage incentive spirometer, and decrease narcotics. These clients may need respiratory support by intubating and placing on a ventilator. If Narcan is given to reverse narcotics, be aware the client will wake suddenly and be very restless, blood pressure and heart rate will be elevated. Narcan is only effective for a few minutes, so be prepared to support ventilations if needed.

Respiratory Alkalosis: increased pH, decreased $PaCO_2$
This is due to **hyperventilation**. Causes include pain, anxiety, hypoxia, pulmonary emboli. Place in High Fowlers. Treat pain or, if anxiety is present, with pharmacological and non-pharmacological interventions. Monitor pulse ox and apply oxygen as needed.

Metabolic Acidosis: decreased pH, decreased HCO_3
This is seen in **severe diarrhea, diabetic ketoacidosis, and lactic acidosis**. Treatment includes administration of sodium bicarbonate.

Metabolic Alkalosis: increased pH, increased HCO_3
This is seen with **excessive vomiting, NG drainage, or excessive use of diuretics**. The client needs to be supported and symptoms treated. Hold diuretics, try and clamp NG tube, or give anti-emetics.

PARTIAL COMPENSATION
The body wants to return the pH to normal—again, it's respiratory opposite/metabolic same. When partial compensation occurs, the pH is still outside normal limits but is moving toward normal. To compensate for respiratory acidosis, HCO_3 is retained; in respiratory alkalosis, HCO_3 is excreted. To compensate for metabolic acidosis, CO_2 is blown off and decreased. Think Kussmaul's respirations. To compensate for metabolic alkalosis, CO_2 is retained (hypoventilation).

COMPENSATED

pH is within normal limits but toward either the acidotic or alkalotic side. CO_2 and HCO_3 are outside normal limits

Examples:

Compensated respiratory acidosis: pH 7.36, PCO_2 48, HCO_3 28
Compensated respiratory alkalosis: pH 7.44, PCO_2 32, HCO_3 20
Compensated metabolic acidosis: pH 7.36, PCO_2 32, HCO_3 20
Compensated metabolic alkalosis: pH 7.44, PCO_2 48, HCO_3 28

When thinking about acid-base balance, it is not enough to be able to recognize the imbalance. You must also be aware of interventions to correct the imbalance.

\

Nursing Management in Musculoskeletal and Integumentary Disorders

Mayola Villarruel, MSN, ANP-BC, NEA-BC
Edited by Sylvia Rayfield & Associates, Inc.

Thou seest I have more flesh than another man, and therefore more frailty.
William Shakespeare (Henry IV)

MOST COMMON TYPES OF MUSCULOSKELETAL DISORDERS

Key Concepts:
- Arthritis
- Gout
- Back Pain
- Musculoskeletal Injuries
- Fractures
- Integumentary (Skin Disorders, Burns)
- Decubitus
- Practice Questions, Answers and Rationale

Musculoskeletal disorders are the most common cause of chronic disabilities. Obesity exacerbates disability. In fact, obesity is the leading cause of functional disability in the musculoskeletal system.

During the last 20 years there has been a dramatic increase in obesity in the United States. The states of Mississippi and Alabama head the list of states where the residents have the highest obesity. Approximately 34% (72 million) adults in the United States are obese (body weight more than 20% above normal). Approximately 17% (12 million) children are also obese.

Motion, the ability to move as we want, is affected in virtually all clients with musculoskeletal disorders. These commonalities affect most of these clients. This acronym will be a useful assistant in remembering these issues. Motion will help us remember the commonalities in these systems.

M	**Movement hurts and causes tiredness.**
O	**0 activity causes weight gain, constipation, and depression.**
T	**Treatment of physical therapy is often painful.**
I	**Income may be severely reduced causing inability to purchase treatment/medications**
O	**Outcomes include protection from falls, teaching about special equipment, and coping to have the best possible standard of living.**
N	**No sleep causes irritability and frustration.**

Arthritis is currently one of the most common causes of disability.

Client Centered Assessments	Client Centered Interventions	Client Disorder Issues
Decreased movement and strength of arms, legs, head, and other body parts	Recommend/intervene in evaluating assistive devices being utilized for mobilization Remember clients gain/lose weight and appliances must be adjusted	If utilizing splint braces, canes, or crutches, assure they fit and function properly. Do not allow to rub skin causing blisters or sores. Make sure size is appropriate for the client and the staff competent in use of devices
Protect the client from injury and falls.	Inspect the agency/home situation for risk areas for falls Recommend bars in the living areas for safety	Fractures Traction Casting Surgical intervention
Inability to walk straight and utilize muscle strength	Recognize the need for referrals and obtain necessary orders to assist client and family Physical therapy Occupational therapy Social Security Disability Assist self-care management in home environment	Assist client to cope with life transitions and performance of ADL's
History of broken bones Osteoporosis Loss of height Spine curvature Genetics	Increase intake of calcium and Vitamin D Increase intake of fruit and vegetables Increase exercise/lose weight Smoking cessation Moderate alcohol intake	Fractures Kyphosis

The **SAFETY** acronym will be used to organize the concepts in a way to help you think about this client.

PASS *NCLEX*®!

S   **System specific assessment**

A   **Assess for risk and respond**

F   **Find change/trends and intervene**

E   **Evaluate pharmacology**

T   **Teach/practice infection control, health promotion**

Y   **Your management—legal/ethical/scope of practice, identity, errors, delegation, faulty equipment/staff, privacy, confidentiality, falls/ hazards**

SYSTEM SPECIFIC ASSESSMENT

Pertinent Diagnostic Tests

SEARCH/RESCUE/FALLOUT
is a simplified version of the nursing process, which is a simplified version of a problem solving process. This analogy allows us to <u>make the complicated simple</u>.

Search (Assess/Analysis)	Rescue (Implementation)	Fallout (Outcome—Good/Bad)
Antibody tests: • Rheumatoid Factor • Anti-CCP	The immune system produces anti-bodies or proteins in response to foreign substances and bind to these foreign substances to destroy them	Anti-CCP test can be positive years before onset of symptoms
ESR—erythrocyte sedimentation	Indicates inflammation resulting in rapid accumulation of red blood cells at the bottom of a test tube	Swollen or inflamed joints
MRI	Non-invasive test utilizing a powerful magnetic field to produce detailed pictures of any internal body structure. A short two minute demonstration of an MRI can be found on: http://www.youtube.com/watch?v=FallWN1uYco	Claustrophobia may interfere with test and therefore may require a sedative during test. Remove all metal as the MRI is a powerful magnet

Search (Assess/Analysis)	Rescue (Implementation)	Fallout (Outcome—Good/Bad)
Muscle/bone/tissue biopsy • **ALS** (amyotrophic lateral sclerosis) • **Muscular dystrophy**	Invasive test requiring local anesthesia. Needle inserted into the bone or small incision made to obtain bone tissue sampling. Elevate extremity to decrease edema Medicate with analgesic Assess area for infection	Pain and swelling at site of sampling Infection at puncture or sampling site
Ultrasound	Non-invasive procedure that produces pictures to help with diagnosis and treatment of medical conditions	Inflammation Malignancy
Myelogram	Invasive diagnostic test utilizing a lumbar puncture and dye to make x-rays of bones and fluid filled space (subarachnoid space) between the bones in the spine (spinal canal). Usually done to find a tumor, infection, herniated disc, or narrowing of the spinal canal caused by arthritis. Fluids are often pushed to help excrete the dye.	Adverse reaction to dye, renal impairment May be immobilized for up to 24 hours in a supine position with head elevated to prevent seizure activity post-procedure
X-ray	Non-invasive diagnostic test	Pain on positioning Inflammation Fracture Malignancy
CT scans	Non-invasive diagnostic test used to visualize internal injuries with or without dye. The test visualizes cross sections of the area Review BUN and creatinine results prior to test Push fluids to clear dye	Altered renal clearance Claustrophobia in scanner which may require sedation
Bone scan	Involves intravenous injection of radioisotopes to visualize increased uptake. Push fluids to excrete radioisotopes	Osteoporosis Arthritis Malignancy
DNA testing for genetic disorders	Usually non-invasive requiring a sample of body fluids from client. Often used to determine genetic disease relationships	Positive test may indicate: • Lupus • Myasthenia gravis • Rheumatoid arthritis
Tensilon Test	Sudden improvement in muscle strength to diagnose myasthenia gravis. Demonstration at: http://www.youtube.com/watch?v=k7YX9kuWrxA	Progressive muscle weakness

On average every person will have two bone fractures in their lifetime

ASSESS FOR RISK AND RESPOND

Fractures		

Search (Assess/analysis)	Rescue (Implementation)	Fallout (Outcome—Good/Bad)
History • Accident (MVA) • Fall **Deformity** • Shorter extremity on injured side • For hip fracture the foot will externally rotate **Confirm by:** • X-ray affected area • CT scan • Bone scan	Immobilization — Splint Pain management (see medications for musculoskeletal disorders below) Remember **RICE**: **R**est **I**ce **C**ompression **E**levation Alignment cannot be delegated to CNA • Traction • Surgery • Consents • NPO • Labs Post-operative evaluation • Screws • Plates • Rods • Infection prevention • CPM (continuous passive motion Deep Vein Thrombosis • LMWH • Compression stockings	**Find, Change, and Prioritize** Fat embolus • 1-3 days after injury • SOB • Agitation • Delirium • Rash Thrombus formation Increased severity of pain Infection at pin and incision site Fever

EVALUATE PHARMACOLOGY

Remember, when we administer medications we must be CAREFUL!

PASS *NCLEX*®!

C	**Calculate correctly**
A	**Assess for allergies**
R	**Rights of administration**
E	**Evaluate response**
F	**Feel free to call provider if intuition alerts**
U	**Utilize assessments in determining ordered parameters**
L	**Lab data pertinence**

Search (Assess/analysis)	Rescue (Implementation)	Fallout (Outcome—Good/Bad)
Pain scale 1-10	Assess the client's ability to complete activities of daily living Rate pain according to scale PAIN MEASUREMENT SCALE	Pain free Chronic pain Total disability
Change in pain may require need for pharmacological agents	Administer drugs for musculoskeletal disorders See Table below	Side effects of medication

Medications for musculoskeletal disorders

Pharmacological measures for pain management

Medication	Prior to Administration	Nursing Actions/Education	Alerts
NSAIDS • ASA (Aspirin) • Ibuprofen (Advil, Motrin) • Naproxen (Aleve, Naprosyn) • Celecoxib(Celebrex) • Acetaminophen (Tylenol) • Tramadol (Ultram) • Meloxicam(Mobic)	Allergies Bleeding tendencies Caution with renal impairment Check renal function	The rights of administration	Not given to children or teenagers GI symptoms Nausea/vomiting Blood in stools
Oral Steroids • Cortisone • Hydrocortisone • Prednisone	Baseline levels of potassium (3.5—5.0) Baseline sodium levels (135—145) Baseline glucose (100+/- 10) Tuberculin skin testing Give with food Check for infection Assess and maintain blood pressure	Administer with food or milk Monitor for excessive weight gain Taper dose Monitor glucose levels by performing diagnostic glucose testing Monitor sodium intake Avoid exposure to communicable diseases and infectious agents	Glaucoma Cushing like symptoms: ▪ Fluid retention ▪ Increased BP ▪ Weight gain ▪ Mood swings ▪ High blood sugar ▪ Increased risk of infection ▪ Moon face Thin skin, easy bruising. Perform skin assessment and implement measures to maintain skin integrity and prevent skin breakdown Potential bleeding Calcium bone loss Bone fractures Osteoporosis Lanoxin toxicity Decreased blood calcium Hypokalemia

Medication	Prior to Administration	Nursing Actions/Education	Alerts
Alternate routes IV/IM/Injectable into joints, bursae, tendons, bones Topical Steroids • Solu-Medrol • Kenalog • Cortisone • Decadron	Same as oral steroids—see above	Same as oral steroids—see above	Same as oral steroids—see above
Muscle relaxants • Carisoprodol (Soma) • Cyclobenzaprine (Flexeril) • Diazepam (Valium)	Avoid alcohol Allergy to Equinil or Motrin Check liver and renal function Check for pregnancy and/or breast-feeding Liver and renal disorders Myasthenia Gravis Allergies to benzodiazapines	Do not stop suddenly Do not use if breast-feeding Educate on withdrawal symptoms: headache, seizures, nausea Overdose: tachycardia, hallucinations, muscle stiffness Increased dose causes sedation	May be habit forming May impair mental and physical function May lead to urinary retention on males May impair driving Excitement Rage Seizures in epileptics Depression
Antirheumatic drugs • Methotrexate (Rheumatrex) • Sulfasalazine (Azulfidine) • Hydroxychloroquine (Plaquenil)	Assess for client allergies especially to sulfa Check CBC Check for liver enzymes	Yellow/Orange urine, tears, sweat Drink plenty of fluids Avoid taking on empty stomach	Check for retinal damage May cause bleeding

Medication	Prior to Administration	Nursing Actions/Education	Alerts
	Baseline retina exam	Avoid taking with antacids Discourage alcoholic beverages, increases liver damage	
Uric acid reducing drugs • Colchicine (Colcryse) • Allopurinol (Zyloprim)	Check uric acid levels	Increase fluid intake to flush crystals to reduce renal calculi formation Decrease purine intake Reduce alcohol intake Reduce stress	May form renal calculi
Anticoagulant Therapy • Warfarin (Coumadin) • Heparin • Low molecular weight heparin (LMWH)	Check for bleeding Ulcers Bleeding disorders, hemophilia Assess client for allergies and intervene Platelet count Pregnancy PT/INR (1 is normal) PTT levels	Vitamin K ▪ Broccoli ▪ Kale ▪ Turnip greens ▪ Soybeans Consistent intake of these foods INR checks to range 2—3 Nose bleeds Institute bleeding precautions Alcohol affects bleeding Report PT/INR and PTT levels to provider	Bruising Bleeding of gums Blood in stool Generalized bleeding

Medication	Prior to Administration	Nursing Actions/Education	Alerts
Common Osteoporosis Medications • Risedronate (Actonel, Atelvia) • Ibandronate (Boniva) • Alendronate (Fosomax) • Zoledronic acid (Reclast) • Teriparatide (Forteo)	Assess GERD, ulcers Assess for allergies to Fosomax and Actonel Cannot give if pregnant or breast feeding Check calcium levels For Forteo: ▪ Determine last dosage ▪ Assess if taking Lanoxin	Must be upright for 30 minutes after taking Take on empty stomach Preventive dental exam For Forteo: ▪ Do not give for more than 2 years ▪ Report pain, leg cramps, injection site reactions ▪ Keep refrigerated ▪ Increases serum calcium ▪ May predispose to Lanoxin toxicity ▪ Contraindicated in bone metastasis	Bleeding Jaw pain Loose teeth Bone loss in jaw Postural hypotension May cause renal calculi
Antichololinesterase • Neostigmine bromide (Prostigmine)	Assess for seizures Assess for swallow reflex	Must be given on time Be alert for severe diarrhea, visual problems, and heart palpitations	Seizures

Clients with a cast can't wait to get it off!

The nurse is responsible for applying, maintaining and removing a cast.

Note the word CAST is used as an acronym to help organize the health issues with a cast

C   **Circulation under the cast is vital!**

> Especially in the first 48 hours because of swelling.
>   • Elevate the extremity to decrease swelling
> Swelling under the cast puts pressure on the skin and may cause more pain than the break. The skin can break down and cause **pressure sores** that go to the bone within less than 48 hours, especially on a small boned person or child.
> Pain is an indication of lack of circulation.
> Compartment syndrome may be caused from a cast that is causing pressure or from severely swollen tissues putting pressure on muscles and nerves. Recognition is the nursing priority. Numbness and paleness of the skin are an early sign.
>   • Severe pain when you move the affected area (for example, a person with compartment syndrome in the foot or lower leg will experience severe pain when moving the toes up and down).
>   • Permanent nerve injury can occur after 12 - 24 hours of compression.
>   • Surgery may be needed and the wounds may be left open for 48—72 hours to relieve the pressure.
>   • Permanent damage may leave affected limb useless or in need of amputation.

A   **Arrange wet cast elevation.**

> Plaster cast takes around 24 hours to dry.
> Handle the wet cast with the flat of the hands to prevent indentions into the skin on the inside of the cast.
> Fiberglass cast is not as susceptible to indentions and long term drying.

TEACH AND PRACTICE INFECTION CONTROL

S   **Smelly cast may be a sign of infection under the cast!**

> Bad smell, bleeding, heat, and pain are indications to get the cast off and take a look or call the provider.
> Casts commonly smell bad after they have been on a few weeks and broken bones usually take 6-8 weeks to heal.
> Smelly cast prevention includes keeping the cast **dry**. Cover with plastic bag when bathing. A hair dryer (on low) may be useful to help dry the cast if it gets wet inside. This trick may also help keep the cast from getting "itchy," causing creative clients to force a coat hanger down inside the cast to scratch/break the skin/cause an infection. **Think infection prevention!**

T **Teach mobilization with the cast.**
> Crutches are often necessary if a walker is not built into the cast.
> - Crutch gait depends on type of injury/cast.
> - Swing through gait works well until the client gets to the stairs. Help clients to remember that **GOOD** foot goes **UP** first. (Good goes to heaven) and the **BAD** foot goes **DOWN** first (Bad goes to ****).
> Cane may be utilized. **Place the cane on the opposite side of the injury.** Fall prevention and protocol is necessary for clients with crutches or canes. We don't need another broken bone.

The most common fractures over the age of 75 are hip fractures in women often caused by osteoporosis.

Hip and Knee Fractures

Search (Assess/Analysis)	Rescue (Implementation)	Fallout (Outcome—Good/Bad)
History • Fall • Loss of bone mass • Osteoporosis Deformity • Shorter extremity on injured side • For hip fracture the foot will externally rotate Confirm by: • X-ray affected area • CT scan • Bone scan Vital signs Pain	Immobilization • Traction Surgery • Consents • NPO • Labs Post-operative evaluation • Circulatory checks • Infection prevention • Alignment and positioning • Abductor pillow • Hip flexion no greater than 90 degrees • No crossing of legs (adduction) • CPM machine Deep vein thrombosis • Lovenox • Compression stockings Administer osteoporosis medications Pain management (see medications for musculoskeletal disorders above)	Fat embolus • 1—3 days after injury • SOB • Agitation • Delirium • Rash Thrombus formation Increased severity of pain Infection at incision site Fever Dislocation of prosthetic Decubitus Compression fractures due to osteoporosis

Fractures often cause the need for traction, particularly if the client needs the bones to be aligned or surgery at a later hour.

Traction needs a pull from opposite ends or it doesn't work!

T Traction is used often for alignment or immobilization of broken bones prior to surgery or casting. It may also decrease muscle spasms. The following link will show several different types of traction. http://www.google.com/search?q=skin+traction&hl=en&client=safari& rls=en&prmd=ivns&tbm=isch&tbo=u&source=univ&sa=X&ei=wftYToKQH8Xh0QG-yZylDQ&ved=0CBkQsAQ&biw=1438&bih=786

R Ropes or cables are used between the traction apparatus on the client and the weights usually at the end of the bed. Nothing (pillows, bed rolls, foot boards) can come between these two factions (the client and the counter-weight) or the traction will not have a pull from the opposite end. The weights must hang freely.

A Attend to the skin of the client as the traction puts pressure on the skin and the client is bedridden until the traction is removed. Remember **decubiti drains protein**, which may cause a need for protein increase in the diet. Decubiti become infected and may have to be surgically repaired.

C Constipation may be an uncomfortable situation due to immobility and awkwardness of using the bedpan. Maintain client privacy.

T Turn, cough, and deep breathing will help keep the client from getting pneumonia and pressure areas. Use ergonomic principles when providing care to protect from harm

I Infection raises it's ugly head everywhere there is a skin break. Prevent infection by keeping client and linens dry and clean. Good hygiene is a must. Elevated temp will be a sign of infection.

O Oxygenation of tissues can be determined by use of the Five Ps
   o Pulses
   o Paresthesia
   o Pain
   o Paralysis
   o Pallor

N Neurovascular checks every 2-4 hours keeps the nurse apprised of the client's safety.

Nutrition is vital and hard when the client is standing on their head in traction. Calcium and protein intake may need to be increased to heal wounds.

Integumentary (Skin Disorders, Burns)

"The skin is the window to health."

"The skin is the mirror to the small intestines."

"The skin is the last line of defense and the largest body system."

A picture is worth a thousand words and this WebMD® video on common adult skin problems is a very useful tool for refreshing your memory on skin lesions. http://www.webmd.com/skin-problems-and-treatments/slideshow-common-adult-skin-problems

The *NCLEX*® exam may have pictures of skin and ask what is the nursing priority for this situation? This brings a question of priorities.

✓ Is this infectious and should infection prevention be considered?
✓ Is this painful and require PRN pain medications for comfort?
✓ Does this itch, drive the client nuts, and need medication or cool baths to stop the itch?
✓ Is this a burn that will need to be debrided and silvadene or other ointment applied?
✓ Was this preventable and what client education needs to happen?

The nursing priority includes maintaining skin integrity and preventing skin breakdown.

The most common skin diseases are acne, eczema, skin cancer, and psoriasis.

➢ Eighty percent of Americans will have **ACNE** at some point in their lives, and 60 percent will continue to experience it into adulthood.
  ▪ Prevention—keep skin clean/maintain skin integrity and avoid skin dryness. Limit contact of hands with face. Avoid "picking at face."
  ▪ Reaches peak at the highest level of growth hormone; most severe in teenagers.
  ▪ May cause serious psychosocial despair because of image.
  ▪ Usually not infectious unless it progresses to cellulitis.
    • Cellulitis may progress to staphylococcal or streptococcal.
    • Treated with Penicillin—check for allergies.
    • Do not assign clients with cellulitis into rooms with clients with compromised immune systems.
    • Acne medication Acutane may cause depression and suicidal tendencies.

➢ **Eczema (atopic dermatitis)** is itching, scaling, blistering, weeping skin causing "misery."

Client Teaching
  ▪ Usually not infectious.
  ▪ Assess for cause/allergies (laundry detergent, soap, lotions, something that comes in contact with the skin) and delete if possible.
  ▪ Avoid tight clothes that makes the itch worse.
  ▪ Avoid scratching/wear gloves at night to minimize.

- Sweating makes itching worse.
- Corticosteroids/emollients.
- Benadryl may help with rash and itch, but causes drowsiness.

➤ **Skin cancer** is the most commonly diagnosed type of cancer and affects 1 in 5 Americans.
- **Basal cell carcinoma**—most common type of skin cancer
- **Squamous cell carcinoma**—occurs approximately 25% as often as basal cell carcinoma
- **Melanoma**—most serious of skin cancers because it can metastasize to other areas of the body. Watch this for further learning:
    http://www.youtube.com/watch?v=cGkujLoAEjY&feature=related

Client Teaching

- Usually not infectious.
- Limit sun exposure. (wear hats, sunscreen)
- Avoid tanning beds.
- Seek Dermatologist
    - If laser or cryosurgery is used, watch for bleeding.
    - Follow up to determine diagnosis by biopsy.

➤ **Psoriasis** is itching. Psoriasis is a skin condition causing skin redness and irritation. People with psoriasis have thick, raised, red skin with flaky, silver-white patches called scales. Watch this YouTube for additional information on psoriasis.
http://www.youtube.com/watch?v=O3sauC5xGFk&feature=mfu in order&list=UL

Treatment may include topicals such as creams/ointments containing cortisone or coal tar, salicylic acid, retinoids, or moisturizers. Moderate to severe cases of psoriasis are treated with systemic or biologic medications that suppress the body's immune system such as:
- Adalimumab (Humira)
- Alefacept (Amevive)
- Etanercept (Enbrel)
- Infliximab (Remicade)
- Stelara

Phototherapy is a medical treatment where the skin is exposed to ultraviolet light with or without a drug that makes the skin sensitive to light.

Burns

Search (Assess/Analysis)	Rescue (Implementation)	Fallout (Outcome—Good/Bad)
• Airway is first. The burns or smoke inhalation may have caused swelling or obstruction	• Provide for secure airway and continually re-evaluate. Supplement with oxygen therapy. Assist with intubation if necessary	• Client may asphyxiate before the burn can be treated
• Assess vital signs and level of consciousness for signs of shock	• Initiate IV away from burn if possible. Secure to provide dislodgement from edema. Needed for pain meds and fluid resuscitation	• Shock compounds the treatment of burns
• Determine level of pain on a pain scale	• Provide pain medication protocol	• Burns are very painful and this should be diminished immediately with medications
• Burn location especially on the face may not only cause airway obstruction, but may impede vision.	• Apply principles of infection control as burns easily become infected. Wound care may be challenging but vital	
• Burns on the body especially the perineum may necessitate an indwelling catheter • Burns on limbs may cause swelling and disability. Watch for jewelry to be removed as soon as possible	• Determine ability or urinate and intake and output. Indwelling catheters are commonly inserted at time of the burn for a more accurate I&O	• Urinary tract infections are common with indwelling catheters
• Determine time and cause of the burn • Assess extent by using the Rule of Nines		• The first 24 hours are for recovery
• Determine provider orders for fluid resuscitation. Half the volume is ordinarily given in the first 8 hours	• An accurate I&O is vital to assist in evaluating fluid overload. Output below 30mL/h should be reported to the provider. • Listen to breath sounds for fluid overload in the lungs • Assess for signs of hypervolemia • Determine vital signs and intervene out of norm	• Pain and swelling at site of IV may occur • Client may succumb to fluid overload • Hypervolemia • Hypovolemia • Shock and infection are common

Search (Assess/Analysis)	Rescue (Implementation)	Fallout (Outcome—Good/Bad)
	• Tachycardia may indicate hypervolemia. Fluid resuscitation is the art of balance • Ringers Lactate is often used • Re-assess for trends and complications	
• Determine electrolyte status. Burns allow potassium to escape from the blood cells causing hyperkalemia • Burns cause hyponatremia	• Analyze lab results and call the provider for shifts especially in the first few hours • Place the client on telemetry as hyperkalemia will cause cardiac dysrhythmias • Administer calcium, diuretics, and insulin in fluids if ordered • Monitor for trends and changes	• Death from cardiac arrest • Dialysis possible for severe hyperkalemia
• Rehabilitation may be prolonged and painful. (See the chart on **Independence** at the end of this chapter)	• Refer client to burn trauma centers for rehabilitation	• Disabilities of a life-long nature • Contractures • Disfigurement • Chronic pain • Psychological issues/ depression

Decubitus Ulcers/Pressure Sores

Sixty-seven percent (67%) of hospitalized clients with decubitus die. Wow! Even though nursing homes get blamed for this lack of nursing care, the highest incidence occurs in acute care hospitals with the sores appearing in the first week of hospitalization. Nine-five percent (95%) of the sores appear in the lower part of the body over bony prominences. This makes a great case for **PREVENTION!**

Identify Clients at Risk: Protect client from injury. Assess client for potential or actual abuse/neglect and intervene when appropriate.

▶ "70% of all pressure sores occur in persons older than 70 years." (J.C. Bacbenel) If abuse or neglect are suspected, comply with requirement for reporting these conditions to the proper authorities.

▶ Clients with lower limb paralysis who do not feel their pain.

▶ Clients on bed rest at the site of bony prominences.

Stage I Prevention:

- Keep the pressure off the bony prominences:
  - Turn/ change position at least every 2 hours
  - Use pressure relieving devices
    - Mattresses filled with water, gel, foam or air with alternation pattern of inflation.
- Provide protein in nutrition plan. Protein heals ulcers and ulcers drain protein.
- Avoid anything that dehydrates the wound.
- Assess for incontinence
- Assess for infection and utilize antibiotics from protocol such as Silvadene or Sulfadiazine. Antibiotics should be administered after culture.

Stage II – IV Management

- Irrigate with mild soap and water. Soak ulcer/debride/remove eschar.
- Occlusive dressings have been found to be better than other types.
- Consider protein supplements.
- Refer to surgery if determined necessary
- Pain relief per protocol.

Treatments that may delay healing

- Dry dressings
- Hydrogen peroxide
- Phisohex
- Betadine
- Iodine
- Castor Oil
- Some antiseptic agents.

The stages of ulcers determine the nursing Management.

Stages	Nursing Priority
Stage I	Non-blanchable erythema of intact skin
Stage II	Superficial ulcer that presents as a shallow crater or clister
State III	Deep ulcer that presents as a deep crater that may have undermining and tunneling
Stage IV	Deep ulcer with extreme necrosis and may have undermining or sinus tracts
Deep Tissue Injury	Purple or maroon localized area of discolored intact skin or blood-filled blister due to damage of underlying soft tissue from pressure and/or shear
Unstageable	Pressure ulcer where base is obscured by eschar or slough

Watch these 2-3 minute YouTube presentations for graphics and explanation of the stages.

http://www.youtube.com/watch?v=Eyuguc7KKC4&feature=fvst
http://www.youtube.com/watch?v=sdXIDpPmuw0

Use of a Wound VAC

A wound VAC (vacuum assisted closure) is a device that allows negative pressure wound therapy to decrease the wound healing time and reduce risk of infection. All devices and equipment used for drainage should be monitored and documented.

A sterile sponge is placed in the wound with a clear film and a tube is in place connected to the wound VAC with a prescribed amount of negative pressure. Watch this for clarification.

http://www.youtube.com/watch?v=KHzqCoDG5NU

Commonalities that flow through client safety of every body system and are heavily weighted on the *NCLEX* ®can be condensed into the following table on MANAGE.

These standards currently count for as much as 23% of the total ***NCLEX*** exam and are always a primary consideration for nursing.

	PASS *NCLEX*®!
M	Make sure of identity, accuracy of orders
A	Arrange privacy/confidentiality/consent/collaboration with other team
N	No injuries, falls, malfunctioning equipment or staff or hazards
A	Address errors, abuse, legalities, scope of practice—document
G	Give (delegate) orders to appropriate people
E	Establish priorities of clients and time

I   Infection leading to septicemia often from pressure sores and pneumonia is the biggest cause of death. Apply all principles of infection control including: hand hygiene, asepsis, and sterile technique.

N   Nutrition will likely need adjusting. Protein is needed for tissue rebuilding. Alternative feeding may be necessary. Guard against aspiration and constipation.

D   Determine venous return. Flaccid muscles allow blood pooling and DVT. It is important to recognize trends and changes in the client's condition. Remember to promote venous return.

E   Everyday ADL is a challenge that must be met. Assess the client's self care ability, especially if the client is heavy and cannot turn, sit, walk, or complete bowel functions on their own.

P   Pressure sores (decubiti) are common. Turn, reposition, use pressure-relieving support surfaces. Document and report to the provider immediately.

E   Equipment and staff to facilitate mobilization may be necessary.

N   Non-verbal may be only communication. Arrange communication with the client.

D   Depression is a common factor. **Coping is the bottom line**. Assess the client for potential for violence and use safety precautions against suicide or other self-destructive behavior.

E   Evaluate home safety prior to discharge. Assess client's ability to manage their care in their home environment. Plan care to include any devices, referrals, or other community services that may be needed.

N   Need for inner strength and family support. Assess the client and the family in coping with these serious and likely permanent life changes. Provide support through education and communication.

C   Collaborate with physiatrist, physical/occupational therapists, and other health team members in care. Unaffected muscles must be strengthened to do the work of paralyzed muscles.

E   Evaluate medication effect on rehabilitation.

Less rehabilitation= More complications
Coping is the bottom line.

1. While caring for a client receiving prophylactic subcutaneous heparin sodium injections for Deep Vein Thrombosis (DVT) prophylaxis, you note bruising on their abdomen. The client asks about why the shots make her bruise and bleed. The most appropriate response would be:
   A. Heparin Sodium thins your blood to prevent clots from forming. This sometimes causes bleeding and bruising at the injection site.
   B. You must be allergic to the injections. I will notify the provider.
   C. When you have a new nurse who is not experienced in administering injections, bruising and bleeding can occur.
   D. The medication you have been given is too strong and is causing you to bleed. We will skip the next dose and restart this medication in the morning.

2. The client reports weakness of the left bicep following a recent workout. To test the strength of the bicep you would apply resistance as the client :
   A. Extends the elbow
   B. Flexes the elbow
   C. Abducts the arm
   D. Adducts the arm

3. The client is inside of a car that has just been involved in a motor vehicle accident and is complaining of back and neck pain. The nursing priority is:
   A. Gathering information about the client's allergies.
   B. Calling the client's family
   C. Stabilizing the client's neck and spine before moving the client
   D. Administering pain medication

4. The client is about to go to surgery for a left total knee replacement and is talking about how afraid they are of the postoperative pain. What is the priority nursing action that will help this client deal with the fear?
   A. Teach the client relaxation techniques like meditation
   B. Teach the client about the medications available to treat their pain
   C. Tell the client that they have nothing to be afraid of.
   D. Listen to the clients concerns about postoperative pain.

5. The client has orders to receive diazepam (Valium) IV for muscle spasms and you notice that the Valium has been diluted with sterile water and that the syringe is cloudy. The appropriate action given this observation is?

    A. To administer the medication as ordered

    B. Dilute the solution with another 5 mLs of sterile water then administer the medication

    C. Waste the medication as this is a sign of incompatibility of the diazepam (Valium) and the sterile water

    D. Shake the syringe to mix the medication and dissolve the particulates, then administer the medication

6. The client has been prescribed alendronate (Fosamax) to treat osteoporosis. What else can the client do to help manage this diagnosis?

    A. Increase calcium and vitamin D intake

    B. Decrease the amount of weight-bearing exercise they do

    C. Begin immunosuppressive therapy

    D. Begin taking steroids on a permanent basis

7. The client is receiving IV Potassium Chloride Replacement 40mEq. They are complaining of 10/10 burning at the IV insertion site. What is the priority nursing intervention?

    A. Stop the infusion

    B. Decrease the infusion rate

    C. Assess the IV site for redness and edema

    D. Remove the IV

8. This is your second day caring for a client who is awaiting surgery for an open reduction internal fixation of the right hip. They have been on bed rest since admission. During your assessment you note unilateral 3+ left lower leg edema and redness and the client states 7/10 pain in that area. What is the priority nursing action?

    A. Elevate the extremity

    B. Notify the provider

    C. Administer pain medication

    D. Ambulate the client

9. One week ago the client was seen in the Emergency Room and was found to have a fracture of the left radius. The client was sent home with a prescription for narcotic pain medication to take PRN and is now experiencing constipation. Which of the following nursing interventions are appropriate? **Select all that apply.**

    A. Encourage the client to ambulate

    B. Encourage fluids

    C. Administer more narcotic pain medication

    D. Encourage use of a stool softener

    E. Encourage a diet high in fiber

10. Which task may be delegated to a Certified Nursing Assistant (CNA)? **Select all that apply**.
    A. Assist the client with activities of daily living or ADL's
    B. Measure and compare the strength of the clients legs
    C. Assess postoperative sutures
    D. Administer medication
    E. Insert an intravenous catheter pre-operatively

11. The RN needs assistance with a client assignment. Which nursing intervention must be delegated only to another Registered Nurse (RN)?
    A. Obtaining the client's vital signs
    B. Applying the continuous passive motion machine to a client who is one day post-op from a left total knee replacement
    C. Performing a bed bath on a client who is on bed rest secondary to a pubic ramus fracture
    D. Performing passive range of motion on a paraplegic client

12. The client is admitted with cellulitis and as prescribed 4.5g piperacillin/tazobactam (Zosyn) IV. It comes to you reconstituted in a 20mL syringe. The order says to administer it over 30 minutes. You set the pump at _____ mL/hr.

13. The client is seen in the Emergency Room for evaluation following a soccer game in which he rolled his left ankle. The X-ray shows no fracture and he is diagnosed with a sprain and sent home. Before leaving, he asks what he can do to treat the swelling. **Select all that apply**.
    A. Elevate the left ankle
    B. Apply an ice pack to the left ankle
    C. Do not bear weight on the ankle for a few days
    D. Apply a warm pack to the left ankle
    E. Walk on the ankle to promote circulation

14. The client has been practicing range of motion exercises for treatment of their rheumatoid arthritis. The exercises are considered effective when:
    A. The client can now flex and extend their effected joints
    B. The client experience pain with movement
    C. The client's ulnar deviation has corrected itself
    D. The client experiences morning stiffness and low-grade fevers

15. A newborn client is found to have asymmetric gluteal folds. What other signs could indicate that this child has hip dysplasia. **Select all that apply**.
    A. Limited range of motion of the affected leg
    B. Signs of pain when using the hip joints
    C. Length of leg on unaffected side is shorter
    D. Popping Noise heard when doing passive range of motion of hips
    E. Length of legs are equal bilaterally

16. The client is admitted with a vesicular zosterform shingles rash. The vesicles are currently oozing. What is the priority nursing action for preventing the spread of this condition?
    A. Wear gloves during exam
    B. Wash hands before entering the clients' room
    C. Drain the vesicles to remove the infection
    D. Have the client soak in the tub to facilitate vesicle drainage

17. The client has a fractured left tibia and is in a full leg cast. The provider should be notified immediately if:
    A. Bilateral pedal pulses are +2 strength, equal, and regular
    B. The client experiences 10/10 pain unrelieved by prescribed analgesia
    C. Capillary refill is brisk on all toes bilaterally
    D. Client complains of itching under the cast

18. The following statement made by a client with osteoarthritis would indicate an understanding of their disease process:
    A. "I expect to have exacerbations that cause me to experience low-grade fevers and fatigue."
    B. "I can help my disease to not progress by participating in physical therapy."
    C. "If I lose weight and take the added pressure off my knees I may experience less pain."
    D. "I will experience stiffness that is worse in the morning and gradually gets better as the day goes on."

19. When caring for a client with a surgical wound that is infected with Methicillin-resistant Staphylococcus aureus or MRSA, the priority nursing action to prevent the spread of the bacteria to others is:
    A. Hand washing before entering and after leaving the clients room
    B. Applying dry sterile dressings to the wound
    C. Educate the client about infection control techniques
    D. Administer the prescribed antibiotics

20. The client with Amyotrophic lateral sclerosis (ALS) is admitted to the hospital during an exacerbation with complaints of increased weakness and fatigue. The client is unsteadily standing beside the bed reaching for the phone. As the client got up from the bed, the bed alarm did not go off. What is the priority nursing action?
    A. Call engineering to fix the bed alarm
    B. Get the client the phone so that they do not need to stand up
    C. Assist the client back to bed
    D. Explain to the client the need to call for assistance with ambulation

21. The client was admitted with osteomyelitis of the third toe on the left foot and is at the end of 6weeks of intravenous antibiotic therapy. Clinical findings indicative of effective treatment include:
    A. Reduction of pain and resolved infection
    B. Increased pain and tenderness of the bone
    C. Client is febrile with a temperature of 101.6°F or 38.6°C
    D. Positive blood cultures drawn

22. When caring for a quadriplegic client who is at risk for developing pressure ulcers, it is important to:
    A. Reposition the client at least every 2 hours to prevent skin breakdown
    B. Keep the client strapped into their wheelchair during the day
    C. Elevate the head of the bed to greater than 45 degrees
    D. Perform a skin assessment every week

23. The client is going to have a magnetic resonance imaging (MRI) test to test for a herniated disk. Which nursing actions need to be completed before the client can have this done? **Select all that apply.**
    A. Gather a client history including any past surgeries
    B. Verify that the MRI Screening form has been completed
    C. Begin an intravenous infusion of normal saline via an infusion pump
    D. Make sure that the client has removed all jewelry and other metal
    E. Assess the client for claustrophobia

24. A delirious client is admitted to the hospital with an ulcer on their coccyx that has full thickness skin loss and both tissue and muscle necrosis with visible bone. The priority nursing intervention for this client would be:
    A. Encourage a diet high in protein
    B. Administer antibiotic medication
    C. Apply a dressing to the wound
    D. Position the client to avoid pressure on the ulcer

25. The client is admitted with a stage 4 pressure ulcer. The priority nursing actions for this client involve:
    A. Airway maintenance
    B. Breathing regulation
    C. Maintaining adequate circulation
    D. Infection control and prevention

Answers and Rationale

1. **Answer A** is correct. It provides the client with a truthful explanation. Answer B is incorrect because the symptoms do not suggest allergy. Answer C is incorrect because the reaction is a result of the medication, not the administration. Answer D is incorrect because skipping a dose will not solve the problem or address the client's concern.

2. **Answer B** is correct. Answer A tests the strength of the triceps and Answers C and D are testing the shoulder.

3. **Answer: C** is correct. If the client has a fracture of the spinal column, this will prevent any further damage from occurring. Answer D is not a correct answer as the administration of a pain medication could disguise any changes in neurological status at this point. Both Answers A and B are not priorities and can be done at a later time without harm coming to the client.

4. **Answer D** is correct because it allows the client to feel like they are being heard and gives the caregiver information needed to help the client deal with the fear. Answers A and B are incorrect because teaching should occur when the client is not anxious and fearful and Answer C is showing that the client is not being listened to.

5. **Answer C** is correct. Diazepam(Valium) cannot be diluted before IV administration. Answers A, B, and D are incorrect because the cloudiness is a sign of incompatibility. This solution would cause harm to the client if it was administered.

6. **Answer A** is correct. All of the other answers add to your risk for developing osteoporosis.

7. **Answer A.** Stop the infusion is correct because that should relieve the pain enough for you to assess what is actually causing the pain and determine your next action. Answers B, C and D are all follow-up actions that may be taken once you have relieved the pain and can gather more data.

8. **Answer B** is correct because this is a dramatic change that could indicate a Deep Vein Thrombosis (DVT) and needs to be evaluated by the provider. Answers A, C, and D are incorrect because if it is a Deep Vein Thrombosis (DVT), these choices risk dislodging the clot.

9. **Answers A,B,D, And E** are the correct answers. These actions are all known to encourage elimination. Answer C, administering narcotic pain medication, is known to contribute to constipation.

10. **Answer A** is correct because these tasks fall under the scope of practice of a CNA. Options B, C, D, and E all require a nursing license.

11. **Answer B** is correct; it is a nursing action. The other actions can be delegated to another healthcare team member.

12. **Answer: 40mL/hr.**

13. Answers A, B, and C. Answers D and E will increase blood flow to the area and increase swelling.

14. Answer A is correct. Answers B and D show symptoms of the disease and Answer C is not possible.

15. Answers: A, B, and D are correct. Answers C and E are incorrect because the affected side would be shorter.

16. Answer A. Personal protective equipment should always be utilized when at risk for coming into contact with any bodily fluid. Answer B is incorrect because it will protect the client but not other clients you may see after coming into contact with the drainage. Answers C and D are incorrect because draining the vesicles will only risk introducing new sources of infection into the clients' body through open skin.

17. Answer B is the correct answer because it could be an indication of compartment syndrome which is a medical emergency. Answers A, C, and D are expected findings for a client with a cast.

18. Answer C is the correct answer. Answers A, B, and D all describe rheumatoid arthritis.

19. Answer A is the correct answer because it stops the transmission of the bacteria from this client to another. Answers B, C, and D are important but are not the priority.

20. Answer C is correct as it addresses the immediate danger. Answers A, B, and D are all important but can be accomplished after the client is in a safe situation.

21. Answer A is the correct answer. Answers B,C, and D can all indicate an infectious process.

22. Answer A is correct. Answers B and C would increase the risk of developing a pressure ulcer and Answer D is incorrect because a skin assessment needs to occur at least every shift on an at risk client.

23. Answers A, B, D and E are all correct. Answer C would not be appropriate because the infusion pump is metal and not allowed in the MRI room.

24. Answer D is correct because this will prevent further damage and will increase blood flow to the area to facilitate healing. Answers A, B and C are all nursing interventions that are appropriate for this condition but will not be effective if further damage is not prevented.

25. Answer D is correct given the diagnosis. Answers A and B do not apply to this client given the information provided. Answer C is important in the healing process; however, infection poses a greater threat to the client.

The Pediatric MUSCULOSKELETAL SYSTEM

Jessica Peck, DNP, RN, MSN, CPNP-PC, CNE
Edited by Sylvia Rayfield & Associates, Inc.

INJURY IS THE LEADING CAUSE OF DEATH IN CHILDREN AND ADOLESCENTS, AND FALLS ARE #1 ON THE LIST!

FOR CONGENITAL NEURO/MUSCULAR DISEASES, EARLY INTERVENTION IS CRITICAL TO OPTIMIZE OUTCOMES!

KEY CONCEPTS TO REMEMBER:

- ❖ Congenital musculoskeletal disorders
- ❖ Chronic neuromusculoskeletal disorders
- ❖ Fractures

MUSCULOSKELETAL DISORDERS

What causes these defects? A **GEM** does. It is a combination of **G**enetic, **E**nvironmental, and **M**echanical factors that contribute to these disorders.

What are the priorities in focused assessment?

Know your **A-B-C's**	**Developmental Dysplasia of the Hip** **(DDH)**	**Talipesequinovarus** **(Clubfoot)**	**Scoliosis**
Ask about the history	Risk Factors: - Female - Breech - Intrauterine position - Family history - Genetics - Culture	Risk Factors: - Intrauterine position - Genetic Syndrome - Idiopathic - Boys *May be one or both feet*	Etiology: - Congenital - Idiopathic - Acquired **Usually presents

	**Monitor for this condition during the first year of life.*	**Usually detected on intrauterine ultrasound or at birth*	*during the preadolescent growth spurt.*
B—Be aware of possible presenting symptoms you might detect on assessment	Get an "**A**" on your assessment for DDH! **A**—Asymmetrical gluteal & thigh folds **A**—Abduction of hips is limited **A**—Allis sign+ (one knee is shorter than the other when infant is supine with thighs flexed) **A**—Audible click when walking or during diaper changes or exam **A**—Abnormal gait	This baby does not have feet made for dancing in the club. Any abnormal flexion, inversion, or eversion that cannot be manually corrected during the exam is abnormal and warrants further investigation.	Curvature of the spine Asymmetry in scapula, ribs, flanks, shoulders and hips when client bends over at the waist. Look for any humps or bumps! www.youtube.com/ watch?v=NuU3pq4U5Ck **Visit here to watch "Scoliosis Girl Diaries"**
C—Care for the client until surgical repair is completed or condition resolves www.youtube.com/wat ch?v=9pMvmRWaJq **Visit here to watch real families care for kids in spica casts**	It's all about the **HiPPPPs**! **P**avlik harness until 5-6 months of age, **_wear it all the time!_**(except for bathing only). **P**rovider visits **_weekly_** for harness adjustments. **P**revent skin breakdown with cotton shirt, diaper	**PASS** the club to care for the foot. **P**—Passive exercises if a minor deformity **A**—Assess neurovascular status for casting **S**—Serial casting once a week immediately after birth	**BRACE** the child for surgery. **B**—Brace worn for 10-20 degree curvature **R**—Remind parent that brace will not correct curve, but stabilize it. **A**—Adherence to wear brace 23-24 hours/day **C**—Catch signs of skin

		breakdown
and socks, limit lotions and powders. **P**roper positioning at all times.	**S**—Surgical correction if serial casting ineffective by 3 months	**E**—Exercise and adhere to physical therapy regime

Therapeutic Interventions	Developmental Dysplasia of the Hip (DDH)	Talipes equinovarus (Clubfoot)	Scoliosis
CAST CARE	HIP **SPICA** CAST (Post-op for hip reduction) Used for infants > 6months who are diagnosed late or had no success with Pavlik. **S**—Skin integrity assessment and maintenance (sponge bathe, waterproof barrier around diaper) **P**—Pain assessment and control **I**—Intake and output, monitor hydration and elimination **C**—Color and temperature of toes, ***FREQUENT NEUROVASCULAR CHECKS!!*** **A**—Ambulate in wagon or stroller, perform ROM exercises with unaffected extremities.	Serial casting of the foot—sometimes responds quickly, sometimes quite extended. Casting begins at birth and usually lasts 8-12 weeks. Casting change initially every few days, then every 1-2 weeks. ***FREQUENT NEUROVASCULAR CHECKS!!*** (Baby is growing and can have compromised circulation if cast becomes too tight). Keep elevated.	Suggest decorating the cast to encourage acceptance. Instruct adolescent to exercise with the brace. Wear a cotton t-shirt under brace and avoid powders, lotions and cosmetics.
Indication for surgery	Closed or open reduction of the hip between 6 months and 4 years if caught late or Pavlik is unsucccessful.	If casting unsuccessful by 3 months of age, indication for corrective surgery with pins and release of tight joints and tendons. Casting maintained 2-3 months after surgery.	If curve is greater than 40 degrees, internal fixation with hardware along with spinal fusion is indicated to realign the spine. The goal is

			to achieve maximum correction and maximum mobility.
	Visit here to see a Pavlik Harness. www.youtube.com/watch?v=gc2 Hs-XIHCw		

HOW TO CARE FOR A SPINAL FUSION PATIENT

	Pre-Operative Care	Post-Operative Care
Nursing Actions	❖Assist to obtain autologous blood-donations. ❖Document baseline H&H and CBC ❖Document results of type and cross blood screen	❖Monitor immediate post-op period in the ICU ❖Monitor pain using age-appropriate tool ❖Treat pain with PCA ❖Turn frequently with log rolls ❖Assess for skin breakdown ❖Monitor surgical drains for signs of infection ❖Observe for paralytic ileus ❖Encourage mobility ASAP ❖Monitor for signs of bleeding such as change in H&H or decreased blood pressure ❖Turn, cough and incentive spirometry every 2 hours
Infection	❖Document baseline CBC values	❖Monitor vital signs. Report fever immediately. ❖Reposition frequently. ❖Use aseptic technique when caring for surgical drains or incision site. ❖Maintain a high fiber diet and encourage fluid intake. ❖Maintain good handwashing and encourage family and visitors to do the same.

Client Education	❖ Prepare client and family for surgery by clarifying expectations and demonstrating equipment such as catheters, NGT, PCA, hemovac. ❖ Review guidelines for visitors and encourage visits from friends and family. ❖ Explain expected path to recovery.	❖ Encourage independence ❖ Emphasize importance of physical therapy ❖ Reinforce the need for follow-up care ❖ Educate family to provide modifications in home environment that allow maximum independence ❖ Provide education on signs and symptoms of infection and when to call provider.

A WORD ABOUT PAIN pediatric pain!

Visit here to read about nurses at the forefront of

http://www.youtube.com/watch?v=H-XJhLT2jUw

Assessing pain in children can be a challenge! Have you tried to ask a 9 month old to rate his pain on a scale of 1-10? Good luck with that! However, it is CRITICAL that nurses OBJECTIVELY measure pain and do not "estimate" pain scores.

For infants and children who are intellectually disabled or for whatever reason are unable to comprehend the use of the number scale, then the FLACC scale is a good choice that is commonly used. The total score should be treated as an equivalent to the 0-10 number scale.

FLACC SCALE

	0	1	2
Face	No particular expression or smile	Occasional grimace or frown, withdrawn, disinterested	Frequent to constant frown, clenched jaw, quivering chin
Legs	Normal position or relaxed	Uneasy, restless, tense	Kicking, legs drawn up
Activity	Lying quietly, normal position, moves easily	Squirming, shifting back and forth, tense	Arched, rigid or jerking
Cry	No cry	Moans or whimpers, occasional complaint	Crying steadily, screams or sobs, frequent complaints
Consolability	Content, relaxed	Reassured by occasional touching, hugging, or talking to; distractible	Difficult to console or comfort.

Merkel, S. et al.; The FLACC: a behavioral scale for scoring postoperative pain in young children, *Pediatric Nursing* 23(3): 293-297, 1997.

Children ages 4-7years may use the Wong and Baker (1988) **FACES** scale. Children point to the picture that best describes their feelings.

Children over the age of 7 years may be assessed for developmental appropriateness of the number scale.

What neuromuscular problems do children face?

Chronic neuromuscular problems affect the muscles, joints, bones, and the brain. What should the nurse keep in mind when assessing a patient with a neuromusculoskeletal problem? Remember your ABC's still apply! The nurse is in a unique position to detect some of the abnormalities that may be early warning signs of a problem. Let's go back to the ABC's we learned earlier in this section.

Ask about the history	**B**—Be aware of possible presenting symptoms you might detect on assessment	**C**—Care for the client with goal to prevent complications of condition

Know your A-B-C's	**Cerebral Palsy** ***most common permanent physical disability in children***	**Spina Bifida** **(myelomeningocele)** ***neural tube defect***	**Muscular Dystrophy** ***progressive skeletal muscle degeneration, terminal***
Ask about the history	Risk Factors: • Anoxic brain injury • Prematurity • Multiple births (twins, triplets) • Very low birth weight • Insufficient placenta • Severe jaundice with kernicterus at birth	Risk Factors: • Occurs at 3-5 weeks en utero. • Inadequate maternal intake of folic acid • Elevated alpha-fetoprotein ***May be visible sac protrusion through the skin or may be invisible to the naked eye (spina*	Risk Factors: • Family history MD is the largest group of disease that affect muscle function in children—hence the annual Labor Day telethon to raise money for research. Characterized by gradual loss of motor function and

		bifida occulta).	previously attained
		*Impairment presents depending on both the level and the severity of the defect.**	developmental milestones.
			Onset and progression depends on type.
		MRI, ultrasound, and CT are helpful in establishing diagnosis.*	
			Duchenne (x-linked trait) is the most common form.
Know your <u>A-B-C's</u>	**Cerebral Palsy**	**Spina Bifida**	**Muscular Dystrophy**
<u>**B**</u>—Be aware of possible presenting symptoms you might detect on assessment	CP presentation is different for every child! Some are severely affected physically and cognitively. Some become independent and productive adults. Parents often first report concerns to the nurse. Listen carefully for these reports!	Inspect the spine at birth to see if it is intact. Check for any openings or dimples.	It's all about the <u>M</u>-<u>M</u>-<u>M</u>-Muscles!
		<u>**B**</u>—Bowel/Bladder incontinence	<u>M</u>uscular weakness in lower extremities
		<u>**I**</u>—Increase in head circumference that may indicate associated hydrocephalus	<u>M</u>uscular hypertrophy, especially calves
			<u>M</u>obility declines
		<u>**F**</u>—Fever or other signs of infection related to exposed structures or use of clean catheterization	<u>M</u>otor skill delay
			<u>M</u>ild cognitive delay
			<u>M</u>arked difficulty running, riding a bike or rising from sitting position
	<u>**P**</u>—*poor* head control, ***p**ersistent **p**rimitive* reflexes	<u>**I**</u>—Impaired skin integrity, may have pressure sores related to diminished sensation	<u>M</u>oves with an awkward gait
	<u>**A**</u>—*absence* of smiling		
	<u>**L**</u>—*limp* or floppy body,	<u>**D**</u>—Developmental	

	limping or altered gait **S**—*spasticity*, **s**its only with *support*, *stiff* arms and legs, "*scissor* legs," **s**peech may be poor **Y**—*involuntary* movements	delays, may or may not have impaired cognition **A**—Allergy—high risk for latex allergy related to chronic exposure	Labs: DNA Analysis PCR Muscle tissue biopsy CK elevated
Know your A-B-C's	**Cerebral Palsy**	**Spina Bifida**	**Muscular Dystrophy**
C—Care for the client until surgical repair is completed or condition resolves www.youtube.com/ watch?v=Kzb1XYGo0IQ **Cohen's Story** www.youtube.com/ watch?v=PqUDdxm-qSA **Abigail's Story**	The goal of therapy is early recognition and promotion of optimal development. Therapy is palliative. May need surgery to correct contractures or spastic deformities.	*If sac is present at birth, immediately cover with a sterile moist dressing. Assess every 2 hours. Keep baby in prone position, turning head and repositioning body every 2 hours.* *Monitor head circumference for signs of increasing intracranial pressure.* A significant portion of care for these patients is bowel and bladder control measures. Clean, intermittent self-catheterization should be taught. Families should monitor for signs of infection. A vesicostomy, or surgically created	Monitor respiratory status closely. As condition deteriorates breathing will be compromised. Use incentive spirometry, positive pressure ventilation, give oxygen as prescribed, maintain ventilator as ordered. Encourage independence and maximize function for as long as possible. Surgery may be necessary to repair contractures, insert a gastrostomy tube or a tracheostomy.

www.youtube.com/ watch?v=cY3M_A_BkG0 **Ian's Story**		urinary stoma is becoming more common practice. Avoid rectal temps to prevent irritation. Give laxatives or enemas as needed to treat constipation.	

A Memorable Patient Encounter

I was once caring for a patient who had severe cerebral palsy, with significant cognitive impairment. His grandparents were his primary caregivers and they very lovingly cared for his every need. He was frequently in the hospital for various complications and on one occasion I came upon the team of residents who were rounding and happened to be discussing his case. He had come in for a tracheostomy infection but I heard the team discussing a new development—seizures. The resident was telling the attending that this child kept hitting himself in the head with one arm in a peculiar jerking motion. The resident ardently advocated for starting anti-epileptic medication. At this point I decided to go and talk to the grandmother to see what was going on. I entered the room and began to tell her about the discussion the residents were having. To my great surprise, she started laughing hysterically. She told me that every time the little boy's grandfather entered the room, he would touch his hand to his head as his way of acknowledging the grandfather, who ALWAYS wore a cowboy hat. To demonstrate, she had the grandfather leave the room and the "seizure" stopped. When he re-entered, it resumed. It was a poignant moment, as I realized how important it is to talk to your patients.

We may be experts in nursing care, but the caregivers are experts in the patients. It is essential

that we partner our expertise to provide the best care possible. It also taught me that patients

who seem unable to communicate may be communicating with me in a language I don't know!

It taught me to be ever vigilant for potential opportunities for communication.

ASSESSMENT OF PATIENTS WITH NEUROMUSCULAR DISORDERS

ASSESSMENT	INTERVENTION
A- **AIRWAY**	Patients may have difficulty managing their secretions. Keep head of bead elevated and make sure suction is readily available.
B- **BREATHING**	Monitor for signs and symptoms of aspiration. Uncoordinated oral motor function can contribute to dysphagia and aspiration. Report tachypnea, adventitious breath sounds, or retractions.
C- **CIRCULATION** Clients are often immobile. They need assistive devices such as wheelchairs, ankle-foot orthoses, and wrist splints. Interdisciplinary care with physical therapy is important to achieve maximum function and capacity for self-care.	Continuously monitor for signs of skin breakdown, being sure to check under splints and braces. Affecting factors may be limited mobility with CP or decreased sensation with SB. Encourage play activities that promote achievement of developmental milestones. Prepare families for palliative surgeries. Perform passive ROM to stretch and exercise muscle groups. Take measures to prevent constipation due to lack of mobility (high fiber diet, adequate fluid intake, exercise as tolerated).
D- **DEVELOPMENT &** **GROWTH** It is critical to promote optimal growth and development so that the patient may attain the greatest quality of life possible within their disease	Cognitive development may be normal or impaired. Physical growth is often delayed because of inability to ingest adequate nutrients. Maintain upright position during feedings. Use specific head positioning and manual jaw control technique as indicated. Provide foods that child enjoys whenever possible. Administer feedings by NGT or GT as ordered.

process.	Monitor daily weight and trending on growth chart.
	Monitor developmental milestones.
	Communicate with child on a developmentally appropriate level, using assistive communication devices as needed.
	Collaborate with interdisciplinary teams to provide best care for the patient (PT, OT, speech therapy, nutrition, school nurses, etc.)
	Ensure adequate rest periods to facilitate optimal growth.
	Encourage good dental hygiene to prevent tooth decay.
E- ERADICATE PAIN Intense pain is possible with muscle spasms. Patients may also experience pain after surgical procedures or during physical therapy.	Administer pain medications as needed (see medication chart).
	Ensure that client is well rested for physical therapy sessions.
	Administer scheduled round-the-clock pain medications post-operatively.
	Use a developmentally appropriate pain scale.
F- FAMILY CENTERED CARE	Assess available family resources.
	Include the family in hospital care. Seek their input and try to maintain home norms.
	Clarify expectations of treatment.
	Assess for issues of body image disturbance and low self-esteem, especially those related to bowel and bladder incontinence.
	Provide understanding and support during problem solving.
	Assess siblings for signs of impaired coping, such as behavioral problems or poor school performance.
	Assist family to find a caring support group.
	Interdisciplinary is a critical element of care. OT, PT, speech therapy, social services, physicians, nurses, and respiratory therapy are all important.
G- GUARD THE PATIENT AGAINST INJURY AND INFECTION	Institute seizure precautions when indicated.
	Make sure side rails are up at all times and patient is securely fastened into assistive ambulation devices.
	Pad side rails and wheelchair arms.

	Use helmets or other protective equipment as necessary. Be especially alert to signs and symptoms of infection. These patients may have decreased sensation or impaired cognition and may not be alert to early signs such as pain or fever. SB: Observe for increasing head circumference, which may be indicative of increasing intracranial pressure from related hydrocephalus. SB: Inquire about latex allergies, as these can be common because of chronic exposure. Use non-latex gloves. Be aware that kiwi, bananas, avocados and chestnuts are often allergens for those with latex allergy.

JUVENILE IDIOPATHIC ARTHRITIS

A chronic autoimmune inflammatory disease of the joint synovium that causes damage of the articular cartilage*

KEY CONCEPTS TO REMEMBER:

❖ JIA is rarely life threatening but it can cause joint deformities and significant disability. It starts before 16 years of age.
❖ Peak incidence is 1-3 years of age and girls are affected twice as often as boys.
❖ There is no specific diagnostic test. There is no cure and therapy is palliative.
❖ Therapy goals are to preserve joint function and promote normal growth and development.

What do you assess in JIA? The **JOINTS** of course!

- **J**—Joint swelling, stiffness, warmth and erythema
- **O**—Ocular changes—uveitis may occur (inflammation in the eye)
- **I**— Impaired mobility
- **N**—Nodules under the skin
- **T**—Trouble with growth and development
- **S**—Scary rash

How do we manage JIA? By giving them **WARMTH**!

- **W**—WARM baths, WARM moist compresses to joints prior to exercise.
- **A**—Activity should be encouraged as tolerated.

- **R**—Recruit help from the school nurse for medication administration and rest needs.

- **M**—Meet their needs for development and socialization. Encourage self-care!

- **T**—Treat pain with NSAIDS

- **H**—Help them sleep better by providing a firm mattress, discouraging fluffy pillows, and not using pillows under the knees. Use warmed blankets for extra warmth. Apply splints at night to prevent contracture deformities.

PEDIATRIC FRACTURES

KEY CONCEPTS TO REMEMBER:

- ❖ Fractures occur most commonly in pediatrics and older adults.
- ❖ Fractures heal more quickly in children because of a thicker periosteum and healthy blood supply
- ❖ Injuries to the epiphyseal plate (growth plate) may result in permanent growth restrictions
- ❖ Multiple fractures in various stages of healing should trigger suspicion for physical abuse or osteogenesis imperfecta (OI).
- ❖ Immediately report severe pain or pain that is unrelieved within one hour of pain medication administration.
- ❖ Consider safe transportation and car seat accommodations after casting.

A WORD ABOUT ABUSE AND NEGLECT

Child maltreatment is one of the most serious social problems affecting children in the U.S. Nearly 1 million children experience abuse or neglect each year.

	Shaken Baby Syndrome	Munchausen Syndrome by Proxy	Physical Abuse	Sexual Abuse
Facts	Babies have large heads and weak neck muscles. They are susceptible to brain injury from shaking!	Caregivers deliberately make their children ill to get attention from medical personnel.	Younger single parents and non-married parental partners are at higher risk to abuse. Children from birth-3 years are at highest risk.	Most is committed by men and by persons known to child. Child is often afraid to disclose the truth for fear of

				retribution.
Signs & Symptoms	Intracranial bleeding, retinal hemorrhages, vomiting, poor feeding, seizures	Nausea, vomiting, diarrhea, seizures, or symptoms only witnessed by the perpetrator	Bruises on face, lips, mouth, back. Regular patterns on marks/bruises. Burns. Multiple fractures in various stages of healing. Lacerations and abrasions, unexplained illness.	Trauma to genitalia, torn or stained underclothing, dysuria, discharge, STI, odor, pregnancy.
Behavior Changes	Irritability, crying, flu-like symptoms	Biting, rocking, sucking, fearfulness, antisocial behavior, extremes in personality, developmental delay	Wary of physical contact with adults, fear of parents, reluctance to go home, refusal to cry, acting out or withdrawn, afraid when other children crying	Inappropriate sexual behavior, withdrawn, poor relationships with peers, anxiety, change in weight
Prevention	EDUCATE PARENTS ON COPING MECHANISMS IN CARING FOR BABIES WITH INCONSOLABLE CRYING!	BE ALERT TO RESOLUTION OF SYMPTOMS WHEN THE PERPETRATOR IS ABSENT	Teach appropriate childcare methods. Utilize an interdisciplinary team in prevention.	EDUCATE CHILDREN TO PROTECT THEMSELVES.

KEY CONCEPTS TO REMEMBER:

❖ Take reports of potential abuse very seriously.
❖ AN INJURY THAT IS INCONSISTENT WITH THE HISTORY IS WORRISOME!
❖ Do not promise children that you will not tell what they reveal.
❖ Accept information in a non-judgmental way and tell them that the abuse is not their fault.
❖ Listen, and avoid using leading statements, which may confuse them.
❖ Determine what needs to be done to keep the child safe.
❖ Be aware of personal biases and report objectively.

MEDICATIONS COMMONLY USED FOR MUSCULOSKELETAL CONDITIONS

MEDICATION	ACTION	NURSING CARE	EDUCATION	ALERTS
Baclofen (Lioresal)	Central-acting skeletal muscle relaxant	Administer ORALLY or INTRATHECALLY via a specially implanted pump. www.youtube.com/watch?v=xFP6VYJBAOl	Follow-up at least once a month to monitor effectiveness. Does not improve muscle coordination but decreases spasticity and contractures.	Report adverse effects such as drowsiness, somnolence, headaches, vomiting, seizures)
Antiepileptics Carbamazepine (Tegretol) Valproic acid (Depakote)	Used to treat seizure disorders associated with CP	Monitor for reports of therapeutic levels	Compliance is important in order to prevent seizures.	Ensure adequate dental care! Some side effects can cause gum hyperplasia.
Diazepam (Valium)	Skeletal muscle relaxant	Monitor for drowsiness and fatigue		Should be used in older children and adolescents
Botulinum toxin A (Botox)	Inhibits release of acetylcholine into muscle groups, preventing spasms.	Apply topical analgesic prior to intramuscular administration. Onset of action is 24-72 hours, peaks at 2 weeks and duration of 3-6 months.	Can prevent contractures and possibly surgeries.	The goal is to relax the muscle and allow ambulation without orthotics.
Oxybutynin chloride (Ditropan) **Tolterodine (Detrol)**	Antispasmodic	Improves continence Increases bladder capacity	Give medications on time.	Compliance with monitoring of therapeutic levels
NSAIDS **Naproxen (Naprelan)** **Ibuprofen (Motrin)**	Anti-inflammatory	Administer with food to prevent GI irritation.	Educate family about s/sx GI bleeding such as changes in stool, abdominal pain, or increased bruising	Can cause GI bleeding! Be alert to s/sx.
Methotrexate (Rheumatrex)	Chemo-therapeutic	Slows joint degeneration	Avoid alcohol consumption (adolescents)	Monitor LFT and CBC

	Used when NSAIDS are ineffective		Use birth control to prevent birth defects.	Can cause immuno-compromised state
Corticosteroids	Anti-inflammatory Used for severe disease and uvetitis	Administer PO, IV, or intraoccularly Taper dose Monitor for excessive weight gain Monitor for slowed linear growth	Avoid exposure to communicable disease and infectious agents	Can cause immuno-compromised state Doses of more than 2mg/kg/day for > 2 weeks increase the risk of immune compromise.

The Girl With the Cast

One of my patients was a 2 year-old girl who had fallen off of her parent's bed and fractured her tibia. The fracture was really quite simple and small and the recovery was projected to be very easy. She was casted from her toes to her hips and sent home. The little girl continued to be in a great deal of pain and her mother called the clinic the next day, concerned about the level of discomfort. She was told that fractures are painful and to give it some time. The next day she called again, still complaining of pain. The mother was then told to fill a prescription for Lortab and to use that in conjunction with the ibuprofen she was already taking. Still, the pain continued and on the third day the mother called again. The clinic began to be annoyed at her persistence and told her that the little girl had a broken bone and of course it is going to hurt! Still, the mother continued to be concerned. On the fourth day, the little girl would cry continuously unless her mother held the cast up at just the right angle. The mother called the clinic again. At this time, the mother felt the clinic had labeled her as "drug-seeking." The mother could not dismiss the feeling that something terrible was wrong and she showed up unannounced at the clinic, demanding to be seen. The physician decided to recast the leg, thinking perhaps it was too tight or something like that. When they removed the cast, they found that the casting technician had evidently not handled the cast with flat palms and there was a very small bump right at her ankle. That very small bump had literally eaten away the back of the poor baby's entire ankle, right down to the bone. There was a gaping hole where flesh should have been. She spent months in recovery, experiencing multiple complications. Sometimes the simple things become the most important.

REVIEW QUESTIONS

1. A 1-year-old patient is in a spica cast for Developmental Dysplasia of the Hip. Which of the following assessment findings would alert the nurse to a potential infection under the cast?

> 1) The infant's toes are cold to the touch and have capillary refill >3 seconds
> 2) The infant's respiratory rate has increased from 24 to 30 breaths per minute
> 3) The infant's temperature is 100.2 degrees Fahrenheit
> 4) The nurse feels a "hot spot" when palpating the cast

Option #4 is correct. Option #1 is indicative of neurovascular compromise, not infection. Option #2 includes a normal range of respiratory rate for this age group. Option #3 could indicate infection but Option #4 specifically indicates possible infection under the cast.

2. The parents of a newborn just diagnosed with myelomeningocele are expressing feelings of guilt and anxiety about the future of their baby. Which of the following is the most appropriate approach by the nurse?

> 1) Sign them up for a support group with other parents who have a baby with the same problem.
> 2) Talk to them about the diagnosis and encourage them to express what they are feeling.
> 3) Call the infant's provider and ask for an interdisciplinary conference to discuss treatment options.
> 4) Tell them that this is preventable with future babies by taking the recommended amount of folic acid.

Option #2 is correct. At this point, the parents need to be able to express their emotions and begin to accept the diagnosis. Options #1 and #3 are not appropriate at this time but will be valuable later down the road. Option #4 will increase their feelings of guilt that this was preventable.

3. A 12-month-old baby girl was diagnosed 3 months ago with cerebral palsy. She is presenting to the clinic today for a well baby check-up. Which of the following statements by the mother indicates that the nurse's teaching has been effective?

> 1) "I have been working on getting her to hold and use a sippy cup by herself."
> 2) "I want to have another baby but plan to get some genetic testing from my healthcare provider first."

3) "I am hoping the provider will prescribe muscle relaxants today to help her start to walk now that she is one-year-old."
4) "I am watching her closely for any signs that her condition might be worsening."

Option #1 is the best way to promote independence and optimal development, the goal of therapy in patients with cerebral palsy. Option #2 is incorrect because the disease is not genetic. Option #3 is incorrect. Muscle relaxants do not improve muscle function, but decrease spasticity and the risk of contractures. Option #4 is incorrect because CP is not a progressive disease.

4. A 5-year-old patient is on his fifth post-op day in skeletal traction for treatment of a vertebral fracture. His pain is being treated with Morphine in a PCA. Upon assessment he appears irritable and points to a "6" on the FACES scale when you inquire about his pain. What is the most appropriate action to take next?

1) Instruct both the patient and his parents on correct use of the PCA
2) Call the provider and request a re-evaluation of his current pain management plan
3) Dim the lights in the room, limit visitors, and give a dose of prn diphenhydramine (Benadryl) to allow him to rest
4) Ask his mother the date and time of his last bowel movement

Option #4 is correct. He has been immobilized for 5 days and is also being treated with Morphine, which has a potential side effect of constipation. Option #1 is a reasonable choice, but chances are that after 5 days of treatment, the parents and patient know how to use the PCA appropriately. Options #2 and #3 may be considered after gathering more data first.

5. A 14-year-old girl is 4 hours post-op after having a spinal fusion and instrumentation to correct scoliosis. When the nurse assesses the client upon admission, she finds that the client's feet are cool to the touch, capillary refill is >5 seconds, and she cannot palpate a pedal pulse. What action should the nurse take at this time?

1) Cover the patient with heated blankets to counteract post-operative hypothermia
2) Call the orthopedic surgeon immediately
3) Reposition the patient and complete the assessment again
4) Start an IV fluid bolus to counteract the early signs of hypovolemic shock

Option #2 is correct. These are critical signs that should be attended to immediately in order to prevent permanent disability.

6. A 4-year-old child has a casted arm for a fracture of the radius. For which of the following should the parent be instructed to contact the provider? **Select all that apply.**

    1) Pain level of 3 on a scale of 1-10
    2) Reddish, warm fingers
    3) Complaints of numbness
    4) Pallor
    5) Inability to wiggle the thumb

The correct options are #3, #4, and #5. Remember the 5 P's of cast care: Pallor, Pain, Pulselessness, Paresthesia, and Paralysis.

7. A 9-year-old child is in skeletal traction following a horseback riding accident. His bed is not working properly and he needs to be placed in another bed. What is the appropriate action of the nurse?

    1) Release the weights, transfer as quickly and carefully as possible, and reattach the weights.
    2) Consult with physical therapy before transferring the patient.
    3) Call the orthopedic surgery team prior to transferring the patient.
    4) Use a transfer board and keep the weights at the same level during the transfer.

The correct option is #3. You should NEVER release or change traction weights for any reason except with approval of the orthopedic provider.

8. A 10-year-old child will be in skeletal traction for 3 weeks. What actions should the nurse take to prevent skin breakdown? Select all that apply.

    1) Use the Modified Braden Q scale to assess the skin.
    2) Change position every hour to relieve pressure.
    3) Provide a low fat diet to prevent excessive weight gain.
    4) Stimulate circulation with gentle massage.
    5) Total body skin checks every hour.

The correct options are #1 and #4. Changing position every two hours is standard. Doing total body skin checks every hour is ridiculous. Once daily is sufficient. The child will need a balanced diet with plenty of protein to facilitate healing.

9. The mother of a 2-month-old infant tells the nurse she suspects her baby may have a dislocated hip because she has heard and felt a "click" twice when changing the diaper. How should the nurse respond?

1) Assess the hips using the Ortolani and Barlow maneuver
2) Assess for symmetry in gluteal skin folds
3) Advise the mother to "double-diaper" the baby to maintain good hip alignment.
4) Call the provider

The correct option at this point is #2. Option #1 is incorrect because this is an advanced practice technique and is not to be performed by a Registered Nurse. Double diapering will not help and ignores a potentially debilitating problem. Further assessment is needed before calling the provider.

10. What is the most critical element of care for an infant in a Pavlik harness?

1) Preventing skin breakdown
2) Keeping follow-up appointments
3) Promoting optimal growth and development
4) Creating an emotional bond

Option #2 is most important. If follow-up appointments are not kept, the child could be permanently disabled.

11. Which statement by a parent of an infant with clubfoot demonstrates good understanding of the condition?

1) "We will come in for new casts or splints every few days for 8-12 weeks."
2) "We will need to stay in a cast for approximately 12 weeks."
3) "We need to be very careful and keep him as still as possible."
4) "We understand that surgery is the only option."

Option #1 is correct. Initial treatment is to provide serial casting or splinting for 8-12 weeks. If optimal alignment is not achieved at that time, surgery is considered. Parents should strive to keep activities as normal as possible to promote optimal development.

12. An adolescent who has just undergone surgery for scoliosis repair says to the nurse "I will never look normal. I hate myself and I want to die." What is the appropriate response of the nurse?

    1) "Don't worry. Everything will be okay. You will feel better tomorrow."
    2)"There is another patient on this floor that had the same surgery. Maybe you two can talk."
    3) "Your pain medication is making you feel down. We can talk to your provider about getting something different."
    4)"Have you ever thought about harming yourself?"

Option #4 is correct. Suicide is a leading cause of death for teens and any mention of it should be taken seriously. If patients say they have thought about self-harm, the nurse should ask if they have considered a plan. If the teen has given thoughts to specific methods, they are at greater risk of self-harm.

13. What should be included in the pre-operative care for an adolescent preparing for surgery to correct scoliosis? **Select all that apply.**

    1) Autologous blood donation
    2) Education about a PCA pump
    3) Demonstration of a Foley catheter
    4) Proper technique for a log-roll
    5) Explanation of a chest tube

All options are correct. The potential for blood loss in this surgery is significant, so advance planning must be made. The teen needs to be equipped to cooperate and fully participate in treatment and recovery while preserving dignity and body image as much as possible. All the other options are part of surgery to correct scoliosis.

14. A nurse is assessing a 14-year-old who is 12 hours post-operative spinal fusion. Vital signs 4 hours ago were: P-98, BP 120/76, R-24. Current vital signs are: P-118, BP-100/64, R-24. What is the appropriate action to take?

    1) Do a pain assessment
    2) Call the provider
    3) Check I&O
    4) Check temperature

The correct option is #2. This is potentially a sign of significant blood loss and early shock. I&O is helpful, but not critical. The patient is not yet at significant risk for post-operative infection, which typically occurs 48-72hours after surgery. These are signs of early shock and the provider should be notified immediately.

15. A child is admitted with osteomyelitis of the foot. Prioritize these nursing actions from most important to least important.

    1) Immobilize the foot
    2) Administer antibiotics
    3) Manage pain
    4) Promote adequate nutrition

Options are #2, #3, #1, #4. Antibiotics are critical for recovery. Pain medication is second. Immobilizing the joint after pain medication facilitates recovery and adequate nutrition is essential to promote rapid healing.

16. A 3-year-old is in pain following an orthopedic surgery. What is the best approach to pain management?

    1) Teach the child how to use his PCA
    2) Use the FLACC scale to assess pain and response to interventions
    3) Use the numbers scale to most accurately assess pain level
    4) Avoid the use of opiate analgesics because of the child's age

Option #2 is correct. The FLACC scale can be used for young children to objectively measure pain. The FACES scale is used for ages 4-9 years, and the numbers scale for 9 years and up. The scale must match the child's developmental ability. It is important to effectively treat pain and opiates are acceptable. This child is likely too young to use the PCA effectively.

17. A mother of a child with Duchenne Muscular Dystrophy calls to report he is having increasing difficulty with swallowing. What is the appropriate response of the nurse?

    1) Review the plan for home care with the mother
    2) Request the mother to come in for an appointment
    3) Suggest repositioning with feeding and use of a straw
    4) Recommend a liquid-only diet

Option #1 is correct. DMD is a terminal disease and deterioration is expected and planned for. When a new symptom of deterioration appears, parents should be coached through it.

18. A newborn is delivered with a large myelomeningocele. What actions should the nurse immediately take? **Select all that apply.**

    1) Cover the sac with a sterile, moist, nonadherent dressing
    2) Monitor vital signs every hour, including a rectal temperature.
    3) Place the infant in an incubator.
    4) Position the infant prone with head turned to the side.
    5) Avoid diapering the infant

All options except #2 are correct. Rectal temperatures are contraindicated with spina bifida because it can cause rectal prolapse. There is no special need to monitor vital signs every hour. The infant should be placed in an incubator for warmth because clothing and diapering should be avoided to prevent damage to the sac.

19. A nurse is assessing a 5-month-old infant. Which of the following should be reported to the provider? **Select all that apply.**

    1) Presence of head lag
    2) Absence of primitive reflexes
    3) Scissoring legs
    4) Inability to sit up without support
    5) Absence of social smile

Options #1, #3, and #5 are all potentially signs of cerebral palsy. Primitive reflexes should fade at 3-4 months, and sitting up without support generally occurs by 7 months. Social smile should be present by 3-4 months of age and scissoring legs are not a normal finding at any age.

20. The parents of a child diagnosed 2 months ago with cerebral palsy are frustrated with the care they are receiving. The father says to the nurse "You are not doing anything to help us! You don't even care!" What is the appropriate response of the nurse?

    1) Allow the father to express his emotions

    2) Leave the room and return after the father has calmed down

    3) Call security

    4) Tell the father it is not appropriate to raise his voice

Option #1 is correct. Parents of children with chronic diseases often feel frustrated and overwhelmed. They need support and encouragement. Leaving the room may exacerbate the father's emotions.

Nursing Management in Neurological and Sensory Perception Disorders

Sylvia Rayfield, MN, RN, CNS
Edited by Sylvia Rayfield & Associates Inc.

Key Concepts:

- § **Head**
  - ◆ **Increased Cranial Pressure (Brain Tumors, Hemorrhages, Head Injuries) Stroke, Seizures**
- § **Nerves**
- § **Cord**
- § **Rehabilitation**
- § **Eye Disorders**
- § **Ear Disorders**
- § **Practice Questions, Answers and Rationale**

The study of the human brain and its diseases remains one of the greatest scientific and philosophical challenges ever undertaken.

Floyd Bloom

Head

One of the most important things to remember about the head is that it is fixed in size. The brain inside the head takes up all of the space in this fixed area. The brain is not always fixed in size. It may have extra fluid (hydrocephalus) or "space taking lesions" (benign or malignant brain tumors) that increase its' size. When the brain size is increased inside a closed head, it is easy to see that there will be increased pressure on the brain called Increased Intracranial Pressure(IICP) or increased cranial pressure (ICP). Easy right?

This important SAFETY acronym allows for the organization of this chapter. And includes:
1. **Safe client care**
2. **Study of heaviest weighted NCLEX® standards**
3. **Study of all body systems for nursing exams**

SAFETY AS A BLUEPRINT

S   **System specific focused assessment/diagnostics**

A   **Assess for risk and respond**

F   **Find change/trends and intervene**

E   **Evaluate pharmacology — 8 rights, effect on client and other meds/foods, therapeutic blood levels**

T   **Teach and practice safety and infection control**

Y   **Your management—legal/ethical/scope of practice, identity, errors, delegation, faulty equipment/staff, privacy/confidentiality, falls/hazards**

Causes of ICP include:

- Brain tumor either benign or malignant still takes up space
- Motor vehicle accidents causing head injury/ traumatic brain injury (TBI), edema, and hematoma.
- Brain infections
- Brain swelling as in increased cerebral spinal fluid (hydrocephalous), brain hemorrhage (Cerebrovascular Accident [CVA]—Stroke)
- Aneurysm
- Certain medications such as Accutane or Lithium

SYSTEM SPECIFIC ASSESSMENT— ICP and Related Issues.
Assess for:
- Headache
- Nausea and vomiting
- Visual disturbances
- Cushing's Triad (increased systolic BP, widened pulse pressure, and bradycardia) Assess and respond to changes in vital signs.
- Bradycardia
- Altered LOC (level of consciousness), anxiety, irritability, restlessness, confusion, stupor, and coma
- Head position (**up**—ICP is up; **down**—ICP is down)
- Seizures

Diagnostic Tests For Neurological Assessment

NCLEX®TESTING OFTEN INCLUDES WHAT THE NURSE SHOULD PROVIDE BEFORE, DURING AND AFTER THE DIAGNOSTIC TESTS.

Search (Assess/Analysis)	Rescue (Implementation)	Fallout (Outcome—Good/Bad)
Skull X-rays	To detect fractures and bone fragments. Assess for fluids coming from ears and nose No prep needed	Missed skull fractures Level of consciousness decreased
MRI—Magnetic Resonance Imaging	Non-invasive test utilizing a powerful magnetic field to produce detailed pictures of any internal body structure. A short two minute demonstration of an MRI can be found on: http://www.youtube.com/watch?v=FallWN1uYco	Claustrophobia may interfere with test and therefore may require a sedative during test Remove all metal as the MRI is a powerful magnet

Search (Assess/Analysis)	Rescue (Implementation)	Fallout (Outcome—Good/Bad)
CT Scans—Computer Tomography	Non-invasive diagnostic test used to visualize internal injuries with or without dye. The test visualizes cross sections of the area Review BUN and creatinine results prior to test Push fluids to clear dye	Altered renal clearance Claustrophobia in scanner which may require sedation
Cerebrospinal Fluid (CSF) sampling—Spinal Tap	Seek informed consent May be contraindicated in ICP Document test and send specimen to lab with correct label Keep client flat for prescribed period Reassess vital signs and level of consciousness	Headache Infection at injection site
EEG—Electroencephalogram	Measures electrical activity in the brain Advise client to wash hair before test No sedatives Advise client to avoid caffeine Client should be NPO	Seizures may be triggered Goo in hair

ASSESS FOR RISK AND RESPOND

- Secure airway, breathing Mechanical ventilation is a possibility. Respond by elevating the head of the bed unless contraindicated. Assess for spinal fluid leaking from nose or ears, especially after accident. Respond by utilizing urine test stick and, if positive for sugar, it is a good indication of spinal fluid.
- Assess altered LOC. GLASGOW Coma Scale testing: eye opening, motor skills, and ability to talk. Normal ranges from 3-15, the lower the score the more altered the consciousness. Document results. Assess blood sugar level
- Cardiac monitoring
- Vital signs monitoring **Remember except for decreased LOC, the vital signs in elevated ICP are opposite from the vital signs in shock.**
- Elevated temperature can increase ICP. Report immediately.
- Elevated blood pressure is an indication for stroke
- Blood gas monitoring

- Neurological checks of cranial nerves
  - 1—Can the client smell?
  - 2—Can the client see using a Snellen chart?
  - 3, 4 and 6—Will the client's eyes follow your pin light?
  - 5—Can the client bite, chew, swallow?
  - 7—Can the client smile?
  - 8—Can the client hear?
  - 9 and10—Can the client feel under their chin?
  - 11—Can the client shrug their shoulders?
  - 12—Can the client stick out their tongue and move it? Recognize non-verbal cues?
- Seizures require client safety:
  - Protect client from falls
  - Manage the client with impaired ventilation
  - Facilitate appropriate and safe use of equipment. Do not try to shove an airway into this client's mouth.
  - Document seizure progression to help determine the pathophysiology and location of the focus in the brain.
  - Educate client regarding his condition. Identify triggers causing seizures and avoid alcohol. Teach use of medications for control.
  - Clients with diagnosed ICP should be on CBR (complete bed rest).
- Clients with ICP are likely to have fluid restrictions. Evaluate client intake and output and intervene as needed.

FIND CHANGE/TRENDS AND INTERVENE

If you can remember only one thing, remember to find change in the level of consciousness!

Strokes often cause a change in the LOC. All strokes are not hemorrhagic, which would increase the ICP. Most strokes are caused from atherosclerosis, which causes hypertension, but not ICP.

Stroke changes things Utilize the National Stroke Association warning signs for assessment acronym **FAST**. The FAST acronym is used because if the client has a blood clot in the brain causing the stroke, it may be dissolved within 3 hours with tPa. After 3 hours it may be too late to dissolve the clot.

F **Face**—Can the client smile?
A **Arms**—Can the client raise both arms and hold
S **Speech**—Can the client talk without slurring?
T **Time to call 9-1-1** or the medical provider if you find any of these changes.

Rehabilitation begins immediately with stroke

FACE

- If the client can't smile or talk, they may not be able to swallow. If they can't swallow, they can't eat. Manage the client's nutritional intake by adjusting the diet. Parenteral nutrition such as TPN may be necessary. A gastric tube, may be necessary for feeding in the first few days post-stroke. See Gastrointestinal Module for tube feeding.
- If the client can't smile or talk they may not be able to communicate. Work out a communication system with them even if it is blinking the eyes once for yes and twice for no. If they are able to use one hand, they may be able to use fingers. Therapeutic communication techniques may be used to provide client support. Recognize non-verbal cues to physical and psychological factors.
- Verify that the client comprehends and consents to care and procedures.
- If the client can physically smile, but does not, evaluate for sadness and grief for loss of body use.
- The face includes the eyes. Are the pupils equal and respond to changes in light? Can the client see? Assess for homonymous hemianopsia (loss of half the vision field). If they can only see half of what they have seen in the past and they do not know this, they will eat half the food on their plate or only see cars coming from one side when crossing the street. They can be run over by a Mack Truck!
- Stroke may cause blindness.

ARMS

- If the **arm** can't be moved, assess for leg paralysis. Hemiplegia with both the arm and leg impaired on the same side is common in stroke. Impaired leg movement means the client must be protected from injury such as a fall.
- If the client can't move —implement measures to promote circulation.
- If they can move it, encourage active exercises.
- The arm/shoulder is easily injured by allowing it to hang down; utilize a splint to prevent this from happening. The joint in a splint must be exercised to prevent a frozen shoulder.
- If there is paralysis, assess for incontinence, bladder and bowel rehabilitation requires persistence and a schedule. Catheters may be necessary to keep the client dry. Catheters lead to infection. Apply principles of infection control when caring for the catheter. Discontinue as soon as possible.
- Perform skin assessment and implement measures to maintain skin integrity and prevent breakdown. Schedule turning, repositioning, coughing and deep breathing. Utilize pressure-relieved support surfaces). See care for decubitus in Musculo-Skeletal/Integumentary Module.
- Assess and intervene in client performance of ADL (Activities of Daily Living). Recognize limitation of self/others and seek assistance especially if the client is heavy and cannot turn, sit or walk on their own. Use ergonomic principles when providing care. Assistive devices may be needed for lifting. Devices utilized to lift clients can be helpful and hazardous! Guard against falls!
- Teach transfer techniques. **Remember strong side leads!**
- Apply and maintain devices used to promote venous return such as anti-embolic stockings or sequential compression devices. These devices are utilized primarily on the legs. Deep vein thrombosis (DVT) is a risk factor in clients with paralysis. Early ambulation is important unless the client has had a brain hemorrhage; then ambulate with caution and/or provider orders.
- Paralysis of any type requires referral to a rehabilitation facility and physical and occupational therapists. Recognize the need for family and client referrals, and obtain necessary orders.

SPEECH—Stroke, especially one causing right-sided paralysis, often leaves the client unable to speak (Aphasia). The inability to communicate is often extremely frustrating and the nurse finds herself working with a very angry client. Ways to assist the client at this time may include:

- Remembering that if the client cannot speak, they may also not be able to swallow. Guard against aspiration.
- Remember the stroke has affected the client's ability to process language, it **has not** affected his/her intelligence!
- Recognize non-verbal cues
- Clients who are paralyzed may be limited in their ability to pantomime or make other gestures.
- Give the client time to answer your questions and discourage family from answering.
- Understanding and speaking both may be affected. Act accordingly.
- Referring the client to a speech therapist is vital as partial or complete recovery is possible.
- **Coping is the bottom line.**

Aphasia is not limited to stroke victims.

Other conditions where aphasia is found include:

- Clients with brain injury or disease,
- Clients with Alzheimer's disease,
- Clients with Parkinson's disease.

When the client is ready for discharge, assess his/her ability to manage care in a home environment and plan care accordingly. Special equipment and community resources should be available to the client. Educate client on home safety issues.

- Watch for throw rugs that may cause the client to slip.
- Utilize safety bars especially in the bathtub area.

EVALUATE PHARMACOLOGY

When administering medication we must be CAREFUL!

Medication Administration Alert

C	**Calculate correctly**	
A	**Assess for allergies**	
R	**Rights of administration**	
E	**Evaluate response**	
F	**Feel free to call provider if intuition alerts**	
U	**Utilize an assessment in determining ordered parameters**	
L	**Lab data pertinence**	

Drug	Action	Evaluation
Fluid management should include Saline or Ringers Lactate. Dextrose or half-normal saline is contraindicated and should be questioned	Maintains fluid balance without increasing ICP	Monitor VS, I&O Rate may be slow. Do not increase without provider order
IV Mannitol	A diuretic that reduces cerebral edema	Should be monitored by accurate intake and output and ICP variations
Loop Diuretics such as furosemide (Lasix)	Utilized to reduce cerebral edema	I&O and ICP variations
Beta Blockers such as atenolol (Tenormin)	Reduces BP and ICP	Monitor BP closely Monitor ICP variations
Dopamine	Increases BP	Monitor BP
Acetazolamide (Diamox)	Diuretic—interferes with CSF production and lowers ICP	Accurate I&O
Phenytoin (Dilantin)	Seizure prevention anticonvulsant Mixes poorly with any other IV medication	Presence/absence of seizures
Morphine	Pain killer	Nausea and vomiting, itching, confusion, respiratory depression, pinpoint pupils, LOC
Fentanyl	**Potent** synthetic narcotic analgesic utilized for pain and sedation	Pain relief, confusion, hypoventilation, apnea, aphasia
Propofol (Diprivan)	Hypnotic used to sedate clients	Decreased BP, apnea, coma
Pentobarbital (Nembutal)	Anticonvulsant Utilized to place the client in a coma to lower ICP	Evaluate liver and kidney prior to administering Addiction, LOC
Nitrates, nitropresside, and nitroglycerin are often contraindicated and should be questioned		

TEACH AND PRACTICE INFECTION CONTROL

> ➤ Always utilize good hand hygiene to help prevent infection.
> ➤ IV lines to keep veins open and administer fluids and medications are sources of introduced infections. Monitor the IV infusion and watch for pain or redness at the site. Evaluate client intake and output and intervene as needed.
> ➤ Intracranial pressure monitoring devices are sources of infection. Perform skin assessment and implement measures to maintain skin integrity.
> ➤ The client with open head injury is prone to infection. Seek orders for prophylactic antibiotics.

YOUR MANAGEMENT

Commonalities that flow through client safety of every body system and are heavily weighted on the *NCLEX*® can be condensed into the following table on MANAGE.

These standards currently count for as much as 23% of the total *NCLEX*® exam and are always a primary consideration for nursing.

PASS *NCLEX*®
M **Make sure of identity, accuracy of orders**
A **Arrange privacy/confidentiality/consent/collaboration with other team**
N **No injuries, falls, malfunctioning equipment or staff or hazards**
A **Address errors, abuse, legalities, scope of practice—document**
G **Give (delegate) orders to appropriate people, report when they are unsafe**
E **Establish priorities of clients and time**

Nerves

Common Causes of Nerve Diseases:

- Parkinson's Disease—resting tremor, rigidity, slowness of movement, and instability in posture.
- ALS (amyotropic lateral sclerosis)
- Huntington's Disease,
- Muscular Dystrophy
- Polymyositis

Common Cranial Nerve Disorders:

- Bell's Palsy (facial pain)
- Trigeminal Neuralgia (facial pain and paralysis)
- Meniere's Disease (severe vertigo, nausea and vomiting)

Common Autoimmune Disorders—the 3F diseases: fever, falling, and fatigue

- Myasthenia Gravis
- Multiple sclerosis
- Guillain-Barré Syndrome

SYSTEM SPECIFIC ASSESSMENT

- ► Assess for altered mobility/balance and protect the client from injury or falls
- ► Assess for involuntary movements
- ► Look for weakness in arms, legs, speaking.
- ► Assess for depression.

Diagnostic tests for neurological assessment

NCLEX® testing often includes what the nurse should provide before, during and after the diagnostic tests.

Monitor the results of diagnostic testing and intervene as needed. (See tables earlier in chapter.)

- ♦ CT scan
- ♦ MRI
- ♦ EEG-electrical activity of the brain
- ♦ Electromyogram (EMG)— Electrical activity between nerves and muscles using mild electrical shocks to stimulate the nerves
- ♦ C-Reactive Protein (CRP)
- ♦ Erythrocyte Sedimentation Rate (ESR)

ASSESS FOR RISK AND RESPOND

The risks can be remembered along with the **3Fs**. The clients are likely to **fall**, be **fatigued**, and may be prone to **fever**. Responses to these issues include:

> Maintain independence as long as possible
> - Refer to Physical Therapy
> - Encourage family to maintain independence
> - Assist the client to compensate for his/her impairment
> Keep safe from falling
> - Evaluate home hazards such as throw rugs, slippery surfaces. Put in hand rails for safety to protect the client from injury.
> Manage postural instability
> - Encourage exercise
> Relieve symptoms
> - Administer medications appropriately (see Evaluate Pharmacology below)
> Refer to Occupational Therapy for assistance in impaired activities of daily living
> Counseling
> - Chronic disease often causes depression
> Encourage to stay active to improve balance, keep limbs limber, and stay connected with friends and support systems. Assess his/her ability to manage care in the home environment and plan care accordingly. Special equipment, education ,and other resources may be needed.
> Reduced symptoms control the autoimmune process; maintain the body's ability to fight disease.
> Corticosteroids (prednisone, azathioprine, cyclopohosphamide) may elevate the BP, suppress the immune system, and cause frequent infections.

FIND CHANGE/TRENDS AND INTERVENE

If you can remember only one thing, remember to be alert to any trend that will cause the client to lose independence. As these are mostly chronic illnesses. The length of time before they lose independence will vary on intervention, personality, severity, and success of medication. As the disease process progresses, changes may present such as:

- Listen to lung sounds for pneumonia, a common complication and encourage mobility as long as possible.
- Bed sores lead to septicemia and elevated temperature
  - Perform skin assessment and implement measures to maintain skin integrity and prevent skin breakdown. See nursing intervention of Decubiti in the Musculo-Skeletal-Integumentary Module
- Pain in the extremity or shortness of breath may be due to emboli. Contact the provider immediately!

EVALUATE PHARMACOLOGY

When administering medication we must be CAREFUL!

MEDICATION ADMINISTRATION ALERT

See box with CAREFUL on page 324

Disease Process	Drug	Action	Evaluation
Parkinson's	Levodopa (Dopar, Larodopa)	Turns into dopamine in the brain	Evaluate decreased tremors, stiffness, spasms, decreased stiffness, nausea and vomiting, uncontrolled movements of face, tongue, eyelids, and behavioral change
Parkinson's	Carbidopa (Lodosyn)	Slows metabolism of levodopa and makes it longer lasting. Has no action when given alone, only utilized with levodopa	Evaluate decreased tremors, stiffness, spasms, decreased stiffness, nausea and vomiting, uncontrolled movements of face, tongue, eyelids, and behavioral change
Parkinson's	Monoamine oxidase inhibitors (MAOI): Rasagline (Azilect) Selegiline (Eldepryl)	Slows the breakdown of dopamine in the brain and extends the action of levodopa	Evaluate for decreased tremors
Amyotrophic Lateral Sclerosis (ALS) (currently incurable)	Riluzole (Rilutek)	May slow disease progression but does not cure	Teach to eliminate caffeine use Evaluate for fatigue, nausea and vomiting, appetite loss
Huntington's (currently incurable)	Tetrabenazine (Xenazine)	Suppresses involuntary jerking	Evaluate for slowed jerking Watch for signs of depression
Muscular Dystrophy (currently incurable) **Polymositis**	Corticosteroids (Prednisone)	Anti inflammatory	Evaluate for symptom relief, hypertension, hyperglycemia, osteoporosis in long-term use, weight gain, blurred vision, and peptic ulcer

Disease Process	Drug	Action	Evaluation
Bell's Palsy	Corticosteroids (Prednisone) Acyclovir (Zovirax) Valacyclovir (Valtrex)	Anti-viral	Evaluate decreased progression, paralysis, and swelling of the face, changes in vision, dizziness, drowsiness, headache, nausea and diarrhea, severe allergic reaction (hives, dyspnea)
Trigeminal Neuralgia	Carbamazepine (Tegretol, Carbatrol) Phenytoin (Dilantin) Gabapentin (Neurontin)	Anticonvulsant	Evaluate for facial paralysis, decreased pain. Dilantin may cause slurred speech, confusion. Neurontin may cause clumsiness, confusion, fainting, twitching
Meniere's Disease (currently incurable)	Meclizine (Antivert) Diazepam (Valium) Promethazine (Phenergan)	Antivert is anti-nausea and anti-vertigo Valium produces a calming effect	Evaluate for allergic reaction, decreased vertigo, decreased nausea, blurred vision, dry mouth, constipation, decreased nervousness
Myasthenia Gravis (currently incurable)	Corticosteroids (Prednisone) Pyridostigmine (Mestinon)	Cholinesterase inhibitor that increases communication between nerves and muscles	Evaluate for difficulty breathing, improvement in severe muscle weakness
Multiple Sclerosis (currently incurable)	Interferon (Avonex, Betaseron)	Boost the immune system to reduce viruses, bacteria, and other foreign substances	Evaluate for fatigue, encourage exercise, evaluate for weight loss due to loss of appetite. Adjust diet to small frequent feedings. Monitor liver enzymes Avoid alcohol

Disease Process	Drug	Action	Evaluation
Guillain-Barré Syndrome	Plasmapheresis, a laboratory treatment	Rids blood plasma of antibodies that may cause the immune system to attack the peripheral nerves	Evaluate for ascending paralysis, difficulty breathing Begin rehabilitation immediately with PT, adaptive devices, and mobility devices

TEACH AND PRACTICE INFECTION CONTROL

➤ Apply principles of infection control and universal precautions on all clients.

➤ IV lines to keep veins open; administered fluids and medications are sources of introduced infections. Evaluate for redness and pain at the site.

➤ Decubiti is a source of infection. Perform skin assessment and implement measures to maintain skin integrity.

➤ The client receiving steroids is prone to infection. Seek orders for prophylactic antibiotics. The client usually does not have the knowledge base to advocate for themselves. Nurses must be client advocates.

YOUR MANAGEMENT

Commonalities that flow through client safety of every body system and are heavily weighted on the *NCLEX*® can be condensed into the acronym on MANAGE.

See box with MANAGE on page 326.

These standards currently count for as much as 23% of the total *NCLEX*® exam and are always a primary consideration for nursing.

Cord

Spinal Cord Injuries

Common causes:
- Motor vehicle accidents
- Violence—gun shot wounds, military wounds
- Falls
- Sports injuries

A spinal cord injury is likely to affect every single body system!

- ABCs: Airway, impaired Breathing, check Circulation
- Tingling or pain
- Paralysis (quadriplegia, paraplegia)
- Loss of control over any body part
- Extreme pain in back, neck, or head
- Monitor vital signs

Diagnostic Tests For Neurological Assessment

NCLEX® testing often includes what the nurse should provide before, during, and after the diagnostic tests.

Search (Assess/Analysis)	Rescue (Implementation)	Fallout (Outcome—Good/Bad)
X-rays	To detect fractures and bone fragments. No prep needed	Permanent disability
MRI—Magnetic Resonance Imaging	Non-invasive test utilizing a powerful magnetic field to produce detailed pictures of any internal body structure. A short two minute demonstration of an MRI can be found on: http://www.youtube.com/watch?v=FallWN1uYco	Claustrophobia may interfere with test and therefore may require a sedative during test Remove all metal as the MRI is a powerful magnet

Search (Assess/Analysis)	Rescue (Implementation)	Fallout (Outcome—Good/Bad)
CT Scans—Computer Tomography	Non-invasive diagnostic test used to visualize internal injuries with or without dye. The test visualizes cross sections of the area Review BUN and creatinine results prior to test Push fluids to clear dye Determine allergies to iodine	Altered renal clearance Claustrophobia in scanner which may require sedation Anaphylaxis
Cerebrospinal Fluid (CSF) sampling—Spinal Tap	Seek informed consent May be contraindicated in ICP Document test and send specimen to lab with correct label Keep client flat for prescribed period Reassess vital signs and level of consciousness	Headache Infection at injection site Changes in vital signs
Electromyography (EMG)	Diagnose nerve dysfunction, muscle dysfunction, or problems with nerve to muscle signal transmissions	Minor bruising where needle electrode was inserted (if used) Possible pain and discomfort
Myelogram (contrast dye is injected into spinal canal)	Dye outlines spinal cord and nerves Can reveal herniated disks, bone spurs, and tumors. Determine allergy to dye (iodine) Keep head slightly elevated	Anaphylaxis Infection at injection site Headache, nausea, or vomiting

ASSESS FOR RISK AND RESPOND

- ♦ Determine vital signs and respond to changes.
  - • Spinal shock: the traumatized cord swells, decreases circulation, and almost in an instant blood pressure drops causing severe hypotension.
  - • Seek orders for fluid resuscitation.
  - • Compromised immune system may lead to elevated temperature.
  - • Pneumonia is a common complication. Encourage deep breathing.

- Secure airway breathing. Mechanical ventilation is a possibility if there are respiratory complications. Use jaw-thrust to open airway if possibility of a cervical spine injury.
- Mobilize to prevent further injury. Log roll to turn. Axial traction possible. Devices will likely be used to promote venous return. These devices such as anti-embolic stockings or other anti DVT measures should be monitored. Special equipment such as pressure-relieving support surfaces may be utilized. If the equipment is not working correctly, it may cause clients to fall. Monitor all equipment
- Cardiac monitoring due to possible arrhythmias, especially bradycardia. The client may be on telemetry and should be monitored.
- Vital signs—spinal shock probable
- Blood gas monitoring
- Sensation loss and possible paralysis level
  - Assess for bowel and bladder incontinence
  - Assess for ability to change positions
- Determine seizure activity and require client safety:
  - Document seizure progression to help determine the location of the focus in the brain.
  - Educate client regarding reasons for seizure activity, auras, or triggers.

FIND CHANGE/TRENDS AND INTERVENE

- Listen to lung sounds for pneumonia, a common complication. Turn every 2 hours.
  - Chills and high fever may be an indication of septicemia. An estimated 80% of clients with SCI have pressure sores, which often lead to septicemia and elevated temperature. Turn every 2 hours; notify provider of any broken skin area. (See nursing intervention of decubiti in the Musculoskeletal—Integumentary Module.
- Tachycardia, tachypnea, and pain in the extremity or shortness of breath may be due to emboli. Contact the provider immediately! Passive exercises if allowed may prevent deep vein thrombosis (DVT).
- Changes in pain level may require medication, surgery, or acupuncture.
- Spasms may require medication or may be useful for transfer due to stiff limbs. Spasticity may be very painful and should be managed with medication.
- Sudden hypertension may be indication of **Autonomic Dysreflexia**. Assess for full bladder, bowel, and skin breakdown. Evaluate the catheter, empty the bladder/bowel, change positions, loosen tight clothing, lie the client down if possible. **QUICKLY! This is life threatening.**
- Determine renal values, as renal failure is a common cause of death. Measure I&O, hydrate

Changes in the spinal cord client are likely incurable. Rehabilitation must start immediately.

Rehabilitation

The goal of all rehabilitation nursing is to assist the client to achieve and maintain independence. This INDEPENDENCE acronym will help you remember the important concepts.

I   Infection leading to septicemia often from pressure sores and pneumonia is the biggest cause of death. Apply all principles of infection control including: hand hygiene, asepsis, and sterile technique.

N   Nutrition will likely need adjusting. Protein is needed for tissue rebuilding. Alternative feeding may be necessary. Guard against aspiration and constipation.

D   Determine venous return. Flaccid muscles allow blood pooling and DVT. It is important to recognize trends and changes in the client's condition. Remember to promote venous return.

E   Everyday ADL is a challenge that must be met. Assess the client's self care ability, especially if the client is heavy and cannot turn, sit, walk, or complete bowel functions on their own.

P   Pressure sores (decubiti) are common. Turn, reposition, use pressure-relieving support surfaces. Document and report to the provider immediately.

E   Equipment and staff to facilitate mobilization may be necessary.

N   Non-verbal may be only communication. Arrange communication with the client.

D   Depression is a common factor. **Coping is the bottom line**. Assess the client for potential for violence and use safety precautions against suicide or other self-destructive behavior.

E   Evaluate home safety prior to discharge. Assess client's ability to manage their care in their home environment. Plan care to include any devices, referrals, or other community services that may be needed.

N   Need for inner strength and family support. Assess the client and the family in coping with these serious and likely permanent life changes. Provide support through education and communication.

C   Collaborate with physiatrist, physical/occupational therapists, and other health team members in care. Unaffected muscles must be strengthened to do the work of paralyzed muscles.

E   Evaluate medication effect on rehabilitation.

More rehabilitation= Less complications
Coping is the bottom line.

Eye Disorders

SYSTEM SPECIFIC ASSESSMENT

Health Fairs and clinics are an excellent place to perform target screening assessments in vision, and hearing. Common eye disorders such as pink eye can be found just by looking at the client's eye. Pink eye causes itching, burning and is highly contagious. The nurse should teach the principles of infection control. The client may not realize that this infection can be spread to everyone in the family. Educate the client for self care. This YouTube will show this process.http://www.youtube.com/watch?v=PPvxac-BqMn8&feature=fvwrel

According to the World Health Organization (WHO), **cataracts** are the leading cause of blindness in the world except for clients under the age of 30 where eye injuries are the leading cause.

ASSESS FOR RISK AND RESPOND

The aging client is at significant risk for cataracts as the lens of the eye is primarily protein, which denatures with age and becomes cloudy. Other common causes of cataracts (clouding of the lens in the eye) are: smoking, sunlight exposure, trauma, diabetes, and steroids. The client complains of blurred vision, glare, and dimness of color vision—all without pain.

FIND CHANGE/TRENDS AND INTERVENE

It is important for the nurse to recognize trends and changes in the client's condition. As the cataract becomes worse, the client looses the ability to see color changes and vision becomes worse. Surgery (removal of the lens in the eye) is currently the most common medical intervention. Removal of the lens utilizes local anesthesia, usually takes about 15 minutes, and is an out patient procedure.

EVALUATE PHARMACOLOGY

Nursing responsibilities include client teaching:
- Prior to surgery, determine if client is taking tamsulosin (Flomax) or other prostate drugs That relax prostate muscles and also relaxes muscles in the eye which may cause detached retina during the procedure. Alert provider regarding medications the client is taking especially Alpha blockers for elevated BP, kidney stones, urinary symptoms.
- Correct insertion of eye drops several times a day. Eye drops accelerate healing and help prevent infection.
  - 1. Pull down and expose the lower eyelid.
    2. Place the drop(s) of medication, being careful to avoid touching the eye with the dropper.
- NSAID eye drops Xibrom, Acular. Proper application and timeliness of eye drops is imperative. Some research shows non-compliance. Usually **ONE** drop. Two drops can be harmful. Make it very clear that compliance with eye drops is of vital importance

- Topical steroids to prevent infection loteprednol etabonate ophthalmic suspension (Lotemax)
- Do not lift over 25 pounds
- Do not bend past knees as this will likely increase IOP (intraocular pressure)
- Minimize exercise
- Keep eyes closed while showering (infection)
- Avoid coughing, sneezing, vomiting, constipation if possible.
- Warn against eye pain, increased sensitivity to bright lights, worsened vision, flashes of light in peripheral vision, and floaters in vision. Curtain across vision field
- Do not share a room with immunosuppressed clients.

Glaucoma is the second leading cause of blindness in US with open-angle glaucoma being the most common. IOC (Increased Ocular Pressure) may be hereditary. Glaucoma is often symptomLess, but causes a slow loss of peripheral vision (tunnel vision). Eye pressure may be reduced with eye drops

- Beta- blockers—timolol (Timoptic)
- Alpha-agonists—apraclonidine (Iopidine) ophthalmic solution
- Miotic eye drops such as pilocarpine and carbachol reduce **intraocular** eye pressure. Educate for headache and blurred vision. Evaluate the response to all eye medications.

Mydriatic eye drops such as atropine may be contraindicated in clients with glaucoma. These drugs are used to dilate the pupils for eye exams.

Eye drops are to clients with glaucoma are as insulin is to diabetics. This is an everyday process. and the clients must be educated.

Blindness

Macular degeneration and **diabetic retinopathy** are the two most common diseases that lead to blindness. This is a severe life-altering situation. Blindness causes adaption in activities of daily living as well as all of life. The goal of rehabilitation in blindness is the same as other rehabilitation: to work toward as much **independence** as possible for the client. One cardinal rule in working with blind clients is: **Don't move anything!** If the client is in their home environment, they likely know where chairs, etc. are located so they do not fall over them. If they are in a new environment, such as a hospital or health care agency, the surroundings should be clearly explained and experienced to prevent injury

Ear Disorders

Common ear problems include:
- Balance such as discussed in Meniere's disease (see pages 10 and 13)
- Blockage such as foreign objects (children) and earwax (cerumen).
  - Earwax is likely to require ear irrigation. To be effective the ear irrigation must follow the anatomy of the ear. Remember, the adult ear must be pulled **up** and the child's ear pulled **down** in order for the irrigation fluid or eardrops to be effective.

- Swimmer's ear—teach client to keep the ears dry. Slant the head to one side to allow the water to drain. Alcohol or vinegar mixtures dropped in the ear allow the trapped water to drain.
- Tinnitus or ringing in the ear is often caused by medication such as aspirin. Contact the provider regarding discontinuing of the medication.

Deafness

This is a severe life-altering situation. Deafness causes adaption in activities of daily living as well as all of life. The goal of rehabilitation in deafness is the same as other rehabilitation and that is to work toward as much independence as possible for the client. If the client is in a new environment such as a hospital or health care agency, the surroundings should be clearly explained and experienced to provide communication.

1. Which of these are needed when assessing cranial nerve number 12?
    A. Tuning fork
    B. Tongue blade
    C. Snellen Chart
    D. Cotton Q-tip and safety pin

2. The client is 5 days post-op craniotomy with no focal areas of weakness. What is the nursing priority in the bowel care for this client?
    A. A daily enema to prevent Valsalva pressure
    B. A low residue diet and increased fluids
    C. A high fiber diet
    D. Regular diet with stool softener

3. What is the nursing priority following a grand mal seizure?
    A. Remain with the client and provide safety from falls
    B. Record description of the seizure before, during, and after the event
    C. Evaluate the airway of the client and suction
    D. Administer Valium per protocol

4. The client receiving phenytoin (Dilantin) should be educated regarding which of the following? **Select all that apply**
    A. No driving until individual action of the drug is determined
    B. Avoiding stress
    C. Rash or difficult breathing
    D. Ringing in the ears
    E. Consistent use of eye drops

5. Which is priority in caring for the client with new spinal cord trauma? **Select all that apply**
    A. Inflammation at the site of the injury
    B. Airway and effective breathing
    C. Pain
    D. Alcohol addiction
    E. Elevated pancreatic enzymes

6. Which is the primary assessment of increased cranial pressure?
    A. Perform the Glasgow Coma Scale
    B. Determine ability to move lower extremities
    C. Rate headache on a pain scale from 1-10
    D. Call the provider to perform a spinal tap for pressure

7. The low-pressure alarm has sounded on the client's ventilator that is providing 15cm positive end expiratory pressure (PEEP) for the client admitted from a motor vehicle accident. Which nursing action is priority?
    A. Increase the ventilator pressure alarm limits
    B. Prepare for chest tube insertion
    C. Suction the client's airway
    D. Check for ventilator disconnection

8. The client with spinal cord dissection is exhibiting a BP of 190/100, sweating, and confusion. What is the priority nursing action?
    A. Raise the head of the bed
    B. Determine bladder fullness
    C. Administer Mannitol from protocol
    D. Check the client's level of consciousness

9. The client with an 8-week-old spinal cord injury is admitted due to "feeling terrible." What are the most important nursing assessments? **Select all that apply**
    A. Vital signs
    B. Skin assessment
    C. Blood glucose assessment
    D. Lung sounds
    E. History of the last 24 hours

10. The goal in rehabilitation for any condition is which of the following?
    A. Secure family support
    B. Provide assurance to the client
    C. Utilize the client and family in the plan of care
    D. Assist the client to maintain independence as long as possible

11. The client states "It's as though a curtain has been pulled over my left eye." The nursing priority includes which of the following?
    A. Refer the client to an ophthalmologist
    B. Assess the first cranial nerve
    C. Escort or involve the family in transporting this client to referral
    D. Administer eye drops from protocol

12. An adolescent client is admitted unconscious to the ED following a motor vehicle accident. There is no identifying material with the client. Which is the priority?
    A. Due to the client's age, withhold treatment until the client can be identified and consent given
    B. Provide emergency treatment and search for identification and consent after the client is stable
    C. Seek a court consent for client treatment
    D. Sign the consent as a Registered Nurse

13. The client with a spinal cord injury has an order for a heating pad for cold feet. Which nursing intervention has the highest priority?
    A. Ensure correct operation of the heating pad
    B. Instruct the client to notify the staff if the heating pad is too warm
    C. Call the provider to determine the accuracy of this order
    D. Assess client's bilateral pedal pulses

14. Which discharge instruction should be provided to the client with glaucoma induced blindness? **Select all that apply**
    A. Return every week for follow-up care with the opthalmologist
    B. Remove throw rugs from the client's living space
    C. Provide education on signs and symptoms of early glaucoma
    D. Recommend that furniture placement in the client's living space be permanent
    E. Test cranial nerve iii

15. Which task should be assigned to the LPN/VN?
    A. Initial assessment of a 17 year-old client with a spinal cord injury
    B. Planning for discharge of the client newly blinded by glaucoma
    C. Assessment of the client recently returned from surgery on the ear
    D. Pain reassessment of a client with a fractured skull

16. The client in ICU is receiving a Mannitol drip. Which is a priority evaluation of the effectiveness of this drug? **Select all that apply**
    A. Intake and output evaluation
    B. Temperature elevation
    C. Level of consciousness
    D. Increased mobility
    E. Blood pressure elevation

17. The CNA working in the ICU raises the head of the bed of a client who is unconscious from a head injury.
    A. Advise the CNA that an error has been made and ask that an incident report be completed
    B. Ascertain why the CNA has been delegated the responsibility for this client
    C. Speak to the nurse manager regarding unit protocol
    D. Document the action of the CNA

18. The client with Trigeminal Neuralgia is complaining of severe facial pain. A pain medication was administered one hour earlier. What is the nursing priority?
    A. Repeat the PRN medication that was administered earlier
    B. Assist the client to exercise the facial muscles
    C. Assess cranial nerve vii
    D. Contact the provider to recommend a stronger medication for the pain

19. A client with Myasthenia Gravis develops a fever of 102°F. Which is the priority action?
    A. Contact the provider immediately for orders
    B. Sponge the client with a cool liquid
    C. Increase the client's IV rate
    D. Administer Tylenol per unit protocol

20. Which task would be best to delegate to a CNA on the neurological unit?
    A. Wound care on a client post-surgery
    B. Application of anti-embolic stockings post-operatively
    C. Using tongue blade to administer antibiotic cream to a wound
    D. Present discharge plan to client and family

21. The client in ICU becomes restless, combative, and yells at the nurse. What is the nursing priority?
    A. Raise the side rails and provide for client safety
    B. Notify the provider of the change in behavior
    C. Notify the family that someone will need to stay with the client at all times
    D. Provide sedative per PRN protocol

Answers and Rationale

1. **Answer B**. A tongue blade is needed to prevent the tongue from moving when the client is asked to move the tongue from side to side. A strong tongue should be able to move the tongue blade.

2. **Answer C** is the least invasive. The high fiber should promote normal elimination.

3. **Answer A**. Keep the client from hurting themselves. B is an answer, but not priority. A suction tube should not be pushed into the client's mouth. Valium may be useful but is not priority.

4. **Answers A and C**. Others are not side effects of Dilantin.

5. **Answers B and C** have the highest priority. Everything else comes later.

6. **Answer A**. Level of consciousness is most important in IOP.

7. **Answer D**. The low-pressure alarm may indicate a build up of moisture in the system decreasing the client's ability to receive optimum oxygenation. It also may indicate the client has accidentally become disconnected from the ventilator. Pressure alarm limits should never be increased to silence alarms as they serve the purpose of protecting the client from injury due to excessive pressures that may lead to the development of a pneumothorax or decreased pressure due to disconnection.

8. **Answer B**. The client is likely having autonomic dysreflexia due to full bladder. Lie the client flat to help with possible hypertension. Mannitol is used for IOP.

9. **Answers A, B and D** are priority as the client is susceptible to infection (increased temperature), decubiti (skin assessment, and pneumonia (lung sounds).

10. **Answer A**. Independence is the ultimate goal of rehabilitation. Family may not be available or willing.

11. **Answer C**. This is an emergency and this client should not be referred to get anywhere without assistance.

12. **Answer B**. Emergency care should be provided even if there is no consent regardless of the client's age. Court consent may take a month. Never sign any consent other than your own.

13. **Answer C**. The client with a cord injury is likely without feeling in the lower extremities. The order should be questioned to protect the client from injury. All other answers are within nursing prerogative, but do not address the question of a possible burn.

14. **Answers B and D**. Throw rugs and out of place furniture is a problem for the blind. This client will not likely need a provider appointment each week and certainly not education on signs and symptoms of early glaucoma. The cranial nerve may be intact so testing is irrelevant.

15. **Answer D**. The LPN/VN is licensed to reassess, but not an initial assessment. Planning for discharge is the RN's responsibility.

16. **Answers A and C** are the primary evaluators of Mannitol which decreases ICP. All other answers are wrong.

17. **Answer C** is the most appropriate answer. All of the other actions should take place, but it is important to follow unit protocol.

18. **Answer D**. Trigeminal Neuralgia is known to cause severe facial pain. Pain management is a nursing responsibility.

19. **Answer A**. This client is susceptible to muscle weakness leading to difficult breathing and the provider should be contacted immediately rather than administering Tylenol and waiting to see if it works. Many of these clients are taking steroids which may exacerbate an infection and should be seen immediately.

20. **Answer A**. Except for the stockings, all other answers are outside of the CNA's scope of practice.

21. **Answer A**. First things first. See that the client is safe. This change in behavior may be ICU psychosis or a change in Increased Cranial Pressure so the provider should be notified as well. Safety is priority.

The Pediatric NEUROLOGICAL SYSTEM

Jessica Peck, DNP, RN, MSN, CPNP-PC, CNE
Edited by Sylvia Rayfield & Associates, Inc.

THERE ARE SOME SLIGHT DIFFERENCES TO BE AWARE OF FOR CHILDREN WITH NEUROLOGICAL DISORDERS. MUCH ABOUT NEURO IS THE SAME AS WITH ADULTS. THIS MODULE WILL FOCUS ON THE THINGS THAT ARE DIFFERENT FOR PEDIATRICS.

KEY CONCEPTS TO REMEMBER:

- ❖ Meningitis
- ❖ Seizures
- ❖ Ventriculoperitoneal Shunts

NEUROLOGIC DISORDERS

Know the differences in presentation of meningitis for infants, children, and adolescents. You don't need to know this to diagnose it because that is not within your scope of practice. However, you need to be alert to early signs so that you can alert the provider to initiate early intervention. Early intervention SAVES lives!!

BACTERIAL MENINGITIS

Know your A-B-C's	Neonates & Infants	Infants & Young Children	Adolescents
Ask about the history	Risk Factors: - History of maternal GBS - No immunizations - Immature immune system - Recent illness **Neonates can go from asymptomatic to dead in as little as 8 hours**	Risk Factors: - Not up-to-date on immunizations - Exposure to communicable disease at school **Strep pneumo is the most common organism in children.*	Risk Factors: - Smoking - Kissing - Sharing food or drink - Close quarters - Swimming in lakes or rivers **Teens are more at risk for meningococcal meningitis**

B—Be aware of possible presenting symptoms you might detect on assessment	Signs are subtle, vague, and non-specific.	Signs are still subtle from 3 mos.-~2years.	Signs are more classic and adult-like
	<ul><li>Behaves poorly</li><li>Poor feeding</li><li>Poor tone</li><li>Weak cry</li><li>Tense fontanel</li></ul> **Typically do NOT have a stiff neck. They don't have a neck period so how can it be stiff?!** *SIGNS OF NEONATAL MENINGITIS ARE NOT CLASSIC.*  **Do you see a neck?!**	<ul><li>Vomiting</li><li>Poor feeding</li><li>Very cranky</li><li>Seizures</li><li>Fever</li><li>Bulging fontanel</li></ul> **Still usually NO stiff neck. Kernig and Brudzinski NOT helpful. Anterior fontanel closes about 18 mos. so assess if it is still open.**  **Cranky Kids!**	<ul><li>Fever</li><li>Nucchal rigidity</li><li>Headache</li><li>Vomiting</li><li>Positive Kernig and Brudzinski</li><li>Photophobia</li><li>Delirium</li><li>Purpura</li><li>Altered LOC</li><li></li></ul>  **Teen signs are classic, just like this car.**

C—Care for the client until condition resolves www.youtube.com/ watch?v=i_IU7eM_TvA **Visit here to see stories of teens who got meningitis.**	TREATMENT IS THE SAME FOR ALL AGE GROUPS **TREATMENT IS DEPENDENT ON THE INFECTING ORGANISM**		
	Drugs: Steroids to decrease inflammation Antibiotics for the organism Anticonvulsants Analgesics	Therapy Aims: <ul><li>ISOLATION 1st!</li><li>ANTIBIOTICS 2nd!</li><li>REDUCE ICP</li><li>HYDRATION</li><li>VENTILATION</li><li>PREVENT SHOCK</li><li>CONTROL SEIZURES</li><li>PREVENT COMPLICATION</li></ul>	10-15% of cases are fatal. Sequelae include: amputation, hearing loss, brain damage, learning disability, death. NEONATES ARE AT HIGHEST RISK OF DEATH!

It is important to note that infants and young children have different presentations of increased intracranial pressure. If the fontanel is open, there is more room to accept increased pressure before symptoms will show. The fluid can expand outward and enlarge the head. If the skull is fused, this is not possible and kids will feel the pressure sooner and differently.

SIGNS OF INCREASED ICP IN CLOSED VS. OPEN FONTANEL

OPEN/INFANTS	CLOSED/OLDER KIDS & TEENS
✓ Change in feeding ✓ Irritability ✓ High-pitched cry ✓ Distended scalp veins ✓ Space between skull sutures ✓ RAPIDLY INCREASING FOC ✓ Bulging fontanel	✓ Restlessness ✓ Confusion ✓ Nausea ✓ Vomiting ✓ Headache ✓ Double Vision ✓ Seizure

LATE SIGNS

HINT YOU WANT TO RECOGNIZE THE EARLY SIGNS!!!!!!

✓ Altered LOC
✓ Bradycardia
✓ Altered motor response
✓ Altered sensorium
✓ Abnormal pupillary reactions
✓ Posturing
✓ Papilledema
✓ Respiratory Distress

THESE VACCINES CAN HELP PREVENT MENINGITIS:

➢ **HIB**
➢ **Pneumococcocal**
➢ **Meningococcal**

HOW TO CARE FOR A CHILD HAVING A SEIZURE

Risk Factors:	Genetics, fever, head trauma, infection, noncompliance with med, tumor, trauma, fluid and electrolyte imbalance, stress, toxins, chemicals, flashing lights or video games	
	During the Seizure	After the Seizure
Nursing Actions	❖STAY CALM! ❖Time the seizure ❖Side-lying position ❖Loosen clothing ❖Cushion the head ❖NEVER restrain! ❖NEVER put anything in the mouth! ❖Give meds as ordered ❖Facilitate recovery	❖Side rails up ❖Hard objects padded ❖Waterproof mattress ❖No swimming or bathing alone ❖Medical identification bracelet ❖Protective helmet or padding as needed for sports ❖Ensure medication compliance ❖Check state laws for driving restrictions if applicable
	Call Rapid Response IF: • Child stops breathing • Child is diabetic • Pregnant adolescent • Seizure lasts longer than 5 minutes • Status epilepticus • Pupils unequal • Continuous vomiting • Post-ictal period is prolonged • Seizure occurs in water • This is child's first seizure 	
Febrile Seizures	❖Scary, but not uncommon. 3-5% occurrence. ❖Recurrence is common. ❖Not related to how HIGH the fever is, but how FAST it rises. ❖Treatment is proactive fever management.	

A WORD ABOUT THE GLASGOW COMA SCALE

Think about it. How could the Glasgow work on a baby?!

Visit here to see the pediatric Glasgow!

http://www.youtube.com/watch?v=a-CC5FvGTK0

Children over the age of 7 years may be assessed for developmental appropriateness of the regular Glasgow scale.

Infants and young children may have a condition called hydrocephalus. This means either there is an excess of CSF or there is the right amount of CSF that is just not getting reabsorbed. To fix it, a VP shunt is sometimes needed. This is a tube that goes from the brain to the stomach to dump the CSF to be reabsorbed into the peritoneum. Fascinating!

What is a ventriculoperitoneal shunt?

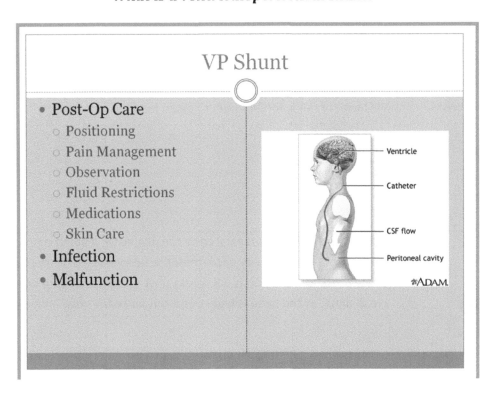

Post-Operative Care of a VP Shunt

Positioning	Keep flat after first shunt placement!! The brain has gotten used to lots of fluid so lowering the level too rapidly can actually shear the cerebral cortex from the dura! This is not necessary for shunt revisions (a revision is putting in a new shunt because the child has grown, there is infection or malfunction).
Pain	Usually okay with just Tylenol, believe it or not. Opioids are acceptable if needed.
Observation	Look for: ➤ INFECTION (remember, surgery in the brain so infection is meningitis!) ➤ INCREASED ICP ➤ BLOOD PRESSURE ➤ NEUROLOGIC ASSESSMENT ➤ ABDOMINAL DISTENTION/ILEUS
Fluid Restrictions	NPO with IV fluids for 24 hours to avoid fluid volume overload
Follow-Up	The family needs support related to the diagnosis. If vomiting occurs, the child must go to the emergency department to be evaluated for malfunction. The greatest risk for infection is ~ 6 weeks post-operatively. Care needs to be taken to avoid injury, as the head is bigger and can make the child a bit wobbly.

Emma's Story	This is a heart-warmer.
www.youtube.com/ watch?v=Nn8NdPAPrYY	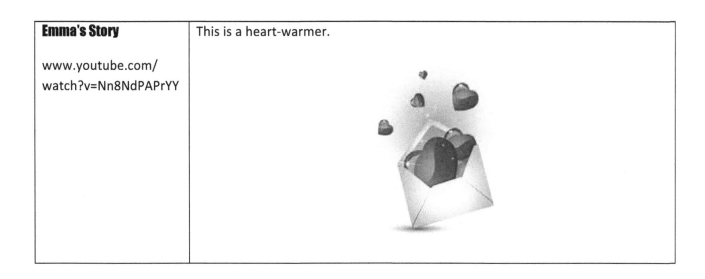

One word about pediatric head trauma: PREVENTION!!

The three most common causes of head injury are:

FALLS, MOTOR VEHICLE INJURIES, and BICYCLE INJURIES.

A Memorable Patient Encounter

I was once caring for a patient who had severe cerebral palsy, with significant cognitive impairment. His grandparents were his primary caregivers and they very lovingly cared for his every need. He was frequently in the hospital for various complications and on one occasion I came upon the team of residents who were rounding and happened to be discussing his case. He had come in for a tracheostomy infection but I heard the team discussing a new development—seizures. The resident was telling the attending that this child kept hitting himself in the head with one arm in a peculiar jerking motion. The resident ardently advocated for starting anti-epileptic medication. At this point I decided to go and talk to the grandmother to see what was going on. I entered the room and began to tell her about the discussion the residents were having. To my great surprise, she started laughing hysterically. She told me that every time the little boy's grandfather entered the room, he would touch his hand to his head as his way of acknowledging the grandfather, who ALWAYS wore a cowboy hat. To demonstrate, she had the grandfather leave the room and the "seizure" stopped. When he re-entered, it resumed. It was a poignant moment, as I realized how important it is to talk to your patients. We may be experts in nursing care, but the caregivers are experts in the patients. It is essential that we partner our expertise to provide the best care possible. It also taught me that patients, who seem unable to communicate, may be communicating with me in a language I don't know! It taught me to be ever vigilant for potential opportunities for communication.

REVIEW QUESTIONS

1. A nurse is caring for an 8-year-old who is brought to the emergency by ambulance after being thrown from a horse. The nurse assesses the child and finds that the child is non-responsive to painful stimuli. What should the nurse do next?

    1) Notify the provider
    2) Call a code
    3) Administer epinephrine
    4) Assess vital signs

Option #1 is correct. This is a sign of a potentially serious neurological injury.

2. A nurse is assessing a toddler who experienced a fall down the stairs. Upon assessment half-way through the shift, the nurse finds one pupil is fixed and dilated. What is the appropriate action of the nurse?

    1) Notify the provider
    2) Call a code
    3) Assess vital signs
    4) Assess cranial nerves

Option #1 is correct. This is a neurosurgical emergency that must be addressed immediately.

3. A nurse arrives in the trauma room and finds an unconscious child in a c-collar on a back-board. The x-ray tech is present to obtain c-spine films as ordered. The tech asks the nurse to remove the collar for the films. How should the nurse respond?

    1) "I don't think so buddy."
    2) "Is there an order to remove the collar?"
    3) "Please step away from the patient."
    4) "How can I contact your supervisor?"

Option #2 is correct. The c-collar should never be removed without an order and all tests involving rotation of the head should be delayed until the c-spine is cleared.

4. A father brings his 2 -month-old infant to the emergency department after a reportedly minor auto accident. The nurse assessing the infant in triage finds a positive Moro reflex. What action should the nurse take at this time?

    1) Document the findings
    2) Notify the physician immediately
    3) Place the infant on a backboard with a c-collar
    4) Assess the infant with the pediatric Glasgow coma scale

Option #1 is correct. A positive Moro reflex is a sign of neurological health in a young infant.

5. A child has been admitted for 72 hours for a closed head injury and is on opioids for pain management. The child is suddenly irritable and restless. What action should the nurse take?

1) Notify the provider
2) Discontinue the opioids
3) Assess vital signs
4) Check chart for last bowel movement

Option #4 is correct. Opioids can cause constipation and should always be given with a stool softener. This child has been receiving them for four days and may be constipated.

6. A nurse witnesses a child fall from a tree at a local park. In what order should the nurse perform these assessments?

1) Check for patent airway
2) Stabilize the head and neck
3) Assess LOC
4) Check pulse
5) Call for help

Options should be ordered 2, 1, 3, 4, 5. Protecting the spine is essential. If the airway is obstructed, cardiac arrest will follow.

7. A child has just had an extraventricular drain placed. The nurse notes that the dressing on the bolts is soiled. What is the appropriate action of the nurse?

1) Change the dressing using sterile technique
2) Change the dressing using clean technique
3) Notify the neurosurgeon
4) Cover the soiled dressing with sterile plastic wrap

Option #3 is correct. Nurses are NEVER supposed to change or even disturb those dressings. Period. Another word about EVDs: be VERY careful about maintaining the level of the collection container. If it is too low, it could quickly cause bleeding and pain. EVDs are SCARY so ask if you don't know.

8. A child has just undergone initial placement of a ventriculoperitoneal shunt. How should the nurse position the child? **Select all that apply**.

1) Supine
2) HOB elevated 30 degrees

3) Head turned to the side
4) Prone
5) Legs flexed

Option #1 is the only correct one. For initial placement, flat is indicated to prevent subdural hemorrhage. Turning the head to the side could cause jugular compression.

9. A nurse is caring for an unconscious child. Which of the following are appropriate nursing care measures? **Select all that apply.**

1) Apply artificial tears as needed
2) Assess the eyes every 1 to 2 hours
3) Perform mouth care once daily
4) Place in side-lying or semi-prone position
5) Support the extremities with pillows

Options 1, 2, 4, and 5 are correct. Oral care should be performed at least two times per day. The corneal reflex can be absent in unconscious children, making them prone to dust and debris irritating their eyes and causing permanent damage.

10. A nurse is caring for a child who has been in a coma for 3 weeks following an injury. The mother expresses to the nurse that she is thinking about going home to sleep and rest for the day, planning to return tomorrow. How should the nurse respond?

1) "You should try to stay here in case your child wakes up."
2) "You will need to find someone to sit with him while you are gone."
3) "I will be sure to call you if there is any change."
4) "It is our policy that at least one relative is here at all times."

Option #3 is correct. It can be very exhausting to sit with a child who is ill for days on end. If the mother voices to the nurse an idea of getting rest, often parents are looking for a blessing or permission to go. They need reassurance their child will be well cared for in their absence.

11. An 11-year-old boy has experienced a head injury during football practice. His mother calls the nurse for advice. What symptoms would prompt the nurse to recommend emergency treatment? **Select all that apply.**

1) One or more episodes of vomiting
2) Any occurrence of loss of consciousness
3) Complaint of headache
4) Presence of neck pain
5) Clear fluid leaking from the nose

Options #2, #4, and #5 are correct. Vomiting may occur but three or more episodes should be reported. Headache is also expected but a worsening headache or one that interferes with sleep or daily activities should prompt the family to seek emergency medical attention. Any loss of consciousness should prompt an emergency visit. Clear fluid leakage could be CSF resulting from a skull fracture.

12. Which physical signs should prompt the nurse to suspect brainstem involvement in a child with a head injury? **Select all that apply**.

      1) Gasping respirations
      2) Fluctuations in BP
      3) Bradycardia
      4) Narrowing pulse pressure
      5) Hypotension

Options #1, #2, and #3 are correct. Widening pulse pressure can be present with brainstem involvement. Hypotension may indicate internal injuries.

13. The emergency team is running a code on a child following a motor vehicle accident. The child's parents arrive shortly after the child arrives. What is the appropriate action of the nurse?

      1) Bring the family to the trauma room and allow them to watch the code
      2) Escort the family to the closest waiting area and give them an update
      3) Ask the family if they desire the services of a chaplain or priest
      4) Tell the family that the doctor will be out to speak with them shortly

Option #1 is correct. Evidence shows that family presence during a code is beneficial.

14. A nurse is admitting a young child for a febrile illness. During the initial assessment, a purpuric rash is noted on the lower extremities. What is the priority action of the nurse?

      1) Institute isolation precautions
      2) Report the rash to the provider
      3) Administer antibiotics
      4) Continue with care as ordered

Option #1 is correct. This indicates possible meningococcal meningitis or meningococcemia, which is highly contagious. Preventing the spread and protecting those exposed is priority.

15. A nurse is caring for a child with bacterial meningitis. Which nursing action has the highest priority?

      1) Administration of antibiotics
      2) Maintenance of hydration

3) Management of pain
4) Minimize external stimuli

Option #1 is correct. Without antibiotics, the risk of death or permanent severe sequelae is likely. The other options are important, but not as important as antibiotics.

16. A 3-year-old child is experiencing a seizure in the hospital playroom. What actions should the nurse take? **Select all that apply.**

1) Restrain the child
2) Pad the child's head
3) Use a tongue depressor to prevent tongue injury
4) Time the seizure
5) Place in side-lying position
6) Provide privacy if possible

Options #2, #4, #5, and #6 are correct. Restraints should never be used. Nothing should ever be put into the child's mouth. Seizures can be upsetting to those around, including the family of the patient, so privacy should be provided if possible.

17. A 4-year-old has just stopped seizing after a 3-minute first time seizure. After 5 minutes, she is still unresponsive to vocal commands. Her vital signs are normal. What action should the nurse take at this time?

1) Request an order for administration of fosphenytoin
2) Notify the provider
3) Time the post-ictal period
4) Try to elicit a response to painful stimulus

Option #3 is correct. After a seizure, it is common to experience a post-ictal period, in which the patient can be extremely drowsy and unresponsive. It is very important to watch for signs of altered vital signs and respiratory distress. The post-ictal period varies from child to child, lasting a few minutes to an hour or more.

18. Which factors during a seizure should prompt the nurse to call for rapid response? **Select all that apply.**

1) Respiratory arrest
2) First seizure
3) Continuous vomiting
4) Seizure occurs in water
5) Child is diabetic

All of these options are correct and reasons for which to notify the rapid response team.

19. A toddler is admitted following a fall down the stairs that occurred in her home. The provider notes papilledema and multiple skull fractures in various healing stages. What is the appropriate action of the nurse at this time?

1) Notify Child Protective Services
2) Order a consult from Social Services
3) Question the parents about the injuries
4) Call security to the child's room

Option #1 is correct. Papilledema is a potential sign of Shaken Baby Syndrome and fractures in various stages of healing can be a sign of abuse.

20. A 2-year-old has experienced a near-drowning event. She was revived and appears fine but was admitted to the hospital for observation. The mother asks the nurse why an admission is necessary. What is the best response of the nurse?

1) "We want to watch closely for any complications that may occur."
2) "We need to make sure your child did not experience any brain damage."
3) "It is routine to have a consult with Child Protective Services after this type of incident."
4) "We need to monitor for possible aspiration and cerebral edema."

Option #1 is correct actually for the reason of #4, but the terminology used in #4 would not be appropriate to use with a parent. Any child with a near-drowning episode should be hospitalized even if asymptomatic. Aspiration pneumonia can occur 48-72 hours after the incident, as can cerebral edema.

Nursing Management in Endocrine Disorders

Melissa Geist, EdD, APRN, CNE
Edited by Sylvia Rayfield & Associates Inc.

"If the ladder is not leaning against the right wall, every step we take just gets us to the wrong place faster."
Stephen R. Covey ·

Key Concepts:

- ﹩ **Diabetes Mellitus (DM)**
- ﹩ **Thyroid Disorders**
- ﹩ **Imbalances of Adrenal Corticotropin Hormone (ACTH)**
  - ◆ **Addison's Disease**
  - ◆ **Cushing's Disease**
- ﹩ **Syndrome of Inappropriate Secretion of ADH (SIADH)**
- ﹩ **Diabetes Insipidus**
- ﹩ **Practice Questions, Answers and Rationale**

THE ENDOCRINE SYSTEM –Basic Physiology

The endocrine system is a complex system involving hormones to orchestrate responses in every body system. Endocrine glands are found throughout the body, each secreting distinct hormones to achieve homeostasis These hormones are controlled in most part by a negative feedback system. A negative feedback loop is a self-regulating system where increasing levels of a hormone will cause the gland to stop producing that hormone. This system maintains a relatively constant level of hormones in the body. Because the glands and hormones in the endocrine system are so diverse in their function, one must consider each hormone separately when considering nursing care. There are, however, some common symptoms that can raise the suspicion that a client is experiencing a problem with the endocrine system. The mnemonic CHANGES will help you remember these key Endocrine assessments as it is important to recognize trends and changes in client condition and intervene as needed.

CHANGES

Changes in thirst and hunger

Habits of urination and bowel elimination change

Altered level of consciousness (LOC)

Nervousness or depression

Gain or loss of weight

Energy level decreases or increases

Sleep disorders

Diabetes Mellitus

Diabetes mellitus is the most common disorder of the endocrine system.
There are two main types:

> **Type I** (formerly known as juvenile diabetes) These clients have an absolute insulin deficiency and will be insulin dependent for life.

> **Type II** (formerly known as non-insulin dependent) These clients have insulin resistance and decreased insulin production. Although the vast majority of Type II diabetics are adults, there is increased incidence in obese children. These clients will rely mainly on oral medications for disease control, but may require insulin therapy in certain circumstances.

Diagnostic Testing for Type I and Type II Diabetes

► Random Blood Glucose Test

This test is just what it sounds like; it can be done at anytime. It can be drawn from a capillary (fingerstick blood sugar (FSBS) or from a vein (serum blood glucose). It is NOT a sensitive test for diagnosis.

► Fasting Blood Glucose Test

Patient does not eat anything or drink anything except water 8-10 hours before the test. Normal = 70-110mg/dl

>126mg/dl = diabetes

► Post-prandial Glucose Test

Serum glucose measured 1 hour after a meal.

>180mg/dl = diabetes (Will need of confirmation with other glucose testing.)

► Oral Glucose Tolerance Test

Begins with a fasting glucose test and then the client drinks a solution containing 75 grams of glucose. Blood glucose levels are measured at specific time intervals (usually 2 hours later) after the test to measure how the system is responding to the glucose level over time.

>200mg/dl = diabetes

► Hemoglobin A1c (HgbA1c) is a diagnostic test, accepted as the best measure of average gucose used in long-term management of diabetes. It is a blood test measured every 3 months.

Goal for diabetics is < 7%

*Disease processes such as anemia will cause the test to be unreliable.

SEARCH/RESCUE/FALLOUT (Diabetes Mellitus)

SEARCH (Assessment, Analysis)	RESCUE (Implementation)	FALLOUT (Outcome—good/bad)
The 3 P's—Polyuria, Polydipsia, Polyphagia Cardinal assessments for diabetes	Assess for increased urination, increased thirst, and increased hunger (Type 1 diabetics may have a significant increase in appetite accompanied by significant weight loss.)	Disease process is discovered before major physiologic changes occur. Avoid major emergencies with DM (DKA, HHNS, hypoglycemia)
High serum glucose levels	Assess and maintain blood glucose levels (norms = 70-110mg/dl depending on research labs) Administer insulin as needed to maintain levels (See Insulin Protocol at your agency) Manage insulin pump	Avoid macro and micro vascular damage Side effects of insulin (hypoglycemia —see PANIC) Side effects of oral antihyperglycemic agents (see chart)

SEARCH (Assessment, Analysis)	RESCUE (Implementation)	FALLOUT (Outcome—good/bad)
	Administer oral antihyperglycemic agents (See chart pages 6-7) Check for medications that increase blood glucose levels (steroids, diuretics) Check for conditions that increase blood glucose levels (physiologic or mental stress, infection, secretion of growth hormone in adolescents)	Avoid DKA and HHNS
Increased risk for infection and poor wound healing	Assess for symptoms or frequent recurrence of common infections such as upper respiratory infections (URI) or urinary tract infections (UTI) Perform skin assessment Examine feet (a common site for infection)	Temperature <100.4ºF No signs/symptoms or URI/UTI or skin infection Loss of digits/limbs due to amputation. Meticulous foot/nail care Bacteremia, sepsis, shock, death
Target organ problems	DM affects every organ system. Think head to toe assessment looking for manifestations. Teach client how to recognize problems • **Head**: Cerebral Vascular Accident (CVA) • **Eyes**: diabetic retinopathy • **Nose**: frequent URI and sinus infections • **Heart**: MI (often "silent"—no pain or atypical presentation) • **GI**: gastroparesis (leading to constipation and blockage) • **Sexual dysfunction**: erectile dysfunction • **Kidneys**: diabetic nephropathy (major cause of chronic renal failure in the United States) • **Legs**: Peripheral neuropathy, stasis ulcers	Patient recognizes problem in early stages and understands when to seek treatment FAST—Face, Arm, Smile/Speech, Time is Brain (3 hours) Present with fatigue, vague complaints BUN < 20 creatinine < 2, no protein in urine

SEARCH (Assessment, Analysis)	RESCUE (Implementation)	FALLOUT (Outcome—good/bad)
Risk Factors	Identify risk factors and teach high-risk patients how to avoid DM. **Risk Factors:** **Type I:** Ask about family history, history of viral infections **Type II:** • **Obesity** (Assess body weight for >20% normal) • **Lifestyle** (sedentary) • **Diet** (high in fat, sugar, and processed foods, fast food) • **Ethnicity** African American and Latino (incidence is almost double the rate of Caucasians, Native Americans/ Alaskan Natives)	Client understands the risk and is empowered to make lifestyle changes to combat the disease Collaborative care with access to nutritionist and diabetes educator
Don't forget the psychosocial factors	Lifetime of lifestyle changes (diet, exercise, medication regimen, checking blood glucose levels) Diabetic retinopathy is one of the leading causes of blindness Diagnosis of life changing disease may cause depression Parents may be overwhelmed when child is diagnosed	Teaching starts at the time of diagnosis and at the client's level of learning Make sure client knows to have yearly eye exam Screen for depression Tell parents about support networks for diabetic children

<h3 style="text-align:center">When administering medication we must be CAREFUL!</h3>

<h3 style="text-align:center">MEDICATION ADMINISTRATION ALERT</h3>

PASS *NCLEX*®!

C	**Calculate correctly**
A	**Assess for allergies**
R	**Rights of administration**
E	**Evaluate response**
F	**Feel free to call provider if intuition alerts**
U	**Utilize assessments in determining ordered parameters**
L	**Lab data pertinence**

Medications for Endocrine Disorders

Manage client experiencing side effects and adverse reactions of medication.

Common Types of Insulin

Insulin Type	Names	Onset	Peak	Duration
Ultra-short acting (rapid acting)	Lispro (Humalog) Aspart (Novolog) Glulisine (Apidra)	10-15 minutes	30-60 minutes	3-5 hours
Short Acting (regular)	Humulin R Novolin R Velosulin (for use in pumps)	30-60 minutes	2-4 hours	5-7 hours
Intermediate	NPH Humulin N Novulin N	1-4 hours	8-12 hours	22 hours
Long-acting	Lantus Levemir	2-4 hours	NONE	24 hours

Insulin Type	Names	Onset	Peak	Duration
Combination	NPH 70:R 30	30 minutes	2-12 hours	10-16 hours
	NPH 50: R 50	30 minutes	2-6 hours	10-16 hours

Peak times are most critical as this is when hypoglycemic reactions will occur.

P = Palpitations/Tachycardia
A = Anxiety/Restless
N = Nausea
I = Intense hunger
C = Cold sweat

Image by MIT OpenCourseWare.

A Few Key Points:

- If you administer lispro or Humalog make sure the client has food immediately available. Very fast onset!
- Ultra-short [rapid], short acting, and long acting insulins are clear. **All others** should be uniformly cloudy.
- Tip: you will all be RN's in a short time, always draw up the regular (R) before the NPH (N).
- **Always** check the insulin dose you are preparing to give with another licensed person (LPN, nurse practitioner, another RN).
- Insulins are given by subcutaneous injection, rotating sites
- Regular insulin is the only one that can be given IV and may be used in insulin pumps.
- Never mix ultra short or long acting insulins with other insulins!
- An insulin pump is very useful to some clients if they are taught proper use and care. The following link will explain the management of the insulin pump. http://www.youtube.com/watch?v=eSJz7vFSZ0Y
- Velosulin is a short acting insulin for use in the insulin pump.
- The subcutaneous catheter apparatus shown in the video is changed every 3 days or as needed.
- The pump can deliver a basal amount and can also deliver a bolus dose if the blood glucose level is high or if the client feels like eating and needs to cover the meal. **15 grams of carb = 1 unit of insulin**

ORAL Antihyperglycemic agents (For Type II Diabetics Only)

Class	Examples	Actions	Nursing Considerations
Sulfonylureas	Chlorpropamide (Diabinese) — 1st generation Glipizide (Glucotrol) Glyburide (DiaBeta) — 2nd generation	Stimulates secretion of insulin Increases sensitivity of cellular receptor site to insulin	Cannot use if no functioning bets cells Check for sulfa allergy **No alcohol!** Can cause hypoglycemic reactions NSAIDs potentiate hypoglycemia
Meglitinides	Nateglinide (Starlix)	Stimulates beta cells to produce insulin Increases cellular insulin response	Cannot use if no functioning beta cells Hypoglycemia Rapid onset/short duration
Bigunide	Metformin (Glucophage)	Decreases hepatic glucose secretion Improved action of insulin at cellular level	Limited hypoglycemia Lactic acidosis in clients with renal problems Watch liver function
Alpha-glucosidase inhibitors	Acarbose (Precose)	Delays digestion and absorption of carbs in small intestine	GI—flatulence, diarrhea, abdominal cramps
Thiazolinedione	Pioglitazone (Actos) Rosiglitazone (Avandia)	Resensitizes body to own insulin Decreases insulin resistance	Cannot use if body cannot produce insulin Edema Weight gain Hyperlipidemia Need liver function test

Class	Examples	Actions	Nursing Considerations
DPP-4 Inhibitor	Sitagliptin (Januvia)	Increases release of insulin, decreases glucose production Only active in hyperglycemic environment	Causes hypoglycemia with sulfonylureas, URI, stuffy nose, sore throat

There are THREE acute life-threatening emergencies for diabetic clients

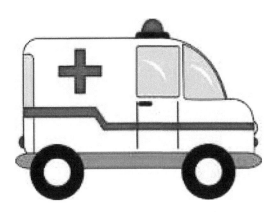

Provide emergency care

One involves low blood glucose values. The other two involve high glucose values.

Low blood Glucose: (Hypoglycemia)
Signs and symptoms: **PANIC**

P = Palpitations/Tachycardia
A = Anxiety/Restless
N = Nausea
 I = Intense hunger
C = Cold sweat

Treatment if conscious:

- Check blood glucose level (but err on the side of treating if clinical picture clearly indicates hypoglycemia)
- If patient is conscious and can swallow:
  15 grams of carb (3 glucose tabs, 4 oz juice, 4 oz regular soda, 6-jelly beans, small tube cake frosting). May repeat if level not normal in 15 minutes

- If blood glucosevlevel is normal (> 70) switch to complex carb like milk, cheese & crackers, PB crackers

Treatment if not conscious:

- IV 20-50 mL of $D_{50}W$ over 1-3 minutes
- Glucagon 0.5-1 mg, IM, SubQ, IV

Compare And Contrast: Two Hyperglycemic emergencies

Diabetic Ketoacidosis (DKA)	Hyperosmolar Hyperglycemic Nonketotic Syndrome (HHNS)
Type I Diabetics and Insulin Dependent Type II Diabetics	Type II Diabetics
Blood glucose values average 300-400mg/dl	Blood glucose values extremely high. Usually 800mg/dl or higher
Hot, dry, flushed, vomiting	Hot, dry, vomiting, osmotic dieresis (urinary output greatly increased)
ABG show pH < 7.35, HCO_3 < 22meq/L = **metabolic acidosis** pCO_2 normal or slightly below normal if compensating Kussmaul respirations are fast and deep respirations that help the patient blow off CO_2—a compensatory response to metabolic acidosis	ABG will be normal, **no** ketosis, **no** free fatty acid formation, **no** acidosis

Diabetic Ketoacidosis (DKA)	Hyperosmolar Hyperglycemic Nonketotic Syndrome (HHNS)
Potassium levels may be high due to compensatory exchange of H^+ for K^+ in the renal tubules (kidneys trying to excrete H^+ to correct acidosis)	Potassium levels low due to loss during osmotic diuresis
Treatment: • Normal saline IV, regular insulin per IV drip (0.1units/kg/hr) • Do not lower blood glucose faster than 100mg/hr • Potassium may be added to normal saline IV solution to correct for potassium entering the cell in the presence of insulin and glucose • When blood glucose level reaches 250mg/dl, the provider will likely change solutions to D_5NS to avoid hypoglycemia	Treatment: • Normal saline IV bolus until urine output returns to normal • Regular insulin per IV drip (0.1units/kg/hr) • Potassium may be added to correct hypokalemia • When blood glucose level reaches 250mg/dl, the provider will likely change solutions to D_5NS to avoid hypoglycemia

Thyroid Disorders

Hypothyroidism (Hashimoto's Thyroiditis being the most common cause) and Hyperthyroidism (Graves' disease) are OPPOSITES

Just think…you only have to know one-half of the information!!

Assessment	Hypothyroid	Hyperthyroid
Skin and Hair	Dry and coarse	Warm/moist and fine/silky
Temperature	Cold intolerance	Complains of being hot
GI Changes	Constipation	Diarrhea
Weight	Weight gain	Weight loss
Cardiovascular	Bradycardia Decreased cardiac output	Tachycardia Premature ventricular contractions (PVCs)
Nervous System	Depression Psychosis Slow DTRs	Emotional irritability Tremor Restlessness Hyperreflexive
Labs	Low T3 and T4 High TSH	High T3 and T4 Low TSH
Medications	Thyroid replacement: Levothyroxine (Synthroid) Take medication morning Hold if HR > 100	Thyroid Antagonist: Methimazole PTU—watch for agranulocytosis

Assessment	Hypothyroid	Hyperthyroid
Life Threatening Emergency	Myxedema Coma—everything low! • Hypothermia • Severe bradycardia • Hypoglycemia • Shock • Hypoventilation • Ileus	Thyroid storm—everything high! • Hyperthermia (high fever) • Tachycardia • Hyperglycemia • Hyperventilation

Important:

Hyperthyroidism is often accompanied by Exophthalmos, a bulging of the eyes, sometimes out of the orbit. An advanced stage of Graves' Disease (hyperthyroidism).

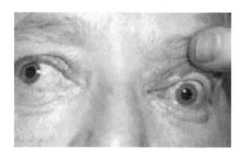

Nursing Implications:

◆ The client may not see well and need assistance with activities of daily living.

◆ The eyeball should be kept moist if the eyelid will not close to prevent damage to the eye.

Imbalances of Adrenal Corticotropin Hormone (ACTH)

Cushing's Disease

Aldosterone ↑

Cortisol ↑

Labs:

Some	Sodium	↑
People	Potassium	↓
Get	Glucose	↑
Cold	Calcium	↓

Blood presure elevated!

Too much steroid on board (aldosterone and cortisol are steroid hormones).
- ► Poor wound healing
- ► Fluid retention
- ► Increased appetite
- ► Mood swings
- ► Osteoporosis
- ► Cataract formation
- ► Buffalo hump/moon face

These are the same symptoms as a client on high-dose and/or long term steroids.

Low sodium/low fat/ low glucose diet (Diabetic diet)

Monitor and treat hypertension with ACE inhibitors which will increase the potassium.

Addison's Disease

Aldosterone ↓

Cortisol ↓

Labs:

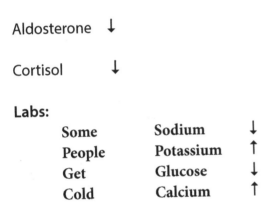

Some	Sodium	↓
People	Potassium	↑
Get	Glucose	↓
Cold	Calcium	↑

Not enough steroids on board. Requires daily steroid replacement usually with predinisone.
**Take ⅔ of daily dose in the morning and ⅓ in the early evening.

Must have frequent rest periods throughout the day.

Stress, fatigue, infection, and not taking steroids can lead to **life threatening** Addisonian crisis.
BP, sodium and glucose are low
Potassium is high

Treatment:
- ▪ Steroids IV
- ▪ Fluid replacement (D_5NS) will help address hypoglycemia and hyponatremia
- ▪ Manage potassium (potassium will enter cell in presence of glucose and insulin)
- ▪ Treat underlying cause

Syndrome of Inappropriate Antidiuretic Hormone (SIADH)

When you think about ADH think about H$_2$O.

- Diureses = peeing
- Anti-diuresing = **not** peeing

➤ **More ADH** = more antidiuretic action = body holds water = more total body water
➤ **Less ADH** = no blockage of antidiuretic action = lose water = less total body water

More ADH:

In **Syndrome of Inappropriate Antidiuretic Hormone (SIADH)**, even though the body already has too much fluid on board, the negative feedback system is not working and the posterior pituitary gland keeps sending out ADH. These people are **soggy!**

Causes: Start with the head!

- Brain tumors
- Head injury
- Lung cancer (and other solid tumor cancers)
- Meningitis

Think about what **hold fluid and increased total body water** means in terms of lab values and signs and symptoms

- Decreased urine output (holding fluid) —leads to high urine specific gravity (very concentrated urine)
- Low serum osmolality (holding so much fluid that the plasma is very dilute)
- Serum sodium less than normal (normal 135-145 meq/L)
- Fluid shift from vascular space to tissues---**watch out**—cerebral edema

Nursing Management of SIADH (aimed at controlling symptoms due to hyponatremia)

- Seizure precautions (cerebral edema)
- Fluid restrictions (500mL/day)
- Managing 3% saline solution (very slow infusion rate, watch renal function, client **must** have adequate urine output or vascular system will be stressed and collapse)

Now reverse these concepts.

Diabetes Insipidus

Less ADH:
Diabetes Insipidus (DI) means that even though the client has **huge** volumes of urine output (can reach 10-15 liters/day!!), the feedback loop does not work and the posterior pituitary does not release ADH. So there is no signal to the kidneys to hold water.

DI is the opposite of SIADH

These people are **dry**!

When should the nurse look for DI? Interesting that the causes are the same as SIADH. Start with the head!

- Brain tumors
- Head injury
- Lung cancer (and other solid tumor cancers)
- Meningitis

Sometimes alcohol or medications such as lithium cause DI by blocking the release of ADH (this is why alcohol is dangerous in the heat; it blocks ADH release which means dieresis)

Think about what **losing fluid and decreased total body water** means in terms of lab values and signs and symptoms.

- Increased urine output (free water loss)—leads to low urine specific gravity
- High serum osmolality (no fluid in the vascular system; it's all in the toilet!)
- Serum sodium higher than normal (normal 135-145meq/L)
- Fluid shifts from the cells/tissues to the intravascular space = cellular dehydration

Nursing Management of DI (aimed at controlling dehydration and circulatory collapse)

- Fluid replacement (sometimes you will replace mL for mL lost + 500 mL just to "stay ahead" of the volume loss)
- Trend vital signs. Must watch for fluid deficit due to disease process **and** fluid overload due to treatment.
- Medications
  - Vasopressin (ADH) administered IV
  - Desmopressin (DDAVP) synthetic ADH (oral, nasal spray)

Commonalities that flow through client safety of every body system and are heavily weighted on the *NCLEX*® can be condensed into the following table on MANAGE.

These standards currently count for as much as 20% of the total *NCLEX*® exam and are always a primary consideration for nursing.

PASS *NCLEX*®!

M   Make sure of identity, accuracy of orders

A   Arrange privacy/confidentiality/consent/collaboration with other team

N   No injuries, falls, malfunctioning equipment or staff or hazards

A   Address errors, abuse, legalities, scope of practice—document

G   Give (delegate) orders to appropriate people

E   Establish priorities of clients and time

---

1. The nurse asks the client to state his name following a thyroidectomy. What is the nurse assessing by this action?
    A. Laryngeal nerve damage
    B. Level of consciousness
    C. Post-op bleeding
    D. Trigeminal nerve damage

2. A client develops hypoglycemia. The nurse institutes the hypoglycemic protocol. What is necessary to be included in the documentation of the event? **Select all that apply.**
    A. The initial glucose result
    B. The treatment given
    C. Repeated glucose level after the treatment given
    D. Client assessment pre and post treatment
    E. HgbA1c result

3. The client is in the midst of an Addisonian crisis. Which of the following is priority?
    A. Assessing for hypertension
    B. Preventing infection
    C. Preventing hypotension
    D. Increasing urine output

4. A client taking propythiouracil (PTU) presents with a lab result of WBC of 4.2, neutrophils of 25%, lymphocytes of 45%, monocytes of 30%. What are the appropriate nursing interventions? **Select all that apply.**
    A. Continue the medication
    B. Alert the provider
    C. Document and report any signs and symptoms of infection
    D. Place the client in reverse isolation
    E. Wash hands before entering room

5. The diabetic client receives 15 units of Humulin N insulin at 0730. The nurse should assess the client for symptoms of hypoglycemia at what time?
    A. 0830 hours
    B. 1030 hours
    C. 1600 hours
    D. 2400 hours

6. The hospitalized client is observed to be perspiring profusely, his hands are shaking following a dose of Humalog® insulin. What is the nursing priority for this client?
    A. Implement the appropriate glycemic protocol
    B. Notify the provider of these symptoms
    C. Offer the client orange juice with sugar added
    D. IV bolus the client with D_{50} and recheck the glucose

7. The client's HgbA1c level is 7.0%. What is the nursing priority?
    A. Treat the elevated glucose level
    B. Document the results on the medical record
    C. Notify the provider
    D. Consult a hematologist

8. Which of the following clients should be evaluated first?
    A. A diabetic client who is demonstrating a deep, rapid respiratory pattern with long expirations
    B. A post-op client verbalizing pain as a #3 on a 0-5 scale
    C. A COPD patent with a pulse ox reading of 89%
    D. A client requesting a laxative

9. A type II diabetic client asks the nurse for recommendations for removing a callus from her foot. How should the nurse advise the client?
    A. "Cleanse the area with rubbing alcohol to dry the callus"
    B. "Soak the area in Epsom® salts and the callus will dry up"
    C. "Use a lava stone to remove the callus"
    D. "Consult a foot doctor to remove the callus"

10. The client is receiving IV insulin. The nurse inspects the site and finds the site to be reddened and edematous. What is the next nursing action?
    A. Apply Emla® to the site
    B. Flush the IV with heparin
    C. Discontinue the present site
    D. Apply warm soaks

11. A newly diagnosed diabetic client refuses to take his insulin. He states, "I am Jewish. I am not permitted to consume anything from a pig and this includes insulin." How should the nurse respond to this situation?
    A. "Please discuss this with your family."
    B. "Please discuss this with your rabbi."
    C. "Insulin may be the only effective treatment."
    D. "This really is your choice."

12. The client with hyperthyroidism is experiencing exophthalmos and asks how she can prevent the complication of corneal irritation or abrasion. Which is the most appropriate response?
    A. Advise the client to massage the eye on a regular interval.
    B. Instruct the client to administer an ophthalmic anesthetic as ordered.
    C. Encourage the client to wear eye protection such as sunglasses.
    D. Cover both eyes in normal saline soaked gauze.

13. The client returns to the nursing unit following a thyroidectomy. His neck is edematous and he complains of having increased dyspnea. Which is the nursing priority action?
    A. Maintain client's airway
    B. Notify the provider for emergency orders
    C. Document the findings as this is expected after surgery
    D. Instruct the client to cough to clear secretions

14. The client is diagnosed with hypothyroidism and is experiencing the signs and symptoms of the disease. Which assessment indicates a need to notify the provider?
    A. Coarse hair
    B. Menorrhagia
    C. Constipation
    D. Bradycardia

15. The client is about to go to surgery for a thyroidectomy and has expressed fear of the postoperative pain. What is the priority nursing action that will help this client deal with the fear? **Select all that apply**
    A. Teach the client relaxation techniques like meditation
    B. Teach the client about the medications available to treat their pain
    C. Assess the client's use of pain medication
    D. Listen to the client's concerns about postoperative pain.
    E. Notify the provider of the client's fear.

16. The client is taking propylthiouracil (PTU) to treat Graves' disease and develops a sore throat and fever. Which is the most appropriate action?
    A. Notify the provider
    B. Recommend forcing fluids
    C. Administer acetaminophen (Tylenol) as ordered for fever
    D. Administer cough drops

17. The client with Type 2 diabetes mellitus presents with decreased feeling in their bilateral lower extremities. To prevent client injury, which is for the discharge plan?
    A. Check the client's feet daily for abrasions or changes in appearance
    B. Always wear socks no matter what the temperature is
    C. Soak the client's feet in hot water every night
    D. Elevate the lower extremities on pillows when in bed

18. A client had a bilateral adrenalectomy to treat Cushing's disease yesterday. The client now has a temperature of 99.4° F. Which is the priority nursing intervention?
    A. Administer intravenous fluids
    B. Encourage coughing and deep breathing every 1 to 2 hours
    C. Assume wound infection and notify the physician
    D. Obtain a urine sample for a urine culture

19. The client is on a patient controlled analgesia (PCA) machine to administer morphine sulfate after a bilateral adrenalectomy. Which of the following nursing interventions are appropriate to prevent constipation? **Select all that apply**
    A. Encourage bedrest
    B. Encourage fluids
    C. Administer more narcotic pain medication
    D. Encourage use of a stool softener
    E. Encourage a diet high in fiber

20. Which task may be delegated to a Certified Nursing Assistant (CNA)?
    A. Assist the client with activities of daily living or ADLs
    B. Measure and report the blood glucose level
    C. Assess postoperative sutures
    D. Administer medication

21. The RN needs assistance with a client assignment. Which nursing intervention must be delegated to another Registered Nurse (RN)?
    A. Obtaining client's vital signs
    B. Start an insulin infusion for a client in diabetic ketoacidosis
    C. Perform a bed bath on a client who is on bedrest secondary to a bilateral adrenalectomy
    D. Ambulate the patient in the hallway

22. The client with diabetes mellitus asks what lifestyle changes they can make to help control their disease. **Select all that apply**
    A. Lose weight and control gain.
    B. Exercise
    C. Increase daily caloric intake
    D. Eat one large meal a day
    E. Self monitor blood glucose frequently

23. The client has diabetes insipidus and is experiencing polydypsia and polyuria. Which is the priority nursing action?
    A. Educate client about daily weight monitoring before discharge
    B. Apply lip balm to dry lips
    C. Teach client to avoid alcohol as it decreases ADH secretion
    D. Monitor fluid and electrolyte status

24. When caring for a diabetic client with a foot wound that is infected with methicillin-resistant Staphylococcus aureus or MRSA, which is the priority nursing action to prevent the spread of this bacteria?
    A. Hand washing before entering and after leaving the clients room
    B. Applying dry sterile dressings to the wound
    C. Educate the client about infection control techniques
    D. Administer the prescribed antibiotics

25. The nurse observes a client leaving their bed yet the activated bed alarm does not go off. What is the priority nursing action?
    A. Call engineering to fix the bed alarm
    B. Get the client the phone so that they do not need to stand up
    C. Assist the client back to bed
    D. Explain to the client the need to call for assistance with ambulation

26. Which is priority when caring for a diabetic quadriplegic client at risk for developing pressure ulcers?
    A. Reposition the client at least every 2 hours to prevent skin breakdown
    B. Keep the client secured into their wheelchair during the day
    C. Elevate the head of the bed to greater than 45 degrees
    D. Perform a skin assessment every week

Answers and Rationale

1. **Answer A** is correct because the laryngeal nerve is very close in proximity to the surgical area of a thyroidectomy. Options B and C are important but do not specifically assess nerve function as a complication to the surgical procedure. Answer D is incorrect as the trigeminal nerve does not lie within the surgical field for a thyroidectomy.

2. **Answers A, B, C, and D** are all elements necessary for complete documentation of a hypoglycemic event. Glucose results are necessary for evaluation of the effectiveness of the treatment plan. Treatment must be documented. Client assessment must also be documented to assess treatment effectiveness. HgbA1c evaluates glycemic control over a period of weeks; therefore, it is not relevant in this acute situation

3. **Answer C** is correct. The client with Addison's disease has a deficiency of adrenal corticosteroids, which may cause severe hypotension due to the uncontrolled loss of sodium in the urine as well as the decreased mineralocorticoid function. These effects result in loss of extracellular fluid and low blood volume. Answer A is incorrect. The pathophysiology of the disease process does not physiologically indicate that hypertension would occur. Option B is incorrect. At this point, preventing infections is not a priority intervention. Answer D is incorrect. With Addison's disease, the important aspect is to decrease the loss of sodium in the urine. Increasing the urine output will increase the chance of hypotension and even hypovolemic shock.

4. **Answers B, C, and E.** Answer B is correct. The physician must be notified of the decreased WBC count and differential as the client is at risk for infection due to the adverse effect of PTU. Option C is correct. The client is at risk for thrombocytopenia and any suspected areas of infection must be addressed and documented for treatment. Answer E is correct. Hand washing is always necessary for the prevention of infection, no matter what the situation. Answer A is incorrect. The medication is most likely the causative factor of the alteration in lab work. Answer D is incorrect. While the WBC count is low, it does not merit reverse isolation.

5. **Answer C** is correct. Depending in the type of insulin, hypoglycema occurs during the time of peak action. Humulin N peaks in 4 to 12 hours after administration.

6. **Answer A** is correct. The client has just received a rapid acting form of insulin and may be demonstrating symptoms of hypoglycemia. By utilizing a protocol, treatment is not delayed in waiting for a physician call back. Answer B is incorrect. The client needs immediate attention, protocols are set up to avoid having to call the physician for orders; thusly, delaying treatment. Option C is incorrect. This will make the situation worse.. Answer D is incorrect. This treatment is reserved for extreme cases of hypoglycemia, especially when the client is unresponsive.

7. **Answer B** is correct. While not an acute indicator of blood glucose levels, knowledge of HbgA1c will assist the provider in overall care and attempts to assure glycemic control of the client. Answers A and C are incorrect because HbgA1c does not indicate acute glucose levels and therefore is not treated nor immediately life threatening. Option D is incorrect. The management of diabetes is not within the focus of practice of a hematologist.

8. **Answer A** demonstrates an abnormal respiratory pattern, i.e., Kusmal's respirations. This may indicate the client is suffering from diabetic ketoacidosis. This is a life-threatening situation and needs immediate attention. Answer B, while the client is uncomfortable, is not life threatening and could be delegated to an LPN to administer pain medication. Option C is not life threatening for a client with COPD as their body is accustomed to lower levels of oxygen and still can sustain bodily function. Answer D is the least of priorities as the patient may be uncomfortable but the situation is not life threatening.

9. **Answer D**. Due to the potential complications of diabetes, the only acceptable answer is Answer D. Diabetic foot care must be performed by a physician or preferably a podiatrist to assure that the care is properly carried out. Answers A, B, and C are incorrect as a diabetic client should not perform any foot care.

10. **Answer C** is correct because the IV site is demonstrating sites of infiltration. The only acceptable action is to discontinue the present site. Option A is incorrect as Emla® is a local anesthetic agent used for clients, especially children, who are sensitive to injections. Emla® does nothing for the patency of the IV site. Answer B is incorrect as the site has infiltrated and heparin flush will only admit heparin into the tissue. Option D is applicable after the angiocatheter has been removed to assist with the pain and swelling of the site.

11. **Answer B** The client's religious beliefs prohibit him from consuming pork products. He is firmly expressing a concern about the potential conflict of medicine and his religious beliefs. Option B is correct, as the rabbi may be able to advise the client on the medicinal use of pork products according to the Jewish faith. Answer A is not the best option, as the family may possess the same opinion as the client. Answers C and D are incorrect as the client's cultural/religious needs are totally being ignored. Perhaps all the client may need is the approval from his rabbi to assure that his faith philosophy is not violated.

12. **Answer C**. Wearing eye protection will prevent any debris from getting into the eye and causing irritation. An anesthetic will address pain but not help prevent this complication. Eye massage and gauze may only introduce more particulates to the eye and increase chances for irritation.

13. **Answer A**. The post-operative edema appears to be compromising the client's airway and as a result increasing their dyspnea. You would get help and have another nurse call the physician while you treat the client. Instructing the client to cough may just irritate the new sutures and cause pain and increased edema.

14. **Answer D**. An abnormally slow heart rate takes priority over the other symptoms of this diagnosis. The other symptoms can be addressed after the heart rate is controlled.

15. **Answers C and E** are priority. If the client is abusing pain medication this may make their pain control more difficult. The provider should be aware of the fear.

16. **Answer A**. A client who is taking propylthiouracil (PTU) should be monitored for any signs of leukopenia or agranulocytosis. With a fever and sore throat the provider needs to be notified

17. **Answer A**. With decreased sensation the client is at risk for developing an abrasion without their knowledge, which could get infected. Soaks do not provide protection. Decreased sensation could cause the client to be unaware of very hot water and cause burns. Elevating the lower extremities will reduce swelling but will not detect any problem with sensation.

18. **Answer B**. Decreased lung expansion is the most common cause of early post-operative fever. If the wound is infected it would take longer for the client to develop a fever and with this surgery a urinary tract infection is not common.

19. **Answers B, D, and E**. These actions are all known to encourage elimination. Not moving will decrease peristalsis and administering narcotic pain medication is known to contribute to constipation.

20. **Answer A is** correct because it falls under the scope of practice of a CNA. Options B, C, and D all require a nursing license.

21. **Answer B** is correct. It is a nursing action requiring a license. The other actions can be delegated to another healthcare team member.

22. **Answers A, B, and D**. These actions decrease insulin resistance, increase insulin sensitivity, and help to keep a better control of levels. Increasing calories will only increase insulin resistance and the client should eat small frequent meals to help maintain glucose levels.

23. Answer D. The nurse is responsible for monitoring the fluid status of the patient and reporting fluid imbalances. Education and lip balm application can take place once the patient is stabilized.

24. Answer A is correct because hand washing stops the transmission of the bacteria from this client to another. Answers B, C, and D are important but are not the priority.

25. Answer C is correct as it addresses the immediate danger. Answers A, B, and D are all important but can be accomplished after the client is in a safe situation.

26. Answer: A is correct. Answers B and C would increase the risk of developing a pressure ulcer and Answer D is incorrect because a skin assessment needs to occur at least every shift on an at risk client.

The Pediatric ENDOCRINE System

Jessica Peck, DNP, RN, MSN, CPNP-PC, CNE
Edited by Sylvia Rayfield & Associates, Inc.

How do endocrine disorders affect children?

DIABETES MELLITUS

DIABETES IS THE MOST COMMON ENDOCRINE DISORDER IN PEDIATRICS, AFFECTING, IN SOME WAY, 1 OUT OF 3 CHILDREN IN THE UNITED STATES!!!

KEY CONCEPTS TO REMEMBER:

- ❖ Diabetes causes 27 million trips to the emergency room per year.
- ❖ The risk for African American and Hispanic children is 1:2.
- ❖ Peak incidence is between 10 and 15 years.
- ❖ Initial diagnosis is often delayed in children because of attribution to other common childhood pathologies such as gastroenteritis, influenza, etc.
- ❖ An interdisciplinary approach is essential for successful therapy.
- ❖ Children have constantly changing insulin needs based on physical growth, frequent pediatric illnesses and varying activity levels.
- ❖ SELF-MANAGEMENT IS CRITICAL! Children should be taught as early as possible to care for themselves and to manage their disease process.

http://www.youtube.com/watch?v=xZc6xqjjX_U

Visit this "Day in the Life of a Toddler with Diabetes

DIABETIC KETOACIDOSIS (DKA)

WHAT TO ASSESS WHEN A CHILD IS A NEWLY DIAGNOSED DIABETIC IN DKA:

ASSESSMENT	INTERVENTION
A- AIRWAY Airway can be compromised	• Admit child to intensive care unit. • Be prepared for emergency airway.

if patient is unconscious.	• Administer gastric suction if unconscious to prevent aspiration.
B- BREATHING Children can experience Kussmaul respirations (deep, rapid respirations) as a result of metabolic acidosis.	• Monitor for signs of respiratory failure. • Give oxygen if arterial O2 is <80%. • Be prepared for emergency intubation. www.youtube.com/watch?v=0YJxz-Sxx90 **This is what those respirations look like.**
C- CIRCULATION Severe dehydration will cause decreased organ and tissue perfusion.	• Place on continuous cardiac monitoring. • Monitor for signs of organ failure. • Check perfusion frequently (cap refill, etc.) • Neuro checks every 15 minutes during acute phase to observe for signs of cerebral edema
D- DEHYDRATION All children in DKA are experiencing dehydration. Severe losses are more than 10% of body weight. This is a life-threatening process with a high mortality rate. Watch for signs of hypovolemic shock.	• Check vital signs every 15 minutes. • Assess skin turgor, mucous membranes, fontanel (if applicable). • Assess frequently for changes in level of consciousness. • If child loses consciousness, should regain quickly with replacement IV fluid bolus administration. • Check urine for ketones. • Avoid indwelling catheter if possible to avoid risk for infection.
E- ELECTROLYTES & LABS Potassium may initially be high, but it drops very quickly with rehydration.	• Monitor serum potassium CLOSELY! • Once UOP is established (at least 25ml/hour), give aggressive potassium replacement therapy. • Monitor Blood Glucose. • Monitor ABG's. • Other labs include H&H, CBC, Calcium and Phosphorus. • If any signs of infection are present, initiate antibiotic treatment.
F- FLUID THERAPY	• Initial fluid therapy is isotonic (0.9% NS) • Restore lost body weight/fluid loss evenly over 24-48 hours. Do not give bolus too rapidly or the risk of cerebral edema will increase. • Weigh daily at same time on same scale. • Monitor for signs of FVO (fluid volume overload)

	• Follow-up bolus with hypotonic fluid (0.45% NS) to hydrate the cells.
G- GLUCOSE LEVELS **INSULIN IS NOT GIVEN IMMEDIATELY FOR SEVERE DKA!!!!** Blood glucose levels fall rapidly during rehydration. A _steady_ descent of 50-100mg/dL/hour is desired.	• Anticipate insulin therapy _after_ IV fluid bolus is given. • Insulin is given at 0.1units/kg/hr • When blood glucose levels approach 250-300mg/dL, add **DEXTROSE 5-10%** to the IVF. This seems contradictory! This is done to MAINTAIN blood glucose levels between 120-240mg/dL. • Check blood glucose every hour until stabilized. • Insulin therapy is the same for both kids and adults.
H- HELP FAMILY TO COPE	• Assess family structure for coping, educational needs, and current diabetes management plan • Assess for interdisciplinary team needs.

I- ILLNESS MANAGEMENT
 	
PLAN
 	
Illness will usually run its course in a similar fashion to a healthy child if the child with diabetes has well-controlled blood glucose. If the child's disease is not well controlled, even a minor illness can be catastrophic. Stress causes hyperglycemia, so it is not uncommon to have an increased insulin need during times of illness. Goals are to:
  1) Restore normal BG levels
  2) Maintain adequate hydration
  3) Treat ketones
	• Check BG and urine ketones at least every 3hours while ill, expect elevations in both
	• Call provider **IMMEDIATELY** if BG >300mg/dL, as this could indicate the onset of DKA.
	• Anticipate greater insulin need throughout illness.
	
	CALL THE PROVIDER IF:
	  1) Blood glucose is >240mg/dL
	  2) >1 episode of vomiting
	  3) +Ketones in urine
	
	• **IT IS CRITICAL FOR THE CHILD TO HAVE ADEQUATE FLUID INTAKE**. Fluids prevent dehydration and flush ketones from the urine, thus preventing DKA.
	
	Visit this link to read a more detailed protocol for DKA management. www.youtube.com/watch?v=dW3GZP6isbQ

J- JUMPSTART DIET AND EXERCISE	• Encourage CONSISTENCY with meals and snacks • Use exchange charts for ease of calculating carbs • Use sugar substitutes sparingly as some have been labeled as potentially carcinogenic and have not been adequately tested in children. Also, most cause some degree of gastric upset and potentially diarrhea. Just because something is sugar-free does not mean it is

		carbohydrate free. Reading labels is essential.
		• Distribution of calories should be tailored to each individual child's activity level. For instance, a child may have increased insulin need in the summer, when activity is greater.
		• **IF THERE IS INCREASED ACTIVITY, ANTICIPATE THE NEED FOR INCREASED FOOD!**
		• Encourage a snack 30 minutes before vigorous exercise. If exercise is prolonged, a snack may be needed mid-way.
		• Toddlers may benefit from shorter-acting insulin because of their notorious picky eating habits and food jags.
K-	**KEEP TRACK OF BLOOD GLUCOSE**	• Children should test their blood glucose at least 6 times a day • Optimal BG levels should be maintained between 80-120mg/dL. • Acceptable Hgb A1C is 6.5-8%, but the goal is <7%. • Encourage children to check their own blood glucose (they do this much younger than you would think!) **Visit here to check out this amazing little girl!** www.youtube.com/watch?v=TC1oZEHcayM

L-	**LEARN SIGNS AND SYMPTOMS AND MANAGEMENT OF HYPO/HYPERGLYCEMIA**
	
	Children often know when they are feeling "low" or "high" but may not know the specific treatment for it.
	
	Another complicating factor is that children may sometimes fake being "low" in order to get a quick sugary treat.
		• HYPOGLYCEMIA
		  1) Most commonly occurs immediately AC
		  2) Treat with 15-20g carbs (1TBS sugar, tubed cake icing, 6 ounces of milk or juice)
		  3) If child is unconscious, give glucagon IM or SQ and check BG in 15 minutes. Place child in recovery position to prevent aspiration if vomiting occurs.
		• HYPERGLYCEMIA
		  1) **IF IN DOUBT ABOUT HYPER/HYPO, THEN GIVE CARBS!!** It will help if they are low and if they are high will not make a significant difference.
		  2) Anticipate hyperglycemia in times of illness, stress, increased growth, and at the onset of menses each month.

M-	**MASTER INSULIN**	• Teach children as soon as possible to administer their

INJECTIONS Sometimes new diabetics are thin because of the physiologic effects. Make sure the injection is given SQ and not IM!	own injections. It is helpful for parents to administer injections a few times a week in hard to reach places in order to rotate sites more frequently. • Choose a site not heavily exercised (for example, if plays tennis, avoid arms and legs). • Practice on an orange or a doll first. • Keep a chart with a child's outlined body on it. Place date at injection site to assist with site rotation. • Teach appropriate technique	
N- NEVER FORGET ABOUT HOW MUCH THIS WILL CHANGE THE FAMILY'S LIFE. REVIEW AND EDUCATE, EDUCATE, EDUCATE!	• Follow-up plans with interdisciplinary team • Prevent and treat hypo/hyperglycemia • Meal and snack plans • Exercise appropriately • Sick day management • Options for insulin administration and BG monitoring • Insulin pumps can be used to administer a continuous dose SQ under the skin starting ~4yrs. Disadvantages: it is expensive, requires math skills, and children experience frequent skin infections. • Encourage family support groups and diabetic camp attendance	

CEREBRAL EDEMA

DEHYDRATION

KUSSMAUL RESPIRATIONS

ACIDOSIS

Diabetic Ketoacidosis
(DKA)

A BOY WITH NEWLY DIAGNOSED DIABETES

An 8-year-old boy came into my clinic complaining of classic polyuria, polydipsia, and polyphagia. He was thin and pale looking, with large dark circles under his eyes. As I suspected, his blood glucose was severely elevated at over 800. How do I try to explain to his mother that no, he doesn't have "bad allergies" as she suspected, but instead has a lifelong disease for which there is currently no cure? How do I go from telling her that no, he doesn't need stronger allergy medicine but in fact needs to be transported immediately by ambulance to the nearest pediatric intensive care unit because he will die if he is not treated? How do I tell her that I am very concerned about potential swelling in his brain? How do I tell her that he will have to check his blood sugar more than ten times a day and will have to learn to give himself shots every day for the rest of his life? How do I tell her that her family life will never be the same as she knows it, that they will always have to care for his disease, and that they cannot even have one day of vacation from it? How do I tell her that even though he will get much better in the hospital and even though he will look "normal" that his disease is still there, waiting to emerge its ugly head? How do I tell her to sleep in peace and not to worry about blood glucose fluctuations in the night? How do I tell her not to worry about her other children developing the disease? How do I coach her to call her husband and give him this news? You see, I have just walked the most enormous elephant straight into her room and now it refuses to leave. I must help her to eat this elephant one bite at a time. I must convey to her that there is hope for her son to have a meaningful and productive life. I must convince her that one day in the future things will not be as bad as they are today. I cannot tell her these things nearly as well as someone who has walked in her shoes. Maybe one day these elephants will be extinct.

This little boy has a message for other children with diabetes. Visit to listen.
http://www.youtube.com/watch?v=yx1t4yZ1nQU

JUVENILE HYPOTHYROIDISM

Here is the down and dirty version of what you need to know:

❖ Congenital hypothyroidism is a major cause of childhood mental retardation.

❖ Early detection and intervention is key to a successful treatment outcome.

❖ Infants need rapid thyroid hormone replacement, but children need a more graduated approach over 4-8 weeks to prevent compensatory hyperthyroidism.

❖ Compliance and monitoring response to therapy is critical.

❖ Children should assume responsibility for care beginning at 8 years of age if developmentally appropriate.

Visit here for more information on congenital hypothyroidism and to see some pictures.

http://www.congenitalhypothyroidism.net

HYPOPITUITARISM

❖ Diminished secretion of pituitary hormones causes Growth Hormone (GH) deficiency, TSH deficiency, somatic growth retardation, and absence or regression of secondary sex characteristics due to absence of gonadotropins.

❖ Severity of clinical manifestations is dependent on the degree of the deficiency.

❖ Risk factors include trauma, surgery, structural defects, and heredity. Most cases are idiopathic.

NURSING CARE:

ASSESSMENT FINDINGS:	• Decreasing growth velocity (height affected more than weight)
	• Skeletal proportions normal, appears well nourished
	• Underdeveloped jaw, dental crowding
	• Sexual development delayed but normal in sequential progression
LAB FINDINGS:	• Plasma insulin-like growth factor I (IGF I) may be low
	• If low, GH should be stimulated and measured at time increments (levels are usually too low to assess unless stimulated by exercise, administration of glucose, or 30 minutes after onset of sleep)
	• Assess for hypothyroidism, hypoadrenalism, and hypoaldosteronism
	• Skeletal surveys usually show skeletal immaturity
NURSING CARE:	• Document growth and plot on growth chart every 6 months for children under 3 years and every year for children over 3 years. Early identification of growth problems is an essential nursing intervention.
	• Administer other concurrent hormone replacements as indicated
	• Provide emotional support to the family about psychosocial issues

(disturbed body image, etc).

- Emphasize the importance of maintaining realistic growth expectations. GH administration will not work miracles by making giants!

- Counseling is advisable.

MEDICATIONS COMMONLY USED FOR PEDIATRIC ENDOCRINE PATIENTS

MEDICATION	ACTION	NURSING CARE	EDUCATION	ALERTS
Growth Hormone	Hormone replacement	Administer SQ injection 6-7 days per week Continue injections until bone maturation occurs	Teach parents how to complete injections at home	OPTIMUM DOSING ACHIEVED AT BEDTIME TO COINCIDE WITH NATURAL GH RELEASE!
Thyroid Hormone	Hormone replacement	Administer PO doses on time.		COMPLIANCE IS KEY TO PREVENT MENTAL RETARDATION!

What is the goal of nursing care for a child with endocrine disorders?

The goal is to cut the **CRAP** this family and child have to deal with.

C-_COMPLIANCE WITH MEDICATION!_

R- _RECOVERY FROM ILLNESS_

A- _ABILITY TO COPE_

P-_PREVENT RECURRENCE_

REVIEW QUESTIONS

1. A 6-year-old girl has been admitted to the pediatric intensive care unit as a newly diagnosed Type I Diabetic with diabetic ketoacidosis (DKA). Her orders include a fluid replacement bolus of 0.9%NS, vital signs every 15 minutes, and neuro checks every hour. Her blood glucose has decreased from 890 mg/dL to 285mg/dL after 8 hours of therapy. What orders would the nurse anticipate at this time? **Select all that apply.**

    1) Administer oxygen @ 2L via nasal cannula
    2) Change IV fluid to 0.45% NS
    3) Add dextrose 5% to IV fluids infusing
    4) Blood Glucose every 15 minutes
    5) Anticipate starting potassium replacement therapy

Options #2, #3, and #5 are correct. When the Blood Glucose approaches 250mg/dL, a hypotonic solution should be started and dextrose should be added to the fluids to maintain a controlled descent. This patient's DKA is beginning to stabilize and so Option #1 would not be anticipated unless the arterial O2 is <80%. Option #4 is incorrect because this child would likely need glucose checks every hour at this point.

2. A child has an order to receive an infusion of Regular insulin at a rate of 0.1units/kg/hour. 100 units of insulin have been mixed in 250mL of 0.45%NS. The child's weight is 84 pounds. What is the appropriate action of the nurse?

    1) Administer the infusion at 95 cc per hour.
    2) Administer the infusion at 9.5 cc per hour.
    3) Question the order because this is an unsafe dose.
    4) Change the solution to an isotonic fluid.

Option #2 is correct. This is an appropriate dosage in an appropriate fluid.

3. The parent of a 13-year-old newly diagnosed with Type I diabetes asks if he will be able to continue on the basketball team. What is the appropriate response of the nurse?

    1) "His condition is too unstable and unpredictable to be able to participate safely in sports."
    2) "He will require extra doses of insulin before each practice and game."
    3) "He will likely need to have an extra snack before practice and games."
    4) "Exercise will dangerously increase his blood glucose level."

Option #3 is the best answer. Exercise is essential for health and modifications can be made to help him participate safely. The other options are incorrect because exercise requires more glucose consumption.

4. The mother of a newborn just diagnosed with hypothyroidism is crying because she read on the internet that hypothyroidism causes mental retardation. She wants to know if this will happen to her baby. What is the appropriate response of the nurse?

1) Allow her to express her fears and concerns, showing concern for her feelings.
2) Tell her that this is unlikely because it was identified early and can be treated with medication
3) Recommend that she seek professional counseling to aid in coping with the grieving process
4) Suggest that she join a support group with parents of other children who have this disorder

Option #2 is correct. The most important factors in a positive outcome are early identification and compliance with medication. There is no need to allow the mother to be distraught about an outcome that is not likely. Professional counseling is likely not needed at this point. A support group is an option but is not the most pressing need at this moment.

5. A nurse is providing education to a family with a child who has been newly diagnosed with hypopituitarism. Which statement by the family indicates understanding of the treatment plan to administer growth hormone?

1) "We know not to hope that she will ever reach 5 feet tall in height."
2) "We need to accept the fact that these injections will be necessary for a lifetime."
3) "We should wait until the teenage growth spurt to start administering these shots."
4) "We understand that we will have to give an injection every day."

Option #4 is correct. Hypopituitarism requires daily subcutaneous injections for an indefinite period of time, not a lifetime. Height attainment is unpredictable. Treatment should begin at diagnosis.

6. A nurse is caring for a child with syndrome of inappropriate antidiuretic hormone. Which nursing intervention has the greatest priority?

1) Restrict fluids to ¼-½ normal maintenance
2) Measuring intake and output
3) Daily weights
4) Implement seizure precautions

Option #1 is correct. Restricting fluids is the priority nursing intervention.

7. A three-year-old boy is in the Pediatric Intensive Care Unit for diabetic ketoacidosis (DKA) with a blood glucose of 729. Which of these provider orders should the nurse question?

    1) Neurologic assessment every 30 minutes
    2) NPH insulin 12 units subcutaneously
    3) Potassium replacement therapy
    4) Rapid IV bolus administration

Option #2 is the correct answer. SQ insulin is not given during acute treatment for DKA. Children with DKA are at risk for developing cerebral edema and should have frequent neuro checks. Potassium replacement and IV rehydration are indicated for acute dehydration associated with DKA.

8. A provider has written an order to administer 100 units of regular insulin in 50ml of D50.9%NS. The insulin is to be administered at 0.1U/kg/hr. The child weighs 20kg. How many cc/hour should be administered?

    1) 12 cc/hour
    2) 10 cc/hour
    3) 2 cc/hour
    4) 1 cc/hour

The correct answer is option #4.

9. A 12-year-old newly diagnosed type one diabetic is being discharged to home. What is the most appropriate goal for the family at this time?

    1) Eliminate simple sugars from her diet until her diabetes is well controlled.
    2) Ensure the mother is comfortable with administering subcutaneous injections of insulin.
    3) Maintain a fasting blood sugar between 150-250 mg/dL.
    4) Self-administer insulin injections using appropriate site selection and technique.

Option #4 is correct. At 12 years of age, it is important for this child to learn to manage her diabetes. Having her mother administer injections when needed is not practical or realistic.

10. The mother of a 2-month-old infant with congenital hypothyroidism has been administering levothyroxine (Synthroid) daily to her baby. She asks the nurse how she can be sure that the medicine is working. What assessment data would demonstrate efficacy of the medication?

    1) Sleeping at least 12 hours at a time.
    2) Maintaining a heart rate of 60-90 beats per minute.
    3) Having 3-4 soft formed stools per day
    4) Drinking 2 ounces of formula every 4 hours.

Option #3 is correct. The other options are all signs of continuing hypothyroidism.

11. A nurse is educating a family about home administration of growth hormone. Which instruction is most appropriate to help achieve the best outcome?

    1) Administer the injection every night at bedtime.
    2) Administer the injection immediately after breakfast.
    3) Do not exercise for 30 minutes after the injection.
    4) Ensure that all immunizations are up to date before starting therapy.

Option #1 is correct. During the first 45-90 minutes of sleep, growth hormone release is normally stimulated and released. Exercise can increase levels of growth hormone. Growth hormone does not compromise the immune system so there are no special precautions that need to be taken.

12. An 8-year-old child is being treated for diabetes insipidus and is on strict fluid restrictions. The child's urine output has increased in the last 24 hours. What is the most appropriate action of the nurse?

    1) Call the provider immediately.
    2) Lock the door to the child's bathroom.
    3) Emphasize the need for compliance to the mother.
    4) Encourage ambulation.

Option #2 is correct. Small children can, sometimes, sneak fluids if they are very thirsty, drinking from sinks, flower vases, even toilets. It is important to be sure there are no accessible fluids in the room. This is not an emergent situation that necessitates an immediate call to the provider and ambulation has no effect on DI. If the condition is worsening and dehydration is occurring, ambulation could potentially be a safety risk.

13. A nurse is preparing to administer an injection of vasopressin (DDAVP) to a child with syndrome of inappropriate antidiuretic hormone. What is the most effective way to prepare the medication?

1) Keep the medication refrigerated until immediately prior to use.
2) Warm the medication under running water for 10-15 minutes prior to use.
3) Discard the medication if any particulate matter appears in the vial.
4) Give the medication in the morning to enhance efficacy.

Option #2 is correct. DDAVP is suspended in oil and must be warmed and shaken vigorously prior to use. Small brown particles should be seen throughout the suspension. This assures that the medication has been evenly dispersed. Medication should be given at night if possible. These children have to make very frequent trips to the bathroom for urination and having the medication at night can help to provide better rest. DDAVP lasts for 48 to 72 hours.

14. A nurse is caring for a 10-year-old patient with syndrome of inappropriate antidiuretic hormone. Upon assessment, the nurse finds that the child is complaining of nausea and malaise. One episode of vomiting has occurred. What is the priority action of the nurse?

1) Administer a prn order for an anti-emetic medication.
2) Remove the breakfast tray from the room.
3) Call the provider immediately to report.
4) Check the child's vital signs.

Option #3 is correct. Nausea, vomiting, and malaise can be signs of impending seizure and coma in patients with this disorder. All of the actions are appropriate but the priority action is to call the provider.

15. A 17-year-old female is 2 days post-op thyroidectomy. Upon assessment, the nurse finds the adolescent anxious and vomiting with a positive Chvostek's sign. In what order should these actions be taken?

1) Call the provider.
2) Institute seizure precautions.
3) Obtain a tracheostomy set.
4) Place calcium gloconate at the bedside.

The options are ordered correctly, #1, #2, #3, #4. This is a sign of hypocalcemia. The most important thing a nurse can do is to recognize it early. Seizures can occur so before leaving the patient to obtain the other supplies, seizure precautions should be instituted. Laryngospasm can occur so preparations for an emergency airway should be close at hand.

16. A 5-year-old who has been diagnosed with Type I diabetes six months ago is experiencing her first acute illness since diagnosis. She is experiencing a fever of 101.2 and a cough. Her parents call the nurse for advice. Which of the following are appropriate instructions? **Select all that apply.**

1) Check blood glucose every hour while febrile.
2) Omit scheduled insulin doses while febrile.
3) Call the provider if any vomiting occurs.
4) Encourage additional fluid intake
5) Call the provider if blood glucose is >240mg/dL.

Options #3, #4, and #5 are correct. Blood glucose should be checked every 3 hours during illness. Insulin should never be omitted during illness, as insulin requirements usually increase. Vomiting and BG >240 should be reported immediately, as those are potential signs of DKA. Fluid intake is essential to maintain hydration and to flush out ketones.

17. A nurse is preparing to administer IV insulin to a child. Which action is necessary for appropriate administration?

1) Prime the tubing with an insulin mixture prior to infusing.
2) Prime the tubing with normal saline.
3) Place a UV protectant bag over the mixture prior to infusing.
4) Warm the IV bag prior to administering.

Option #1 is correct. Insulin can have a chemical bind to the plastic tubing, which reduces the amount actually infused. In other words, if you have an order to infuse 100U of insulin in a 1000mL bag and you add 100U and then prime the tubing, you will lose some of those 100 units as the tubing absorbs the insulin. So, you prime with an insulin mixture to saturate the tubing, NOT counting the units you are supposed to administer and then administer your infusion.

18. A 10-year-old who was diagnosed at the age of 4 years is going to diabetes camp for the first time. What advice is most appropriate for him at this time?

1) Do not let anyone else use your lancet.
2) Be sure to stay well hydrated.
3) You may need extra insulin for vigorous activities.
4) It is important to get plenty of rest.

Option #1 is correct. This child will be around other children with diabetes and checking blood glucose is "normal" to them. It is important to educate and protect him from the risk of communicable bloodborne diseases. The other options are valid but these are all things he would have encountered at home.

19. A nurse is caring for a 7-year-old who is experiencing her 4th admission for DKA in less than one year. The parents have recently divorced this year and the mother has started a new full time job and a part time job at night, leaving her 15-year-old daughter to care for the 7-year-old. What is likely to be the most effective intervention for this family to prevent future episodes of DKA?

    1) Call CPS (Child Protective Services) to report child endangerment.
    2) Enroll the mother in diabetes education classes.
    3) Encourage the family to attend a support group.
    4) Have a family conference with the interdisciplinary health team.

Option #4 is correct. At this point, there is no data to indicate a CPS referral. Having the mother's burdened schedule increasingly burdened with an additional time commitment is not likely to be seen as a valuable experience, but an obligation. Setting mutual goals and a family management plan is most likely to be successful.

20. A 16-year-old boy is in the emergency department for the 7th time in the last year for hyperglycemic episodes. What is the best question for the nurse to ask?

    1) Do you drink alcohol on a regular basis?
    2) Do you know that your Hgb A1C shows us you aren't even trying?
    3) What do your friends think about your illness?
    4) How is diabetes affecting your life?

Option #4 is correct. The first two are closed-ended questions. #3 is a good question, but the best question is to assess the patient's perception of his illness and to determine his priorities, creating a management plan to help maintain control while preserving his desired quality of life. Peer pressure, growth spurts, poor diet and sleep patterns can all be typical in adolescence and can affect his diabetes.

Nursing Management in Psychosocial Disorders

Darlene Franklin RN MSN
Edited by
Sylvia Rayfield & Associates, Inc.

"Feelings of self worth are the outcome of treating others with dignity and respect."

Key Concepts:

- § Suicide
- § Dementia/Alzheimer's Disease
- § Therapeutic Communication
- § Depression
- § Psychosis (Schizophrenia, Bi-Polar Disorder)
- § Substance Abuse
- § Eating Disorders (Anorexia, Bulimia, Pica)
- § Psychiatric Pharmacology
- § Death and After Death Care
- § Practice Questions, Answers and Rationale

Our approach to easy learning and remembering is to provide the acronym **SAFETY** as a powerful tool. Utilize this tool every time you walk into a client's room or answer an **NCLEX**® question. All of these are standards tested on the current **NCLEX**® exam.

PASS *NCLEX*®!

S **System specific assessment**

A **Accurate orders and assignments**

F **First priorities**

E **Evaluate pharmacology**

T **Try infection control**

Y **Your assets in MANAGEMENT**

Suicide

Suicide is often ranked as the tenth cause of death in the United States. The people who attempt and complete suicide consider that there is "no solution" to their situation and no other way to remove themselves from the pain. This makes for the most perilous psychiatric condition for nursing. Statistics show that over 80% of the clients that end their own life have a psychiatric illness. Each client should be assessed for psychosocial and spiritual factors affecting the plan of care.

SYSTEM SPECIFIC ASSESSMENT

Suicidal/Homicidal Ideation: Assess the potential for violence and use safety precautions (e.g., suicide, homicide, and self-destructive behavior). Documents show that the majority of clients who try to end their lives have some type of mental illness. Nursing interventions include:
- Identify thoughts of harm to self/others. Use therapeutic communication techniques to provide client support.
- Identify plan, lethality, and means to achieve. Ascertain if they have a gun? Drugs? Sharps? All must be removed from client.
  - Evaluate the environment for safety. Unit safety **first**: No harm to befall client
    - No breakable glass—windows, mirrors, drinking utensils, etc.
    - Collapsible shower curtain rods, etc.
    - Belts, shoelaces, anything that the client may use for the purpose of suicide.

- ♦ Provide a therapeutic environment for clients with emotional/behavioral issues.
- ♦ Establish no harm to self or others contract—verbal and/or written. Protect the client from injury. Participate in institution security plan.
- ♦ Sentinel Event Alert, #46 Suicide on Medical/Surgical Units and ER (JCAHO, 2010). http://www.jointcommission.org/assets/1/18/SEA_46.pdf

Mental Status—orientation to person, place, time. Include history of current symptoms such as headache, nausea and vomiting. Any positive symptoms especially behavioral change will indicate the need for an MRI to determine possible brain tumor or other neurological impairment.

Depression (also see section on this topic later in this chapter):
- ▪ Physiological status must be assessed.
- ▪ Laboratory studies include:
  - • CBC to rule out anemia (tiredness and low energy)
  - • Thyroid function for hypothyroidism (hold lithium if the client is receiving it as it will affect the test). Hypothyroidism has similar symptoms of depression .
  - • Schilling's test for B12 to diagnose pernicious anemia, which may cause depression or dementia.

Dementia and Alzheimer's Disease

Clients with dementia and Alzheimer's disease are susceptible to anxiety and suicide. Symptoms that may indicate dementia include confusion, short term memory loss which may result in confabulation (made up information to fill in for lapses of memory), or getting lost while driving. They may become combative especially if confronted. Do not argue with these clients as this makes their behavior more aggressive. Later symptoms that may cause safety risks (e.g., suicide) include: roaming, getting lost, wandering, and depression. Consistency and assisting the client in decision making are useful tools for decreasing their anxiety.

SYSTEM SPECIFIC ASSESSMENT—for all psychiatric illnesses.

The initial assessment of a client will determine when to conduct the head to toe assessment. Psychotic clients actively harming self and/or other are an indication of priority need to maintain safety.
Head to toe assessment—ideally on admission; in client gown. Assess and ask about scars and check and seize contraband. Provide care and education for acute and chronic behavioral health issues (e.g., anxiety, depression, dementia, eating disorders).

Often medical/surgical nurses avoid psychosocial needs and psychiatric nurses shun the physiological needs of clients? Do clients shed these parts of their beings when in different inpatient units? Does this mean the spiritual aspects of clients require a separate venue? Recently I was involved in an online professional discussion where the question was raised, "Should head to toe assessments even be conducted on admission of inpatient psychiatric clients?" My response was, unequivocally, "YES!" Clients are physio, psycho, social, sexual, spiritual, beings. How can we provide care by assessing only one aspect of the person? Trust is being established during this assessment as well. Here are only a few experiences to support a physiological, hands on assessment:

- Build trust by listening, direct eye contact, not interrupting, physically sitting or standing on the same level as the client, being consistent, being non-judgmental!
- To ensure the client that both physiological and psychological needs are being assessed and addressed
  - Gown only
  - Privacy of and in client's room
  - Non-licensed personnel may be present to examine the client's belongings for sharps.
  - Outcomes have included:
    - Head: lice (pediculosis)—not common but may be present and require the client to be on contact isolation until treatment is complete. How would I know this without this investigation?
    - Skin Assessments: perform skin assessment and implement measures to maintain skin integrity and prevent skin breakdown. Should include the documentation of any breakdown or self inflicted injury. Remember, while performing all assessments, to apply principles of infection control.
    - Ensure proper identification of the client
    - Maintain client confidentiality and privacy.
    - Scars on a person's body tell a person's life story, including past suicide attempts, as do fresh scabs and wounds. Once during the skin assessment portion of the admission assessment of an eating disordered client, I noticed lesions on the lower back and asked if I could look further to which she agreed. Unknown to anyone, she was using coarse steel wool to clean herself after voiding and defecation and now had serious open lesions that would have been missed without this assessment. This is only one of many examples—fungi, melanomas, scars from abuse, etc.
    - Assess the client for abuse or neglect and intervene.
    - Recognize ethical dilemmas and take appropriate action.
    - Identification of complications from coexisting diseases. Clients with mental illness may lack the energy and/or the ability to care for themselves and their diseases. Diabetic clients with peripheral neuropathies, who no longer experience the feeling of pain in extremities, may ignore treatment not realizing that paralysis is a more serious complication. Recognize trends and changes in the client's condition and intervene as needed.
- Withdrawal risk from alcohol. Assess client for drug/alcohol dependencies, withdrawal, or toxicities and intervene as appropriate. Assess for signs and symptoms of increased heart rate (usually 24-72 hours of the last drink of alcohol). This often may be seen when the client is in the hospital for surgery. They may stop drinking for the surgery because they have so much pain from a disease process or automobile accident. Even though they are administered medication for pain their pulse and BP will remain elevated and they may have fever. If gone untreated, alcohols may say, "I feel bugs crawling on me." This is a big red flag for withdrawal. Ativan is often the drug of choice to bring the BP down. If the vital signs are still elevated, the client may be given magnesium sulfate to prevent convulsions.

ACCURATE ORDERS/ASSIGNMENTS

Room Placement

▶ **Room Together**: Depressed--Match-Making Support Systems for the future. Psychiatric nurses read the obituaries when clients do not return for inpatient care to determine, if the client killed themselves—a sad but common ritual. *A few years ago a nursing graduate totally reframed my thinking and obituary ritual. She changed my life. I was teaching about the importance of rooming depressed people together; finding individuals with common problems to share with the goal of establishing life long support systems. I noticed tears running down the nursing graduate's face as she whispered aloud, "It worked, it worked!" When asked what she meant, the girl explained that several years ago her mother had been admitted for depression and met two other women while hospitalized. One was her roommate. The women called themselves "The Three Musketeers," experiencing life's ups and downs together. "I'm closer to those two other women than my own aunts," the young nurse's mother had remarked. "Did those nurses put my mom in the room with that roommate on purpose?" I nodded yes with tears in my eyes then and even now. "It worked...it worked!"* Rarely did I ever find a client in the obituaries. Why? Because, rooming depressed clients together works! It really works!

▶ **Room Alone—SAFETY** is the goal
  - Homicidal
  - Intermittent Explosive Disorder
  - High Risk for Violence

▶ **Separate Clients with Eating Disorders**
  - To avoid competition
  - To avoid sharing weight loss ideas

Bottom line—the registered nurse is responsible for delegating the care of the client to the nurse who is not only the most knowledgeable about the client's condition, but also has the most humanitarian approach.

Assign and supervise care provided by others (e.g., LPN/LVN, assistive personnel, other RNs). Report unsafe practice of health care personnel and intervene as appropriate.

Therapeutic Communication

FIRSTS PRIORITIES INCLUDE TRUST, ASSESS AND TREAT

Trust—build and maintain therapeutic communication techniques to provide client support.

Convey Respect
Establishing trust and rapport with clients is vital **particularly with clients who exhibit anxiety or have been diagnosed with schizophrenia (paranoia) or bipolar disease.** This may be thwarted if the nurse

fails to treat clients with dignity and respect. Individuals admitted to inpatient psychiatric units are in crisis and at the lowest point in life. Addressing people honorably sends the message of value and worthiness. The goal is not to coddle or enable clients, but to arm them with methods to succeed in life on their own. This is accomplished by identifying effective coping skills that previously worked for clients and applying the same strategies to present situations. However, if clients are managed like children, i.e., nurses taking on parental roles, the clients will respond like children, not problem solvers. If clients are addressed condescendingly and no time is spent with them, how can they be expected to fulfill the role of well-functioning adults? First, and foremost, the psychiatric mental-health nurse must truly hold others in high esteem, otherwise trust, safety and effective communication is compromised and thus positive client outcomes altered. How can the client ever learn to feel good about him/herself if others fail to treat the person well?

Other important nursing responsibilities include:
- Assess psychosocial, spiritual, and occupational factors affecting care and plan interventions.
- Assess client in coping with life changes and provide support.
- Collaborate with health care members in other disciplines when providing client care.

Calm-Cool-Collected
"Be Calm, Be Cool, Be Collected, Be Collected Be the CCC"
In the 1970's when a high school ball game was heated and the players began making careless errors, the cheerleaders would lead the crowd to chant this idiom: "We don't care, what the people may say, cause we can beat the tigers (other team's mascot), any old day...be calm, be cool, be collected, be collected, be the CCC." The psychiatric mental health nurse must be CCC no matter the circumstance.

Have you ever been on a plane and hit turbulence? Serious turbulence? How do you know if you are safe? You watch the flight attendants' behaviors for cues of uneasiness but nothing is more comforting than the pilot's voice over the intercom calmly saying, "Well, ladies and gentlemen, we hit a few bumps, but just stay buckled in your seat belts and we will get you safely to your destination for an on time arrival." Can you imagine how passengers would respond if the pilot's voice was shaky and screamed, "We're going to crash!"? Chaos would erupt!

You, the professional nurse, are the pilot of your unit! If you are not in control of the unit, then no one is in control, just like if the pilot is not operating the plane then all passengers are in trouble! Inpatients must believe you can resolve unit issues or trust will be lost and unit safety negatively affected. Sometimes the nurse must use academy award winning skills to convey this calmness, but that is why psychiatric nurses wear dark pants rather than whites. When to be CCC: escalating behaviors, agitation, and manipulation. Manage conflict among clients and health care staff. Other concepts that begin with a C include **communication, community and consistency.**

Communication (Facilitative)
First Know Thyself

Role modeling communication is as critically important with staff as with clients because the clients are watching and imitating the nurses' behaviors. Utilizing facilitative communication requires ongoing self analysis, nursing staff analysis, and interdisciplinary team analysis of how effective or ineffective one or the group is at communicating messages and achieving the entire program's mission. Consistency is often violated by mere miscommunication that results in unit chaos. For example, one night a nurse allows clients to stay up and watch a movie past the set bedtime hour while another nurse enforces the rules as set by the interdisciplinary team, reminding clients that this is part of their contract and sends them to bed on time. Bedtime wars? Oh yes! Nursing staff will split in half over such issues. Arguments will persist for weeks and often months. Some staff will become so angry they resign—yes, over a bedtime! This is why it is so important that all staff follow the rules and not be taken in by pleading clients. Technology exists to record good movies and ballgames but it is not as easy to replace good staff; however, many of those who leave under such circumstances probably needed to resign because they did not comprehend the scope of the treatment plan for the clients.

Ineffective communication can be literally deadly. JCAHO 2004-2011 Root Cause Events cites insufficient communication as the third cause of death or permanent injury in all reported sentinel events and ranked it the number one cause of injury or death when related to delay in treatment. Communication errors ranked second in both suicides and restraint events. This is only voluntarily submitted data and fails to represent actual numbers.

Insufficient communication penetrates all nursing venues and one common problem that I have personally observed lead to death is irritability. So often in report I hear medical/surgical nurses explain how they ignored or distanced themselves from an irritable client because he/she was "difficult to deal with!" Irritability is a red flag symptom of many different complications that demands further assessment, not isolation. The problem? Communication! Nurses feel uncomfortable determining if the client's mood is normal versus unusual, fearing such questions will offend family members. It is important to advocate for client rights and needs. Ask family members out of the client's room and say, "I do not know your family (client) like you do and need your help. He seems irritable to me today. Is this normal behavior for him?" Sometimes the family will say, "Yes, he's feeling better. He's always irritable and picking on people!" This is good news, but more frequently the answer is, "No, this is very unlike him, I don't know what's wrong with him today." Unexpected irritability requires further investigation and can mean:
  ◆ Hypoxia
  ◆ Hypoglycemia
  ◆ Hyperkalemia
  ◆ Hepatoencephalopathy
  ◆ Increased Intracranial Pressure
  ◆ Escalating behavior toward agitation
  ◆ Substance abuse withdrawal
  ◆ Undesired effect of a medication
  ◆ Among other possibilities
The point? Ignoring irritable clients will create more serious complications. Irritability is a **RED FLAG** to focus on, not to ignore!

Ignoring uncomfortable situations can cause complications. Effective communication is often the critical bridge between life and death.

Another example: the lack of accurate ongoing mental status exams conducted in nursing practice may often be related to the nurses' fear of belittling clients by asking redundant questions. Most nurses assess orientation to person, place, and time at the beginning of each shift but consider the client responding to his/her name accurately as orientation to person. Unfortunately, some client complications go unrecognized due to the lack of these critical ongoing assessments. To prevent this problem, at the beginning of the shift, nurses need to express the rationale for asking the questions and explain how frequently the client will be assessed. Clients learn to expect the questions and sometimes with humor, spontaneously offer answers upon entry into the room, which verifies intact short-term memory.

Which is more uncomfortable as a nurse, communicating with the client and family even if it means asking hard questions, or finding the client unexpectedly dead?

Community (Therapeutic)

Nurses are responsible for maintaining a therapeutic environment on the inpatient unit and collaborating with health care members in other disciplines when providing care. Clients are admitted in life crises. The psychiatric unit is not an escape from reality nor stress free but invites less threatening problem solving opportunities to exercise coping skills utilized in the past that may be tried and applied to the current life-threatening situation. The nurse must first observe the client's individual negotiating abilities such as television programing, outgoing telephone times, etc., which may create interpersonal issues between clients and/or staff. Observation of such communication exchanges is invaluable in recognizing a clients' strengths and limitations regarding social skills and coping skills used. More important is the early recognition of escalation behaviors in clients at risk for agitation and physical violence so harm to others may be thwarted through intervention. Assess the potential for violence and use safety precautions. When nurses remain at the nurses' station and not a part of the client population throughout the entire shift, the likelihood of incident is increased. Remember to acknowledge and document any practice error that occurs.

"To err is human, to forgive divine." Alexander Pope

Staff are imperfect people. It is important to recognize limitation of self/others and seek assistance. Even nurses and doctors make mistakes; so capitalize on interpersonal faux pas that occur in the presence of clients to model how to deal with real life situations. One of two approaches works well. Either acknowledge to the client population during an interdisciplinary community group meeting that a public exchange was inappropriate and the involved staff apologize to one another in front of the entire group, or do the same but to only those who were part of the encounter soon after the event occurred. Demonstration of forgiveness is a way to role play effective communication by an n outward voicing of the situation and accountability, "I admit I did wrong and take responsibility for my own actions," as well as the release of guilt, "I regret my actions and now forgive myself and the other person for the action."

A second method is to stage an apology in front of the clients. This is a planned event following an inappropriate encounter. *One example occurred while working as faculty in an inpatient clinical setting. A nursing student was waiting in line on the unit for the locked staff restroom. Another student nurse jumped in front of her when the room became vacant. The student beat on the door and said, "I was first, you jumped line you idiot," not realizing that the first student had a female emergency. Of course the two apologized in private and there were no hard feelings, but the damage was done because the restroom was in front of the dayroom where all the clients watched the interaction. As their nursing faculty, I helped them plan an "apology encounter" to occur in front of the client population. The two students practiced a couple of times, went to the day room, and when the opportunity presented itself, apologized for the door scene to each other and laughed about it, without relaying too many details. The clients smiled afterwards.*

Later, the client assigned to the student left in the hallway said, "I was so mad at that girl who got in front of you...but then I saw you weren't mad and thought, 'Hmm..Why am I?' I saw you two laugh about a toilet and thought, 'a toilet is a silly thing to get mad about'...and I have laughed about it ever since!" Role modeling is a critical aspect of psychiatric nursing. **You** might be the most effective problem solver the client has ever experienced.

Consistency vs. Chaos

Consistent implementation of a unit's rules builds trust while erratic enforcement of the policies breeds confusion and loss of trust among people. For example, speeding on the interstate will result in a fined ticket from the highway patrol. Citizens detest speeding tickets but feel safe and secure on the roads knowing that reckless drivers will be punished and are only a cell phone three-digit number call away from notifying an officer who will come to aid if need be. If, however, officers working on Mondays and Fridays never issued speeding tickets, the interstates would be perhaps more fun to drive but certainly not as safe. People would be killed and/or permanently injured. Chaos would prevail on the roads. The same is true on a psychiatric unit. When unit rules are homogeneously applied, the client population learns to depend on and trust the staff. However, if a unit rule is enforced on one shift and not another, clients are left confused and uncertain about what are acceptable versus unacceptable behaviors. Clients, who utilize manipulation to problem solve, attempt to split nurses against each other even with a unified staff. This type of behavior is often exhibited by clients with borderline personality disorders or antisocial disorders. A lack of continuity in enforcing rules is like giving the manipulative client ammunition to puppet control the staff in order to distract which is the purposes of the milieu. It leaves all clients wondering who has control of the unit? Like who has the control of the interstate? If the nursing staff fails to maintain control of the unit, the clients will rightfully be terrified—*I would be*. Use precautions to prevent injury and/or complications associated with any diagnosis and collaborate with health care members in other disciplines when providing client care.

Consistency, confidentiality, and privacy starts on admission, if appropriate, by reviewing with each client the unit's rules and consequences for failure to comply. Be sure to maintain client confidentiality and privacy. The admission nurse and client sign and date the Unit Rules and Consequences document. The original is placed in the client's medical record and a copy given to the client. The first time a rule is broken, the nurse confronts the client in an adult-to-adult manner and reviews the written contract. Another signature of both the nurse and the client's is obtained on the original document and a second copy given to the client. This process is repeated with each offense so that the official written and oral message is clear for both professionals and the client. On the third, forth, and fifth offenses, the medical record makes confrontation a straightforward task for interdisciplinary team members to accomplish with the client.

Depression

The Center for Disease Control (CDC) cites that approximately 1 in 10 adults suffer from depression. **Assess problems early & intervene to prevent injuries**. Incorporate behavioral management techniques when caring for a client (e.g., setting limits, positive reinforcement). Initiate, evaluate, and update plan of care We learn so much from our clients by listening. It is one of the most important assets that we have as nurses.

Treat behaviors accurately

- **Harmful to self/others**—must assess on admission, at beginning of each shift, and p.r.n.—which means the nurse must be on the unit to watch for signs and symptoms of clients becoming agitated, depressed, or suicidal. Follow requirement for use of restraints and/or safety device (e.g., the least restrictive restraints, timed client monitoring).

- **Safe to self and others**—suicidal and/or homicidal ideation. Verbally assess on admission, beginning of each shift, and p.r.n.—as needed during shift based on client's behavior(s). Visual rounds every 10-15 minutes, intermittent checks. Recognize non-verbal cues to physical and/or psychological stressors.

- **Sad Affect** —many depressed clients do not feel like eating. Manage the client's nutritional intake (e.g., adjusting diet when necessary.)They may "take to their bed," withdraw from activities, or become unclean from the lack of bathing. Their face may look sad with their eyes downturned.

- **Resting Patterns and Response to Meds** is an important nursing intervention A plan may need to be determined so that the client's need for rest and sleep are provided.

- **Interactions**—initiates interactions vs. isolates from others

- **Self Care**—kempt vs. unkempt. Determine the ability of the client to perform everyday activities of daily living

---

Psychosis, Schizophrenia, and Bi-Polar Disorders

These clients exhibit the following symptoms:
- **Hallucinations**—alteration of a sense
  - Auditory: hearing voices
  - Visual: seeing things that are not present
  - Tactile: feeling something on the skin
  - Olfactory: smelling nonexistent aromas
  - Taste: taste that is not present in mouth
- **Delusions**—a thought that is not real or true.

Antipsychotic drugs treat these problems Note: these clients are most often having delusions and/or hallucinations that may cause them to kill themselves or someone else. These medications are very toxic, but their positive outcomes are direly needed. See Evaluate Pharmacology on page 411.

Substance Abuse

Substance abuse or the use of any substance that causes the mood to be altered is both harmful and expensive to the client, family, and the economy. There is a strong correlation to abuse and jail. Assess client for drug/alcohol dependencies, withdrawal, or toxicities and intervene as appropriate. Substance abuse leads to craving and addiction.

- **Tobacco**, a commonly abused substance, is linked with cancer. Over 70 million Americans smoke cigarettes and have severe complications of lung diseases such as emphysema. Nursing is responsible for providing information for prevention and treatment of high-risk heath behaviors such as smoking cessation and drug education. Education is a major component of treatment.

- **ETOH (alcohol)** is abused by more than 22 million people and is a leading cause of liver damage, esophageal varices, and death. Alcoholics Anonymous (AA) is one of the most effective organizations to help clients reduce alcohol use. Recognize the need for referrals and obtain necessary orders. Again, education is a major component of treatment. These clients may choose to drink rather than eat, leading to a severe nutritional deficiency in vitamins. Vitamin deficiency may cause lesions on nerves (painful extremities), fatigue, weakness, weight loss, or Wernicke-Korsakoff syndrome (psychosis) Family dynamics often play an important role in the treatment of the alcoholic. Assess family dynamics to determine plan of care (structure, communication, boundaries, coping mechanisms). Incorporate behavioral management techniques when caring for a client (setting limits). Sudden withdrawal from alcohol can be deadly. The first 24-72 hours are crucial. The client often is admitted to the health agency for an automobile accident or other emergent health issue and be unable to drink. They may exhibit signs of anxiety, irregular heartbeat, hallucinations, or "pill rolling" leading to seizures.

  - **Lorazepam (Ativan)** is a common drug administered to these clients and is often the choice for ETOH detoxification. This is a powerful drug and often causes drowsiness, dizziness (protect the client from injuries/falls), blurred vision, shuffling walk, and/or a persistent fine tremor. Recognize signs and symptoms of complications and intervene appropriately when providing care.

  - If the Ativan is ineffective and it is too late, give **Magnesium Sulfate**!
    An easy way to remember signs and symptoms of magnesium sulfate toxicity can be found in this song sung to the tune of *Achy Breaky Heart*.

Magnesium Sulfate

Darlene Franklin
Lyrics©
Tune to "Achy Breaky Heart"

Decreased BP, decreased pee pee,
These are toxic signs of Mag Sulfate.

Drop in respiratory rate, patellar reflex one there ain't,
Give the antidote Calcium Gluconate

- **Disulfiram (Antabuse)** is a drug that may be offered to the client who wishes to stop drinking. They must be educated regarding the violent nausea and vomiting that occurs if they drink anything with alcohol, including cough medicines, shaving lotions, or using any substance on their skin that contains alcohol.

- **Prescription drugs**, especially pain medications, are often abused by taking a friend's or a relative's painkiller not only for pain, but to get high. Clients who abuse these types of drugs, often crush the pill or capsule and "sniff it" or turn it into liquid and inject it. Withdrawal from many of these drugs includes nausea, vomiting, diarrhea, chills, and muscle pain.

Eating Disorders (Anorexia, Bulimia, Pica)

Anorexia and **bulimia** are the most common, examples of eating disorders often caused by anxiety and a feeling of loss of control. The acronym **WAKES** will help in remembering the intervention concepts for eating disorders. Always wake the patient to weigh or they will drink copious amounts of water to alter their weight.

- **W**eigh different times, in client gown only and **W**atch them eat for only 30 minutes. They have ingenious ways to hide food. Vaginal packing gains a whole new meaning for these clients.
- **A**lways make the client void first
- **K** (potassium—fluid & electrolyte imbalance may be life threatening)
- **E**valuate outcomes; weight gain—the client obtains privileges based on weight gain. Monitor the client's weight.
- **S**cales—use the same balanced scale each day and turn client's back to the scale.

Pica is a disorder of eating nonfood substances such as Argo starch, hair, dirt, detergent, and copious amounts of ice. Assess for Argo starch in the environment, note broken hair, and ask client if they are eating these items. Nursing goal is to minimize eating these nonfood items and maintain good nutrition.

Anxiety may be caused from such disorders as:

- **Obsessive compulsive disorder (OCD)** characterized by irrational thoughts and fears leading to compulsive repetitive behaviors
- **Post traumatic stress disorder (PTSD)** triggered by a terrifying event causing severe anxiety and uncontrollable thoughts about a past event.
- **Generalized anxiety disorder (GAD)** Excessive uncontrolled anxiety and worry lasting more than 6 months
- **Panic disorder**—a period of severe fear
- **Social phobia** (agoraphobia-—fear of leaving home)
- **Sleep deprivation**—nursing intervention calls for **cool, calm and collected** behavior, as well as **communication, community and consistency.**

EVALUATE PHARMACOLOGY

When administering medication we must be CAREFUL!
Medication Administration Alert

C	**Calculate correctly**
A	**Assess for allergies**
R	**Rights of administration**
E	**Evaluate response**
F	**Feel free to call provider if intuition alerts**
U	**Utilize assessments in determining ordered parameters**
L	**Lab data pertinence**

Anxiety Drugs

Drug	Prior to Administration	Alerts
Anxiety/Escalating Behavior Medication ■ Lorazepam (Ativan) ■ Diazepam (Valium) ■ Alprazolam (Xanax) ■ Clonazepam (Klonopin) ■ Chlordiazepoxide (Librium) ■ Oxazepam (Serax) ■ Hydroxyaine (Atarax) ■ Buspirone (BuSpar)	Determine allergies Determine if the medication should be administered with food Determine lab values, especially liver function Document client behavior prior to administration	May be addictive. Should be administered under controlled substances guidelines Do not stop without provider notification May cause withdrawal symptoms May have an antihistamine effect of dry mouth Avoid alcohol Watch for drowsiness Avoid driving until effect is known May Take 2-3 weeks before the client feels the effect

Anxiety drugs are often controlled substances and should be administered within regulatory guidelines.

➢ **Fast acting.**
  ♦ **Benzodiazepine drugs** such as lorazepam (Ativan), diazepam (Valium), alprazolam (Xanax), clonazepam (Klonopin), and chlordiazepoxide (Librium). Addictive but drug of choice when client is escalating abnormal behavior and verbal and exercise techniques become ineffective.

An easy way to remember these drugs is this song, which is sung to the tune of *Spiderman:*

Anti-Anxiety Medications

Darlene Franklin, RN MSN
Lyrics ©
To the tune "Spiderman"

Ativan, Ativan, does whatever a Valium can.
CNS gets depressed
Alcohol can cause arrest
Driving banned.
          That's it for Ativan.

Serax, Atarax, Xanax
Puts anxiety on the nix.
But when taken long term
Withdrawal causes nerves to squirm
That's the facts—
          Serax, Atarax, Xanax.

+ **Benadryl** is an antihistamine that decreases anxiety. Use caution in the elderly as it may cause depression, excitement, visual disturbances, dry mouth, urinary retention, constipation, and decreased cognitive function.
+ **Beta Blockers**: propanalol (Inderal), atenolol (Tenormin) may be administered to prevent panic attacks—one before a test to think your very best. Lowers heart rate, thus no tachypnea.

➤ **Long acting antianxiety/antidepressants** used for antianxiety take 2-3 weeks to be effective
  + **Non-Benzodiazepine drugs** such as buspirone (BuSpar) has a calming effect. Administer with food, do not drive heavy equipment until body has adjustment time.
  + **Anti-Depressants**
    ▪ Selective Serotonin Reuptake Inhibitor (SSRI) often utilized for adolescents for anxiety and depression. **Watch for suicide**
       • Citalopram(Celexa)
       • Escitalopram (Lexapro)
       • Paroxetine (Paxil)
       • Fluoxetine (Prozac)
       • Sertraline (Zoloft)
  + **Beta Blockers** often used for panic attacks
    ▪ Propranolol (Inderal)

Drugs for Depression

Drugs	Prior to Administration	Alerts
Selective Seratonin Reuptake Inhibitors (SSRI) • Citalopram (Celexa) • Escitalopram (Lexapro) • Paroxetine (Paxil) • Fluoxetine (Prozac) • Sertraline (Zoloft)	Often used for adolescents Notify provider if the client is taking blood thinners. May increase bleeding tendencies in clients taking Coumadin Determine allergies Contraindicated in clients taking MAOI	Suicide risk in children and adlescents Nausea Dry mouth Agitation Weight gain Rash Drowsiness or insomnia Sexual dysfunction Withdrawal syndrome May take 2-3 weeks before the client feels the effect Bleeding tendencies May increase toxicity with Dilantin, Clozaril, beta blockers
Selective Serotonin Norepinephrine Reuptake Inhibitor (SSNRI) • Duloxetine (Cymbalta) • Venlafaxine (Effexor)	Determine allergies Blood pressure	Hypotension Hypertension Sexual dysfunction Drowsiness
• Bupropion (Wellbutrin, Zyban)	Determine seizure disorder May be administered to help clients stop smoking	May cause seizure Alcohol increases seizure risk Suicide alert

Drugs	Prior to Administration	Alerts
	Notify provider if client is taking MAOI within the last 2-3 weeks Contraindicated in conjunction together (Wellbutrin and Zyban)	Extended release capsule may show up in stool. Does not mean the medication has been ineffective Driving alert
Monoamine Oxidase Inhibitors (MAOIs) ■ Isocarboxazid (Marplan) ■ Phenelzine (Naradil) ■ Tranylcypromine (Parnate)	Determine allergies Document symptoms such as panic attacks, agoraphobia	Reacts with aged foods that contain tyramine such as aged cheese, wine, soy sauce, raisins, prunes Reacts with many over-the-counter cold preparations Administration with Demerol may cause hypertensive crisis Withdrawal syndrome Depression Weight gain
Tricyclic Antidepressants ■ Amitriptyline (Elavil) ■ Nortriptyline (Pamelor) ■ Protriptyline (Vivactil) ■ Doxepin (Sinequan) ■ Desipramine (Norpramin)	Determine baseline vital signs Determine baseline bowel sounds Document client behavior such as obsessive compulsive disorder, panic, bulimia, migraine, phantom limb pain Notify provider if client is taking cimetidine, other antipsychotic drugs, or calcium channel blockers	Hypotension Anticholenergic effects of dry mouth Sedation Syncope Disorientation Altered mental status Sensitivity to sun Seizures Weight gain Cardio-toxicity Withdrawal syndrome

An easy way to remember these drugs is to learn this song sung to the tune of *Zippity-Do-Dah.*

Antidepressants

Darlene Franklin, RN MSN
Lyrics ©
To the tune: "Zippity Doo Dah"

Chorus
        Antidepressants brings smiles—replace sighs
                SSRIs and Tricyclics these are two types
        If these do not work MAOs may be tried
                But take measures so that the client won't die.

        Celexa, Prozac, Paxil, Zoloft.
                No antacids for GI upset.
        Or absorption you will forfeit
                These are the meds we call SSRIs
                Assess response and signs of suicide.

Chorus

        Tricylclic meds Ela-vil, Tofranil
                Pamelor, Norpramine, Sin-e-quan, Vi-vac-til
        Hold MAOs so the BP won't swell
                No Ci-me-ti-dine or Syn-throid as well.

Chorus

        MAOs Par-nate, Mar-plan, and Nardil.
                Mixed with certain drugs and foods can the client kill.
        Teach and assess before giving the pill.
                Less complications will decrease health bills

        Never mix with Ci-me-ti-dine
                Or with the pain med Me-per-dine
        Or death and lawsuit might be seen.
                Antidepressants brings smiles replace sighs.
                But take measures so that the client won't die.

Antipsychotic Drugs

Drugs	Action	Alerts
Risperdone (Risperdal) Olanzapine (Xyprexa)	Decreased psychotic behavior	Extrapyramidal effects (pill rolling, tremors, shuffle gate, thick tongue)
Quetiapine (Seroquel)	Decreased psychotic behavior	Contraindicated in dementia, may cause death Weight gain, elevated blood sugar/diabetes Increased cholesterol Extrapyramidal effects
Clozapine (Clozaril)	Decreased symptoms of schizophrenia	Risk of suicide Agranulocytosis (watch white cell count) Hypotension Risk of seizures
Ziprasidone (Geodon)	Decreased symptoms of schizophrenia and mania in bipolar disorders	Contraindicated in dementia, heart failure Fainting If taken with many drugs (e.g., Biaxin, erythromycin, Cordarone, Zofran) may cause death producing arrhythmias
Clozapine (Clozaril)	Changes in brain chemicals Reduces suicidal behavior in clients with schizophrenia or other psychotic disorders	Contraindicated in dementia, epilepsy, bone marrow disorder Prednisone must be evaluated
Haloperidol (Haldol)	Decreases elderly behavioral problems	Extrapyramidal effects Pneumonia, CHF
Chlorpromazine (Thorazine)	Decreases symptoms of schizophrenia and bipolar disorders	Extrapyramidal effects Contraindicated in dementia Caution in hypertension

Drugs	Action	Alerts
		Glaucoma, hypocalcemia, seizures, Parkinson's
Lithium (Eskalith, Lithabid)	Effective for bipolar disorders	Dependent on sodium balance. Avoid activity that causes sweating. Therapeutic blood levels required. Normal less than 2meq/L
Lamotrigine (Lamictal)	Anti-epileptic currently used as mood stabilizer especially in bipolar disorders	Kidney or liver disease, fever, sore throat, rash, suicidal ideation Allergy to seizure meds
Benztropine (Cogentin)	Controls movement from anti-psychotic drugs	Confusion, eye pain, skin rash

Non-Prescription Drugs

Drug	Action	Alerts
Herbs are alternative remedies for depression. Their flowers and leaves are used to make the medication. **St. John's Wort**	Notify provider if client is taking blood thinners. May decrease clotting time Notify provider if client is taking antianxiety prescription drugs Determine liver enzyme level Effective for mild to moderate depression, OCD, smoking cessation May take up to 6 weeks to be effective	Alcohol exaggerates sedation Driver precaution Rash Should not be administered with any other anti-depressant medication Contraindicated in pregnancy. May decrease the effectiveness of birth control pills May cause significant sunburn Topical remedies may not be safe When taken with digoxin (Lanoxin), may cause arrhythmias May prolong the effects of narcotics Do not administer with Demerol

Drug	Action	Alerts
KavaKava, a Greek word for intoxicating. Found to have a calming effect. Reported to prevent convulsions and relax muscles. Promotes sleep.	Notify provider if client is taking blood thinners. May decrease clotting time Notify provider if client is taking anti-anxiety prescription drugs Determine liver enzyme level	Alcohol exaggerates sedation Driver precaution Rash Should not be administered with any other anti-depressant medication Contraindicated in pregnancy. May decrease the effectiveness of birth control pills Possible liver damage Should not be administered to children May prolong anesthesia effects May increase effects of Dilantin Do not administer with Thorazine

TRY INFECTION CONTROL by applying principles of hand hygiene.

- ◆ **Admission assessment for all clients**
  - • Many clients are unable to care for their own daily medical needs. Assess for communicable disease—pediculosis, fungi, etc.
  - • Assess for body scars, cuts, and scabs.
  - • Assess bedridden clients for decubitus
- ◆ **Clients with paranoia** are afraid of eating or drinking anything. Use sealed meds and feeds for these clients.
- ◆ **Clients with Bi-Polar disorder**—eat on the run, infection control with hand hygiene
- ◆ **Self-mutilating clients** have scabs and wounds that become infected. Utilize wound care with sterile dressing change.

YOUR ASSETS AND YOUR MANAGEMENT

What is the management in psycho- social nursing as it is tested on *NCLEX®*?

It is defined by the NCSBN® as "performing and directing activities that manage client cares such as: client rights, confidentiality, information security, establishing priorities, ethical practice, legal rights and responsibilities, collaboration with interdisciplinary team, client advocacy, quality improvement, referrals, resource management, informed consent, staff education and supervision".

THIS TRANSLATES TO THE FOLLOWING:

	PASS *NCLEX®*!
M	**Make sure of identity, accuracy of orders**
A	**Arrange privacy/confidentiality/consent/collaboration with other team**
N	**No injuries, falls, malfunctioning equipment or staff or hazards**
A	**Address errors, abuse, legalities, scope of practice—document**
G	**Give (delegate) orders to appropriate people**
E	**Establish priorities of clients and time**

► Ensure proper identification of client when providing care. Clients with delusional behaviors may tell you their name is Jesus Christ or Elvis Presley. If you do not know the client, it is imperative to obtain 2 sources of identification.

► People are often curious about psychiatric clients and may ask inappropriate questions concerning them. The client's confidentiality must be secured. Telephone calls on inpatient units may be problematic as clients may be called. If the nurse confirms that the client is on the unit, the nurse has breeched confidentiality.

► Legal consents must be available on the chart. It is preferable that clients sign themselves into the unit but if they refuse to seek treatment, a court order may be needed. The psychiatric clients often cannot legally sign the consents so family members or officers of the court arrange appropriate signatures. Involuntary Commitments—state laws are different regarding involuntary commitments! Be sure that you know what is legal in your state.

► Prevention of injury is important on a psychiatric inpatient unit as restraints may be needed as a last resort to prevent the client from harming themselves or others. If restraints become necessary, documentation by the nurse indicating communication with the provider regarding the required need is vital. Without proper documentation the professional staff may be charged with assault and battery.

▶ Standards of Practice are set that protect the client and are evident in this YouTube: *Policies Regarding Restraints Reflect Standards of Practice*. *APNA Standard of Practice*: http://www.apna.org/i4a/pages/index.cfm?pageid=3730

▶ Refuse Treatment—Pushing medications with the client who is paranoid may be considered "not refusing treatment." These clients are fearful/paranoid of being poisoned. The nurse must gain trust in order for this client to be compliant with treatment.

▶ Without the antipsychotic medication, the client will not improve. It is critical to do the following:
  ▪ Assign the same nurse to allow consistency and establish trust to administer meds each shift
  ▪ Provide medications and food in sealed containers to decrease paranoia
  ▪ Allow time for client to examine sealed medication and sealed fluids prior to taking meds.

Each of us experience situations where we are ignored or treated as "low lifes," but psychiatric units should be the most accepting places on the planet. We should assign no negative labels of any type. A sign of a burned out psychiatric nurse is when he or she brands all clients as "personality disordered" or as "unreliable." It is impossible for every inpatient to be "unreliable," but perhaps the nurse's perception is unreliable?

Objectively documenting specific behaviors the client actually exhibits is a required responsibility of the nurse especially to support or disclaim specific DSM IV-TR diagnoses. But nurses who suspect all clients to be liars and manipulators need to conduct self-reflection exercises to identify if personal, unaddressed, emotional issues exist and/or if burnout is occurring. A change in practice venue may be indicated. Nursing is not the best career choice for those who do not value and respect all peoples, but certainly not mental health nursing. Mental health clients seek psychiatric services as a desperate resort for help, not to be further damaged. Recognize ethical dilemmas and take appropriate action.

Why do people select nursing as a profession especially psychiatric nursing? I have asked this question of nursing students and graduates in my almost thirty years in nursing education and receive a similar answer every time—to give back to others—that is, generativity. Nurses are Erik Erikson's prodigies of generativity. Rarely does a person enter nursing education to make money; in fact, this is a humorous thought. Nurses choose to care for clients because they care about people. Why does this section end with this sentiment? Because the psycho-social-emotional aspect of nursing care makes the difference in a client and their family's perception of the healthcare experience. So often well meaning nurses fail to communicate critical aspects of care that would clarify the family's concern. A good example is baths. Families often judge nursing care based on the following being addressed in a timely manner: pain, complications, and daily baths. Nurses sometimes share the rationale for withholding a bath; however families view such an omission as a lack of attention and care when actually the problem is ineffective communication. Clients experiencing respiratory distress should not be bathed—this is how to include the family in the decision.

Nurse (in front of client to family member): "*Have you noticed your mom's O$_2$ sats have continued to drop today and she has required more and more oxygen to breathe?*"

Family member: "*Yes, I have.*"

Nurse: *"I'm concerned that if we give her a bath it will wear her out—use up her energy that she needs to breathe.* (pause) *What do you think?"*

Family member: *"Oh, let's don't give her a bath."*

Nurse: *"I agree with you. We'll let her use her energy to breathe. I will wash her face and hands just to help her feel refreshed but nothing more. If she is much better this afternoon, meaning her O$_2$ sats are up, she needs less oxygen and she has more energy, we might give her a quick bath just cleaning the most important areas, but for now, I agree she needs her energy to breathe."*

Such an interaction is family centered care and takes less than 30-45 seconds of time. Document that the family was consulted and recommended the bath be deferred. If you want to be reassured this yields positive outcomes, stand outside the door and listen after the interaction. Typically the conversation goes like this, *"That's the best nurse we've ever had...she's not going to give you a bath because it might cause you to stop breathing."* The nurse did not actually say this but truly this is a fear, but the point was absorbed, the family involved, and you are the best nurse because you included them in the decision.

Death and After-Death Care

One of my favorite roles in nursing is working with the dying client and their family. Why? Birth and death are the most intimate experiences of life. Most people consider birth as positive and death as a negative occurrence; however, as a nurse, both are opportunities to assist clients' and families through maturational crises—especially death.

The word death typically yields a fearful response from most individuals—"the end of life," "pain and suffering." Nurses can often make death experiences peaceful and sweet memories for loved ones or the opposite. An important issue for the nurse caring for the dying is to determine any advance directives that the client may have and the family's clear understanding of these directives. Advance directives should be a part of client care.

There are several critical needs of the dying client and family.

- Assess family dynamics to determine plan of care.
- A higher calling for nurses may be to help the client in their transition or **pass** to the next life. Assess client in coping with life changes and provide support to both client and family.
- Pain—assess and address. Hospice care, working with the primary health care providers, most often can titrate medication to comfortable levels for the client.
- Avoidance of client and family is contraindicated
- Spiritual and cultural preferences—

Acknowledge your own spiritual needs and use them appropriately. I am Christian. When a client with the same spiritual beliefs as mine is dying, I assess the family and their beliefs and determine if their beliefs are similar. If so, I use those similarities to hopefully provide an illuminating experience for the family. For example, I ask the family if they believe the spirit separates from the body? If they say, "Yes" then I tell them that I do too and that I have no idea exactly when this occurs but as a nurse, I feel this is the most intimate of times in my practice and that if alone with a client I lay my hand on the client's heart until he or she is gone— knowing the spirit is passing through to heaven at some point. I ask if this is something that the family might want to do. Typically I get an overwhelming, "YES" and, after the death, hear these words, "I wouldn't trade that experience for anything in this world—it was beautiful—thank you!" This is the spiritual aspect of nursing. Remember, when the client is gone, the family remains.

Death and After Death Care

Rituals and Beliefs of Various Religions It is a nursing responsibility to provide end of life care and education to clients. Perform post-mortem care.

- **Buddhism**
  - Allow client peace and quiet during dying process to meditate. No other critical customs.
- **Catholicism—**
  - Dying newborn—most critical to call priest in to baptize infant to save the baby's soul. If no time, a Catholic in good faith or a nurse may perform the baptism.
  - Dying other—Last rites performed by a priest is ideal. The family, if available, is an excellent resource. Many hospital agencies have chaplains or social service departments with appropriate guidelines.
- **Christianity**
  - Some Baptists/Church of Christ—if a client requests to be baptized even if dying, immersion baptism is performed.
- **Hinduism**
  - Contact Hindu priest to perform last rites.
  - Post-mortem care provided by family
  - Do not remove jewelry and religious objects
- **Judaism**
  - May request Rabbi for confession
  - When death is imminent need to be with Jewish others
  - No post-mortem care
  - Cover with white sheet—handle body as little as possible post-mortem.
- **Islam**
  - Do not perform post-mortem care. The Muslim religion believes that if anyone other than a Muslim touches the client after death, the spirit is inhibited. This religion requires that after death a male provide care if the client is a man. Leave body alone for family to perform rituals.
  - Buried within 24 hours.
- **Sikhism**
  - Family may want to be reciting "Waheguru" (Wonderful Lord) while dying—private room may be appropriate.
  - Family may prefer to perform post-mortem care
  - Never trim or cut beard or hair from body

Seek family's needs.
Include family in the hospice/nursing care of their loved one. Often family members are afraid of the physiological changes the client may exhibit during the dying process. Anticipatory guidance is critical. Describe possible scenarios for the family so they are prepared. Incorporate client cultural practices and beliefs when planning and providing care.

Lawsuits have been filed because a client's body has not been treated with respect or in accord with the appropriate religious guidelines. Being innocent of these practices is no excuse under the law. It is a nursing responsibility to be knowledgeable regarding these issues. It is vital to provide care within the legal scope of practice.

1. A client is admitted with demand auditory hallucinations and paranoid ideation. Which nursing interventions are important? **Select all that apply**
    A. Assess the client's concept of the content of the hallucinations to determine safety risk each shift and p.r.n.
    B. Assign the same nursing staff each shift.
    C. Keep medications, foods, and drinks sealed for client to open.
    D. Explain to client, "The voices are not real. I don't hear them."
    E. Assign one-to-one staff/client ratio.

2. After a two-week vacation, the psychiatric inpatient charge nurse returns and is working at the desk. A client approaches and says, "I think I'm gonna hurt somebody!" Select the best action by the nurse.
    A. Take a step back, make eye contact with the client and say, "Not on my unit. Hello, I'm the charge nurse, I don't believe we've met."
    B. "You think you're gonna hurt somebody? When did you start thinking this?"
    C. "Have you talked to your doctor about these thoughts?"
    D. "Sit down where I can watch you and, as soon as I take off these orders, we will talk."

3. On admission to the ER, the client begins beating his head on the floor screaming, "Get the devil out of me." Blood is gushing from a deep laceration to the scalp. The client fails to respond to verbal commands. The best response by the nurse is:
    A. Obtain a stat order for an IM antipsychotic to calm the client.
    B. Restrain client with 4-point leather restraints.
    C. Call a Psychiatric code.
    D. Start an IV stat for medication administration.

4. A psychiatric client's vital signs are B/P 107/64, HR 88, RR 20, Temp. 101.1 F. Which nursing actions are indicated? **Select all that apply.**
    A. Place client in isolation until infection identified.
    B. Assess for enlarged lymph nodes
    C. Ask client if throat is sore.
    D. Contact healthcare provider for blood cultures.
    E. Hold risperdone (Risperdal) and contact healthcare provider.

5. A 24- hour post-op client is reassessed 30 minutes after administering pain medication. His pain is reduced to a 2 (0-10 scale), but vital signs are increasing—BP 146/88, HR 92, RR 22, T 99.2. Two hours later he says, "I think there are bedbugs in this bed." Which is the best action of the nurse?
    A. Check the bed for bedbugs, especially in the seams of the mattress.
    B. Ask the client, "When was the last time you had a drink of alcohol?"
    C. Reassess the client for pain and vital signs.
    D. Contact the healthcare provider for an increase in pain medication.

6. Which nursing actions are important to prepare the client for Electroconvulsive Therapy? **Select all that apply**
    A. Obtain Informed Consent from client to perform ECT for schizophrenia diagnosis.
    B. Ascertain updated crash cart at site of ECT procedure.
    C. Ensure at least one, preferably two intact 18 gauge IVs NS.
    D. Defibrillator at bedside.
    E. Antipsychotic medication withheld prior to ECT.

7. Which nursing action by the LPN/LVN indicates a need for further teaching when caring for a manic client with paranoia?
    A. Ensures the client receives a well-balanced diet on her plate.
    B. Assists the client to dress appropriately for group.
    C. Removes the client from over stimulating activities.
    D. Documents the client's inappropriate interactions.

8. A client is admitted with a major mood disorder and a co-existing diagnosis of hypothyroidism. An order is written for amitriptyline (Elavil). What is the priority nursing action?
    A. Determine if the client has any drug allergies before administering medication.
    B. Question the order.
    C. Assess the client for orthostatic hypotension.
    D. Teach client about the possibility of weight gain with this drug.

9. Which of the following statements made by the new RN teaching a client about lithium (Eskalith or Lithobid) indicates a need for further nursing education? **Select all that apply.**
    A. "Be consistent with sodium intake."
    B. "Be cautious with your fluid intake."
    C. "Maintain a thorough exercise plan to stay in shape."
    D. "Take this medication every day."
    E. "Return to the provider for blood levels."

10. A delusional client comes to the nurses' station complaining that his tongue feels thick and heavy. What action by the nurse is indicated?
    A. Contact the healthcare provider for further orders.
    B. Administer benztropine (Cogentin) according to orders from protocol.
    C. Assess vital signs.
    D. Administer diphenhydramine (Benadryl) according to orders from protocol.

11. In the morning, a client taking protriptyline (Vivactil) says, "I'm so tired and my mouth is so dry, may I go to my room and sleep?" The best response by the nurse is:
    A. "Your medication causes these side effects. Yes, go get some water and some rest."
    B. "Remember your agreement when you were admitted. Go get some water, and go to group."
    C. "No, everyone must attend group."
    D. "I can see you are tired. How long have you felt this way?"

12. A client is admitted for an eating disorder. **Select all that apply**
    A. Weigh client with back to scales at the same time daily.
    B. Allow only 30 minutes to eat meals while being observed during mealtime.
    C. Assign room with other eating disordered client.
    D. Have client empty bladder before weighing.
    E. Weigh in client gown.

13. A violent client is in four point leather restraints. **Select all that apply.**
    A. Assess vital signs hourly and p.r.n.
    B. Assess for compartmental syndrome distal to each restraint every hour and p.r.n.
    C. Document incident leading to restraint use, other methods attempted, and ongoing client response.
    D. Ideally provide 1:1 visual to ensure adequate ventilation and safety.
    E. Offer fluids and toileting every 4 hours and p.r.n.

14. The nurse notices that a depressed client's affect and mood are considerably improved and the client states, "I'm feeling so much better." Which of the following assessments is most critical?
    A. "Why is there an end in sight? Are you thinking of harming yourself?"
    B. "It sounds like your antidepressant is starting to work."
    C. "What do you think is the reason?"
    D. " I'm so glad you found some hope!"

15. A client with a dual diagnosis of major depression and alcoholism is suddenly disoriented to place and time. Which actions by the nurse are indicated? **Select all that apply.**
    A. Contact the healthcare provider for an ammonia level.
    B. Palpate liver to determine if enlarged
    C. Assess orders to determine if client is receiving Thiamin and B Complexes.
    D. Hold amitriptyline (Elavil) order and contact healthcare provider.
    E. Contact psychologist for further testing and evaluation.

16. A new RN needs to conduct a body search for sharps on a new client admitted for suicidal ideation. Which of the following techniques would best preserve the client's dignity and provide thorough outcomes?
    A. Explain to the client that this search head to toe procedure is used on every client to determine if he/she is hiding sharp objects that they may use to hurt themselves or others.
    B. Do not explain the procedure; it is too overwhelming at this point. Simply search the client for objects.
    C. Ask the client to undress and put on a patient gown so that an assessment may be completed to ensure his safety and physical well being.
    D. Ask the client to turn over any sharps to staff that may be on his/her person. A body search is needless—it is too demeaning.

17. An inpatient is found to be washing her hands 50-60 times/day. Which of the following nursing actions is most appropriate?
    A. Replace hand-washing ritual with hand sanitizer.
    B. Redirect the client to other activities when the urge to cleanse hands occurs.
    C. Assess client following the hand-washing ritual.
    D. Require client to stop ritual due to risk for alteration in skin integrity.

18. During the morning assessment, an adolescent client with a head injury yells at the nurse saying, "Leave me alone…let me sleep." What is the priority nursing action?
    A. Allow client to rest.
    B. This is an expected developmental outcome for this client who is attempting to gain control.
    C. Complete Glasgow Coma Scale assessment stat.
    D. Ask the family if this is typical behavior for this client.

19. A psychiatric inpatient says, "You're the only person I can trust, the only one who listens to me. If I tell you something, do you promise not to tell anyone else?" The best response by the nurse is:
    A. "This is a manipulative ploy. No, I will not make that promise."
    B. "Thank you. Yes, I promise not to tell anyone."
    C. "Anything you say to me will only be shared with your healthcare provider, staff caring for you, and documented in your chart."
    D. "I appreciate and honor your trust. Tell me more about what concerns you."

20. A client with Intermittent Explosive Disorder [IED] is in group therapy. Place in correct order the nursing interventions to prevent injury to others.
    A. Nurse asks client, "What are you experiencing physically at this moment?"
    B. Nurse explains to client to flee anxiety- producing situations.
    C. Nurse gives client a prearranged non-verbal cue to leave the group session.
    D. Nurse assesses clenched jaw and slight rocking behavior.

21. During lunch, a psychiatric inpatient loudly shouts obscenities at an LPN who responds saying, "If you continue to talk like that, you will end up in restraints." What is the legal responsibility of the charge nurse?
    A. Remove the client from the dining room and begin de-escalation techniques.
    B. Explain to the LPN/LVN that this behavior is inappropriate and the client must be more self-aware in the future.
    C. Privately, review the definition of assault with the LPN/LVN.
    D. Take privileges away from client for using obscenities.

22. A young adult, exhibiting manic behaviors, is admitted with R/O bipolar disorder. Which of the following actions is indicated first before administering the lithium?
    A. Teach about lithium toxicity.
    B. Check for two client identifiers.
    C. Ascertain T3 and T4 have been obtained.
    D. Teach about steady sodium intake.

23. A newly admitted psychiatric inpatient refuses to agree to a verbal no harm to self or others contract saying, "I just want to end it all. You can't stop me." When asked about a plan, the client states, "You've taken away my gun and pills. I'll find some other way." What action by the nurse is priority?
    A. Assign a private room closest to the nurses' station.
    B. Place on 1:1 observation with a certified nurse assistant.
    C. Continue to attempt to obtain a verbal no harm to self and/or others agreement.
    D. Document the client's comments.

24. Attempts to de-escalate a psychotic client are unsuccessful. Which medication should be questioned if ordered to reduce the client's current anxiety?
    A. Lorazepam (Ativan)
    B. Chlordiazepoxide (Librium)
    C. Buspirone (Buspar)
    D. Diazepam (Valium)

25. Which of the following clients are at highest risk of violence to self and/or others?
    A. Newly admitted paranoid schizophrenic with command auditory hallucinations.
    B. Client with Intermittent Explosive Disorder admitted two days ago.
    C. Bipolar client in manic phase who thinks she is a butterfly, flapping arms around unit and perching on furniture.
    D. Young adult female admitted from the medical/surgical unit today with an eating disorder.

26. An inpatient with a diagnosis of major depression and alcoholism returns from a day pass at 4 p.m. At 9 p.m. the nurse notices the client's speech to be more slurred, gait staggered, and sclera reddened. What is the highest priority nursing action?
    A. Confront the client regarding his appearance and behaviors and ask if he's been drinking today.
    B. Confiscate the source from the client.
    C. Set limits with the client regarding his breech of unit rules and remove privileges.
    D. Contact healthcare provider for blood alcohol level.

Answers and Rationale

1. Answers B and C. Assign the same nursing staff to assist in developing trust with the paranoid client. Keep medications, foods, and drinks sealed so paranoid client feels less likely he/she is being poisoned. Expect the first few medication administration attempts to take extra time—20-45 minutes. Answer A, document content of voice command hallucinations on admission. Assess the client each shift and p.r.n., i.e., when noting client appears to be hearing voices, by asking if the voices are saying the same things/content. If so, do not ask client to repeat—this only reinforces the hallucination; however, if the voices are saying something different, the nurse must determine the content to assess safety risk. Examples, if client says voices are now telling him to harm his/her roommate, then action to move roommate would be indicated. Answer D, when a client asks the nurse, "Don't you hear the voices?" the best response is, "I don't hear the voices, but I believe you do." Do not destroy trust by disagreeing with the client. These clients **are** hearing voices; that is why they need antipsychotic medication. Answer E, there is no indication in the question that the client is demonstrating immediate harm to self or others.

2. Answer A. Clients become afraid, when a new nurse is on the unit, that the staff is not in control. It is important to ensure the clients that the nurse is competent and in control; otherwise chaos will erupt. Follow this statement with the following, "I'm the charge nurse and take my job seriously. I won't let you hurt anyone or anyone else hurt you. Do you have a plan?" Answer B, when the thinking started is not as critical as asking the client if he has a plan and if so, what the plan is. Answers C and D. Both of these answers avoid the current situation, which could be lethal, and needs limits set, trust built, and further investigation.

3. Answer C. It is unknown if the client is on drugs or psychotic from mental illness. For the safety of both the client and staff the best option is Answer C, obtaining help from a group trained to safely take the client down and then place him in restraints for his own well being. All other answers put the staff at risk for injury. Answer B will follow Answer C but remember healthcare provider orders must be obtained.

4. Answers B, C, and E. Agranulocytosis is associated with antipsychotic medications and includes symptoms such as fever, sore throat, and swollen lymph nodes. Hold the antipsychotic medication and contact the provider for Complete Blood Count (CBC) to rule/out.

5. Answer B. Clients, who exhibit signs and symptoms of alcohol withdrawal including increased heart rate, change in level of consciousness, sweating, and especially the tactile hallucination of bugs crawling on the skin, must be treated for withdrawal. The first 12-24 up to 72 hours post alcohol intake is the highest risk for delirium tremens. Vital signs should be taken; however, need for pain assessment is not applicable.
http://www.ncbi.nlm.nih.gov/pubmedhealth/PMH0001771/

6. Answers B, C, and D. ECT is used to treat severe depression that is unresponsive to multiple antidepressant medication attempts. ECT is **not** used to treat schizophrenia.

7. **Answer A**. Paranoid clients need food in sealed containers especially bipolar clients who take little if any time to wash hands which is an infection control issue. All other answers are appropriate nursing activities.

8. **Answer B**. Tricyclic antidepressants, such as amitriptyline (Elavil) are contraindicated with levothyroxine (Synthroid) [drug-drug interaction] which this client will be taking since he/she has hypothyroidism.

9. **Answers B and C**. Lithium (Eskalith, Lithabid) is a salt and will make the client thirsty. Drinking more water is expected and recommended. However, our bodies excrete sodium in sweat so if the client does exercise it must be done in a climate-controlled environment and preferably without much sweating so as not to affect the lithium levels or to keep the levels the same daily.

10. **Answer B**. Benztropine (Cogentin) is used to treat extrapyramidal side effects of antipsychotic medications. Diphenhydramine (Benadryl) is used as a second medication with Cogentin if needed.

11. **Answer B**. Remind the client of the contract to attend group sessions. The tricyclic medications do cause dry mouth and sleepiness but the client must attend the group sessions—it's part of the therapeutic process. Answer D avoids the client's question.

12. **Answers B, D, and E**. Eating disorder clients must be awakened at different times early in the morning, empty bladder (so they do not drink copious amounts of water to alter weight gain), and weighed in only a client gown on the same balanced scales every day with their backs to the scales. These measures are taken to prevent manipulation of water versus real weight gain. These clients are not roomed together in order to prevent competition and sharing of ideas of how to control weight gain.

13. **Answers A, B, C, and D**. Clients should be offered fluids and toileting minimally every 2 hours and p.r.n. See Nursing Standards of Practice regarding Restraint Use: http://www.apna.org/files/public/APNA_SR_Standards-Final.pdf

14. **Answer A**. I know what you're thinking; I was taught never to ask "Why" because it puts the client on the defensive. But look back at the answers, my friend. Your client is suicidal! Which answer assesses for this problem? You will find if you will ask "Why" and the world won't collapse, clients won't jump out of windows. When you really care about people and you ask why, they will tell you the right answer because they don't want to do this final act. So, the important issue is to develop trust…then you can ask about anything.

15. **Answers A and C**. High ammonia levels would indicate hepatoencephalopathy. All clients with a history of alcoholism are at risk for Wernicke's advancing to Korsakoff's syndrome—an advancing dementia like disease caused by lack of thiamin and B complex. http://www.nlm.nih.gov/medlineplus/ency/article/000771.htm Korsakoff syndrome is irreversible. Supplemental Thiamin and B complexes are indicated for clients with alcoholic histories on each hospitalization regardless of diagnosis as prevention.

16. **Answer C**. A physical assessment is required during the admission process and is the perfect time to assess for contraband and sharps without drawing attention to this process. This also allows the RN to conduct a thorough skin assessment, which tells a life story—scars—past surgeries, accidents, suicide attempts, etc. The other answers are **incorrect**—a body search is critical to insure the safety of the client, the unit, and the staff.

17. **Answer C**. The ritual decreases anxiety. Gathering information from the client is most appropriate when levels of anxiety are at lowest levels.

18. **Answer D**. Irritability is the first symptom of increased intracranial pressure. Communication with the family is critical to determine baseline behavior before the injury to compare to current behavior to ascertain if a potential problem exists.

19. **Answer C**. Although this is often a manipulative ploy, the best response is to clarify and reinforce the multi-disciplinary team approach. Answers B and D set the nurse up to lie to the client. What if the client is suicidal and/or homicidal? Such information must be shared with the team and action taken.

20. **Answer in correct order is D, C, A, B**. The client with IED is at high risk of harming others which is often related to response to anxiety. The client possesses all fight no flight to fearful situations. The role of the nurse is to help the client identify when he/she is anxious and to run from the incident—"Run, Forrest, Run!" Typical symptoms include: clenched teeth, increased heart rate and respiratory rate, slight rocking, slight tremor of one hand.

21. **Answer C**. The legal definition of assault is the threat of harming another person. Battery is the actual harm to another human. http://definitions.uslegal.com/a/assault-and-battery/ Threatening to restrain a client is considered assault especially without just cause. If anyone actually uses restraints on a client without sufficient evidence to support such use, not only is the nurse's license at risk, such action is considered battery and can be punishable by jail time and fines.

22. **Answer C**. Manic behaviors—pressured speech, lack of need for sleep, energy, etc.—may actually be hyperthyroidism/Graves' disease. Lithium masks an abnormal T3 and T4. Lithium must be held until the T3 and T4 are drawn in order to obtain accurate results.

23. **Answer B**. Answers A and D are also good answers but will not keep the client as safe from him/herself as Answer B—constant observation.

24. **Answer C**. Buspar is an anti-anxiety medication but takes 2-3 weeks to reach therapeutic levels.

25. **Answer A**. Newly admitted clients are at risk for violence especially if they are psychotic or have conditions that put them at risk for violence. This is because they usually do not have trust established with the staff and are not on psychotropic medications or at least not at therapeutic levels. Most critical is for the nurse to determine the content of client A's hallucinations for the safety of the individual, other clients, and staff

26. Answer B. Alcohol is usually stored and sold in glass containers which is a safety hazard for all on the unit thus the bottle must be confiscated immediately.

Pediatric HEALTH PROMOTION

Jessica Peck, DNP, RN, MSN, CPNP-PC, CNE

Edited by Sylvia Rayfield & Associates, Inc.

What are the best ways to promote safety and prevention?

"Children are the world's most valuable resource and its best hope for the future."
~John Fitzgerald Kennedy

http://www.youtube.com/watch?v=55476dCgSsw
Whitney Houston sings, "I believe the children are our future ..."

KEY CONCEPTS TO REMEMBER:

❖ Safety risks are directly related to developmental ability!!
❖ Infancy and growth are the greatest times of physical and emotional growth in the entire lifespan!! There are lots of changes there!
❖ Childhood obesity and childhood mental health disorders are currently two very important focus areas of health prevention.

NORMAL PHYSICAL ASSESSMENT *VARIANCES* FOR CHILDREN:

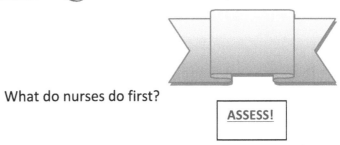

What do nurses do first?

ASSESS!

Do you remember that little song your mother might have sung to you as a child? "Stop, look and listen before you cross the street. Use your eyes, use your ears, and then use your feet!"

Well, I would like for you to consider an alternative. "Stop, look and listen before you touch the baby. Use your eyes, use your ears, and then use your hands!" Try this in your best singsong voice so you will remember it! Throw the order of head-to-toe out the window for kids! We do *least* invasive to *most* invasive. Start with assessment by observation, then auscultation, then palpation.

STOP!

LOOK!!

LISTEN!

ASSESSMENT	INTERVENTION
A- **ADDRESS THE CHILD AND FAMILY**	▪ Be friendly and natural! Be yourself! ▪ Allow the child to stay where he/she is most comfortable. This may be on mom's lap or under the table!

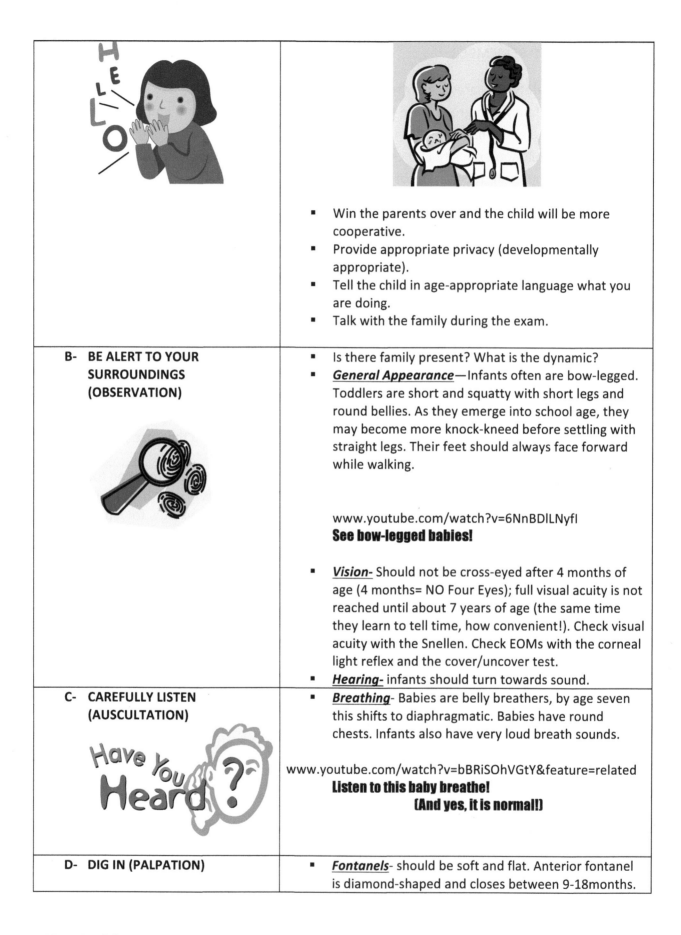

	<ul><li>Win the parents over and the child will be more cooperative.</li><li>Provide appropriate privacy (developmentally appropriate).</li><li>Tell the child in age-appropriate language what you are doing.</li><li>Talk with the family during the exam.</li></ul>
B- BE ALERT TO YOUR SURROUNDINGS (OBSERVATION)	<ul><li>Is there family present? What is the dynamic?</li><li>***General Appearance***—Infants often are bow-legged. Toddlers are short and squatty with short legs and round bellies. As they emerge into school age, they may become more knock-kneed before settling with straight legs. Their feet should always face forward while walking.</li></ul> www.youtube.com/watch?v=6NnBDlLNyfl **See bow-legged babies!** <ul><li>***Vision-*** Should not be cross-eyed after 4 months of age (4 months= NO Four Eyes); full visual acuity is not reached until about 7 years of age (the same time they learn to tell time, how convenient!). Check visual acuity with the Snellen. Check EOMs with the corneal light reflex and the cover/uncover test.</li><li>***Hearing-*** infants should turn towards sound.</li></ul>
C- CAREFULLY LISTEN (AUSCULTATION)	<ul><li>***Breathing-*** Babies are belly breathers, by age seven this shifts to diaphragmatic. Babies have round chests. Infants also have very loud breath sounds.</li></ul> www.youtube.com/watch?v=bBRiSOhVGtY&feature=related **Listen to this baby breathe!** **(And yes, it is normal!)**
D- DIG IN (PALPATION)	<ul><li>***Fontanels-*** should be soft and flat. Anterior fontanel is diamond-shaped and closes between 9-18months.</li></ul>

Posterior fontanel is triangle-shaped and closes at 2-3 months. Remember that a triangle has 3 sides! It closes at 3 months!

www.youtube.com/watch?v=_IS_fyIDHc8
How to examine a baby's head.

- *Pulses-* Babies have necks that are short and squatty. Jugular? Not a pulse option! Go for the femoral, brachial, or apical pulse until about 2 years of age, when you can palpate the radial pulse.

E- **EVALUATE DEVELOPMENT**	

- Fine Motor
- Gross Motor
- Psychosocial
- Cognitive

www.youtube.com/watch?v=i0fnBTUuRIA&feature=related
Explore development, the down and dirty

F- **FIND THE DIFFERENCES**	

dare to be different

- *Secondary sex characteristics*—should not be present before the age of 9 years. If present, indicates evaluation for abnormality.

- *Ear Structure*—short and straight Eustachian tube= tunnel to trouble (otitis media). For infants, pull the pinna down and back. After 3 years, they move on up (like the Jeffersons) and you pull up and back!

- *Mouth*—teething starts at about 7 months. Kids have 20 baby teeth and 32 permanent teeth. They should have an intact hard and soft palate. You may not be able to see a baby's tonsils, but it is quite common for kids to have HUGE tonsils. They typically atrophy as they move towards adulthood.

- *Genitalia*—in uncircumcised males, the foreskin may not be fully retractable until 3 years of age. DO NOT FORCE IT BACK!!!

LET'S GET PHYSICAL, PHYSICAL!!

	Infant	Toddler	Preschooler
Growth Trends	_Weight_: Double by 6 months, triple by 1 year _Height_: 1inch per month for 6 months, then 0.5inch per month _FOC_: 1.5cm per month for 6months, then 0.5cm per month	_Weight_: Weigh 4 times birth weight at 30 months _Height_: grow about 3inches a year _FOC_: Anterior fontanel closes 9-18mos	_Weight_: Gain 4-6 pounds/year _Height_: Grow 2-3inches per year
Gross Motor Trends	_3mo_: Can lift head & shoulders while prone _5mo_: Rolls over both ways _7mo:_ Bears full weight _8mo_: SITS UNSUPPORTED _9mo:_ Pulls to a stand _11mo_: Cruises around the furniture	_15mo_: Walks well without any help... probably running! _18mo_: Gets up to stand from any position _2yrs:_ Up and down the stairs my friend! _2 1/2yrs:_ JUMPS WITH BOTH FEET & STANDS ON	_3yrs_: Rides a tricycle! _4yrs:_ Skips with both feet, throws a ball overhand _5yrs:_ Jumps rope, walks backward, takes the stairs with alternating feet.

		ONE FOOT!	
Fine Motor Trends	_3mo:_ Grasp reflex fading, keeps hands in open position _4mo:_ Puts everything in the mouth! _6mo:_ Can hold a bottle or sippy cup _9mo:_ PINCER GRASP- time to start finger foods! _11mo:_ Nesting objects _12mo:_ Stacks 2 blocks	_15mo:_ Can stack two blocks. _18mo:_ Uses a spoon (in very messy, interesting ways!) Can turn the pages of a book. Holds a crayon _2yrs:_ Up to stacking 6 or 7 blocks now! _2 1/2yrs:_ BETTER HAND COORDINATION! IS BEGINNING TO DRAW AND COPY SHAPES.	_3-5yrs:_ Begins to learn to make letters and copy shapes. Crude drawings of stick figures. .
Personal Social	• _Cooing_ • _Laughs & Squeals_ • _Single Syllables_ • _1 word by 1 year_ • Separation Anxiety • Stranger Anxiety www.youtube.com/watch?v=wyo127dqgZU **Check out baby Ethan. Yes, he is adorable but see how many developmental milestones you can pick up!**	• _2 word sentences at 2 years_ • _400 word vocab by 3 years of age_ • _3 word sentences by 3 years_ • _Intentional Jargon_ • _Telegraphic Speech_	• _Vocabulary continues to increase_ • _Identifies colors and shapes_ • _Defines words_ • _Simple Opposites_
Cognitive	**Piaget- Sensorimotor** _(birth-24months)_ • Separation • Object Permanence • Mental Representation **Erikson- Trust vs. Mistrust** _(birth-one year)_ Primary task of the baby is to	**Piaget- Sensorimotor** _(birth-24months)_ • Separation • Object Permanence • Mental Representation **Erikson- Autonomy vs. Shame and Doubt**	**Piaget- Preconceptual** • Artificialism • Animism • Imminent Justice Crude concept of time **Erikson- Initiative vs. Guilt**

	bond with the caregiver.	*(1-3 years)* They want to be independent but are afraid when their caregivers leave!	Want to try new tasks but feel guilty when they fail.
Self-Concept	The major task of a baby is to realize they are a separate individual.	EGOCENTRIC Increasingly separate from parents. GENDER IDENTITY BY 3 YEARS OF AGE	Starting to feel independent but during stress may regress. INTENSE FEAR OF BODILY HARM! Sex-role identification maturing.
Nutrition www.youtube.com/watch?v=MBPhMYHQpKk **Visit here to see some do's and don'ts**	▪ BREAST IS BEST! 6 months of exclusive breastfeeding! ▪ Iron-fortified cereal after 6 months, then fruits and veggies. ▪ Finger foods when pincer grasp established. ▪ NO-NO's: Honey, egg yolk, citrus, choking foods (citrus, nuts, chips, hot dogs, popcorn), cow's milk	▪ VERY PICKY EATERS! ▪ Intense food jags ▪ 24-30oz milk/day ▪ <6oz juice/day ▪ Regular meals ▪ Snacks while seated ▪ Eat healthy ▪ Prevent choking ▪ Takes an average of 13xs to try a new food before liking it	▪ Growth rate slows ▪ More open to try new foods ▪ Increase protein intake ▪ Limit sugars, fats, and refined/pro-cessed foods
Health Promotion	*Burns:* bath water, sunscreen, electrical outlets *Drowning:* NEVER leave unattended in a bathtub *Falls:* Cribs low, don't leave unattended on bed or counters, use safety gates *Poison:* avoid lead paint, keep meds and cleaners locked away, carbon monoxide monitor	*Burns:* pot handles to the back of the stove *Drowning:* #1 cause of death in this age group, close toilets, constant supervision in tub and pool, teach how to swim *Falls:* close windows, safety gates on stairs *Poison:* avoid lead paint, keep meds and cleaners locked away, carbon	*Burns:* pot handles to the back of the stove *Drowning:* #1 cause of death in this age group, close toilets, constant supervision in tub and pool, teach how to swim *Sleep:* nightmares and night terrors, keep a consistent bedtime routine.

	SIDS: Use a pacifier, no smoking!, minimal bedding, no plastic bags or drawstrings. *Car Safety:* Rear facing until 2 years of age in a 5-point harness www.youtube.com/watch?v=K-h6XAIMDlc **Visit here to see a video about child safety at home. It is a little scary, I won't lie. I hope it makes you a little uncomfortable so you remember!**	monoxide monitor *Safety:* Teach address, stranger safety, strange animals caution, gun safety *Car Safety:* Rear facing until 2 years of age in a 5-point harness, then forward facing in a 5-point convertible until 40 pounds. *Toilet Training:* Show interest, positive reinforcement, need to be able to walk backwards and pull pants up and down. *Temper Tantrums:* Make sure child is safe and ignore.	*Poison:* avoid lead paint, keep meds and cleaners locked away, carbon monoxide monitor *Safety:* Teach address, stranger safety, strange animals caution, gun safety *Car Safety:* forward facing in a 5-point convertible until 40 pounds, then in a booster until 80 pounds and 4'9".
Immunizations	DTaP, HIB, IPV, HepB, Rotavirus, PCV, *ANNUAL FLU SHOT for ages 6 months+*	*New at one year are the MMR, varicella, and Hep A vaccines. They are also eligible for the Live intranasal spray flu vaccine.*	*4 year boosters (DTaP, MMR, Varivax, IPV)*
Developmental Play Activities	▪ *Tactile (cuddling)* ▪ *Kinetic (rocking)* ▪ *Acoustic (singing and talking)* ▪ *Visual (mobiles)*	▪ Parallel Play ▪ Playing ball ▪ Reading picture books ▪ Sorting ▪ Push toys	▪ Pretend Play ▪ Puzzles ▪ Reading picture books ▪ Painting & crafting ▪ Tricycles

	School-Aged (6-12years)	Adolescent (12-18 years)
Growth Trends	*Weight*: Average gain is 4-8 pounds/year *Height*: Average growth 2inches/year www.youtube.com/watch?v=jFhqNNfNKR4 **Visit here to see a hilarious remix of old sex-ed videos. Maybe you will remember one of these!**	*Weight*: Boys usually gain 15-60 pounds during puberty, with girls gaining 15-50 pounds). *Height*: The final 20% of height is achieved during puberty. Boys will grown 4-12 inches and stop between 18-20years of age. Girls grow 2-8 inches and stop growing at the onset of menarche. Final height is tied to Tanner staging maturity. If teen is in an early Tanner stage, more height achievement is possible.

Pubertal Changes	Girls: Breast buds, appearance of pubic hair, hips widen, onset of menarche Boys: Enlarging testicles, appearance of pubic hair, voice deepens, shoulders widen	Sexual maturity never occurs at the same time but it always occurs in the same progression. Girls: breast buds, pubic hair, menarche. Boys: enlarged testicles, pubic hair, change in voice.
Growth Maturation	Coordination improves. Visual acuity approaches 20/20. Permanent teeth erupt.	Adolescents need lots of extra sleep. They haven't done this much growing since they were infants! View themselves as invincible! Often engage in risky behaviors.
Personal Social	<ul><li>*Peer groups become very important.*</li><li>*Same-sex friendships.*</li><li>*Clubs with rules*</li></ul>	<ul><li>*Peer Jargon*</li><li>*Increased interest in romantic relationships*</li></ul>
Cognitive	**Piaget- Sensorimotor** *(Concrete Operations)* <ul><li>Able to tell time starting at age 7</li><li>Comprehends simple analogies</li><li>Weight and volume fixed</li><li>Increased problem-solving ability</li></ul> **Erikson-** *(Industry vs. Inferiority)* Very into learning tasks. They are very proud of their accomplishments and gain self-worth. They are also intensely afraid of ridicule. Everything revolves around an infamous three words: "***That's not FAIR***!" It is all about the best deal, the best way, you-help-me and I'll-help-you. Just think of them as little politicians!	**Piaget- Sensorimotor** *(Formal Operations)* <ul><li>Thinks at an adult level</li><li>Thinks abstractly</li><li>No longer all black and white, but also shades of gray (rules are not absolute)</li><li>Idealistic and creative</li><li>Thinks about the perspective of others</li><li>Uses decision making and reasoning skills</li></ul> **Erikson-** *(Identity vs. Role Confusion)* Future-oriented. Often identify with peer groups and label themselves as "popular," "jock," "geek," etc. Creating and fulfilling plans for the future.
Self-Concept	Children develop feelings of self-esteem	Achieve a healthy self-image through

by excelling at tasks (academics, sports, liberal arts, etc.). They thrive on the encouragement of others.

It is normal to have a curiosity about body development and sex and they begin to be more modest.

It's all about cooties! At this age they are alive and well and same-sex friendships are the order of the day. Best friends are present and constantly changing. Children may begin to show a healthy rivalry of the same-sex parent.

www.youtube.com/watch?v=kl1ujzRidmU

Visit here to see one dad's experience raising a teen in a Facebook world.

healthy relationships with friends/family.

Participation in a sport or hobby or organized activity with success has a positive outcome on self-worth.

Consumed with body image, media portrayal of peers, self-comparison to peers.

Depression and eating disorders can result from poor body image.

Cutting: Self-inflicted injury from a variety of potential objects (knife, razor, broken glass, stones, etc.) as a result of poor self-esteem. 60% of reported cases occur in 7th and 8th grade girls. Cutting is treated as an addiction and requires therapy and a 12-step program.

WARNING SIGNS OF CUTTING:
Unusual injuries with a history that doesn't match patterned injuries, wearing long sleeves and pants in warm weather, bloodstains on clothing, and social isolation.

| Nutrition | <ul><li>Obesity is a prevalent concern.</li><li>HEALTHY snacks and food choices.</li><li>No sodas, excessive sugar or processed foods.</li><li>Encourage physical activity.</li><li>Don't use food as a reward.</li><li>Snacks should be measured in portions, not eaten out of the bag in front of the TV.</li></ul>
www.youtube.com/watch?v=s-9A0OuEr14

This video is for kids who are going to be checked for scoliosis. | Rapid periods of growth require increase in caloric intake, healthy choices essential!

Diagnostic criteria for Anorexia Nervosa:
Intense fear of being fat, refusal to acknowledge seriousness of low BMI, amenorrhea of at least 3 cycles, body weight <85% of expected.

Diagnostic criteria for Bulimia Nervosa:
Recurrent binge eating, recurrent abuse of laxatives or self-induced vomiting, episodes occurring at least 2x/week for 3 months.

ASSESSMENT WARNING SIGNS:
Profound weight loss, secondary amenorrhea, bradycardia, low body temperature, hypotension, dry skin, thin hair, brittle nails, and cold intolerance. |

Health Promotion www.youtube.com/watch?v=DzjTJ6oSt2g **Visit this car seat safety video!**	_Scoliosis:_ Screenings for POSSIBLE curvature of the spine should be completed in the schools. _Drowning:_ Always supervise children in a pool. Teach them how to swim. _Safety:_ keep firearms in locked cabinets with the ammunition locked away separately, teach children to never play with guns, stranger safety, WEAR HELMETS DURING SPORTING ACTIVITIES—the best chance of achieving this is through parental modeling. _Burns_: Teach fire safety, "stop-drop-and-roll," smoke detectors, fire evacuation, and USE SUNSCREEN! _Poison:_ keep cleaning materials and chemicals locked away, "Say NO to drugs." _Dentist:_ Children can brush their own teeth at about 7 years of age. Get regular check-ups. _Car Safety:_ Booster seat (with a high back) until 9 years, 80 pounds, AND 4'9". ALL school-aged children should sit in the back seat.	_Burns:_ encourage use of sunscreen and DISCOURAGE USE OF TANNING BEDS! _Drowning:_ adolescents should not swim alone. Avoid risky behaviors such as horseplay in the pool and diving in shallow waters. _Safety:_ Gun safety. _Car Safety:_ MVA is the #1 cause of death for adolescents. MAKE SURE THEY WEAR A SEAT BELT!! They should not EVER use a cell phone to talk or text while driving. The best chance for car safety is for parents to model the appropriate behavior. _Suicide:_ Suicide risk should be taken seriously. If an adolescent has a history of a suicide attempt, they should be taken very seriously. Half of adolescents who commit suicide have a history of a previous attempt. If the adolescent has considered a method, they should be watched continuously and all firearms should be removed from the home. WARNING SIGNS OF SUICIDE: _Preoccupation with death, change in sleep pattern, non-specific physical complaints, repeated visits to healthcare provider, heavy alcohol or drug use, fighting, cutting, flat affect, dramatic mood swings, change in appetite._
Immunizations	_There are recently recommended vaccines for the "tweenagers."_ • _HPV-_ Human Papilloma Virus, recommended for girls AND boys ages 9-12yrs. HPV is a highly contagious disease (you can get from genital-to-genital contact) that can potentially cause cervical dysplasia and cervical cancer.	_Verify that records are up to date for:_ • _HPV_ • _Tdap_ • _Meningococcal Meningitis_ • _Hep A_ • _Hep B_ • _Varicella_ • _MMR_ • **_INFLUENZA_**

	• *Tdap*- There has been an epidemic rise in cases of pertussis in the U.S. Boosters with Tdap cover tetanus and pertussis. • *Meningococcal meningitis*—now recommended for this age group and also required for most colleges. • Catch-up for Hepatitis A, Hepatitis B, varicella and MMR boosters if needed. • Don't forget the annual flu vaccine for ALL children! Remember if they are 9, they are fine. (Meaning that if they are 9 and have never had a flu shot before, NO booster is needed). If this is the first flu shot before the age of 9 yrs, a booster in 30 days is indicated.	
Developmental Play Activities	• *Physical activities for younger school-aged children- think fun on the playground! Jump rope, hopscotch, simple games, organized sports with an emphasis on skill building and COLLECTIONS of things—rocks, jewelry, small toys, etc. These things enhance GROSS motor skill.* • *For older children, switch to fine motor and social skill development: board games, puzzles, lego models, organized sports with an emphasis on competition.*	• **NON-VIOLENT** video games and music • Organized sports • Career-preparedness courses • Positive social events • Nurturing positive friendships • Encourage family time

KIDS ARE LITERAL

My four-year-old son recently developed an obsession with a frontier hero, Davy Crockett. He continually dresses as Davy Crockett, acts like Davy Crockett, reads books about Davy Crockett, watches the Davy Crockett movie—you get the picture. The other day he came to me in full Davy Crockett regalia complete with "authentic" coonskin cap. On top of the coonskin cap sat a golden crown (thanks to Prince Caspian of Narnia). I asked him why he was wearing the crown and he looked at me like I had lost my ever-loving mind. He simply pointed to the crown and said, "Mom. Davy Crockett? King of the Wild Frontier!"

Kids are literal and interpret things literally. They also don't "pretend" to be characters. They use their magical thinking to BECOME their favorite characters. We should take such a lesson!

REVIEW QUESTIONS

1. Which of these grouped assessment findings should a nurse find in a healthy 4-month-old with normal development?

   1) Bears some weight on his legs, palmar grasp is fading, holds head up when prone
   2) Puts syllables together such as "dada", transfers objects from one hand to another, rolls over from prone to supine
   3) Sits steadily unsupported, uses thumb and index finger in crude pincer grasp, exhibits social smile
   4) Head lag when pulled to sit, releases cubes into a cup, verbalizes single syllables such as "da" and "ooh"

1. Option #1 is correct. Option #2 is incorrect because rolling over occurs by 5 months and transferring objects at 6 months. Option #3 is incorrect because sitting unsupported occurs by 8 months and a crude pincer grasp by 9 months. Option #4 is incorrect because a head lag persisting to 4 months is an abnormal finding and a 4 month old is not able to release objects into a cup.

2. A group of girls ages 9 and 10 have formed a "girls only" club. They invite neighborhood and school friends who have a popular brand of a doll. This should be interpreted as

   1) Behavior that encourages bullying and low self-esteem.
   2) Characteristic of social development of the school-aged child.
   3) Behavior that fosters the development of unhealthy "cliques."
   4) Characteristic of children whose parents have a sexual bias.

2. Option #2 is correct. This type of behavior is very typical for school-aged children.

3. A nurse is doing a physical assessment for a 13-month-old infant. It is noted that the infant cannot pull to a standing position. Which assessment would provide more information to report to the provider?

   1) Check symmetry of the gluteal skin folds
   2) Perform the Ortolani and Barlow assessment
   3) Assess for head lag
   4) Look for Kernig and Brudzinski sign

Option #1 is correct. This could potentially be a sign of developmental dysplasia of the hip. Ortolani and Barlow is an advanced practice technique, head lag is not necessarily related, and Kernig and Brudzinski is a neurologic assessment used to check for meningitis.

4. A mother is talking to the nurse about her 9-month-old infant who used to say "mama" all the time but hasn't said it in several weeks now, saying only "dada" instead. How should the nurse respond?

    1) You should talk to the provider about your concerns.
    2) Perhaps you were mistaken about her saying it earlier.
    3) It is common for infants this age to prefer their fathers.
    4) When infants learn new words, they often stop using recently acquired words.

Option #4 is correct. It is common for infants to regress as they concentrate on learning new tasks.

5. A mother of a 2 week-old infant is in the clinic for a newborn check-up. The infant is crying and the nurse notes that the mother does not respond to the infant's cry, but sits away from the infant sending text messages on her phone. What action should the nurse take?

    1) Alert the provider to assess for possible post-partum depression
    2) Ask the mother to put her cell phone away during the visit
    3) Notify CPS of possible neglect
    4) Ask the mother if she feels depressed

Option #1 is correct. If a mother does not respond to infant crying, it could be a sign of post-partum depression. Asking the mother if she feels depressed is a closed-ended question and does not give adequate information.

6. A mother reports her infant is teething and asks for recommendations on comfort measures. Which should the nurse advise? **Select all that apply**.

    1) Over-the-counter numbing topical gel
    2) Cold teething rings
    3) Teething biscuits
    4) Acetaminophen

Options #2 and #4 are correct. However, acetaminophen should only be used for 3 days or less and only if necessary. Numbing gel can create a choking hazard as can teething biscuits.

7. A mother asks a nurse on an inpatient unit where she can go to microwave expressed breastmilk for her infant. What is the best response of the nurse?

    1) Ensure the bottle is freshly made and has not been sitting out
    2) Make sure the mother tests the milk temperature before giving to the infant

3) Advise the mother to heat the bottle under warm water instead
4) Tell the mother there is no need to heat breast milk, as it may be given at any temperature

Option #3 is correct. Breastmilk should never be microwaved because it destroys proteins and immune properties.

8. Which symptoms should parents report to the provider following routine vaccination?

1) Redness at the injection site
2) Fussiness
3) Low grade temperature
4) Inconsolable crying

Option #4 is correct. The first three options are expected reactions.

9. A 7-year-old is getting her very first influenza vaccination. Which of the following represents appropriate action by the nurse? **Select all that apply**.

1) Administer 0.25cc subcutaneously into the arm
2) Advise the mother to return for a booster in 30 days
3) Give the mother a Vaccine Information Sheet prior to administration
4) Check to see if the child is eligible for the live intranasal vaccine

Options #2, #3 and #4are correct. Children less than 9 years of age who are receiving their first flu shot need to get a booster for optimal immunity. Federal law prior to each vaccine dose requires a VIS. The vaccine is administered IM and 0.5cc unless the child is less than 3 years of age. Most vaccines for children are standardly dosed at 0.5cc. She is eligible for the LAIV, which would save her from having to get a shot. Asthma is a contraindication for LAIV.

10. A 5-year-old child is receiving his measles mumps rubella (MMR) booster. His mother asks if it is safe for him to have the vaccine, because she is pregnant and in her second trimester. How should the nurse respond?

1) "It is safe for you and your baby."
2) "You should wait until the baby is born."
3) "Let's ask the provider if it is okay."
4) "Please call your obstetrician and ask."

Option #1 is okay. There is no contraindication for the child to be vaccinated. The mother should not be vaccinated while she is pregnant.

11. A child is due to receive his varicella booster vaccine but the mother tells you that he had an injection of gamma globulin for a hepatitis A outbreak at his daycare. How should the nurse respond?

    1) "How long ago did he receive the gamma globulin?"
    2) "There is no contraindication to be vaccinated today."
    3)"You will have to return in 3-6 months for this immunization."
    4) "The gamma globulin protects him against varicella."

Option #1 is correct. If gamma globulin is administered, live vaccines should be deferred for 3-6 months. That makes option #3 incorrect because we don't know how long it has been since his injection of gamma globulin.

12. A mother inquires about choosing the best car seat for her 9-month-old 22-pound infant. What should the nurse recommend?

    1) A forward-facing 5-point harness restraint
    2) A rear-facing 5-point harness restraint
    3) A forward facing convertible booster
    4) A rear-facing booster seat

Option #2 is correct. Infants should remain rear-facing until age 2 years, in a 5-point harness until 40 pounds, and a booster seat until 80 pounds and ~4'9". Height and weight may vary slightly from state-to-state.

13. A mother calls and reports her child ingested an unknown quantity of acetaminophen. What should the nurse advise the mother to do?

    1) Administer syrup of ipecac
    2) Call 911
    3) Go the emergency room
    4) Call poison control

Option #4 is the correct response and should be the first step. Ipecac is no longer recommended or commercially available.

14. A mother asks a nurse how she will know when her child is ready for toilet training. What should the nurse advise the mother to watch for? **Select all that apply**.

    1) Stays dry for periods of 2 hours or more
    2) Can walk, sit and squat
    3) Can communicate to caregiver wet or dirty diaper

4) Walks backward

5) Curiosity about toilet

All options are correct. Parents should never force a child to train who is not exhibiting signs of readiness. Training will likely be prolonged in such a scenario. Boys usually train by age 3yrs and girls by 2 1/2 years.

15. The siblings of a child hospitalized for cancer are exhibiting hostility and jealousy. They ask the mother repeatedly if they can go home. How should the nurse respond?

1) Suggest the names of counselors to the mother

2) Advise the mother to set guidelines on expected behavior

3) Admonish the children and encourage them to be compassionate

4) Reassure the mother that this behavior is normal

Option #4 is correct. Sibling rivalry is normal and can be exacerbated in times of illness. Patience is required.

16. A nurse is caring for a six-year-old female patient who reports to the nurse that "Daddy touches me in my private parts when I don't want him to." What is the appropriate action of the nurse?

1) Do nothing at this point because children this age often tell stories

2) Discuss the conversation with the father to clarify any misunderstanding

3) Call Child Protective Services

4) Do whatever is necessary to ensure the child is safe while the complaint is investigated.

Option #4 is correct. Children very rarely lie when reporting abuse. The first priority is to make sure the child is safe. Child reports of abuse should ALWAYS be reported.

17. A teenaged patient whose girlfriend has just broken up with him tells the nurse he is thinking about suicide. How should the nurse respond?

1) "You should talk to your parents about how you feel."

2) "You shouldn't talk like that, I am sure you don't mean it."

3) "I am going to have to report this to your physician."

4) "Have you thought about how you would do it?"

Option #4 is correct. If the teen has contemplated a method, his threat should be taken very seriously. All threats of suicide should always be taken seriously.

18. A school-aged child cheated on a test at school and lied to the parents about it. The parents ask if the should be concerned. How should the nurse respond?

    1) "Children this age often lie to escape punishment."
    2) "This can be an early sign of pathological behavior. You should consult a therapist."
    3) "Has there been any additional stress in your home that could have contributed to this?"
    4) "You should evaluate the child's group of friends and see if they are being a poor influence."

Option #1 is correct. Children who are normally good as gold may steal, lie, and cheat which can cause severe parental distress. They understand rules and justice and know they will be punished if they are disobedient. They sometimes have difficulty distinguishing fantasy from reality. It is also very difficult for school-age children to lose. Parents should be consistent in setting examples of honesty.

19. Which of the following signs should cause concern for possible signs of depression in a child? **Select all that apply.**

    1) Preference to be alone
    2) Worsening school performance
    3) Diarrhea
    4) Sleeplessness
    5) Hypersomnia

All options except #3 are correct. Diarrhea can be present with anxiety, but constipation is more common with depression.

20. A nurse is assessing an adolescent girl and notes the following findings: bradycardia, hypotension, dry skin, brittle nails and lanugo. What is the appropriate action of the nurse at this time? **Select all that apply.**

    1) Alert the provider to possible signs of hypothyroidism
    2) Assess the teen's body mass index
    3) Inquire about bowel habits
    4) Perform an oral assessment

Options #2 and #4 are correct. This teen is exhibiting signs of anorexia nervosa. An oral assessment may show signs of enamel erosion if bulimia is involved.

Nursing Management in Health Promotion

Tina Rayfield, RN, PA-C
Sylvia Rayfield, MN, RN, CNS
Edited by Sylvia Rayfield & Associates, Inc.

Treat the causes rather than the symptoms. So what are the root causes?
They are the lifestyle choices that we make each day: What we eat, how we respond
to stress, whether or not we smoke, how much we exercise, and how much love,
intimacy and social support we have in our lives.
Dean Ornish, MD

Key Concepts:
- § Preventable Health Issues
- § Women's Health Problems
- § Health Promotion in Maternity Care
- § Men's Health Problems
- § Practice Questions, Answers and Rationale

Preventable Health Issues

We will utilize **Search, Rescue, and Fallout** as the organizational method of this chapter.

Obesity

Two-thirds of adults and one-third of children in the United States are overweight or obese. The approximate annual cost to treat obesity—related illnesses is over $190 billion dollars

Search (Assess/Analysis)	Rescue (Implementation)	Fallout (Outcome—Good/Bad)
Assessment of vital signs	Centers for Disease Control and Prevention (CDC)	Weight loss to normal prevents complications
Body weight	Increase fruit and vegetable consumption	Hypertension
Exercise capacity		Heart disease
Dietary habits	Decrease consumption of energy-dense foods	High cholesterol level
	Increase physical activity	Diabetes
	Decrease television viewing and sitting	Cancer
		Ulcers
	Decrease consumption of sugar-sweetened beverages	Gallstones
	In pregnancy, increase breast-feeding initiation, duration, and exclusivity	Skin infections
		Costly bariatric surgery

Tobacco

More deaths are caused each year by tobacco use than all deaths from HIV, illegal drug use, alcohol use, motor vehicle injuries, suicides, and murders combined. Smoking in any form increases the risk of cancer (especially lung, esophagus, larynx, and oral cavity). Smokeless tobacco is a known risk for sudden death due to heart arrhythmias.

Search (Assess/Analysis)	Rescue (Implementation)	Fallout (Outcome—Good/Bad)
Assess smoking inception	Counseling of sufficient length and intensity increases the likelihood of cessation	Cessation prevents complications
Assess number of cigarettes/day		Shortness of breath (SOB)
Determine current illnesses, drug use		Chronic obstructive pulmonary disease (COPD)

	The Food and Drug Administration has approved six first-line medications for cessation • Nicotine gum • Nicotine patch • Nasal spray • Inhaler • Lozenge • Bupropion SR (sustained release)	Coronary heart disease Emphysema Cancer Peripheral vascular disease Aortic aneurysm Cataracts
	Smoking cessation begins to reverse fallout after the client is successful	Osteoporosis Smoking is known to have an effect on the unborn child

Alcohol

Alcohol affects all age groups. Women are the most vulnerable.

Search (Assess/Analysis)	Rescue (Implementation)	Fallout (Outcome—Good/Bad)
Assess vital signs	Rescue is preventable and difficult	Complete recovery with rehabilitation
Inception of drinking habit	Alcoholics Anonymous indicates efficiency with the 12 step program	Diminishes brain function from brain shrinkage, causes seizures
Amount of drinks/day		
Assess for blackouts and memory loss	This is often a full family issue. Refer family members to Al-Anon and Alateen	Difficulty walking and blackouts
Assess for blurred vision and speech		Severe anemia, blurred vision/ slurred speech, peripheral vascular disease
Assess dietary habits		Slow reaction times causing motor vehicles accidents
Assess family history		Severe nutritional deficiency in B12, Folate, and other vitamins
Assess for acute withdrawal		Destroyed marriages and relationships
Watch for DTs		Premature death

Substance Abuse

Prescription and street drugs are a major public health problem affecting individuals, families, and communities.

Search (Assess/Analysis)	Rescue (Implementation)	Fallout (Outcome—Good/Bad)
Inception	Monitor behavior	Recovery with rehabilitation
Usage and type of drug	Refer to Narcotics Anonymous 12 step program	Increases the blood pressure, cardiac arrythmias, liver disease
Drugs primarily abused include:	Provide support for families	Brain damage
• Amphetamines (speed, meth, ice, and tina)		Aggressive behavior
• Anabolic steroids used to enhance athletic performance or muscle building		Miscarriages
• Cocaine stimulates the brain (crack)		Addiction is costly and may lead to crimes in order to "feed the habit"
• Marijuana (weed, pot, hash)		
• Methylenedioxymethamphea-mine (Ectasy, XTC, Lover's speed)		Loss of productivity in the workplace
• Narcotics (pain killers, sedatives, stimulants)		Divorce
• Rohypnol (roophies, forget me pills)		Destruction of personal relationships
Teenagers will try anything to make themselves high or to change their consciousness		Overdose
Assess for withdrawal (muscle pain, diarrhea, vomiting, and cold flashes)		Premature death

Women's Health Problems

Search (Assessment)	Rescue (Intervention)	Fallout (Outcome—Good/Bad)

Community issues in women's health includes:
 	
• Heart disease
• Skin cancer
• Sexually transmitted disease
• Osteoporosis
• Breast cancer—40,000 women a year die from breast cancer die
• Obesity
• Alcohol and tobacco abuse
	▪ Exercise is one of the most important interventions. It reduces heart disease and osteoporosis
	▪ Sun protection reduces skin cancer
	▪ Safe sex reduces sexually transmitted diseases
	▪ Screening exams:
	  • Add routine yearly gynecological exam at age 18 or onset of sexual activity
	  • Bone density exams monitors osteoporosis
	  • Mammograms monitor for breast cancer in the early treatable stages. Self breast exams
	  • Skin exams identify skin cancer in early treatable stages
	  • Dental exams promote health
	  • Colonoscopy detects early colon cancer
	  • Vaccinations—routine from CDC protocol
	▪ Eating healthy includes fruits, vegetables, whole grains, high-fiber, lean sources of protein. Reduces obesity
	▪ Maintaining healthy weight reduces obesity
	▪ Smoking cessation reduces cancer
	▪ Limiting alcohol consumption limits alcoholism
	▪ Education regarding fallout
		A healthy productive woman
		
		Lung cancer
		
		Colorectal cancers
		
		Alcoholism
		
		Obesity
		
		Diabetes
		
		Hypertension
		
		High cholesterol
		
		Skin cancer
		
		Sterility from sexually transmitted diseases
		
		Breast removal
		
		Stress
		
		Blindness
		
		Broken bones
		
		Expense
		
		Death

Health Promotion in Maternity Care

Although pregnancy is not ordinarily a health problem, it may become one without prenatal care which permits early identification of modifiable risk factors. Positive outcomes include a healthy mother and baby. Safety will be utilized for organization

PASS *NCLEX*®!

S   System specific assessment

A   Assess for risk and respond

F   Find change/trends and intervene

E   Evaluate pharmacology

T   Teach/practice infection control, health promotion

Y   Your management—legal/ethical/scope of practice, identity, errors, delegation, faulty equipment/staff, privacy, confidentiality, falls/ hazards

System Specific Assessment

Antepartum	Labor and Delivery	Postpartum
Baseline Height, weight, BP, vital signs, urine protein, glucose	Vital signs	Determine vital signs for hypertension, hemorrhage, or fever
Laboratory Diagnostics to determine renal profile	Labor timing pattern Assessment of contractions	Assess for uterine height. Should be 3 fingers above the umbilicus and at midline and firm
■ Sexually Transmitted Disease (STD) ■ Alpha Fetal Protein (AFD)	Vaginal discharge and bleeding Compare historical and current lab work.	Determine lochia amount, odor, and character
■ CBC and Hemaglobin ■ RH Factor ■ Blood type	If positive for Beta strep, begin treatment per protocol	Assess for fever, hemorrhoids, voiding capability

Antepartum	Labor and Delivery	Postpartum
	Assess birth plan for pain control and seek order from provider	Massage fundus for bleeding control
		Assess episiotomy for hematoma
		Assess breasts for discharge
		This client is at risk for deep vein thrombosis (DVT)

Assess for risk and respond

Antepartum	Labor and Delivery	Postpartum
Report any urinary tract infection Common diagnostic tests include: • Ultrasound to determine fetal risk is non-invasive • Blood tests including hemoglobin, pregnancy-associated plasma protein screening (PAPP-A), human chorionic gonadotropin (hCG), alpha-fetoprotein screening (AFP) to determine fetal risk • Amniocentesis (removal of small amount of fluid from placental sac) determines genetic defects including chromosomal disorders or neural tube defects • At 35-37 weeks, test for Group B strep culture	Provide newborn with warmth Nursing management at delivery involves safety of the mother and baby Assess for anoxia in the infant, keep airway open and assess with an APGAR score. Birth asphyxia is a leading cause of infant risk. The APGAR score includes: • Breathing scored 0-2 from not breathing to cries lustily • Heart rate scored 0-2 from no heart sound to minimum of 100 beats per minute • Muscle tone scored from 0-2 from floppy muscles to active motion	Evaluate for postpartum psychosis Assess for bleeding—shock Assess for hypertension and seizures Reassess fundul priority. Should be at midline—deviation suggests full bladder Bogginess indicates need for uterine massage and bleeding assessment Assess for the Ws (wind, wound, water, and walk) Cesarean section should be assessed for pain. Pain management protocol should be followed

Antepartum	Labor and Delivery	Postpartum
	• Grimace scored 0-2 from no response on stimulation to grimacing, coughing, sneezing, or lusty cry • Skin color is scored from 0-2 from a pale blue color to a pink body • As you can see the perfect score would be a 10, but as low as 7 is considered normal • Check the infant's identity and place identifier on the infant • Warm the infant to reduce brain injury • Obtain weight, length, and head circumference • Determine blood sugar if the mother is a diabetic • Provide for mother and infant bonding	

Evaluate Pharmacology

Antepartum	Labor and Delivery	Postpartum
Pain control if needed The fewer medications in antepartum is better for the fetus Administer flu shot Most commonly needed are anti-infectives for upper respiratory infections, urinary tract infections, and sexually transmitted diseases Anti hypertensive drugs such as Aldomet and Magnesium Sulfate may be administered for pregnancy induced hypertension (PIH).Watch for seizure control	Spinal anesthesia is most prevalent for pain relief. Monitor skin, injury below the waist, initiate an indwelling catheter and monitor vital signs for hypotension Pitocin may be utilized to increase strength of contractions Assess for continuous contractions and uterine tetany Magnesium sulfate is utilized to reduce hypertension Evaluate for shortness of breath less than 12 and assess tendon reflexes	Pain control Analgesics, Lortab, narcotics. Standard for narcotic protocol Anti-infectives for infection Assess for allergies

Try/Practice Infection Control

Antepartum	Labor and Delivery	Postpartum
Assess beta strep status and administer Penicillin G if required	Monitor for sterility in the delivery room Utilize hand washing protocols	Assess for cracked, sore nipples, and episiotomy suture line for pain, redness, and burning on urination Determine vital signs for elevated temperature Assess beta strep status and, if positive, follow CDC protocol

Your Management

These standards currently count for as much as **23%** of the total *NCLEX*® exam and are always a primary consideration for nursing.

PASS *NCLEX*®!

M   Make sure of identity, accuracy of orders

A   Arrange privacy/confidentiality/consent/collaboration with other team

N   No injuries, falls, malfunctioning equipment or staff or hazards

A   Address errors, abuse, legalities, scope of practice—document

G   Give (delegate) orders to appropriate people

E   Establish priorities of clients and time

Men's Health Problems

Many of these problems are preventable if the client is proactive. Vaccinations administered recommended according to CDC protocol. Some of the problems that require intervention are:

- Heart disease—exercise is one of the most important interventions. It reduces heart disease and osteoporosis. Managing stress reduces heart disease and hypertension.

- Hypertension—exercise and healthy eating reduce risk of stroke, heart attacks, and high cholesterol

- Smoking cessation reduces cancer and COPD.

- Alcohol consumption. Managing alcohol intake reduces alcoholism.

- Obesity—eating healthy to include fruits, vegetables, whole grains, high fiber, and lean sources of protein reduces obesity. Exercise is vital to reduce weight.

- Sexually transmitted diseases—safe sex reduces STDs. Teach importance of routine physical exams starting at age 20.

- Cancer—lung cancer, skin cancer, colon cancer, prostate cancer. Interventions in heart disease, smoking cessation, and alcohol/drug consumption reduces cancer. Colorectal cancers may be detected early with colonoscopy. Prostate cancer—the screening exam for the prostate specific antigen (PSA) may detect early disease and the need for prostatectomy. Skin cancer—skin exams find skin cancer in early treatable stages. Testicular cancer—teach testicular exams through life.

- Osteoporosis, although uncommon in men, may be reduced with exercise and utilization of calcium.

- Diabetic control prevents blindness, peripheral vascular disease, hyper-and hypoglycemia, and infection

Compliance with health promotion guidelines results in reduced illnesses and a healthy life.

1. What would be priority to include in the health promotion plan of a newly diagnosed insulin dependent client with diabetes? **Select all that apply.**
   A. Continue to take the prescribed prednisone medication
   B. Check blood glucose consistently
   C. Reduce exercise
   D. Observe feet for blisters or redness
   E. Never mix the "cloudy" insulin with the "clear insulin"

2. Which of these screening tests should be recommended for the teenager? **Select all that apply.**
   A. Height and weight
   B. PSA (prostate specific antigen)
   C. Mammogram
   D. Chicken Pox vaccination
   E. Hepatitis B (HepB) injection

3. Which response by the client indicates an understanding of antibiotic therapy?
   A. "I can stop taking the pills when I feel better."
   B. "I should take my antibiotics with milk."
   C. "If I have a cold, I should stop taking the antibiotic."
   D. "I should take every pill until all of them are gone."

4. Which is the highest priority in the teaching plan of a new mother with a 2-year-old?
   A. Plan frequent outings
   B. Set strict limits on the toddler
   C. Call the provider with a temp. of 99 degrees
   D. Lock the kitchen cabinets

5. Which are the highest priorities in the teaching plan of an 80-year-old to prevent falls? **Select all that apply**
   A. Include the normal changes in aging
   B. Install grab bars in the bathroom
   C. Remove all throw rugs
   D. Read the label on all medications
   E. Avoid all stairs

6. Yesterday the older adult, with an indwelling catheter, had a urine output of 50mL/hour. Today's output is 15mL/hour. What is the nursing priority?

    A. Remove the indwelling catheter and reinsert
    B. Irrigate the existing catheter and measure
    C. Change the client's position for better flow
    D. Notify the provider

7. Two hours after removal of a gastric tube, the client begins vomiting. What is the priority?

    A. Administer the client's PRN medication for nausea
    B. Provide cold compresses to the forehead
    C. Assess the client's vital signs
    D. Notify the provider

8. Which client has the highest risk of a pulmonary embolism?

    A. The 1-day postpartum client
    B. A client with a hemoglobin of 9 and a hematocrit of 28
    C. A client 10 days post surgery, walking with a boot
    D. The 350 pound male admitted following a motor vehicle accident

9. Which clinical finding is most appropriate to report to the provider?

    A. A client with a pacemaker and a pulse rate of 46
    B. The client complaining of a severe headache
    C. A client with an overnight weight loss of 3 pounds
    D. A client with a serum potassium level of 4.3

10. What is the priority for a client who has attempted suicide?

    A. Determine the identity and age
    B. Notify the provider
    C. Present the client a contract of behavior
    D. Assess for prior suicide attempts.

11. What is the initial assessment of the newly admitted client who cannot remember the evening before?

    A. Determine the client's cultural practices
    B. Assess blood work for possible anemia
    C. Assess for drug/alcohol intake
    D. Determine the client's closest kin

12. The client receiving Lithium is considering joining a baseball team. Which is the teaching plan?
    A. Agree with the client's decision for exercise
    B. Warn the client that sweating may interfere with the medication
    C. Notify the family of the client's plan
    D. Determine the Lithium therapeutic level

13. The nurse receives a report on a client who is confused. Which is priority?
    A. Implement fall protocol
    B. Assess for alcohol and drug use
    C. Notify the family
    D. Insert an IV to keep a vein open

14. Which client may be delegated to the Certified Nursing Assistant?
    A. The early postpartum client
    B. A client in traction
    C. The sweating diabetic client
    D. The client receiving a discharge conference

15. The client is complaining of pain and redness at the blood transfusion site. Which are the best nursing interventions. **Select all that apply**
    A. Irrigate the tubing and reassess
    B. Remove the IV line and restart in another location
    C. Place compresses on the site according to protocol
    D. Utilize a different type of solution in the IV
    E. Begin the second IV with a smaller needle

16. Which is the safest client to delegate to the LPN?
    A. The 6- hour postpartum client
    B. A premature infant
    C. A client returning from having gallbladder surgery
    D. The client receiving Dopamine

17. The newspaper reporter is inquiring about the hospital admission of the mayor. Which is the best response?
    A. "Due to HIPAA policies I can not tell you anything except that the mayor has been admitted."
    B. "I'm sorry, but the nurses' initial assessment in incomplete."
    C. "Confidentiality policies prevent sharing any information."
    D. " Please return at a later more convenient time."

18. What is the priority of care of a client with a new prescription order of insulin? **Select all that apply**
    A. Always keep refrigerated
    B. Reconciliation of insulin and food
    C. Keep source of low-density sugar available for possible insulin reaction
    D. Utilize a clean syringe every dose
    E. Minimize exercise

19. The second hour postpartum client has the following vital signs.
    • Respirations 26/minute
    • Blood pressure 85/50
    • Pulse bounding at 110/minute
    What is the highest nursing priority?
    A. Reposition the client into a Trendelenberg position
    B. Reassess vital signs
    C. Notify the provider
    D. Call a code

20. The nurse is asked to perform diagnostic testing. Which of the tests is within the nurse's scope of practice? **Select all that apply**
    A. Perform an electrocardiogram
    B. Secure blood for blood gases assessment
    C. Perform an oxygen saturation exam
    D. Perform an ultrasound
    E. Perform an amniocentesis

21. The maternity client in labor has a sudden rupture of membranes. What is the nursing priority?
    A. Determine vital sighs for mother
    B. Determine the fetal heart rate
    C. Notify the provider
    D. Assess for prolapsed cord

22. Which is priority assessment after hearing a high-pitched cry in the newborn?
    A. Assess the feeding patterns of the newborn
    B. Determine a history of maternal drug use
    C. Determine the temperature of the crying infant.
    D. Determine the weight of the mother prior to birth

23. What is the best answer for the pregnant client who asks if an amniocentesis will hurt?
    A. "This is a non-invasive procedure and there will be no pain."
    B. "A small amount of fluid will be withdrawn from the fetal sac, causing some discomfort."
    C. "A bowel prep is needed prior to this exam and may be uncomfortable."
    D. "Any allergies must be identified before the test can be begun."

24. What would the priority for assessing the client who is receiving Magnesium Sulfate?
    A. Assess the IV site for pain and redness
    B. Determining blurred vision
    C. Check reflexes
    D. Reassess vital signs every 30 minutes

25. Which interventions are key prior to a 64-year-old client being discharged after hip replacement surgery? **Select all that apply**
    A. Determine client's ability for self care
    B. Remove throw rugs
    C. Place handicap bars in the bathroom
    D. Advise sitting on a low stool for rehabilitation
    E. Encourage client to go to group therapy

26. Which would be the priority for the new mother experiencing postpartum psychosis?
    A. Determine past psychiatric problems
    B. Provide safety to prevent suicide or infanticide
    C. Advise the mother that it takes a long time to get through these feelings
    D. Administer anti-psychotic drugs from protocol

Answers and Rationale

1. **Answers B, D, and E** are correct. The client's order for prednisone should be confirmed with the provider as this drug increases the blood sugar level. Exercise is indicated as exercise reduces the blood sugar level.

2. **Answers A, D, and E.** The PSA is utilized in older males and the mammogram is utilized in older females

3. **Answer D.** Antibiotics used inappropriately are responsible for resistance. All antibiotics should not be taken with milk.

4. **Answer D.** While outings and limits are necessary, most providers want to know when the infant's temp is over 100 degrees.

5. **Answers B, C, and D** are priority. The others are important, but not priority.

6. **Answer A.** This much drop in output is very significant and is not likely the fault of the client's position or the catheter.

7. **Answer C.** It is very appropriate to notify the provider, but not before there is information to share. Answers A and B will likely to be useful to the client, but are not priority.

8. **Answer D.** The obese client is at severe risk for pulmonary embolism. The postpartum client is at risk, but not the highest. Although the hemoglobin and hematocrit is lower than normal and deserves intervention, there is not the most significant risk. Ambulation with a boot is desirable, as this kind of exercise will likely reduce the risk.

9. **Answer A.** Bradycardia may lead to ventricular tachycardia and a rate of 46 is too low to sustain perfusion. Answers B and C deserve attention, but not first. The potassium level is within normal limits.

10. **Answer A.** Identity would be priority to any of the other interventions, which are appropriate.

11. **Answer C.** Alcohol and drugs are known for blackouts. The other answers will not be useful at this time.

12. **Answer B.** Lithium works on a sodium balance. Sweating will lose sodium. The other responses are inappropriate.

13. **Answer A.** All other intervention may be considered later. Safety first

14. **Answer B.** All others are outside of the CNA scope of practice.

15. Answers B and C. Irrigating the IV line is not likely to reduce the problem. The nurse does not prescribe the IV infusion and a smaller needle is detrimental for the client receiving blood products

16. Answer A. The LPN will be useful for the late postpartum client. All other clients should be assessed by the RN first or is outside the LPN scope of practice unless they have had additional certification

17. Answer C. HIPAA policies require confidentiality and privacy. Admission to the unit would be a violation. All others are inappropriate

18. Answers B. C, and D. Insulin, if kept in a cool place, does not always have to be refrigerated. Exercise reduces the need for higher insulin dosage.

19. Answer A. Keeping venous return is vital to a client exhibiting shock symptoms. Answers B and C should be performed after the client is repositioned. If intervention is successful, no code will have to be called.

20. Answers A, B and C are all within the nurses scope of practice. Answers D and E are not.

21. Answer D. Safety of the fetus first. Prolapsed cord is a possibility. Answer B is a good distracter, but the fetus rate can decline in rate while the nurse is assessing the rate. A&C come later.

22. Answer B. A high-pitched cry in the infant is an indication of possible drug withdrawal. History of the mother's use prior to delivery is priority. Other answers are not priority.

23. Answer B. The client may feel pressure and the stick of the needle used during this diagnostic test. Answers A and C are inaccurate. There are no dyes utilized in amniocentesis.

24. Answer D. The client's blood pressure may drop significantly; therefore the vital signs should be checked often. Answers A, B, and C are secondary options, but not priority.

25. Answers A, B, C. Sitting on a low stool may cause the hip replacement to fail. Talking to other people with similar experiences may be useful at a later time.

26. Answer B. There is a risk of the mother killing the baby and herself. Answer A is important information as clients with bi-polar disease are susceptible, but Safety first! Anti-psychotic drugs may be prescribed, but life is priority.

INDEX

INDEX

INDEX

INDEX

INDEX

INDEX

INDEX

INDEX

INDEX